The
Good Holiday
Cottage Guide
2002

Stop Press: At a late stage of production we were pleased to feature (on Page 423) Lower Pethills Farm, in Cheshire.

Cover

This year's cover is not meant as a reminder to send a holiday postcard to Aunt Sally but is a snapshot of the range of properties available in the guide. Clockwise from top left they are Glengorm Castle, on the Isle of Mull, Cefn Old Farmhouse, near Caernarfon, and Erbistock Mill, near Llangollen. They're featured respectively on Pages 140, 201 and 209/339.

The
Good Holiday
Cottage Guide

2002

Edited by
Bryn Frank

Feedback from readers is the lifeblood of this guide. During 2001
we heard from two couples, from Leeds and Northamptonshire,
who stayed at Monkhouse Hill in Cumbria. One described 'a
fantastic break'. They were 'all stressed out' and say 'the leisure
club added the finishing touches'. The other reported: 'This is the
best self catering accommodation we have ever stayed in. We
loved the thoughtful extras like the toy box, which kept
the children occupied for hours'.

A family of five on their third visit to Vere Lodge, in Norfolk,
were thrilled by the new Enchanted Wood: 'the grown -ups
enjoyed it as much as the children...and Mrs Bowlby's
two dogs are such treasures'...

The help of the following in preparing this guide is gratefully acknowledged:
Leyla Ali, Richard Bamforth, Diane Davies, Carole Frank, John Harrison, Nicky
Phillips, Paul Phillips, Debbie Richardson, John Ruler and Gillian Thomas.

Bryn Frank, Hertford, December 2001

Printed by Stephen Austin & Sons Ltd, Caxton Hill, Hertford SG13 7LU.
Telephone (01992) 584955.

Distributed by Portfolio Ltd, Unit 5, Perivale Industrial Park, Perivale, Middlesex
UB6 7RL. Telephone 020-8997 9000. Fax 020-8997 9097.

Distributed in the USA and Canada by SunWelcome Inc, PO Box 991, McLean,
VA 22101-0991. Telephone/fax 1 703 757 2080 or (in USA and Canada)
1 800 430 8096, or email: frank@cottageguide.co.uk

ISBN 0-946238-22-7

Note: the advertisement and advertisement feature on Colour section C, Page 8,
and 379 respectively contain information about 'Cottages4You', a state-of-the-art
website operated by The Holiday Cottages Group.

Note also: as well as the sophisticated systems operated by the Holiday Cottages
Group (see our features on Blakes, Country Holidays and English Country Holidays),
Hoseasons and Welcome Cottage Holidays, two agencies that have put extra resources
into their website have asked us especially to note that they now offer a complete 'real
time' – ie literally up to the minute – on-line availability and booking service. These
are Interhome (Pages 32 and 371) and Sykes Cottages (Page 29).

Interhome is the biggest holiday home agency in Europe and at any given time
their website shows properties 'that are definitely available to match your criteria,
so that you can book and confirm instantly'. You can pay by credit card or cheque.

Sykes Cottages, with 300 cottages in the North, the Heart of England, and North
Wales also offers real, up to the minute on line availability and booking
information, and has won accolades. They have twice been regional winners of the
DTI sponsored E-commerce awards and in 2001 were voted one of the UK's top
100 'visionary companies' by the Cranfield School of Management.

Catering for change...

Last year's foot and mouth fiasco has made holidaymakers all the keener to secure their cottages for 2002. This has all the hallmarks of a bumper year, so early booking even for the late season (September, October, perhaps November) is advisable.

This edition of *The Good Holiday Cottage Guide* is the 20th. How things have changed since the first edition. Then, only about two thirds of cottages had TVs (mostly black and white), big houses were a liability for owners rather than the magnet they are now, ensuite bathrooms were rare, and the best kitchens were like 1950s ads from *Ideal Home* magazine.

Where will the constant raising of standards take us? Already there's resistance even among the most assiduous owners to the merry-go-round of 'improvements'. It's a competitive business, and for years now many properties have been more comfortable than most guests' own homes. Not many of us have jacuzzis, full size snooker tables, the drying rooms that are so appreciated by walkers and fishermen and fireplaces that will take six foot logs, but quite a few cottages do.

Perhaps there'll be a backlash? We've noticed how cottages without frills (though clean, well cared for and well situated) do very well, and not necessarily because they are cheaper. And who'd have thought 20 years ago, when we began, how the first question potential guests ask today is often: 'Is there an open fire?'. And that's not just in winter...

Regular readers may notice that a number of properties that have appeared in several previous editions are absent. Because standards are always on the up and up – see above! – even some of the most well intentioned owners have not been able to keep up with holidaymakers' expectations. (But it might also be that properties no longer featured here are unavailable because of retirement, or because they have been sold or continue, say, to be let only to family members or friends....)

BED AND BREAKFAST/HOTEL ACCOMMODATION

The Good Holiday Cottage Guide frequently receives requests from readers wanting information about places to stay en route to distant cottages and for friends and family to stay for a night or two while visiting people staying in a cottage (or apartment, chalet etc). They can sometimes stay as extra people in the cottage, but not usually. So we now include information about hotels and 'b & b' near the end of this edition: see Pages 390 to 395.

Contents

Colour sections: Pages 193-200, 265-272 and 337-344.

The direct approach

A few years ago people used to say 'What is this Premier thing?' Now they ask: 'Has the Premier brochure arrived yet?' Owners of historically interesting holiday cottages with lovingly cared-for interiors revel in the chance the glossy Premier Cottages Direct brochure gives to blow their own trumpet. As one of the Premier owners we feature in The Good Holiday Cottage Guide said: 'We don't know how we ever managed without 'Premier'. It's changed our lives.'

The large-format brochure, now in its fifth annual edition, is a winner. Featuring around 150 cottage set-ups and individual properties in good quality colour, it is on the way to becoming essential reading for serious self caterers looking only for the very best.

All properties are owner operated and all are characterised by a warm personal welcome, which is becoming increasingly important to holidaymakers. Letting agencies provide a useful service, but cottage-goers seem to divide into two camps, preferring the (usually) more impersonal type of contact or, instead, to strike a more direct relationship with owners. There is a view that holiday tenants can save money by going direct, and there is a view, expressed by one of our readers, that 'It's nice to be able to ring up at odd times just to re-assure ourselves about certain details: such as "Is the swimming pool available all weekend"..."Is there definitely a king sized bed in the main bedroom?" '

A strength of Premier is its healthy geographical spread, and there are already signs that people who have sampled a holiday with one of the members (say, for example, Gladwins Farm, on the edge of Constable country, in Suffolk) look at the organisation's brochure again and then book in a different location – say Combermere Abbey, in Shropshire.

The Good Holiday Cottage Guide knows almost all the Premier members, and features about 50 of them in the pages of this guide.

For a copy of the Premier brochure phone (01271) 336050. Fax 328422.

email: premiercottages@responseuk.co.uk
www. premiercottages.co.uk

(The website has an excellent search facility, with links to most owners' individual sites)

Advertisement feature

Welcome Cottage Holidays*

Welcome Holidays' 2002 brochure brims with notably *affordable* properties of a consisently high standard. They actually turn down *two out of every three* properties offered to them, and each one they take on is constantly reinspected to check it is still 'up to scratch'.

The grading system is clear and simple, from 'Comfortable' ("everything you will need for an enjoyable self-catering break") up through 'Good Quality' ("slightly more holiday cottage than home") and 'Lovely' ("more

Near Lavenham, Suffolk, this 300-year-old cottage fits prettily into its village.

This handsome 16th century house, sleeping 8, is near Bala, in North Wales.

like a home than a holiday cottage") to 'Beautiful' ("that very rare property featuring furniture, furnishings and decor chosen with the express purpose of creating a beautiful holiday home"). Intriguingly, a high proportion of the sprinkling of 'Beautiful' properties is in Brontë country, around Haworth!

Old favourites include a substantial family house (**sleeping 6**) on a steep hillside overlooking Lamorna Cove, just six miles from Penzance. With open fires *and* central heating, it falls fair and square into the 'Lovely' category. Ref 2802. And in Devon, we have been struck by a Grade II terraced character cottage, **sleeping 4**, at Musbury, about five miles from Lyme Regis and Seaton. One dog is welcome. 'Good Quality'; ref 1137.

There are few places with a bigger helping of peace-and-quiet than the 'Lovely', Grade II listed cottage at Hewood, near Lyme Regis. **Sleeping 2/3**, it has a four-poster bed and views over farmland towards partly-Tudor Forde Abbey, famous for its gardens. Ref 2585.

Five miles from quaint, cobbled Rye, in East Sussex, a detached barn conversion lies appropriately in the grounds of a 16th century manor house. There are even studded oak doors and a galleried landing. **Sleeps 6**. Ref 2804; 'Lovely'. Just yards from one of the forest paths in the heart of the New Forest, yet under a mile from the centre of Lyndhurst, is a detached character cottage **sleeping 3/4**. 'Comfortable'; ref 7858.

Well suited for annual house parties or reunions of friends or family are two barn conversions at Somersal Herbert, near Ashbourne, **sleeping 8/11** and **12/17** or a **total of 28** if taken together. There's a floodlit tennis court; pets welcome. Refs 7921 and 7922. Or at Deiniolen, near Mount Snowdon in North Wales, a detached cottage with spectacular mountain views **sleeps 14** and has the bonus of two sitting rooms, a games room and a large and enclosed lawned garden. 'Good Quality'; ref 4530.

Close to the centre of Bath and thus ideal for those keen to see its Roman Baths and Pump Room, Bath Abbey, Costume Museum, as well as the

Royal Crescent, Pulteney Bridge and all those quirky little alleyways dotted with surprising antique and gift shops and little eateries is a handsome detached house within its own lawned garden. **Sleeps 6**; 'Good Quality'; ref 4573. One pet welcome.

There are several properties available on the Isle of Wight, from three converted boathouses at Yarmouth (stunning sea views!) to a detached house **sleeping 10** close to the coast path at Fishbourne.

At Auchencairn, near Castle Douglas, is a 'Comfortable' detached tower

This admirable barn conversion near Otley (handy for Harrogate) sleeps 8...

...and this (neither is featured) is in Northumberland's South Tyne Valley...

house **sleeping 4** with a spiral staircase, panoramic sea views and its very own private beach. A fisherman's cottage **sleeps 4** in a four-poster double room and a twin room close to the harbour in the lovely village of Pennan, near Banff. Golf, sailing, surfing and fishing are nearby, so, too, are the castle trail and distilleries on the famous whisky trail. This is 'Beautiful', in terms of both category and location. Ref 2560. Spectacular views of Clashnessie Bay and the Sutherland hills beyond make the trek to a converted cottage set on a working croft in the far north west well worthwhile. This falls in the 'Comfortable' bracket, as are some of the remoter, more deeply rural properties. **Sleeps 4**, with up to two pets welcome. Ref 2721. Also **sleeping 4**, this time in the 'Lovely' category, is a detached house at Strathconon, near Muir of Ord, in the highlands. With a studio cottage, old estate office and gunroom, this is away-from-it-all stuff in a quiet glen.

A 200 year old detached country house at Otterburn, near the Kielder Forest, is on our list of 'must-see specials'. In its own grounds, and surrounded by 100 acres of woodland and pasture, it retains features such as period fireplaces, four poster beds, wooden window shutters. The spacious hallway exposes the grand staircase and has one of many exquisite chandeliers here. **Sleeps 11/13**; 'Beautiful'; ref 7699.

The busy brochure has something for everyone: whether traditional, modern, fit for a house party or just for 2, bustling or remote. There's a former school, log cabins, barn conversions, fishermen's cottages, farmhouses, apartments and a 16th century Welsh longhouse. Contact Welcome Holidays, Embsay Mills, Embsay, Skipton, North Yorkshire BD23 6QR. Telephone (01756) 697737.

See also Pages 89 and 373.

www.welcome.cottages.co.uk

11

Magnificent seven...

The Good Holiday Cottage Guide is happy to be associated with seven outstandingly conscientious regional holiday letting agencies, who market themselves as 'Cottage Line' – though they are also known informally as 'Ask A Local'. Recommending each other's properties, and meeting regularly, each is a family-owned organisation operating in its home area and able to answer questions about individual properties. Together offering a thousand properties covering a large part of England and Wales, and touching Scotland, they provide a network of reliable contacts for the holidaymaker. Their joint website is: **www.cottageline.com**

Norfolk Country Cottages (Page 57):
'Norfolk is a county for connoisseurs: unspoilt villages, pretty countryside, wide sandy beaches and huge skies. There are miles of waterways on the Broads, traditional seaside resorts, pretty rural villages and, of course, the city of Norwich, with its castle, cathedral and shops. Within this fabulous part of England, the agency offers an huge variety of quality properties.'

Norfolk Country Cottages, Carlton House, Market Place, Reepham, Norfolk NR10 4JJ. Telephone (01603) 871872. Fax 870304.
www.norfolkcottages.co.uk   email: info@norfolkcottages.co.uk

Northumbria Coast and Country Cottages (Page 113):
'Wild country, fabulous sandy beaches, the romance of the Scottish borders, the Roman Wall. These (and more) fall within the ambit of Northumbria Coast and Country Cottages, one of the most effective regional cottage agencies in Britain. Their 200 or so properties are a great introduction to the far North Country.'

Northumbria Coast and Country Cottages, Carpenters Court, Riverbank Road, Alnmouth, near Alnwick, Northumberland. Telephone Alnmouth (01665) 830783/830902. Fax 830071.
www.northumbriacottages.com   email: cottages@nccc.demon.co.uk

Menai Holiday Cottages (Page 204):
'Clear descriptions in an excellent brochure and friendly staff familiar with the houses will help you choose from the wide variety of properties (about 100) offered by Menai Holiday Cottages. On Anglesey, Snowdonia and the Lleyn Peninsula, with wonderful mountain views and a sweeping coastline, there is everything from a tiny cottage for two to a manor house for 20.'

Menai Holiday Cottages, 1 Greenfield Terrace, Hill Street, Menai Bridge, Anglesey LL59 5AY. Telephone (01248) 71713
www menaiholidays.co.uk   email:ghc@menaiholidays.co.uk

Salcombe Holiday Homes (Page 285):
At the southernmost point of Devon, between Plymouth and Torquay, the small seaside town and sailing resort is known for its sheltered estuary and sandy beaches, its spectacular National Trust coastal walks, its picturesque

town centre and water sports such as boating, windsurfing, diving and fishing. There is a huge demand for holiday houses, and the agency looks after over 100 of the very best ones available.'

Salcombe Holiday Homes, 3 Island Square, Island Street, Salcombe, Devon TQ8 8DP. Telephone Salcombe (01548) 843485. Fax 843489.

www.salcombe.co.uk
email: shh@salcombe.co.uk

Toad Hall Cottages (Page 286):
'Leafy lanes leading to hidden sandy coves, secret creeks where one can watch badgers and rare birds from the window of one's secluded waterside cottage, isolated medieval farms with stunning views, outstanding sandy beaches, film-set villages: such locations make South West specialist Toad Hall Cottages so successful. With properties recently added, notably on beautiful Exmoor, they have about 250 in total.'

Toad Hall Cottages, Elliott House, Church Street, Kingsbridge, South Devon TQ7 1BY. Telephone (01548) 853089. Fax 853086.

www.toadhallcottages.com
email: thc@toadhallcottages.com

New Forest Cottages (Page 306):
'William the Conqueror set aside the New Forest – soon to be a National Park – as his private deer hunting preserve, and many unique customs date back to this time. This incomparable countryside is home to ponies, cattle and other livestock roaming free. The 100 or so properties range from quaint thatched cottages with ponies grazing at the gate to comfortable modern townhouses.'

New Forest Cottages, 4 Quay Hill, Lymington, Hampshire SO41 3AR. Telephone (01590) 679655. Fax (01590) 670989.

www.newforestcottages.co.uk
email: holidays@newforestcottages.co.uk

Cottage in the Country/Cottage Holidays (Pages 360):
'Specialising in Oxfordshire, the Cotswolds, Shakespeare Country and the Welsh borders, this long established agency has the big advantage in most of its 250 properties of being easily accessible (within two hours or even less of London, for example). Though many also enjoy pin-drop quiet in a tranquil and historic part of England, famous for its thatched and half timbered cottages.'

Cottage in the Country/Cottage Holidays, Forest Gate, Frog Lane, Milton-under-Wychwood, Oxfordshire OX7 6JZ. Telephone (01993) 831495, fax 831095.

www.cottageinthecountry.co.uk
email: ghc@cottageinthecountry.co.uk

Advertisement feature

Icing on the cake...

(Quite a few of the cottages we feature offer more than just accommodation)

The owners of *Barkham* (Page 276) are closely associated with The Two Moors Festival (18-26 October), the South West's major classical music festival. There are fifteen concerts taking place in rural churches, including Tavistock, Ashburton, Dunster and Lynton. Artists feature the brilliant young cellist, Guy Johnston, the Britten Sinfonia, Julius Drake, Michael Chance and Nicholas Daniel. Ring 01643 831006 for details.

At *Nannerth Fawr* (see Pages 178 and 179) a farm and wildlife trail starts at the farmhouse and takes in peaceful riverside – the home of otters – through wetlands where rare dragonflies breed, then among the ancient oaks of the owner's woodland where badgers excavate their setts, and up to the open moor where red kites soar above the mountains.

The owners of one of the most memorable properties we found during our recent travels (*The Tallet*, Page 336) offer walking holidays staying at the cottage, with daily guided walks among the glorious Cotswolds hills.

A huge hit with children are the guided farm walks at *Ross Farm*, Northumberland (Page 114), on which little ones meet cows and calves, ewes and lambs, and observe coastal wildlife such as swans, geese and curlews. There are horses and ponies to help groom, and skills such as plaiting and brushing to learn. And much more...

The owners of *Wye Lea* (Page 324/325) offer 'a full range' of beauty treatments, including facials, eyelash and eyebrow tinting, manicures, pedicures, waxing and make-up. 'For a totally de-stressing experience', as they put it, guests are invited to try the half hour head, neck, back and shoulders massage or the one-hour full body massage.

And *Combermere Abbey*, in Shropshire (Page 319), add an extra touch to their exceptional cottages in the form of their Combermere Pure Indulgence Spa package, half-day series of treatments at the Madison Spa.

The main business of the owners of *Hillside Cottage* and *The Bothy* (Page 352) is designing and selling Baltic pine garden furniture. Their most popular products are two- and three-seater swings, two-position dining and relaxing chair, tables, rocking chairs and sunbeds. A discount is available to cottage guests.

Several of the cottage set-ups we feature offer, along with other good things, fine restaurants 'on site'. Though some are open to the public, they add greatly to the appeal and ambience of staying in one of their cottages. We have eaten in most of those featured...

Wye Lea, near Ross on Wye, (see Pages 324/325), features an elegant, spacious, light and airy restaurant that has become a talking point, and outsiders come from quite a distance to enjoy such dishes as *bouillabaisse*, roast duck breast with baby roast rosemary potatoes, tournedos rossini, perhaps preceded by grilled goats' cheese with a pesto dressing, caesar salad or *moules marinières*.

Owlpen, in Gloucestershire (see Page 326), has a restaurant with lots of character; in a converted former cider house, but quite plush, it is a cross between a smart restaurant for an occasion and a cosy pub. Dishes that among other reasons get people returning time and time again include wild boar and bramley apple sausages with onion mash and mustard sauce, or spinach and mushroom roulade served with a tomato coulis.

Trefanny Hill (Pages 220/221) are known not just for the leafy, uncrowded villagey atmosphere of their quiet, well spaced properties but also the charming small pub, mostly used only by cottage people. For example, they serve tiger prawn tails in garlic butter, Cornish crab soup, a range of fish so fresh it winks at you (such as sea bass and John Dory), venison and walnut casserole, chestnut and wild mushroom pie.

Glebe House Cottages (see Page 254), on the Devon/Cornwall border near Holsworthy, have a most welcoming restaurant in the converted cellars of the historic main house, open several evenings a week. The dedicated and energetic owners produce dishes, such as crispy crab cakes and *fondue bourguignonne*, that are said to match anything served locally.

Holidaymakers who have been to Northumberland rave about the notably inexpensive dishes prepared for the freezer by local chef Jo Jackson for the properties at *Beacon Hill* (Page 110) – such as Hungarian goulash, pheasant breasts in marsala and fisherman's pie – and the meals in the spacious Harvey's restaurant at *Akeld* (Page 107) that include for example fresh crab and fennel soup, roast shoulder of lamb, fresh lemon cheesecake with frosted grapes. There is also a bistro-type menu.

Also in Northumberland, guests at *Ross Farm* (Page 114) can enjoy home-grown Lindisfarne oysters from the cottage proprietors' own beds.

A number of properties in this guide will be of interest to holidaymakers who like to ride, want to learn to ride, or like to take their own horses with them on holiday. Riding-orientated places include *Grange Farm* (Lincolnshire, Page 69), *Farsyde Mews* (North Yorkshire, Page 84), *Beacon Hill, Shilbottle* and *Cresswell Wing* (Northumberland, Page 110, 109 and 112), *Bailey Mill* (Cumbria, Page 149), *Sir Johns Hill Farm* (Wales, Page 211) and *Foxes Reach* (Cotswolds/Heart of England, Page 327). *Bailey Mill,* for example, offers full-day stable management courses.

Hoseasons Country Cottages*

Thatched cottage, Scottish croft, manor house, converted barn. These and more feature in Hoseasons' nearly-1500 quality properties spread across the whole of Britain and Ireland. *All are inspected annually,* 400 are new in 2002, and over half accept pets.

Saunas, jacuzzis, outdoor hot tubs, fishing lakes, sunbeds, even a rowing boat or kayak, make many cottages much more than just a place to stay. You'll often find videos, stereos, four-poster beds, open fires and bicycles too – and occasionally even stabling for your own horse. Garden furniture, barbecues and highchairs are standard in cottages for families.

Hoseasons have always been based in East Anglia, so it's not surprising that they offer a good choice there. Many are handy for the Norfolk Broads, reflecting the company's high reputation amongst boating enthusiasts.

One we especially want to see for ourselves is *Black Horse Cottage*

This peaceful house in deepest Derbyshire has its own orchard garden.

This 17th century Welsh farmhouse is near Porthmadog and a Blue Flag beach.

(**sleeping 6**) at Wroxham, six miles from Norwich. Part of a quiet private marina which includes an indoor pool, sauna and coffee shop, it comes with its own launch. There are two twin bedrooms, a double, open-plan living/dining room and waterside sun terrace. Ref E1207.

Ivy House Farm at Wortham, near Diss, on the Norfolk/Suffolk border, has an idyllic setting on the edge of a large common where sheep and horses graze. Its four properties, *Ivy House* (**sleeping 8-10**), *Owl Cottage* (**sleeping 6-7**) and *Suffolk Punch* and *Clydesdale* (both **sleeping 4**) share an indoor heated pool, games room, snooker room/library, croquet lawn and children's play area. Cycles can be loaned and tennis and riding are available nearby. Ref E1532-5.

Among properties we have visited is the 16th-century *Rookery Cottage* at St Margaret's, South Elmham, Suffolk, which looks like something you find on the lid of a chocolate box. It has its own south-facing garden as well as a meadow for games. Holiday tenants also have the use of an enchanting private lake with dinghy and the possibility of fishing. The spacious interior is a delight too, combining a sense of history (it's full of beams) with all mod cons. **Sleeping up to 5**, it has a double bedroom with en-suite shower/toilet and a twin room (up steep stairs) on the second floor. Ref E1275.

In Derbyshire, *Knockerdown Cottages* – two new ones and five converted from 19th-century farm buildings – are grouped around a pretty

16

courtyard, less than a mile from the Carsington Water windsurfing and sailing centre. **Sleeping from 2 to 8,** they are perfect for children as there's a 34-foot indoor pool (3ft-5ft 9in deep), table-tennis and well-equipped play area. Canadian canoes (great for families) and fishing are available on the lake. Ref E1242.

Readers with children who love to scamper across Wales's golden sands have also praised the two *Nant Cottages,* near Aberaeron, on Cardigan Bay. *Polly* (**sleeping 6**), which dates back to the 18th century, has a double and two twin bedrooms and a large enclosed garden, while *Henny Penny* (**sleeping 2**) has just one double bedroom. Birdwatchers will probably already know that this is a red kite area. Dolphin-watching boat trips operate from the harbour at New Quay village, four miles away. Ref W7022-3.

Also in Wales, we know and admire the cottages at *Cwmconnell Farm,* Moylgrove. They are tucked away well out of sight down a narrow lane, and in easy walking distance of the most spectacular part of the Pembrokeshire coast. Sandy beaches are quickly and easily accessible. A

Just 300 yards from a super sandy beach, this Norfolk cottage is also near a pub...

Loch Ness Cottages: each has an open fire, its own garden and loch views.

special feature here, apart from the likelihood of seeing badgers, is the acre of garden planted to encourage wildlife, including a shallow (unfenced) 'conservation pond'. **Sleep from 2 to 6.**

The Stationmaster's House at Rannoch, in Perthshire, is always popular with railway buffs. A handsome granite bungalow (**sleeping 5**), it's close to Rannoch's Grade II listed station, on the famous West Highland Line, one of the world's most scenic railways; a two-hour ride takes you to Fort William and the Silver Sands of Morar. Ref S4258.

Monster spotters should consider one of the four *Loch Ness Cottages,* four miles from Drumnadrochit, which have a glorious panoramic view across the mysterious loch. Each has oak beams, a log fire, its own sheltered garden and access to a shingle beach. Two **sleep 2** in four-posters and **two sleep 4.** Ref S4105.

Details from Hoseasons Holidays Ltd, Sunway House, Lowestoft NR32 2LW. Telephone 0870 534 2342. Fax 0870 902 2090.

On-line booking and 'real time' availability on the web:

www.hoseasons.co.uk   email: mail@hoseasons.co.uk

National Trust Cottages

The National Trust now offers over 300 cottages – by definition in out-standing locations – from which to choose your holiday home in England, Wales or Northern Ireland. (All profits from these holiday cottages go towards funding the upkeep of the great estates or glorious countryside of which they are a part, so it's a bonus to know that your holiday helps preserve this heritage.)

There is an enormous range of accommodation: examples include many within or adjacent to National Trust properties, former coastguard and cosy fishermen's cottages, a recently available and quite extraordinary 1970s house on the Isle of Wight, a lighthouse keeper's cottage, *The Triumphal Arch* at Berrington Hall, in Herefordshire, and the conversion of a former Isolation Hospital in Dorset. Talking about the unusual, how about the *Engineer's Cottage, The Keeper's Cottage,* both **sleeping 4**, and

The Birdcage, in Port Isaac, Cornwall is quite something. Sleeps 2 (small) people!

Mill Cottage is on the Blickling Estate, in Norfolk. Pretty as a picture, sleeping 6.

the more basic *Lookout Cottage,* **sleeping 4**, centred on Souter Lighthouse, near South Shields? In 1871 it was one of the most advanced in the world. You can still clamber up to the Lantern Room and try your hand at Morse Code.

Close to another popular coast is the *Mustard Pot Cottage*, on the Felbrigg Estate in Norfolk, a delightful cottage with direct access to the estate's park and woodland. **Sleeping 4**, it has a charming octagonal sitting room and bedroom above, and its own large fenced garden.

The 2002 brochure helpfully has a Quick Look section at the front from which you can see at a glance which cottages welcome dogs, have been adapted to suit visitors with disabilities, are quirky and unusual, are within Trust properties, in romantic locations, have a double bed, or are in remote places. This year sees the piloting of a quality grading scheme in some areas where properties are awarded between 1 and 5 Acorns, depending on criteria that include location, interiors and facilities.

In splendid isolation on White Edge Moor, within the Peak District National Park, with outstanding views over the Derwent Valley (yet only ten miles from the centre of Sheffield), the former gamekeeper's cottage on the Duke of Rutland's Longshaw Estate (*White Edge Lodge*) has just been converted into an environmentally friendly holiday home. **Sleeping 5**, it has an Aga and a woodburning stove, an enclosed garden and great views. At a little-used entrance to Calke Abbey, a Trust property virtually unaltered since the last Baronet died in 1924, and crammed with fascinating possessions, the Grade II listed *Heath End Lodge* – built in 1806 – has been converted into a charming holiday home **for 3**.

Renovated for the 2002 season are *2 & 3 Bonemill Cottages*, two 19th century, former farm workers' cottages, at the heart of the Dudmaston Estate near Quatford, Bridgnorth. Full of character, each **sleeps 3**.

The Lake District is peppered with properties that appeal to people drawn to the water's edge, such as *The Waterside Cottages*, close to the Lake Windermere shoreline. *The Fell Cottages*, at Low and High Hallgarth, are remote, in glorious surroundings.

Over in Yorkshire, a favourite location for many is the 17th century fishing village of Robin Hood's Bay; the Trust is able to offer the second floor of the *Old Coastguard Station* for holiday use **for 2 people.** (Trust displays and educational facilities take up the lower floors.) There are, of course, stunning sea views! *The Old Smithy* is a small single-storeyed building set in the hillside, and near a tumbling stream, in a quiet corner of popular Buckden, in the heart of the Yorkshire Dales. **Sleeps 2**. Eight miles north-west of York, *The Victorian Laundry*, in a courtyard fifty yards from Beningbrough Hall, is the unique setting for a first floor flat **sleeping 4.** And handily in the centre of York are two apartments in a medieval building close to the Treasurer's House and Minster.

In the south of the country, *Old Forge House* is a classic Georgian house **sleeping 8**, close to Compton Castle and enjoying easy access to the South Devon coast and countryside. Or choose *The Watchtower*, built into the wall of Compton Castle, and enjoy access during property opening hours to the castle and gardens. It **sleeps 2**.

Dorset is famous for Brownsea Island, with its 500 acres of heath and woodland, and one can stay in *Quay Cottage*. Ideal for birdwatchers and ramblers, the waterside terraced cottage **sleeps 4**. In the neighbouring county of Wiltshire, a gardener's delight must surely be *89 Church Lawn*, a stone cottage **sleeping up to 7**, smack at the entrance to Stourhead. The rare trees, plants, temples and monuments give these gardens great appeal. Convenient for visiting Bath, Bristol, Somerset and down into the West Country, is *Rose Cottage, 6 Blaise Hamlet*; **sleeps 3**. One of a hamlet of nine picturesque cottages around a green, they were designed by John Nash in 1809 to accommodate Blaise Estate pensioners.

For a brochure contact The National Trust (Enterprises) Ltd, Holiday Booking Office, P O Box 536, Melksham, Wiltshire SN12 8SX. Telephone (0870) 458 4422, fax 458 4400. (A card suggesting a voluntary £2 contribution towards production, postage and packing is included.)

www.nationaltrustcottages.co.uk

This historic cottage is close to the cathedral in ancient Lincoln...

This one-time 'dame's school' is near Portscatho, and marvellous beaches.

The Vivat Trust

A charity devoted to rescuing and restoring historic buildings that in most cases are available for holiday letting, The Vivat Trust has (in a short space of time) built up a reputation for very well managed properties that combine a feeling for the past with comfort and style.

The highlight of two journeys we made to Yorkshire and Lancashire last year was definitely seeing a little jewel of a cottage called *Church Brow*. On the outskirts of the small town of Kirkby Lonsdale, just inside the Cumbrian border, it is both fascinating in itself and eye-poppingly situated, on a 'brow' indeed, on a steep bank above the River Lune, with panoramic views over the valley (described by John Ruskin in 1875 as 'one of the finest views in England'). Both outwardly and inwardly, three-storeyed Church Brow is pure delight, with an irresistible sitting room, with open fire, that leads on to a formal garden terrace.

Perhaps more by chance than design, there is a useful geographical spread, which could be the makings of a voyage of discovery for holiday-makers with an interest in British history and architecture. As well as Church Brow, the properties include the early 14th century stone-built *Chantry*, at Bridport, Dorset, a 17th century 'banqueting house' (*The Summer House*) in Shropshire, and, also in Shropshire, an 18th century folly called *The Temple*. The biggest Vivat property is *The Cloister House*, at Melrose, in the Scottish borders. It is an early 19th century Manse in the precincts of Melrose Abbey. And there are two fabulous restored tower houses: *North Lees Hall*, at Hathersage, in Derbyshire, designed by the same architect as nearby Hardwick Hall, and *The Tower of Hallbar*, in Lanarkshire, a romantic 16th century idyll among woods.

Vivat handle two of the very attractive and stylish cottages in the

This is The Temple, in 40 'picturesque' acres: complete seclusion, full of history...

The Summer House is all that remains of a great country seat. Amazing views...

converted Jacobean stable block of Combermere Abbey, in Shropshire.

Despite the seriousness of the purpose behind Vivat, there is nothing austere about the accommodation. Though it varies, the interior style tends to be country-house-with-flair, with good country antiques, deep armchairs and a strong sense of the historical importance of these very special buildings. The properties feel like lived-in homes, not museums. There are open fires or woodburners in several.

For a brochure, contact The Vivat Trust, 61 Pall Mall, London SW1Y 5HZ. Telephone 0845 0900194. Fax 0900174. See also Page 68.

www.vivat.org.uk   email: enquiries@vivat.org.uk

Dales Holiday Cottages*

Browsing through the Dales Holiday Cottages brochure is like taking a tour through the best of England's North Country, with an invigorating detour into some of the most scenic corners of Scotland. Heathery moors, tree-lined rivers with a ruined castle on the bank, ancient market towns, villages that seem hardly to have changed for two or three hundred years: all of these add flavour to a very interesting portfolio.

During a 2000 journey right through Yorkshire and into Cumbria we visited, at random, two properties: the first on a farm near Giggleswick, the second at Feizor, a tiny, farmy hamlet close to the Cumbria border. They both **sleep 6.** Refs 2372 and 2953.

The Lake District hardly needs any introduction from us, but readers who dislike the Lakes' tourist honeypots might prefer a cottage at the rear of a Grade II listed coach-house at Mealsgate, near Bassenthwaite. It **sleeps 4.** Ref 2075.

And there are two self catering suites within the precincts of the Dalehead Hall Hotel, on the shores of one of our favourite lakes, which is Thirlmere. Both *The Stables* and *The Hayloft* **sleep 2** in an ensuite double. The bonus here is that one can wine and dine in the highly regarded hotel. Refs 2063/2064.

Extended families should note that the agency has a good number of big houses, among them *The Turrets*, **sleeping 17-19**, at The Courtyard, Sedbergh, a magnificent 16th century building close to the spectacular Howgill Fells and the Dales Way. Ref 2821.

We rate the countryside where England meets Scotland somewhere among the Cheviot Hills very highly, and in Kirk Yetholm, just inside

The Stables and the Hayloft are close to the shores of Thirlmere and fine dining.

Hillview Cottage is very close to the northern end of the Pennine Way...

Scotland, 18th century *Hillview* (**sleeping 4**) makes a very useful base from which to explore the lonely hills or to make forays to the glorious Northumberland coast. Ref 2043

Details/brochures from: Dales Holiday Cottages, Carleton Business Park, Carleton New Road, Skipton, North Yorkshire BD23 2AA. Booking hotline: (01756) 799821/790919.

www.dalesholcot.com
email: info@dalesholcot.com

English Country Cottages*

Whether you're after something big or small, very smart or just 'intriguing', you're going to find it within English Country Cottages' extra-thick 468-page brochure, which includes Wales. Filled with tempting pictures and descriptions, it makes the point that the British Isles may be the most beautiful country, mile for mile, in the world.

All properties are grouped into nine English regions, plus Wales. Each section begins with an introduction by a travel writer who knows the area well. It also highlights cottages conveniently located for exploring cities such as London, Bath, Chester, Cheltenham and York. In London, for example, you can choose from Chelsea, Kensington or the Barbican.

English Country Cottages is well-known for promoting properties of historic and local interest and has thus indirectly encouraged valuable conservation. Staying in these, you get a genuine sense of history. One of the oldest, on Reen Manor Farm at Perranporth, in Cornwall, is *Manor Barn*

Tuckenhay Mill, in South Devon, is extraordinary, with 21 properties to consider. This is the shared outdoor pool.

Glas Y Dorlan, at Llangynog, near Bala, has antique furniture and – a first for us – a pedal organ...

(**sleeping 8**), a medieval church building complete with Norman arches and stone-flagged floors. Ref GFT.

At High House at Dunster, in Somerset, you can sleep in a Victorian four-poster beneath beams made from ships wrecked in the Spanish Armada. This three-storey Georgian building (**sleeping 10**) is in the heart of the famous old Somerset village that inspired the hymn 'All Things Bright and Beautiful'. Exmoor and the lively seaside resort of Minehead are within easy reach. Ref EKA.

At Iwerne Courtney, a Dorset village in an area of outstanding natural beauty, *The Old Post Office* is a Grade II listed 18th-century thatched

Allerton Cottage, in North Yorkshire, is well placed for touring the whole county.

Riverside is an excellent apartment, with a river view, in Alcester, Worcestershire.

building which still has its red letter box in the wall. It's now divided into two cottages, Hambledon and Hod, named after local hills. They **sleep 6-7** and **2-5** respectively and each has its own small garden. Holiday tenants have complimentary membership of the nearby school club which has a swimming pool, tennis courts and gym. Refs DJY and DJZ.

Tuckenhay Mill near Totnes in South Devon once produced top quality paper, but now its buildings have been converted into 21 cottages and apartments (**sleeping 2 to 10**) in a tranquil wooded setting just five miles from Dartmouth. Most have a garden, terrace or patio. Guests have access to two exotic indoor pools, sauna, steam room, jacuzzi, snooker and bad-minton. There's also an outdoor pool, tennis and croquet. Ref FUB.

In Northumberland, *Akeld Manor House* (**sleeping 15**) stands at the foot of the Cheviot Hills near Wooler, fifteen miles from the sea. Ten cottages around it, converted from old byres and cart sheds, are available too, **sleeping 4-6**, with indoor heated pool, jacuzzi, sauna, sunbed, games

High House, at Dunster, in Somerset, sleeps up to 10 people in great style and comfort. The main bedroom is amazing...

In a beautifully situated Dorset village, The Old Post Office is Grade II listed and dates mainly from the 18th century...

room and licensed bistro. Ref MDW.

Glas Y Dorlan is an 18th-century cottage (**sleeping 2-4**) at Llangynog, in Powys. The lounge/dining room has antique oak furniture and unusually a pedal organ which should keep music-makers happy for hours. There's a sun room too, with breathtaking views across the Eirth Valley and a sofa-bed where a second couple can sleep. Ref JBQ.

Hill walkers love *Cefn Canal*, a converted barn (**sleeping 2-3**), with splendid mountain views. It's on a small sheep farm at Rhydlanfair, near Betws-y-Coed, and has a double bedroom, plus a sofa bed in the living/dining room. Snowdonia's fourteen peaks are temptingly near and there are interesting river walks to bridges and waterfalls. Ref OHL.

In the Lake District, walking, cycling and pony-trekking are all on the menu at *Fox Hollow*, an attractive 19th-century stone house in the hamlet of Matterdale End. **Sleeping 5-6**, it has two double bedrooms, a single and a pull-out bed. Ullswater is nearby for fishing, boating, sailing and steam-cruises. Ref LWK.

English Country Cottages, Stoney Bank, Earby, Barnoldswick BB94 0AA. Telephone (0870) 5851155. You can also dial-a-brochure: (0870) 5851111.

www.english-country-cottages.co.uk

Quote ref EMA 94.

A number of cottage owners known to us, plus a small number of cottage agencies, now market themselves exclusively or almost exclusively through the internet, including The Good Holiday Cottage Guide's website (www.goodcottageguide.com). Although they do not appear in the guide proper, we can still vouch for them ...

*Southfields, Hertfordshire (near Buntingford). A pair of quiet, semi-detached 'traditional' cottages on a farm. Telephone (01763) 281224. **email: The Good Holiday Cottage Guide: frank@cottageguide.co.uk**

*Old Farm Cottages, Norfolk (near Wroxham). Six excellent, stylish, secluded barn conversions plus leisure centre. Sleep 2/6. Telephone (01692) 536612. **email: The Good Holiday Cottage Guide: frank@cottageguide.co.uk**

*Peartree Cottage, Brancaster Staithe. A comfortable three-storey cottage with excellent views over marshland. Sleeps 6. Telephone (01485) 518318. **www.peartreecottages.co.uk. email: peartreecottage@farming.co.uk**

*Woodthorpe, Lincolnshire (near Alford). Attractive, well equipped cottages near superb sandy beaches. Sleep 2/6. Telephone (01507) 450294. **www.woodthorpehall.com. email: Bookings@woodthorpehall.com**

*Lilac Cottage, East Yorkshire. Small, charming cottage close to coast. Sleeps 4. Telephone (01964) 527645. email: nick@seasideroad.freeserve.co.uk **www.dialspace.dial.pipex.com/town/walk/aer96/lilac-cottage**

*Keld Head, Pickering. Seven well equipped and cosy stone farm cottages, by North York Moors. Four-posters. Sleep 2/7. Telephone (01751) 473974. **www.keldheadcottages.com. email: julian@keldheadcottages.com**

*Burton, Turbine, Greystones, Charlie's Stables, Reeth. Stone-built in a calm setting, views to the Pennines, ideal for the Yorkshire Dales. Sleep 2/5. Telephone (01748) 884273. **www.uk-cottages.com. email: cprocter@aol.com**

*Holiday Homes in Yorkshire. Over 80 cottages throughout Yorkshire. **www.holidayhomesgroup.co.uk. email; holidayhomesgroup.york@virgin.net**

*Bolehill, Bakewell. Eight award-winning cottages in 20 acres. (01629) 812359. **www.bolehillfarmcottages.co.uk. email: tonystaley@hotmail.com**

*The Old Byre, Northumberland (near Hexham).Traditionally built farm-steading in 30 acres; panoramic views. Sleeps 6/9. Telephone (01434) 673259. **www.ryehillfarm.co.uk. email: enquiries@consult-courage.co.uk**

*Kinlochlaich House, Appin, Argyll. Apartments/cottage within period house and grounds in spectacular Highlands. Telephone (01631) 730342. **www.kinlochlaich-house.co.uk.**
email: hutchison@kinlochlaich-house.co.uk

*Lochinver, Sutherland. Seven lodges by the sea. Sleep 4. Tel 01571 844282. **www.watersidehomes.demon.co.uk email: lochlarder@btinternet.com**

*Armadale Castle, Isle of Skye. Six comfortable log cottages plus suite with sea/mountain views, by Clan Donald Visitor Centre. Sleep 4/6. (01471) 844305. **www.cland.demon.co.uk. email: office@cland.demon.co.uk**

*Bridge End, Eskdale, Cumbria. Award-winning, characterful, Grade II listed cottages in small hamlet in valley beneath Scafell Pike. Tel (01242) 679900. **www.selectcottages.com. email: greg@selectcottages.com**

*Staffield Hall, Cumbria (near Penrith). Seven elegant apartments in mansion in Eden Valley. Sleep 2/5. Telephone (01768) 898656. **www.eden-in-cumbria.co.uk/staffieldhall. email: dawson.staffieldhall@talk21.com**

*Fell View, Cumbria. Cottages/apartments in peaceful grounds close by Lake Ullswater and half a mile from Helvellyn. Telephone (017684) 82342. **email: The Good Holiday Cottage Guide: frank@cottageguide.co.uk**

*Stoneleigh, near Wasdale and Eskdale. A detached sandstone house in one acre gardens; views to Wasdale and surrounding fells. Sleeps 16. Telephone (019467) 25506. **email: dw@elltech.fsnet.co.uk**

*Penffynnon, Aberporth. Characterful, well equipped properties by sandy beaches. Tel (01239) 810387. **www.aberporth.com. email: tt@lineone-net**

*Ivy Court, mid Pembrokeshire. A clutch of warm stone cottages by 350 acres of parkland. Swimming pool, tennis court, croquet. Tel (01437) 532473. **www.ivycourt.co.uk. email:holidays@ivycourt.co.uk**

*Barlings Barn, Powys. The Barn (private squash court) sleeps 16/18; The Cottage sleeps 10/12. Indoor swimming pool; rural location. (01650) 521479. **www.barlbarn.zetnet.co.uk. email:barlbarn@zetnet.co.uk**

*Houndapitt, Bude, Cornwall. Traditional farm cottages set in 100 acre estate overlooking Sandymouth Bay. Sleep 2/9. Telephone (01288) 355455. **www.houndapitt.co.uk. email: info@houndapitt.co.uk**

*Broomhill Manor, Cornwall (near Bude). 17 cottages and wing of manor house in beautiful 9-acre gardens. Sleep 2/6. Telephone (01288) 352940. **www.broomhillmanor.co.uk. email: chris@broomhillmanor.co.uk**

*The Old Post Office, Wiltshire (near Marlborough). A thatched, elegant 18th century listed cottage in glorious countryside. Sleeps 4. **email: The Good Holiday Cottage Guide: frank@cottageguide.co.uk**

*Westley, Chalford, Stroud. Five cottages scattered over a Cotswold hill farm. Sleep 2/6. Telephone (01285) 760262. **www.westleyfarm.co.uk email: westleyfarm@compuserve.com**

*Cyder Barn,Preston Wynne. Two quiet, cosy cottages by a picture book farm, close to Hereford. Sleep 4/6. Telephone (01432) 820621. **www.ukholidaycottage.com. email: rachael@themail.co.uk**

Country Holidays*

'Nothing compares to staying in the heart of the British countryside or right by the sea' states the Country Holidays brochure. But if anyone was in doubt, they'd be convinced by its descriptions and colourful pictures of over 3000 properties spread across England, Scotland and Wales. We have checked out several, obviously not all, and found them always tidy, clean and good value.

Properties are grouped geographically and ranked by a simple grading system covering comfort, space and facilities. Indexes list those sleeping at least 10 people and those with pools. Also a special symbol denotes

There are so many excellent Lake District properties : this is Brothersfield...

In rural Shropshire, this handsome 'black and white' house is 400 years old.

those with no internal steps or stairs, or having at least one bedroom and bathroom on the ground floor.

So making your choice is easy, from a one star "Acceptable overall level of quality; adequate provision of furniture, furnishings and fittings" up to Five Stars for 'Exceptional overall level of quality; high levels of decor, fixtures and fittings, together with an excellent range of accessories and personal touches'. In addition a clear set of symbols beside each property's picture shows its price band, the number of bedrooms and how many people it accommodates, whether pets are accepted and whether short breaks are available.

Lovers of the Lake District should consider the Five Star-graded Coach House at Loweswater (**sleeping 8**). Originally part of a gentleman's farm, it now has an interesting multi-level interior with two double bedrooms and two twins (though the steps could be difficult for toddlers or the disabled); the living room and open plan dining-room/kitchen are at the top. All around, you get glorious views of the fells, with Crummock Water in the distance, and superb walks from the door. Red squirrels regularly visit the garden. Ref 8368.

Shoreview, a ground floor apartment (4 stars) on the seafront at Troon in Ayrshire, attracts golf addicts as well as lovers of this attractive part of Scotland. Nine courses are within easy reach, including the championship ones at Troon and Turnberry. **Sleeping 4**, it has a double bedroom and a twin. Ref 12125.

Anyone looking for somewhere for a group or extended family to stay could consider either of two former chapels (both 3 stars), just north of Derby. *The Ebenezer Chapel* in the historic conservation village of Milford was built in 1846. Subtly converted, it now includes a 38-foot beamed and galleried lounge, sauna and two stairlifts. The eight bed-rooms can **sleep 20-22**. Or the *Old Baptist Chapel* at Belper, dating from 1817, has a 40-foot beamed lounge with dining area and gallery, and a sauna. Its eight bedrooms **sleep 18-20**. Walkers should note that both properties are on the edge of the Dales in the Peak District, and families are within easy reach of Alton Towers. Ref 12613 & 11621.

We rate the Welsh borders very highly, and love the beautifully restored 16th century half timbered house in Shropshire called *The Pound*, **sleep-ing 6**. It is full of original features, including exposed cruck beams, oak studding, but sympathetically and comfortably restored. There's lots to see and do around here, including the marvellous Ironbridge Gorge

This is one of many classic thatched cottages in Norfolk. Ref 15051.

The Scottish section contains some rare properties: this one is in Fife...

Museum. Almost on the English/Welsh border, at Brilley, near Hay on Wye, *Fern Hill Cottage* is another fine half timbered 17th century prop-erty **sleeping 4** and adjoining the owner's house. It is in the heart of rural tranquillity, with lots of good walking. Refs 12221 and 9384.

A possibility for larger groups, which we know well, is *Barlings Cottage* and/or the adjacent *Barn* at Llanbrynmair (both 4 stars) which are tucked away amid glorious unspoilt countryside in the mid-Welsh hills, about 25 miles north-east of Aberystwyth. The Cottage, an extended 18th-century stone longhouse, **sleeps up to 12** in five bedrooms and the Barn **sleeps up to 16** in seven bedrooms. Pets aren't allowed at the Cottage but one is permitted at the Barn, which also has its own squash court. Both share a heated indoor pool (14 x 28 feet) which is suitable for children as the depth goes from 3 feet to 6 feet. There's a sauna too. Brochure refs 15798 & 15799.

Country Holidays also have a good choice for those at the other end of the scale who simply want a quiet retreat for two, though a friend of ours regularly seeks a little hideaway just for one so she can work on her TV scripts. "All I need is a bed, a microwave and my laptop", she says. One of her recent discoveries is *North End Barn* (3 stars), a timber-clad con-verted barn (**sleeping 2**) at Stelling Minnis, seven miles south of Canterbury. It has a double bedroom, small enclosed garden and is easy to reach from London, being only ten minutes from the M20. Ref 15645.

Details from Country Holidays, Spring Mill, Barnoldswick, Lancashire BB94 0AA. For bookings, telephone 08700 723723; brochures: 08700 725725. **Quote ref CMA 96.**

Live search and book at: www.country-holidays.co.uk.

MANY ARE CALLED...

The days when worthwhile holiday properties sat empty and unloved are long gone. And that applies all year round, not just at the height of the season. The thatched beauty by the mill stream you've had your eye on, the rare 1930s bungalow right on a sandy beach in North Norfolk, the rambling Georgian rectory in its own extensive grounds, may no longer be available by the time you phone about them.

Other equally interesting places are certainly available, but how would you know this?

This is where a well regarded organisation called UK One Call comes in. With nearly 700 properties on its books, and rising, it will field enquiries from holidaymakers mainly wanting a last-minute booking but sometimes looking well ahead, and identify vacancies from their database. It can also help satisfy particular requirements, such as wheelchair access, open fires and four poster beds. Owners on their books keep UK One Call up to date with availability, which saves the cottage-goer time and hassle. At busy times of the year (for example, when the Lake District is full) enquirers might even be offered a different part of the country, and explore new horizons.

There is no charge to holidaymakers, as an annual fee is paid to UK One Call by owners.

Potential self catering clients can log on to the organisation's busy website or phone: see the advertisement on Page 9.

As we found in late 2001 the organisation is also very useful for potentially tricky bookings like those for Christmas and New Year, when demand is huge (many desirable properties being booked two years ahead).

Please note: many but not all the properties on the UK One Call database are featured in The Good Holiday Cottage Guide.

Advertisement feature

Sykes Cottages*

Sykes Cottages, long-established and highly regarded, is based in Chester. The agency focuses on holiday properties in the Peak District, Yorkshire, Northumberland, Cumbria and the Lake District, Shropshire and the Marches and North Wales, with a handful in Dumfries and Galloway in Scotland, and the Cotswolds. Ninety per cent are graded by the relevant tourist board.

The Northumberland National Park covers nearly 400 square miles. Within it, ten miles from Rothbury, Alwinton is a tiny, truly rural village in the Upper Coquet Valley – a great base for walkers, with Hadrian's Wall and the glorious coastline within reach. *Priests House* is a stone-built property of character in a delightful position with over half an acre of grounds. There's a large, well equipped kitchen with Aga and a spacious sitting room with open fire. **Sleeps 8/12**. Ref 187. *Summer House,*

Anchorage House is a spanking new property in an amazing location...

Four Winds is in a secluded position on the edge of Bakewell, in Derbyshire...

in the attractive fishing village of Craster, has fabulous views across Craster Harbour and straight out to sea. Part 17th century, it is perhaps the most impressively situated house in a memorable place. **Sleeps 6**. Ref 797.

Four Winds is a traditional stone-built detached cottage in a secluded position on the edge of the market town of Bakewell, in the Peak District National Park. **Sleeps 7**, with a private garden and drive. Ref 460. At Ashbourne – another market town – *Smith's Yard* is a Grade II listed, terraced cottage with oodles of character. **Sleeps 3/4**. Ref 698.

There's a modern, end-of-terrace house close to the harbour and shops in the quaint seaside village of Staithes. **Sleeps 4**. Ref 733. Or a stone farmhouse built in about 1750 in over 125 acres of pasture and woodland, two miles from Wark. Both the sitting room and the hall have an open fire, and there is a piano. **Sleeps 10/12**. Ref 683.

Overlooking Trearddur Bay, on the west shore of Anglesey, *Anchorage House* and *Porth House* (**sleeping 8/9** and **6**) are two magnificent new 'upside down' detached houses finished to the highest standards with, for example, polished wooden floors, open log fires, balconies and a six person sauna and spa pool. WTB Five Stars (of course!), Refs 658 and 761. But there are so many other good things within the Sykes portfolio: we can only scratch the surface here...

Details from Sykes Cottages, York House, York Street, Chester CH1 3LR. Telephone 01244 345700; fax 01244 321442.

www.sykescottages.co.uk   email: info@sykescottages.co.uk

Blakes*

With nearly a century of holiday cottage experience behind them, Blakes have a massive following among people who book with them year after year. Every property is quality assessed by their regional managers who, from this year, are using the English Tourism Council's Star rating for quality (whether the location is in England, Scotland or Wales).

New too for 2002 is a red 'added value' tick for properties providing facilities and services at no extra cost, such as bedlinen, towels and fuel.

If you want somewhere special, many properties achieve the top grade of 5 ticks for being 'excellent' in every respect. At the other end of the scale, 1-tick cottages will suit people who are happy with somewhere more

Dutch Cottage is one of several places on the water at Horning, in Norfolk.

The Farmhouse, at Glenure, Scotland, is not palatial, but the setting is fantastic...

basic but still want to be assured of cleanliness and comfort.

The Blakes brochure is also handy for people looking for short breaks of, say, two, three or four nights. A special symbol indicates whether a property is available and, if so, for how many nights and at what times of the year. If you can get away midweek, a four night midweek break costs the same as a three-night weekend one in the same period.

One of the most splendid properties (we know it: definitely worth its 5 stars) is *Buckland House*, a Grade II mansion at Buckland Filleigh, deep in glorious Devon countryside. **Sleeping 26**, it's ideal for a big family gathering or group of friends who want to holiday together. The 289-acre grounds feature a lake, 25-yard outdoor pool, croquet lawn and even the village church. The accommodation includes a ballroom with grand piano and gallery, snooker room and children's playroom with table tennis, darts and billiards. Several of the bedrooms have four-poster beds, some are en-suite and many have gas coal/log effect fires. Ref B5039.

Very much smaller, but just the sort of simple property that many people look for, is *Heyhoe* (1 star), at Walcott, in north-east Norfolk (**sleeping 4**). A timber holiday bungalow, it has a sitting/dining room/kitchen and two bedrooms (double and twin). For those who like to be close to a beach, its position is ideal, as it stands at the top of the sea wall giving immediate access to the sand and sea. Ref AB38.

Further north, anyone who enjoys dreaming of trains but does not want to be disturbed by them would enjoy *The Station House* at Brompton by Sawdon, about six miles inland from Scarborough. The picturesque building, part of the former Scarborough-Pickering line, still has its original platform, now turned into a neat terrace above the lawn and garden. Inside are three south-facing apartments (3 stars); two **sleep 2-4** and one **sleeps 3-5**. Ref NM1401/NM1404/NM15.

In Scotland, *Mar House* (4 star) at Inverey, is hidden away in a remote spot amid glorious Highland scenery a few miles west of Balmoral (**sleeping 8**). Nestling in a secluded wooded position overlooking the River Dee valley, it has been lavishly refurbished with full central heating plus an open fire (logs included) in the drawing room. Each of the four bedrooms (two doubles, two twins) has its own bathroom and stunning views. In the evenings, herds of deer graze by the river. Ref B5786.

Four Winds at St Monans (4 stars) has spectacular views over the Firth of Forth from every window, including the loo! It's a traditional end-of-terrace fisherman's cottage (**sleeping 4**), now cosily renovated with kitchen/dining room, sitting room and bathroom downstairs and two bedrooms – an en-suite double and twin – upstairs. Ref B5743.

This fabulous converted Kentish barn, near Benenden, embraces three cottages.

Sleeping – yes! – up to 17, this Welsh treasure is 500 yards from the sea...

A really remote property is *Park* (2 stars), a single-storey stone croft built in 1884 on Sanday Island in the north-east of Orkney. **Sleeping 3**, it stands alone, 200 yards from the sea, amid acres of grassland with only a lighthouse (half a mile away), birds and seals for company. Simply but comfortably furnished, it has two bedrooms (double and single) and solid-fuel central heating. Ref 90290. Cedar Rest, on the mid-Wales coast (4 stars), at Llanaber (**sleeping 2**), is part of a 16th-century farmhouse overlooking Cardigan Bay in an Area of Outstanding Natural Beauty. Holiday tenants can use the owners' extensive terrace garden, or enjoy the Blue Flag sandy beach which is just a third of a mile away. Ref WN82.

Blakes, Stoney Bank Road, Earby, Barnoldswick BB94 0AA. To book, telephone 08700 708090. Brochures : 08700 708099. Quote ref BMA 82.

Live search, availability and booking: www.blakes-cottages.co.uk

Watermeadow Farmhouse, in Suffolk, is one of our East Anglian favourites...

Deep in the Scottish Highlands, well placed for walking, fishing and golf...

Interhome UK*

Internationally known for the range of accommodation in almost every corner of Europe, including Eastern Europe, and also with a strong presence in Florida, Interhome quickly got the measure of the self catering scene in the UK, where, more than anywhere else in Europe and beyond, location, size, character, facilities, architectural style and much more vary such a lot. In the space available, web and brochure information is *admirably full of detail*. (All properties, by the way, can be booked online: see Page 4.)

One of our favourite places in Wales is St David's, and a house with a history (it was once a pumphouse), and **sleeping 6**, is available between there and the utterly charming village of Solva. It is just five minutes' walk from a rocky cove and a coastal footpath. Ref G6157/100. And a semi-detached house with fine views, **sleeping 4**, within the Pembrokeshire Coast National Park and close to Fishguard, is handy for sea-trips to Ireland from that port. Ref G6158/100.

We know a good number of the places on Interhome's UK programme, and have stayed in several. One is near Appleby, in Cumbria, a two storeyed cottage of great character separate from the owner's home. **Sleeps 4.** Ref G1580/100.

In one of the most spectacular parts of the Scottish Highlands, but little frequented, Kinloch Laggan is a favourite of ours. Interhome feature a

This Fishguard cottage, sleeping 4, is also handy for trips by sea to Ireland!

This cottage is superbly situated by Loch Laggan, one of our own favourites.

rare example of a traditional longhouse, **sleeping 4** and with good views of woods and mountains. But it's only a short walk to the nearest shop and pub. There's the big advantage of a woodburning stove in the sitting room. Ref G8815/110.

Interhome also have a number of properties in central and Greater London, such as a comfortable three-bedroom apartment in Richmond (about 25 minutes by underground to the West End), and some most attractive properties in Twickenham, also in easy reach of central London. A much cheaper option than staying in the centre.

Details/brochure from Interhome Ltd, 383 Richmond Road, Twickenham TW1 2EF. Telephone 020-8891 1294. Fax 020-8891 5331.

www.interhome.co.uk
email: info@interhome.co.uk

Bed and breakfast/hotel accommodation

The Good Holiday Cottage Guide frequently receives requests from
readers wanting information about places to stay en route to
distant cottages and for friends and family to stay for a night or
two while visiting people staying in a cottage (or apartment, chalet
etc). They are sometimes able to stay as 'extra people' in the
cottage, but not usually. So we are now including information
about hotels and 'b & b' near the end of this edition.

Cottages big and small

*A number of cottages featured can accommodate large numbers of
people. Some owners and agents have asked us to point out that you do
not have to be a group of 8, 10, 12, etc. Depending on demand, smaller
numbers can normally be accommodated, usually at a lower price, and
we know a lot of readers like having space to 'spread themselves'...

Pets

Between half and two thirds of the cottage owners featured in this guide
accept dogs, and acceptance of dogs usually but not always means other
pets too (a small number exclude cats). Most owners charge extra –
usually between £12 and £17 per week per dog – for the inevitable extra
wear and tear on properties, though this is without exception much less
than what kennels would charge. Please do not arrive with more dogs
than you have permission to take, and please do not sneak a dog into a
cottage where it is not welcome. Do note that, even when cottage owners
say 'No dogs', dog lovers may still find themselves 'among friends': it
could be that visiting town dogs may not take well to cottages
surrounded by farmland with lots of sheep, or that the owners' dogs
don't like strange animals.

Short breaks

Readers often write or phone about short breaks, and sometimes ask why
we don't list the properties that offer these. It's because about ninety per
cent do. This can almost be taken for granted, depending on the time of
year, and it is usually worth asking about a short break even during the
main holiday season. Winter weekends especially can still be a bargain,
but are more realistically priced than they used to be, when some owners
were happy 'just to keep the places lived in'...

Please note: while the individually owned properties and property letting agencies we feature are hand-picked and endorsed by us, we cannot vouch for every single property on an agency's books or within a particular ownership. We do however stand by places we do feature...

We always recommend telephone discussions with an owner or agent about any properties that appeal, and the more detail you can give about particular concerns and requirements the better. It is possible to book direct from this guide, and readers often do so late in the season or at short notice, but in general we recommend that readers send off first for brochures and other information. Elements essential to readers' holiday enjoyment and peace of mind should be double checked prior to making any commitment. This applies for example to the number of people a property comfortably sleeps, whether bedrooms are all upstairs, the types of bed ('firm', 'soft', etc), whether en suite, and whether bathrooms have bath or shower or both.

The Good Holiday Cottage Guide contains a mass of information, some of which, such as tourist board gradings, is as supplied by cottage owners and agents.

Prices given are per property per week, and may be subject to change. They generally include VAT where applicable.

Agencies are marked with an asterisk in the text and are underlined on maps. Those maps are necessarily sketchy and can give only a rough idea of a cottage or agency location. You cannot do better than Ordnance Survey maps, whose Landranger series usually (for we are dealing with rural areas) shows the very property you are booking. Numbers given on maps are not page numbers: to identify a property whose geographical location appeals, refer back to the map reference at the top of the feature (top left or right) in the relevant geographical section of the guide.

East Anglia, East Midlands and The Shires

Glorious sandy beaches, sleepy villages with houses that date back 400 years (some of them the colour of sugared almonds – pink, white, yellow or pale blue), world-class bird sanctuaries, romantic tidal rivers. Much of East Anglia is 'on the road to nowhere', and very nice it is too. There are 'bucket-and-spade' family resorts with end-of-the-pier shows, remote castles, National Trust houses, the nostalgic North Norfolk steam railway: just some elements that make East Anglia so special. A maximum of three hours' drive from London or about two hours by train brings one into the best of the region. From Scotland, about four, from the Midlands perhaps two. Roofs are thatched with Norfolk reed that lasts up to about 80 years. Churches that are the size of cathedrals dominate the skyline, meandering rivers are the haunt of wildfowl, country mansions attract connoisseurs rather than hordes. Even if you are holidaying near the coast, do visit Norwich: the cathedral, the castle, the open-air market. Even if you are staying in a cottage, you can hire a boat on the Broads by the hour or the day. To the west lie the prosperous farms of Leicestershire and Northamptonshire, underrated counties of golden limestone villages and elegant churches. To the north are the Lincolnshire Wolds and the haunting, flat fenland, and well into Lincolnshire are some of the finest sandy beaches in England.

Thaxted map 1/1
Thaxted Holiday Cottages

As neat and pretty a barn conversion – making up a pair of semi-detached cottages – as we have seen, this is set well back from the road. Almost identical, all but mirror-images of each other, they've been lovingly furnished and decorated. (We liked the rugs on oak floors, stylish, pale wood modern furniture – all colour co-ordinated.) The lounge-diner has TV/video, CD/cassette/radio, with a selection of videos and music, plus books and games. Facing west at the rear on to fields and meadows, with the spire of Thaxted's ancient church in view, visitors are virtually guaranteed glorious sunsets from their private patio. Memorable views can also be enjoyed upstairs from well-placed Velux windows in the family bedroom. The cottages are a few minutes' walk from historic Thaxted (and buses, shops and pubs), with Stansted Airport just 7 miles away.

This is an ideal base for exploring the pretty and diverse county of Essex...

ETC Four Stars. Each **sleeps 4** in a double and a set of bunk beds. Linen and towels included. Not suitable for pets. No smoking. Cost: about £200 to £400. Details from Yolanda de Bono, Totman's Farm, Dunmow Road, Thaxted, Essex CM6 2LU. Telephone (01371) 830233.

www.thaxtedholidaycottages.co.uk
email: enquiries@thaxtedholidaycottages.co.uk

St Osyth, near Clacton on Sea
Park Hall Cottages

As we turned off the road that links the little-known village of St Osyth and Clacton-on-Sea, we guessed we were on to something good.

We left traffic sounds behind, spotted a substantial farmstead across the fields and soon found ourselves in a leafy, well tended enclave that could have been 'a hundred miles from anywhere'. But for the record it is only ten minutes from the much-loved traditional family seaside resort of Clacton, an hour from London and 20 minutes from Colchester – once an important Roman settlement, and full of history.

We were met by two cheery Norfolk Terriers (puppies had just been born), saw peacocks and ponies, and in company with owner Trisha Ford looked at two beautifully finished and spacious single storeyed houses whose interiors reminded us of rural five star hotels. Both properties are open plan, with deep sofas, lots of beams, a very effective combination of new (such as in the superbly well fitted kitchen areas) and old pine. We liked the most attractive table lamps.

Everything is 'spot on': scrupulously clean, combining a traditional cottagey mood with 21st century comforts – exceptional.

Among so many impressive details, we also noticed the owl theme: a painted owl here, a porcelain owl there. Appropriately, among a number of activities on offer, such as clay pigeon shooting and fishing in well stocked lakes, guests are able to join the owners on early evening 'owl walks': it is that rural here.

Both cottages – *Old Stables* and *Carriage House* – have a double and a twin, the double being a five foot king size, the twin beds in Old Stables being zip-linkable so as to make that great boon of a six foot bed.

Outstanding properties close to the seaside but deep in the country...

...with quite exceptionally harmonious, 'no-expense-spared' interiors.

Carriage House has a particularly appealing ceiling-to-floor window in the double bedroom. Not surprisingly each is ETC Five Stars. Linen and towels included. There are TVs with integral videos, plus high quality music centres. Cost: about £330 to £560.

Details from Trisha or David Ford, Park Hall, St Osyth, Essex CO16 8HG. Telephone: (01255) 820922. Fax 821230.
www.parkhall-countrycottages.com
email: Trish@parkhall.fslife.co.uk
Note: you can take a day trip to Holland from nearby Harwich.

Edwardstone, near Lavenham
Grove Cottages

As you meander along West Suffolk's sleepy country lanes you might feel as if you are 200 miles from any big city. But check the map: as you approach this charming and inviting group of converted 300-year-old cottages you will see that they are just two hours' drive from London.

The location is ideal for pursuing a whole host of activities such as walking, cycling (free bikes here), exploring the beautiful River Stour on canoes (for hire), horse-riding, golfing, touring and 'pubbing'. Though you may actually want to stay put or just go strolling and simply enjoy these very thoughtfully restored and designed properties, run with tremendous flair by film director Mark and his Austrian partner Stefanie. They have made these into something *very special indeed*.

We admired and noted so many good things. Such as charming 'ragged' walls, an original bread oven in *The Bakery*, original brick walls, wooden floors, beams. Plus personal touches such as fresh flowers, locally handmade soaps, fridges stocked for you with the makings of a full English breakfast, a communal fridge-freezer.

We met several guests enjoying the afternoon sun in the beautiful orchard garden. They were planning a barbecue – barbecues are provided, as well as a party-sized barbecue with refectory tables – had enjoyed the owners' home produced honey, and a couple spoke of the friendly welcome they'd had from Mark and Stefanie's dogs and ducks.

If you can drag yourself away from all this you will not want to miss picture postcard Kersey and a remarkable throwback to the medieval age, preserved-in-aspic Lavenham. Bury St Edmunds and Cambridge are an easy meander (avoiding main roads) and Norwich is not a lot further.

With a great commitment both to the history of the properties and to 21st century comfort, these are very special.

All the (very pretty and cottagey) main bedrooms have five-foot beds, and four of the five cottages have an open fire.

Sleep from 2 to 6. TV, stereo, CD/MC player, selection of music and books. Spacious power showers, no baths. Finest cotton linen and towels provided. Pets welcome. Non-smokers or very considerate smokers preferred. ETC Four Stars. Cost: about £150 to £599. Details and a brochure from Mark Scott/Stefanie Wege, The Grove Cottages, Priory Green, Edwardstone, Suffolk CO10 5PP. Telephone (01787) 211115. Fax 211220 or 211511.

www.grove-cottages.co.uk email: stefanie@edwardstone.demon.co.uk

Dalham Vale, near Newmarket
Jockey Cottage

This is an exceptionally attractive and 'traditional' thatched cottage. Situated very close to the Suffolk/ Cambridgeshire border, a few easy furlongs from horsey Newmarket, it is well placed for exploring the best of rural Suffolk, a good part of Norfolk, Cambridge, Ely and the fascinating Fen Country. Handy for a good village pub, it is one of those places that makes a really pleasant base to return to after touring (we

Fitting prettily into its village setting, this makes a stylish and comfortable base to which to hurry home after a day out.

have heard this from a number of overseas readers). Standing well back from the quiet road through this charming, off-the-beaten-track conservation village, it has been very tastefully and considerately restored and furnished. For example, there is a skilful blend of country furniture and top-notch contemporary soft furnishings. It has a wood-burning stove set in an inglenook fireplace and **sleeps 4**. Remote control television. You'll find a welcome pack, a payphone and a garden.

Pets possible by arrangement. Linen/towels included. Cost: about £140 to £325. Weekend breaks available. Details from Richard Williams, Scorrie House, Redruth, Cornwall TR16 5AU. Telephone (01209) 820264.

Claydon, near Ipswich
Mockbeggars Flat   map 1/5

Handy for the junction of the A14 trunk road and the Ipswich/Norwich road, but out of sight of those, this rare Jacobean house is the home of Priscilla Clayton-Mead and family. Separate from the house is their spacious, quiet and private first floor self catering apartment. It has eye-catching framed black and white photos in the sitting/dining room,

On two levels, the flat is very nicely understated and uncluttered...

expensive cream sofas, a good sized TV/video and hi-fi, a big landing, good-size ensuite bedrooms, a top-notch fitted kitchen. A good find at a central point from which to explore east and west Suffolk, it is just half an hour from the old fashioned seaside resort of Felixstowe. Bed and breakfast and sailing also available: there is a 35-foot yacht moored at nearby Levington. **Sleeps 4 'plus 1'**. ETC Four Stars. Well behaved pets welcome. Short breaks. Daily maid service available. Linen and towels included. Cost: about £190 to £380. Details from Mrs P Clayton-Mead, Mockbeggars Hall, Claydon, Ipswich, Suffolk IP6 0AH. Telephone (01473) 830239. Fax 832989. Mobile: 0770 2627770.

www.mockbeggars.co.uk email: pru@mockbeggars.co.uk

Dedham Vale, near Nayland
Gladwins Farm Cottages

Perfectly poised for exploring both east and west Suffolk, this extraordinarily well situated group of cottages enjoys impressively high standards throughout. When we revisited during last year's warm late summer, we were delighted to see again the glorious location and excellent facilities, and to be reminded of the professionalism of the owners.

Though it feels 'far from anywhere', Gladwins is in fact very accessible – for example, less than two hours' drive from London, less than three from Birmingham. We have seen for ourselves the warm and friendly welcome extended by the Yorkshire-born owners, the far-reaching country views and the joys of the splendid indoor pool, not to mention the delight with which children have got to know the goats and the pigs!

All but two properties face on to a courtyard. One of these is the newest, *Chelsworth Cottage*, **sleeping 8**, which is very private and has spectacular views over the Vale of Dedham (and a sitting-out area from which to enjoy them). It has a four-poster bed, TV and ensuites in *all* bedrooms, a log burner and central heating, stereo, and more. A particular bonus is that is has a specially adapted ground floor twin room for disabled people.

Hadleigh **sleeps 4/5** and is attached to the owners' home; *Constable* **sleeps 6**, *Gainsborough* and *Dedham* both **sleep 4**, *Lavenham* **sleeps 4 'plus 1'**, *Melford* **sleeps 2** in a four poster 'for that special occasion' and *Kersey* **sleeps 2 plus 1**. All could be described as 'little showhouses' with their cosy, comfortable interiors, woodburners, modern pine, good fitted carpets and local pictures.

There is access to 22 acres, an air-conditioned pool and sauna building (which even has an 'aromatherapy capsule'), an adventure playground, an all-weather tennis court and a trout lake.

Dogs welcome, except in Lavenham, Hadleigh and Chelsworth. Small-screen TVs/video players. Cost: £215 to £1230. **Sleep 2 to 8**. Open all year; short breaks. Gainsborough has been adapted for accompanied disabled visitors. Details from Pauline and Robert Dossor, Gladwins Farm, Harpers Hill, Nayland, Suffolk CO6 4NU. Telephone Nayland (01206) 262261, fax 263001. Bed and breakfast is also available.

www.gladwinsfarm.co.uk

email: GladwinsFarm@compuserve.com

Beautifully situated, highly professional and with most impressive facilities ...

Interiors are well planned and welcoming. This is Constable ...

Woodbridge, Orford and around
Jane Good's Holiday Cottages*

We don't operate a league table, but if we did we would put this family-run organisation very high indeed among the regional cottage agencies. Dealing exclusively with rural and coastal Suffolk, it is reliably painstaking and conscientious: a pleasure to deal with. Though it's true that they have a head start on account of the part of England in which they operate, for there is something magical about Suffolk's thatched cottages, its ancient churches, picture-postcard pastel-coloured villages, wide skies and ever-changing seascapes.

Based in the heart of the countryside near Woodbridge, one of the most handsome market towns in England, Jane Good has a good range of prop-

Quay View, Orford, is one of our favourites. From its big windows you can see boats of all sizes coming and going.

If the musicians have not got there ahead of you, the apartments at Snape Maltings are very convenient places to stay...

erties both on or very close to the exceptional coast, much of which is an Area of Outstanding Natural Beauty, and among the meadows and historic, chocolate box villages of the interior.

We have never, in seventeen years, had anything but warm praise about this agency from readers of the guide.

Only just inside Suffolk from Essex, *Gilly Parva* is tucked away down a narrow lane off the main street of Stoke-by-Nayland. **Sleeps 2** in a good sized bedroom (double bed). There is a terrace with garden furniture, and guests are welcome to use the owners' garden too.

And there are a number of properties in exquisite Woodbridge. We were delighted by two town houses, *Treetops* (**sleeping 3**) – 'small but perfectly formed'– and (our favourite) the outwardly attractive and internally just-right little jewel that is *2 Fairfield Cottages*, **sleeping 2** in a handsome five foot pine bed.

Also in Woodbridge, *Cape Cottage* (26 Brook Street) is a sympathetically converted Victorian terraced cottage. With an open fire, it **sleeps 4** in a double and a twin.

Note: Woodbridge is served – most prettily – by the railway, and a holiday is possible here without a car.

A number of properties satisfy the demand for bigger houses. Between Snape and Aldeburgh, again in a much sought after location, *Ramillies* is a 300-year-old detached village property with a good pub within walking distance, and an open fire. It has an enclosed private garden and **sleeps 5**, with room for a baby. Near Orford, one of those villages that people seem to go back to year after year once they have found it, *The Brink* is a traditional cottage in a good-sized secluded garden. This too is used by the owners. **Sleeps 4**.

In Orford itself *Quay View* – which one day we'll choose for ouselves – enjoys a commanding situation beside the River Ore and Orford Quay. On a bustling Saturday morning, with boats to-ing and fro-ing (we took an excursion boat), we found this to be a bright, light, spacious and altogether desirable house, **sleeping 4**.

A bonus for visitors to Orford is the proximity of the marvellous music to be heard at The Maltings at Snape, and it is a great coup for Jane Good to have secured the apartments that occupy part of the original Victorian frontage, surrounding the handsome archway. One of the three, *The Clock Flat* (**sleeping 6/8**), has impressive views of the river and the marshes.

Near historic and absolutely charming Framlingham, Colston Hall Cottage is spacious and full of character.

Three apartments (not featured) are right by the water in historic and beautifully preserved Woodbridge...

On the outskirts of Snape, *Valley Farm Barns* incorporates three self contained self-catering units – highly graded by the English Tourism Council – **sleeping 2, 2 and 4** respectively. A very skilful conversion, fitting in very well with its attractive farm surroundings, it offers spacious, easy-living in a building that combines a number of original features and 21st century comforts. At Tunstall, between Woodbridge and Aldeburgh, *2 Snape Road* is a smallish 19th century terraced Victorian cottage **sleeping 2 adults and 2 children**. At the back there is a patio-style garden with a small ornamental pond and garden furniture.

We like the full and factual fact sheets detailing all the 75 or so properties on Jane Good's books – though you should not expect a glossy brochure – and the star rating each cottage gets. A very honest assessment, from five stars for 'excellent' to one for 'basic'.

Even most of the 'expensive' properties cost only about £350/£750 high season, and many that we know to be perfectly acceptable and big enough for a family are only a little over £300 a week high season.

For a copy of the 'brochure', which is inexpensively produced, illustrated by line drawings and is certainly 'a good read', write to Mrs Jane Good Ltd, Blandings, Hasketon, near Woodbridge, Suffolk IP13 6JA.

Dogs, by the way, are welcome in about half the properties at no extra cost. Telephone Woodbridge (01394) 382770. Fax 380914.

www.mrsjanegoodltd.co.uk
email: theoffice@mrsjanegoodltd.co.uk

41

Cransford, near Framlingham
Wood Lodge

Many years in our guide, this is a house of great character deep in rural Suffolk. (It's tucked away, and really quiet.) We revisited recently, and admired again its high ceilings, tall windows, deep armchairs, its big wood stove guaranteed to create a warm and cosy atmosphere, and off which the central heating runs, its masses of space, its character, its history (it dates from about 1800),

One of our all-time favourites, down a woodland track amid eighteen acres (with a half acre lawn in front).

and its most attractive pictures. We have long thought it would make an exceptional base for a happy family holiday. It even boasts a complete Encyclopedia Britannica! The kitchen is well equipped, and includes a dishwasher, the dining room just demands convivial get-togethers, bedrooms are spacious, beds are comfortable. It's not 'over the top' but is 'the genuine article'. **Sleeps 8** plus cot. ETC Three Stars. TV and video, stereo and CD player. Dogs by arrangement. Free logs. Cost: £200 to £550. Linen and towels for hire. 'B & B' available. Details from Tim and Sarah Kindred, High House Farm, Cransford, near Woodbridge, Suffolk IP13 9PD. Telephone (01728) 663461. Fax 663409.

www.highhousefarm.co.uk email:Woodlodge@highhousefarm.co.uk

Waldringfield, nr Woodbridge/Bawdsey
Deben Vale/Ferry Cottage

Readers who like to be near the buzz of yachting activity will delight in *Deben Vale*, a characterful cottage **(map 1/9)** furnished mainly in antique pine, only 50 yards from the River Deben. Here are boat trips, a small sandy beach, a riverside inn/restaurant. **Sleeping 6**, it has a secluded patio garden and is only five miles from the popular and attractive

Sleeping 6, Deben Vale is just yards from the pretty, unspoiled River Deben...

market town of Woodbridge. Dinghy hire (at cost) can be arranged. Brochure ref: BGU. *Ferry Cottage*, at Bawdsey **(map 1/10)**, is 400 yards from the Suffolk Heritage coast and half a mile from Bawdsey Quay. Formerly an estate cottage (but completely renovated) it has rural views and its own large garden. The seasonal ferry from Bawdsey Quay links directly with Felixstowe, Aldeburgh and Snape (whose Maltings are famous for concerts). Woodbridge and Ipswich are readily accessible. **Sleeps 5** in spacious and modern accommodation. Brochure ref: BKD.

English Country Cottages, Stoney Bank, Earby, Barnoldswick BB94 0AA. Telephone (0870) 5851155. You can also dial-a-brochure: (0870) 5851111. **www.english-country-cottages.co.uk Quote ref EMA 94.**

Elveden and Stradbroke, near Eye
Cranhouse/Kumari House

Ideal for a large gathering of family or friends is *Cranhouse*, an attractive brick/flint house deep in the country a mile down a quiet lane. **Sleeping 12** in six bedrooms (four are ensuite) it has been refurbished to *extremely high standards* and has ETC Five Stars. On a 23,000-acre parkland estate, it has a walled garden and many rooms have rural views. There is a large living/dining room with wood burner and open fire, a spa-

Cranhouse is great in its own right, and for a large group it is 'just the ticket'.

cious drawing room with French doors on to the garden, a farmhouse-style kitchen. Well behaved pets are welcome. Brochure ref: CKC.

Deep in rural Suffolk is *Kumari House*, a detached house **sleeping 4 plus 1**, with a large conservatory, utility room, two cloakrooms, double (5 foot bed) room, twin room with extra single bed, private south facing garden and, best of all, an indoor heated pool with exercise bike, shower room/cloakroom and changing room. Brochure ref: BHX.

English Country Cottages, Stoney Bank, Earby, Barnoldswick BB94 0AA. Telephone (0870) 5851155. You can also 'dial a brochure': (0870) 5851111. **www.english-country-cottages.co.uk**   **Quote ref EMA 94.**

Suffolk/Norfolk   map 1
Suffolk and Norfolk Country Cottages*

Following a recent change of ownership this much-liked agency is the only one we know that embraces the two magical counties of Suffolk and Norfolk. There is a good range of inland and coastal properties, several of which we know well.

Among their outstanding houses is *99 Tangham*, one of a pair of period cottages hidden away in the heart of Rendlesham Forest. This is a rare find if you long to get away from it all, set in half an acre of fenced garden, reached along forest tracks. Straddling the Norfolk/Suffolk border is *Slade Holding,* in Thelnetham, between Diss and Thetford, a large pink painted farmhouse renovated a few years ago to a very high standard. Very spacious, and set in two acres of meadow, it has wood burners in inglenooks in both the sitting room and dining room. It will comfortably **sleep 8** in four bedrooms, but with the addition of a further two single beds and a bed settee can easily absorb another four.

A final example of the diversity of this small agency is *4 Red Lion Yard*, Wells next the Sea. Tucked away in one of the little yards formerly made up of fishermen's cottages, this Grade II listed cottage has wonderful views from the upper rooms across the harbour to the sea and pinewoods.

More information about Suffolk & Norfolk Country Cottages on **www.suffolkandnorfolkcottages.co.uk** or telephone (01223) 207946.

South Elmham and Aldeburgh
Rookery Cottage and Half Past Six Cottage

Firstly: enjoying its own south-facing garden and the use of the owners' summerhouse, a private lake and a large games meadow, three-storeyed, 16th century *Rookery Cottage* has been skilfully refurbished to 21st century standards. It oozes character: oak beams and floors, curving oak stairs, a woodburner in an inglenook, a five-foot brass bed. It is located in a very peaceful part of North Suffolk, just five miles from Bungay. **Sleeps 4**.

Rookery is exceptional, and well placed for seeing both Suffolk and Norfolk...

Secondly: we don't know the history of the name, but we do know the location. An easy stroll from the beach at this ever-popular coastal village stands *Half Past Six Cottage*, a small former fisherman's cottage **sleeping 3 'plus 1'**. The accommodation is cosy and comfortable, in easy reach of Snape (concerts, galleries, craft shops), Dunwich, Minsmere Bird Reserve and Orford. Details from Hoseasons Holidays Ltd, Sunway House, Lowestoft NR32 2LW. Telephone 0870 534 2342. Fax 0870 902 2090.

**On-line booking and 'real time' availability on the web:
www.hoseasons.co.uk email: mail@hoseasons.co.uk**

Corpusty and Pentney, near King's Lynn
Mallard Cottage/The Old Coach House

Mallard Cottage **(map 1/16)** is a 200-year-old cottage on the River Bure, ten miles from the Broads and coast. **Sleeping 4**, it has its own riverside garden – on *both* banks, courtesy of a bridge over the river: an ideal hideaway. The large living/dining room has a log burner in an inglenook; the conservatory looks directly over the river. The cottage is well equipped with linen/towels provided; sorry, no

Mallard is detached and romantic...

pets, smokers or young children. Brochure ref: CJY. In unspoilt countryside, with sandy beaches accessible (Hunstanton and Brancaster are 20 miles), *The Old Coach House* **(map 1/17)** has its own heated indoor pool and games room. Converted from an 18th century stable, close to the owner's home, it has lots of space – a wood burner in the beamed living room, a four-poster bedroom. There's easy walking and excellent bird watching nearby; pets are welcome. **Sleeps 6**. Brochure ref: CCL.

English Country Cottages, Stoney Bank, Earby, Barnoldswick BB94 0AA. Telephone (0870) 5851155. You can also dial-a-brochure: (0870) 5851111.
www.english-country-cottages.co.uk Ref EMA 94.

Wortham, near Diss
Ivy House Farm

Well placed for enjoying the charms of both Suffolk and Norfolk, and set well back from a quiet road, accommodation here consists of three new cottages all in a row, a detached cottage and, across the yard, a fine, historic Suffolk 'long house'. The impressive detached modern cottage,

The farmhouse is full of character and history, the cottages very well planned...

built to high specifications, is designated as a retirement home for the owners. Here we found four very contented ladies who had been before and thought it 'brilliant'. **Sleeps 6**. The three opposite (not uncomfortably close) have well thought out, mainly open plan living areas and warm, comfortable bedrooms. Each **sleeps 4**.

The farmhouse itself is packed with character: we admired the cosy kitchen, the inglenook log fire in one sitting room, a superb dining room, spacious bedrooms (the 'master bedroom' is triple-aspect), good views from most bedrooms. **Sleeps up to 10**.

The leisure centre has a pool table and a full-sized snooker table, and there is an excellent indoor swimming pool. Dogs welcome. Linen/towels included. TVs, videos and CD players. Cost: £218 to £1116. Details from Paul and Jacky Bradley, Ivy House Farm, Wortham, Diss, Norfolk IP22 1RD. Telephone/fax (01379) 898395. **email: prjsbrad@aol.com**

Redisham, near Beccles   map 1/19
Redisham Hall

Dominating a 400-acre park is a fine Grade II listed mansion in which there are two spacious apartments, each with a high-ceilinged sitting room and a double and a twin bedroom that ooze with comfort and old fashioned elegance. We visited on a warm afternoon in September, and thought what a civilised base this would make for exploring most of Suffolk and Norfolk. *The Courtyard*

Parkland or garden views – a place from which to see both Suffolk and Norfolk.

(Ref 9799) and *The Garden Wing* (Ref 13899) have the same facilities but have a different layout. Among many details we admired were absolute quiet, lots of books, impressive garden or parkland views, sympathetic lighting, and some antique furniture. There is a delightful walled garden, and organically grown fruit and vegetables are usually available. No smoking. There is a croquet lawn and two swimming pools are available within three miles. There are tennis courts in the village.

Country Holidays, Spring Mill, Earby, Lancashire BB94 0AA. To book, telephone 08700 723723. Brochures: 08700 725725. **Quote ref CMA 96**.

Live search and book: www.country-holidays.co.uk

Norfolk, countywide
The Great Escape Holiday Company*

Among the counties rated highly by holidaymakers, especially self caterers, Norfolk has an especially good range of cottages and houses of great character.

'The Great Escape Holiday Company' has made a name for itself by dealing exclusively with houses of extra-special quality and style, available when owners are not in residence. During a summer 2001 visit we looked at a good handful of what they have on their books.

Quietly located on the quayside at Burnham Overy Staithe, for example, is *Beam Cottage*, **sleeping 7**. This property is on three floors and the first-floor sitting room takes full advantage of the magnificent and uninterrupted views of the estuary. There is a kitchen with modern amenities, a dining area with large pine table, chairs and additional bench seating, French doors on to a sheltered, enclosed patio. The sitting room has a woodburning stove and stripped pine floors. The main bedroom is on the first floor, and there are two other bedrooms on second floor. If you book here, do not forget your binoculars!

Tucked away behind other houses in the very attractive village of Docking we thought *Mission House*, an old building recently converted for self catering, a real charmer. We especially liked the sleeping gallery accessed by a new pine staircase, the neat and pretty kitchen, the 'old pine and rugs' ambiance downstairs . **Sleeps 2**.

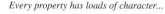

Every property has loads of character...   *...and easy access to the best of Norfolk.*

Hidden away in the tranquil village of Great Snoring (you'll sleep well!) is *The Manor House*, a memorable 16th century property in an acre and a half of grounds. It **sleeps 12**. Within those grounds are the *Shelton Cottages*, done out to the same degree of comfort.

All these properties have such a lot going for them. On our list to see in the spring of 2002 are, among others, the super, 'last word' *Blue Tiles Barn* at Brancaster, **sleeping 9**; an Edwardian beauty near the beach in Old Hunstanton, **sleeping 10**; a part-15th century house in an enviable position by the harbour at Burnham Overy Staithe, **sleeping 10**.

Details/brochures from Marian Rose-Cartwright, The Great Escape Holiday Company, The Granary, Docking, Norfolk PE31 8LY. Telephone (01485) 518717. Fax 518937.

www.thegreatescapeholiday.co.uk
email: bookings@thegreatescapeholiday.co.uk

Castle Acre, near King's Lynn
Heron Cottage

It was a pleasure to revisit this in 2001. A few feet from an impressive 13th century Bailey gate in this historic and unspoilt village, *Heron* is a comfortable, spacious, fully double glazed, modern, red-brick and pan-tiled house. The North Norfolk coast is about 45 minutes away, Royal Sandringham about 25 minutes. Castle Acre itself is off-the-beaten-track – a delight to explore. The cot-

A comfortable cottage in a village full of charm and historical associations.

tage **sleeps 4** in a five foot double and a twin, is clean and well cared for, warm (the open fire also heats radiators, and there are storage radiators), and has TV, hi-fi, radio, good lighting, recliner armchair, fitted carpets. There is a lock-up garage.

We liked the good-sized sitting room and the light, bright bedrooms, and noticed pictures, prints and other details. Our readers like it too: over several years, we have had many enthusiastic reports about this cottage. Not least for its *very reasonable price*.

Not suitable for dogs. Linen included but not towels. Patio garden. Cost: about £160 to £280, available all year for short or long breaks. Further details/location map from Mrs A E Crutchley, 2 Petts Lane, Shepperton, Middlesex TW17 0DT. Telephone Walton-on-Thames (01932) 225620.

Castle Acre, near King's Lynn
Peddars Cottage   map 1/22

First seen by us in 2001, and warmly endorsed by regular visitors ('lots of space, loads of books and board games'...'a super village – just right if you fancy an out-of-season break') this is a 20-year-old house that fits well into its historic surroundings: see our photo! The cosy interior incorporates an open fire, repro oak furniture, a traditional 'cottage suite',

A modern house but 'cottagey' with it. Not 'pretty-pretty' but rather cosy.

old local prints, a mostly pine modern fitted kitchen. There are attractive table and standard lamps and (we also noticed!) lots of good books. There are carpets virtually throughout and Laura Ashley wallpaper.

Castle Acre is a village of great character, and the cottage is at one end of a charming village street. TV. One pet possible by arrangement. Garage. Linen and towels included. ETC Three Stars. **Sleeps 6** in a double, a twin and an adult-sized two-bunk-bed room. Cost: a *very modest* £200 to £295. Details: Mrs Angela Swindell, St Saviour's Rectory, St Saviour, Jersey, Channel Isles JE2 7NP. Telephone/fax (01534) 727480.

email: jsyedu71@localdial.com

Gunthorpe, near Blakeney/Cley
White Horse Farm Barns

The location is superb, deep in rural Norfolk but not too remote, with some of England's best beaches a short drive. Guests wax lyrical about the gardens, the high-pitched roofs with great scrubbed beams, about clean lines, spaciousness, a merciful lack of chintz, well organised kitchen and comfortable living areas with 'squashy' sofas, fluffy towels, top quality linens, log fires and a degree of sophistication. Beds are

One of our readers wrote that her cottage here was 'a joy, a real home from home'.

'big and new', power showers are big enough for two! Surrounded by farmland where sheep and cattle graze among water meadows, a major feature of these places is the flexibility over bookings: you are not tied to 'a changeover day'. Being warm and well insulated, these make very good autumn and winter bases. TVs. Linen and towels included. Non smoking. Cost: (per night) from £55 *(Stables)*, to £65 *(Cartshed)* – both **sleeping 2 plus 'sleeper couches'** – to £75 *(Great Barn,* **sleeping 4**). Details from Dianne Cutterham, White Horse Farm, Gunthorpe, Melton Constable, Norfolk NR24 2PB. Telephone (01263) 860693.

www.white-horse-farm.co.uk email: dianne.c@virgin.net

Brancaster Staithe
Peartree Cottage   map 1/24

This is a beauty. Stylishly decorated and furnished, it backs on to the coast road but has fabulous rear views over one of the most inspiring marshland panoramas in this part of North Norfolk. (It's not surprising that the main, third-floor double bedroom has a telescope trained on the more distant muddy creeks and

Spacious, light and sunny, this super house is partly open-plan...

yachts.) With well chosen pictures, excellent lamps and lots of reclaimed pine, the house has a fine woodburner in the good-sized sitting room, an enclosed courtyard-style garden area with well tended shrubs and borders.

The garden area is overlooked by a well appointed kitchen and an open plan style dining room. TV/video. Not suitable for pets. No smoking. Linen and towels included. **Sleeps 6** in two doubles (one with a king-size bed) and one twin. Short breaks available. Cost: about £350 to £1000. Details from Suzy Lyles, Muckleton Farm, Burnham Market, King's Lynn, Norfolk PE31 8JT. Telephone (01485) 518318.

www.peartreecottages.co.uk
email:peartreecottage@farming.co.uk

Brancaster
Brancaster Farms Cottages

We revisited in 2001, and thought again: these delightful cottages sum up the very best of Norfolk in location and accommodation. Attractively situated, deep in the country, they are only minutes from fine beaches and bird-haunted marshes. You can smell the sea, and will find that the beaches, exceptional pubs and seafood restaurants of the North Norfolk coast are to hand. Combining original character with modern day comfort, the properties are admirably cared for.

The two separate locations are only about a mile apart, a very short distance (a pleasant walk of about two miles, with very little traffic to bother you, or just five minutes by car) from the coast. In fact, both Sussex Farm, where there are five cottages, and Field House Farm, where there are six, are a perfect marriage of countryside and seaside.

In the pretty enclave of cottages near Sussex Farm, absolutely quiet, and protected by old trees, are detached *Park Drive, The Pheasantry, One Hundred Acre* and semi-detached *Apple Tree* and *Beech Tree,* **sleeping 8/10, 8, 7, 6/8 and 6/8** respectively. They are spacious and full of character. Two of these are suitable for people of limited mobility. On each visit we have made we have found the cottages sunny, very clean and tidy and with original features that add to the charm, with 'cottagey' doors, good carpets, microwave ovens, radio cassette players, televisions and videos, and most larger houses have dishwashers and large freezers.

'Norfolk at its best': deep in the country, yet only minutes from excellent beaches.

Traditional and characterful properties, but enjoying 21st century comforts.

At Field House Farm there are five neat and comfortable terraced cottages, **each sleeping 4**, though four of them can be linked. They share an attractive enclosed garden. There is also pretty-as-a-picture *Foremans Cottage,* detached and **sleeping 5**.

Places of interest within easy reach include the traditional family seaside resort of Hunstanton, just-inland Burnham Market and Wells-next-the-Sea – also good for families – from where a delightful narrow gauge railway runs across fields to fascinating Walsingham.

All have central heating *and* open fires (logs included). All linen and towels included. Dogs (one per property) welcome throughout. Cost: about £195 to £900. Short breaks welcome. Details and a good brochure from Sue Lane, Field House, Brancaster, King's Lynn, Norfolk PE31 8AG. Telephone 07885 269538 (mobile). Fax 01485 210261.

Brancaster Staithe
Vista Cottage/Carpenter's Cottage

In *Vista* and *Carpenter's* you can almost reach out and touch one of the most beautiful coastlines in Britain. To be exact, you can walk down the cottage gardens right on to the salty marshes and join the coastal footpath, or make your way somewhat more directly towards the water.

From the back windows of both the properties in the ownership of the Smith family, muddy inlets dotted with yachts and fishing boats snake as prettily as in any sailor's favourite picture out towards the North Sea. Bring your binoculars!

Whether in hazy high summer, crisp autumn or when the winds buffet the backs of the cottages, these are full of character (but, being on the A149 Cromer to Hunstanton coast road, are not remote or irritatingly difficult to find after a long journey).

In Vista Cottage, **sleeping 6**, we met a family who were enjoying spending time in a 'family-friendly' kitchen/diner with original stone flags and excellent fittings, such as washing machine and microwave. There is a

Vista has a big garden and unforgettable views out to sea. We met a family of six who love it and are regulars here.

Carpenter's (also with some marvellous views) is a pretty 'upside down' cottage – one of those 'just for two' properties.

very cosy sitting room with open fire. On the first floor, via a steep staircase, there is a double, a twin and a bunk bedded room (adult sized). The house is well carpeted and there is plenty of heating. The family we met were just off for a late lunch in one of the two village pubs they had discovered and liked a lot; they had also used the excellent barbecue.

Next door is Carpenter's Cottage, set back from the road by a small, safely enclosed courtyard. In the owners' family for over a hundred years, it is a delightful 'upside down' house with a sitting room/kitchen/diner on the first floor and a very cosy, 'compact' double bedded room on the ground floor. The original fireplace has been restored: a lovely focal point on an autumn or spring evening, and there is a well planned window seat from which to enjoy those fabulous views. **Sleeps 2**.

Dogs are welcome in both. Linen and towels are included. Cost: approximately £180 to £600. (Pro-rata off season short breaks are available: minimum three nights.) TVs. English Tourism Council Three Stars.

Further details are available from Mrs G J Smith, Dale View, Main Road, Brancaster Staithe, King's Lynn, Norfolk PE31 8BY. Telephone/fax (01485) 210497.

Hempton, near Fakenham
Claire's Cottage

With a splendid rear garden that backs on to fields, a quiet location within very easy reach of Fakenham (restaurants and pubs), this is a neat and attractive flint and tiled cottage that is used from time to time by the owners themselves, and is therefore reliably comfortable and well organised inside. It is also *very reasonably priced*. Among so many good things in its favour are a coal-effect gas fire in the sitting room – a big bonus during those winter breaks that are so pleasant in North Norfolk: all those empty beaches. There is central heating too. Usefully, the main bedroom has twin zip-link beds *that can be converted to a 6-foot double*.

A very handy, inexpensive base from which to enjoy incomparable North Norfolk.

There is a well appointed galley-style kitchen with a microwave, a dishwasher, a washing machine and a larger than average fridge-freezer. **Sleeps 4.** Dogs possible by arrangement. TV. Linen included but not towels. Cost: about £190 to £250.

Further details from Stephen Joyce, P O Box 21, Hertford, Hertfordshire SG14 2DD. Telephone (014388) 69489.

Blakeney
Jenny's Cottage   map 1/28

Blakeney is one of the most appealing coastal places in Norfolk. It is notable for the beauty of the tidal shore, the walks to Blakeney Point, the birdlife, boat trips to see the seals, good pubs and restaurants. Comfortable holiday cottages are hard to come by here, but happily this is a small-scale, Grade II listed, flint and tiled gem (dating from 1839), with a pretty courtyard garden that in summer overflows with hollyhocks. In the heart of the village, near a welcoming pub and a well stocked shop, it is ideal for a couple with a small child (a double and small single). It is full of charm and comfort: a wood burner in an inglenook fireplace, thoughtfully arranged lighting. Though space is limited, the main bedroom,

A rare example of a traditional, reasonably priced cottage in a famous and sought-after place...

reached via steep and narrow stairs, is quite a good size, and there is even a bath. We thought this would make a particularly good – and inexpensive – base for a winter holiday.

Well behaved dogs are welcome. Linen and towels can be hired. TV. Non smokers only. Cost: about £160 to £300. Details from Simon Flint, Sherwood, Sandy Lane, South Wootton, King's Lynn, Norfolk PE30 3NX. Telephone (01553) 672208.

South Raynham, near Fakenham
Vere Lodge

This is a beautiful, caring, tranquil place in which to enjoy a self-catering holiday. *We have long rated it both as one of the very best set-ups we know – not just in Norfolk but in England as a whole.*

We visited in the late summer of 2001, looked again at several cottages, and – as always – found everything 'just right'.

Set most peacefully in rural North Norfolk, Jane Bowlby's creeper-clad, part Regency, part-Georgian home is the focal point of a clutch of comfortable cottages, each with its own individual character. Amid lovely, wooded, undulating countryside – just half an hour's drive from the sea – we always feel ourselves unwinding.

Over many years we have visited and revisited the individual cottages of which there are now fourteen, and found their advertising slogan – 'Peace, Beauty, Excellence' – more than justified. There is a magic to this place which even the detailed and colourful brochure fails to capture. Children relish the eight acres of freedom, the company of new friends, the daily feeding-round of the many tame animals and birds. Parents can relax, knowing their young are safe and happy.

Vere Lodge is ideally placed for exploring. Vast sandy beaches backed by sand-dunes or pinewoods are barely twenty minutes away, as are coastal resorts which range from the picturesque to the larger, more commercial

Vere Lodge is a place for all seasons.   *Rose Cottage is handsome and relaxing.*

holiday centres. Within easy reach are dinosaur parks, steam-engine exhibitions, stately homes such as Holkham and Blickling, and scores of other attractions: one of our favourites is the steam museum at Thursford.

An impressive leisure centre is the icing on the Vere Lodge cake. There's a large, very warm covered pool (36 feet by 18), with a shallow end with steps for children, and a slide. There's a sauna, solarium, games room with table tennis and pool table, and a centrally heated lounge looking on to the pool. Doors open on to two grass and paved sun patios, so that on hot summer days this effectively becomes an open air pool. There's also a small shop, a launderette and a range of home-cooked frozen foods. If you *are* considering a break between, say, October and March, you'll find the pool as warm then (80° plus) as in high summer, and all the other facilities are available.

Which brings us to the cottages themselves and details of the accommodation available. It has always struck us that much thought and effort has

52

been given to providing those little touches – good pictures, stylish flower arrangements, pretty ornaments – which help to set Vere Lodge out of the ordinary. Not surprisingly, Vere Lodge enjoys a high English Tourism Council grading.

Secret Garden and *The Robin's Nest* are two spacious single-storey cottages built on what was once the kitchen garden to Vere Lodge. We thought them delightful, noting especially masses of space and privacy, deep sofas, good carpets, a combination of character and comfort. Both are extremely quiet and secluded with about half an acre each of garden, mainly lawn, surrounded by high flint walls. They **sleep 6** in three bedrooms – one double, one twin, one bunk-bedded – and have an impressive lounge with an open fire. They are approached via Church Lane, a narrow and barely-used lane which forms the southern boundary to Vere Lodge and leads only to the tiny church and former rectory. On the other side of the lane lie the leisure centre and the seven acre grounds of Vere Lodge with all their amenities.

The other properties are more part of the Vere Lodge 'family'. *Apple Cottage* is a spacious and entirely self-contained ground-floor apartment, plush and comfortable, which faces on to a large landscaped courtyard. Suitable for retired couples, young couples with a baby, or the elderly or disabled. **Sleeps 3**. *Dahlia* and *Thyme* are two cottages which face west over fields of corn or bright yellow mustard. They therefore enjoy not only lovely views but also all the afternoon and evening sun. This is particularly true of Thyme, an 'upside-down' cottage, with a large upstairs living room. **Both sleep 6**. Both have their own sitting-out patios.

Apple, suitable for the partially disabled.

Children and animals are welcome here.

The Dolls House is a small, simple 'budget' cottage, the ground floor of which was once a part of a gun room. Complete with huge doll, it looks out over lawns to the horseshoe of beeches and flowering cherries beyond. It is warm, comfortable and compact. **Sleeps 4**. *Dove Cottage* is furnished to a standard not generally found in a holiday cottage. It has panoramic views of the grounds, woods, and surrounding countryside from the upstairs living room which opens on to its own completely private roof-terrace. We very much like the cool, soft, grey blue ambiance, and the open fireplace. **Sleeps 2 plus 2**. *Garden Wing* is undoubtedly the most popular of all the cottages: ground-floor throughout, it is especially suitable for the disabled. The large and elegant sitting-room looks out over the croquet lawn to woodland beyond. **Sleeps 4**. *Lavender Cottage*, large and west facing, once housed coaches and a harness room. It is a long raised-level cottage, outside which is a large terrace screened by a conifer hedge, with a flight of steps leading up to the front door.

Furnished in log-cabin style, but to standards such as original log-cabins never enjoyed with, for example, carpets on polished wood floors. **Sleeps 6**. *Possum's*, once a full-size billiard-room, is a spacious and unusual apartment called after Miss 'Possum' Smith, who cared for the Bowlby children for over thirty years. Tall Georgian windows face on to formal yew-hedges and flower borders flood-lit by night. **Sleeps 3**. *Pump Cottage* was purpose-built and 'incorporates the lessons learned from 25 years' experience of self-catering'. All the accommodation is on the ground floor and is suitable for the elderly or disabled. Open fireplace here too. **Sleeps 2**. *Rose Cottage*, the largest of all the cottages, is south-facing and therefore very sunny, with its own entirely private walled garden. It is bright and airy, with deep, comfy armchairs and sofa, an open fire and a downstairs shower and loo. **Sleeps 7**. *Rowan* and *Honeysuckle* are an identical pair of 19th century cottages. An unusual feature is the central fireplace, raised for the protection of young children, with a log-burning fire facing into the lounge and behind it an electric fire to warm the dining room. Both are furnished in 'country-style', with a raised south-facing terrace in front of each.

Among the many things they do so well at Vere Lodge are short breaks in late autumn, winter or early spring. To enhance that 'baby it's cold outside' mood, several cottages have open fires. Better yet, prices even in these sumptuously comfortable properties for a three-day break – starting

Lavender Cottage once housed coaches.

The most popular cottage is Garden Wing.

or finishing on any day of the week – can be as low as £14.00 per night per person (6 persons), which includes the use of the leisure centre.

Vere Lodge is something of an animal sanctuary, too, delightful for young children. At feeding time (9.00 am daily) there are tame rabbits to be hand-fed, freshly-laid eggs to be gathered, often from under an indignant hen. In the centre paddock, tame and gentle miniature Angora goats stand on their hind legs against the fence awaiting their turn, while Mingo the donkey, and Toby the docile pony, await theirs. Meanwhile, Asher and Blue, the two border collies, make new friends at every turn.

Children will also love the Enchanted Wood: we won't spoil the surprise!

You do not need to bring anything when you come to Vere Lodge other than you would to a hotel. Dogs are welcome, and remote-control videos, televisions and clock radios are standard throughout. Details and a copy of an impressive full colour brochure from Vere Lodge, South Raynham, near Fakenham, Norfolk NR21 7HE. Telephone (01328) 838261.

www.verelodge.co.uk

email: major@verelodge.fsnet.co.uk

Horning, near Norwich
Premiere Marina Cottages

Readers who've stayed here over the years have told us what a bonus it is to have 'instant access' to the Broads from their cottage. During several summer visits we too have enjoyed the breeze off the water! The village of Horning lies at the heart of the Norfolk Broads, but it retains its character. At the Ferry Boatyard they make (and hire out) superior holiday craft, and offer comfortable, purpose-built holiday houses and apartments

On hot summer days cool breezes from the water have made our visits a delight.

on the water; some have their own mooring, garages and balconies. We looked at the four or five types, which vary in size, and were impressed. They are neat and tidy, all with views of cruisers and yachts. There is a leisure centre, with free use of swimming pool.

Sleep 2 to 8. TV. Linen provided, but not towels. Dogs welcome in some units (extra charge). Out of season reductions on boat hire. ETC Three Stars. Details from Premiere Marina Cottages, Ferry Boatyard, Ferry Road, Horning, near Norwich NR12 8PS. Telephone Horning (01692) 630392/fax 631040.

www.ferry-marina.co.uk email: sales@ferry-marina.co.uk

Hickling, near Potter Heigham
Long Gores   map 1/31

We revisited this exceptional cottage in 2000: it was and is sheer delight. Hidden down a marshland lane near Hickling Broad, only about five minutes' drive from the Broads centre of Potter Heigham but apparently miles from anywhere, the brick and pan-tiled cottage has not lost its character in over a century. We noted the low ceilings, the old fashioned bedrooms

The owners holiday here themselves: this is always a good sign!

– comfy beds, however – the low, cosy, sitting room (open fireplace), the kitchen-diner that in warm weather opens its sliding windows, bringing the well stocked cottage garden straight to you. The sitting-room, one twin bedroom and a children's bunk room are also accessible via the fascinating garden. There is no TV, but reception is fine if you bring your own. Do note that the staircase is steep and winding.

Pets only by prior arrangement. **Sleeps up to 7.** Hi-fi, games and children's books. Linen is provided but towels are extra. Payphone. Cost: from £250 to about £400. Details and an inspiring brochure from Dominic Vlasto, Long Gores Studio, Hickling, Norfolk NR12 0BE. Telephone/fax (01692) 598185.

Cromer
The Grove Cottages

Only a few minutes' walk from the beach and the famous pier, and very well screened from the Cromer to Overstrand road in the grounds of their large guest house, Mr and Mrs Graveling have six properties. You therefore have all the pleasures of a traditional seaside resort and all the advantages of your own place. One is

Just a short walk from the beach, and with your own indoor swimming pool.

a cosy bungalow, four are very skilful conversions of older farm buildings, the sixth is a traditional flint and tile cottage. The four conversions retain several original features – a hay rack in *Stables*, for example – but offer plenty of 21st century comfort. We admired plain white walls setting off dark oak beams, good carpets, stylish duvets, dried flowers: all the things that betoken caring and painstaking owners. *Barn,* **sleeping 6**, is the biggest, and very nice too. A heated indoor swimming pool has been recently built for the use of cottage guests. So when the sea is too chilly or the beach too crowded...

One small dog is welcome. TVs. English Tourism Council Three Stars. Linen and towels are included. Cost: about £160 to £540. Further details are available from Mr and Mrs Graveling, The Grove, Overstrand Road, Cromer, Norfolk. Telephone (01263) 512412. Fax (01263) 513416.

Clippesby, near Great Yarmouth   map 1/33
Clippesby Holiday Cottages   Colour section A, Page 1

Family run but very professionally and welcomingly so, these appealing properties lie within the Norfolk Broads National Park. Most recent additions in the landscaped park are the two excellent *Pine Lodges* **sleeping 6**. We also like the three quiet, comfy bungalows overlooking cornfields (two **sleep 4,** two **sleep 6**). These have unspoilt country views. Closer to the heart of things, surrounding courtyards, we located

Modestly priced family accommodation near the seaside but in the country.

Summertime Apartments, in single-and two-storeyed 'practical' family accommodation **(sleeping 2 to 8)** near well tended gardens, a heated open air pool, grass tennis courts, a family pub and play areas. (Tucked away among trees, there are touring caravans.) TV, central heating and bed-linen; some have open fires too. ETC Two/Three Stars. David Bellamy Gold Award. Cost: £159 to £599. Colour brochure: the Lindsay family, Clippesby Holidays, Clippesby Hall, near Great Yarmouth, Norfolk NR29 3BL. Telephone (01493) 367800; fax (01493) 367809.

www.clippesby.com email: holidays@clippesby.com

Norfolk and beyond
Norfolk Country Cottages*

Based just off the market place in the very attractive small town of Reepham (visitors are welcome to visit the office) this is one of those cottage agencies of a type we much admire. Recently merged with 'Norfolk Country Cousins', these two family-owned companies used to constantly vie with each other to attract the best self catering properties. Now combined, they offer about 230 properties covering the whole of Norfolk and also North Suffolk.

Among so many gems, we love the magnificent *Burnham House*, at Burnham Market, which we first saw on a bright sunny morning when this much-loved large village was bustling with visitors. Beautifully spacious, comfortably **sleeping 12** but with special rates for up to 7, and with a fine and private garden, it is a memorable and elegant base from which to enjoy North Norfolk.

Among others, we have also visited *The Old Rectory*, a substantial property in Suffield, North Norfolk. Situated in eleven acres, **sleeping 10**, this impressive house is part of what was the village rectory. Carefully renovated, with wooden floors and original features, it has a marvellously

Claremont House is a splendid family house at much-sought-after Blakeney.

Meadowsweet is, indeed, 'sweet'. It is at Coltishall, which is handy for Norwich.

well-equipped family kitchen with woodburner, easy chairs and lots of character. There are three bedrooms on the first floor, and a second floor attic room with TV, which would be ideal for 4 children. The owners, together with their cats, dogs and children, live next door.

On a warm and sunny evening we stopped in Great Snoring, among cornfield and woods, to see *Dorothy's Cottage*, **sleeping 4**. Lucky Dorothy! There is a very pretty and well cared for and safely enclosed garden, a most welcoming sitting room with an open fire, and a garage.

We saw several properties just inland from some of England's best sandy beaches, including *Lodge Cottage*, a fine Victorian gatehouse in the historic village of Salle, *Jots Cottage*, a sensitively converted old dairy and milking shed at Bawdeswell, and *Stone Cottage*, in the quiet village of Sharrington. (But there are many, many other good things...)

Details/brochure from Norfolk Country Cottages, Carlton House, Market Place, Reepham, Norfolk NR10 4JJ. Telephone: (01603) 871872 Fax: (01603) 870304.

www.norfolkcottages.co.uk email: info@norfolkcottages.co.uk

Hunstanton, Brancaster and beyond
Norfolk Holiday Homes*

We have a very high regard for this organisation, which is reliable for pin-pointing comfortable self catering in that far north west corner of Norfolk that offers fine sandy beaches, tranquil and unspoilt villages, lonely churches, the traditional seaside resort of Hunstanton, excellent antique hunting, bird watching and more.

The agency has featured in this guide every year without a break since we first appeared in 1983, and we have never once had any kind of complaint. We have visited and revisited many times and never seen a dud. This would be admirable in a private cottage set-up – in an agency of any size it is a tremendous accolade.

Swiss Cottage at Thornham is an excellent and very popular property that has recently undergone alterations and re-decoration. For a large family it is ideal, as it **sleeps up to 9** and a baby.

A most unusual property, with a following of its own, is *Ethelville*, a converted railway carriage **sleeping up to 6**. It will appeal to train buffs and bird watchers, as it overlooks a lake visited by many species.

Also well recommended within this stable of properties is *Island Cottage*, at Brancaster Staithe. This *basic* but pretty cottage (do *not* expect Sanderson fabrics or a bidet, but do expect blissful silence and lots of character) has exquisite views over the salt marshes from the sea and is almost on an island, though just a stone's throw from the National Trust-owned village green and the main part of Brancaster Staithe.

A rather superior property is *The Cottage* at Tudor Lodge, Holme-next-the-Sea, in secure grounds of over five acres. **Sleeping 5**, it offers excellent private accommodation of a very high standard. Also recommended are two very clever conversions, one in Thornham, **sleeping 2,** the other in Great Bircham, **sleeping 2 'plus 2'**.

Other recommended properties of a very good standard are *Courtyard Cottage* and *Norfolk House,* at Docking, which are both ETC Five Stars

Orchard House, at Ringstead, near Hunstanton, is a super new acquisition.

Crossways is both deep in the country and close to the superb beaches...

and 'close to perfection'! *Orchard House* at Ringstead is a house new to the agency which should prove very popular.

Among other new properties added to their books there are, for example, two in the much sought after Old Hunstanton. which has all the advantages of a slightly old fashioned seaside atmosphere with easy access not only to a glorious sandy beach of its own but also to the bright lights of the lively 'family resort' of Hunstanton-proper. *Sandpiper Cottage* is a modern, clean, bright property **sleeping 6** (a king size double in the main bedroom). *Spindrift*, also recently built, is literally a minute's walk from the beach, and also pubs, restaurants and shops. There is a pretty, enclosed courtyard garden, and the property **sleeps 5 'plus 1'** (a king size double in the main bedroom).

Also in Old Hunstanton, overlooking the golf course, *Cleeks* is another modern house of a very high standard. In a private cul-de-sac, it feels very private. It has a secure, enclosed garden that children will probably enjoy gambolling in as much as they enjoy Hunstanton's beaches. **Sleeps 6 'plus 1'**.

Linzel Cottage is a superb, 17th century, chalk and brick cottage just off the village green at Thornham, which has been tastefully restored to a very high standard to reveal its original beauty and charm. **Sleeping 6**, the accommodation incorporates a galleried hall and landing, bathrooms with cast iron baths (one free-standing), Yorkstone flooring and terracotta floor in the kitchen, plus a multitude of other interesting features. Not to be missed! The nearby pond – full of greedy ducks – is an added bonus for children.

It's worth remembering – especially if you don't already know Norfolk – that even a cottage that on the map appears to be well inland is probably just a few minutes' drive from the coast. Some coast! The wide sandy beaches, typically set off by pine trees, are remarkable, but everyone comments on how quiet they are even at the height of the season. There is lots going on to appeal to the whole family: children will especially like the entertainments at Thursford, the North Norfolk steam railway, and the less well known narrow gauge railway that runs from Wells next the Sea to Walsingham.

Dogs are welcome in over half the properties on the agency's books, and several cottages have open fires, which can be the makings of an autumn or winter break. Also, short breaks and discounts may be available. All properties are inspected and graded by the English Tourism Council.

Island Cottage (a bit of a 'one-off'!) has featured in this guide since 1983...

Linzel, at Thornham, is an exceptional property, full of style.

An exceptionally good brochure, fully illustrated in colour, is available from Sandra Hohol, Norfolk Holiday Homes, 62 Westgate, Hunstanton, Norfolk PE36 5EL. Telephone Hunstanton (01485) 534267/fax 535230.

www. norfolkholidayhomes-birds.co.uk
email: shohol@ birdsnorfolkholidayhomes.co.uk

Overstrand, near Cromer
Poppyland Holiday Cottages

Lucky for some: these seven properties, five very nice ones by the sea and two absolute gems in a pleasant rural hamlet a few miles inland, offer some of the very best self catering in Norfolk.

Family-run, with admirably high standards, ETC Four Stars, the cottages in Overstrand **sleep 4-6**, and range from the large Victorian *Forsythia House* to the charming, cosy *Gardener's Cottage*. All are a few minutes' walk from safe, sandy beaches and local shops, and close enough to each other to suit larger parties. (*The Old Bakehouse* and *Hardy's Cottage* share a courtyard.)

The greatest pleasure of one recent Norfolk visit was seeing *Swallow Cottages*, each **sleeping 4**, in Wickmere, near Blickling. They are among the most comfortable cottages we have ever come across, and have a superb sense of design, colour and comfort.

All the cottages are open all year round and are properly and unstintingly decorated for Christmas. They are ideal 'home from home' bases, whether for winter breaks, birdwatching, walking, cycling, or simply a traditional family holiday. Everything is included in the prices, ranging from £165 to £499 per week depending on when you go, short breaks are available on request. No pets.

For further details/colour brochure please phone Tracy Riches: (01263) 577473. Fax 570087.

www.broadland.com/poppyland   email: poppyland@totalise.co.uk

Exterior of Swallows: outstandingly comfortable, in a quiet village setting.

Sitting room of one of the Swallows cottages: an example of 'how to do it'!

Blickling Hall
National Trust Cottages   map 1/36

The National Trust has some outstanding houses in the east of England, several in Norfolk. One of our favourites is Blickling Hall, close to which (actually on or very close to the estate) are four lovely, very skilfully converted cottages, with the well chosen fabrics and furniture that are increasingly a National Trust hallmark. They are both beautifully in keeping with their surroundings and reliably inviting in themselves. Details from the National Trust Booking Office, PO Box 536, Melksham, Wiltshire SN12 8SX. Telephone, for bookings, (01225) 791199.

See also our main feature on Pages 18 and 19.

Blakeney
Sandpiper/Hollyhocks/Buttercup Cottages

On a summer afternoon in 2001 we re-inspected all three cottages, none more than three minutes' walk from the small harbour of this much-loved coastal resort. Upgrading is going on year by year without any loss of the original character. *Sandpiper,* **sleeping up to 7** in three bedrooms, is on the village street, but is quiet, the other two are tucked away off the lane, especially *Hollyhocks* (sleeping **up to 4** in two bedrooms). Each fits neatly into its surroundings, all three

Buttercup was once a fisherman's cottage. It has a games room and garage.

are deceptively spacious – particularly Sandpiper and *Buttercup*, sleeping **up to 6** in a double plus-bunk-beds, and a twin, has a pool table in a basement games room and, unusually, a garage. We liked Hollyhocks's good sized sitting room (with open fire), the good use of pine, the many books.

Dogs by arrangement. Linen available. Open fires. Cost: from £140 to £335. Further details from Veronica Alvarez, New Wellbury Farmhouse, Wellbury Park, Hitchin, Herts SG5 3BP. Telephone (01462) 768627.

www.Blakeneycottages.co.uk
email: VeronicaAlvarez@compuserve.com

Wiveton, near Blakeney
Bones Cottage   map 1/38

Prettily tucked away out of sight, yet very near one of the best stretches of the incomparable north Norfolk coast, this is a charming place **just for 2**, which one of our readers called 'a piece of old England'. It is only about ten minutes' walk from the invigorating saltmarshes at Cley and twenty minutes from the quay at exquisite Blakeney. There is also a good pub just a short walk away. The owners' home (bed and breakfast

Notably inexpensive, very private, very close to one of the best parts of the coast.

also available) is adjacent, but the cottage feels very private. There is a neat and perfectly adequate kitchenette, a shower and (in short) a charming atmosphere.

We liked the big window that seems to light up the whole cottage. It looks on to the front garden and gets the sun all day long. *Bones* would make an excellent base from which to enjoy the coast, and is inexpensive.

Linen is provided, but not towels. Small TV. Not suitable for dogs. Cost: about £160 to £210. Further details from Mrs Stocks, Bones Cottage, Hall Lane, Wiveton, Holt, Norfolk NR25 7TG. Telephone (01263) 740840.

61

Burnham Overy Staithe
Flagstaff House, Cottage and Barn

Especially since their recent makeover, these charming, interesting and superbly well situated cottages, right by the so-picturesque water, have become even more desirable than they were before. They are a quartet of spectacularly situated properties on the harbour-side of this much-sought-after village, a perfect marriage of land and sea.

The skipper of the famous tea-clipper 'The Cutty Sark' (you can still climb aboard it at Greenwich) once lived in Flagstaff House, a quite superb property: the two halves of which can be rented separately. *It is in fact one of the best properties in this guide.*

West Wing, Flagstaff House, **sleeping 6**, which adjoins stylish *East Wing*, **sleeping 5**, is beautifully situated: the view of the salt marshes from the upstairs sitting-room is, summer or winter, very fine. Well equipped, with dishwasher, spin dryer and a telephone, the house is roomy and comfortable without being so chic that families with children can't relax. The enclosed wooden spiral staircase is a gem. The house is quiet and should appeal both to active and 'peace and quiet' visitors. East Wing has an

Lots of character and easy-going comfort in a fantastic coastal location.

The views are amazing: nobody will blame you if you just sit in the window.

especially comfortable, more conventional ground floor sitting room. Taken as one, the house can **sleep 11**.

Across the gravelled drive, which leads off the cul-de-sac to the harbour, is *Flagstaff Cottage*, a bungalow whose exterior belies its apparent size. A sitting-out platform, reached by stairs in the large sitting-room, gives a wonderful view of the sand dunes and salt marshes.

The Barn, next door, was converted in 1987: it has two large windows off the sitting-room (giving, similarly, the best views in Overy Staithe), with kitchenette off and two bedrooms, each of which **sleeps 2**, overlooking the creek. There is a large, enclosed garden, in which there stands the detached *Garden House,* also **sleeping 2**. This can be rented separately but is also just right for grandma and grandpa travelling with the family but wanting a bit of privacy.

Sleep 2 to 11. TV/video in all properties. Not suitable for pets. Cost: about £216 to £713. Details from Mrs C W C Green, Red House Farm, Badingham, Woodbridge, Suffolk IP13 8LL. Telephone (014388) 69489, fax (014388) 69589.

email: frank@cottageguide.demon.co.uk

Holt
No 6 Carpenters Cottages

This was a good find, an unassuming but attractive flint and pantiled terraced cottage close to the centre of Holt, a small, busy Georgian town of character, with good pubs and restaurants, two department stores, antique shops and two fishmongers. But best of all is the easy access to the coast (delightful Blakeney is only

A cosy, very convenient town house that is only minutes away from the exceptional North Norfolk coast.

about ten minutes away) and to such attractions as Felbrigg, Blickling and Holkham Hall. There's a well-equipped kitchen and a bright and cheerful sitting/dining room, informal, comfortable and altogether inviting, opening on to a secluded walled garden area. The cottage is often used by the owners themselves, and its good standards reflect this fact. We spotted well chosen local pictures, books, including a number about Norfolk, board games and puzzles. The cottage **sleeps 3** in a good-sized twin room and a smallish single.

Cost: about £150 to £310. Small, well behaved dogs are welcome. Further details are available from Mrs Sally Beament, Higher Moorlake, Crediton, Devon EX17 5EL. Telephone (01363) 773789.

email: justinbeament@beeb.net

Holt   map 1/41
Sunnyside Cottage

This is a super cottage. Tucked away in a quiet mews in the lively and chic little town of Holt, just a 20 minute drive from the North Norfolk coast, it is light, bright and spacious. Dating from the 1880s, it is furnished to a high standard in Victorian style but with present-day comforts. We endorse the enthusiastic comments sent in by readers: 'So beautifully furnished and equipped'...'immaculate and spotlessly clean'...'excellent colour schemes'

A very special place indeed...

...'beds made up with excellent linen – better than I have at home!'...'gorgeous, polished wood floors'. The owners are perfectionists, who have spent much time working to make Sunnyside Cottage the welcoming haven it is.

Sleeps 5 in a double and two other bedrooms. TV, video, radio, CD player, books and games. Heating, electricity and bedlinen included, but bring your own towels. Stay for as short or long a period as you wish. Cost: *very reasonable*, at about £100 to £295 per week. 'Sorry, no pets.' Details from Michael Drake, Broadland House, Station New Road, Brundall, Norwich, Norfolk NR13 5PQ. Telephone/fax (01603) 712524.

email: michael.drake@ukgateway.net

Weybourne, near Holt/Cley
Bolding Way Cottages

In 2001 we turned into a driveway to revisit – and to see the changes at – these three (soon to be four) properties. Visitors appreciate such a lot about them, notably their proximity to the coast and the North Norfolk Steam Railway. Within the group, *The Cottage* is impressive. **Sleeping 8 'plus 2',** it's actually an Edwardian

'The Cottage' is rather modestly named!

mansion: a huge sitting room, a big, well appointed kitchen, a dining room overlooking well tended communal gardens, with croquet, badminton and other games, and animals. Cost: about £400 to £1100. Adjoining The Cottage is *East Cottage*. This has a large, lofty room and an open plan sitting room/dining room/kitchen overlooking its own garden. **Sleeps 6.** Cost: about £275 to £500. Together, they **sleep 14-plus**: £575 to £1460. *Do enquire (details below) about the two other properties.*

ETC Four Stars. TVs. One or two are suitable for dogs. There is a full sized snooker table. Linen and towels included. Free membership of Pinewood Leisure Park, with swimming pool (three miles). Details: Charlie Harrison, The Stables, Bolding Way, Weybourne, Holt, Norfolk NR25 7SW. Telephone/fax (0800) 0560996 or (01263) 588666.

www.boldingway.co.uk email: Holidays@boldingway.co.uk

Edgefield, near Holt   map 1/43
Wood Farm Cottages

Along a farm track, well away from any busy roads, lies this congenial arrangement of cottages, single and two storeyed, converted (with lots of space) from original barns and stables, *ideal for larger groups holidaying together*. We immediately felt at home amid this clutch of eight cottages, and noted lots of pine, plain cream walls, original features such as exposed interior flint walls, pleasant

Larger families or groups of friends find this ideal: children especially like the adventure area...

views in some cases, deep armchairs, woodburners, very well equipped kitchens, some exposed beams and a very uncramped atmosphere: just right for families or couples wanting space and tranquillity. **Sleep 2 to 6.** ETC Three/Four Stars. TVs and video players, stereos, microwaves. (*Holly*, **sleeping 5**, has a four-poster.) Linen provided. Large outdoor garden and adventure play area with Zip Wire. Indoor games room. Dogs welcome. Cost: about £150 to £595. Details and a brochure from Mrs D Elsby, Wood Farm, Edgefield, Melton Constable, Norfolk NR24 2AQ. Telephone/fax 01263 587347.

www.wood-farm.com email: diana@wood-farm.com

North Norfolk
Swallow Tail Holiday Homes*

This busy agency deals exclusively with the much-loved Norfolk/-Suffolk borders, and offers a hand picked selection (several seen by us) of ETC 'quality-assured' properties, including a Norfolk windmill, a most attractive lighthouse, quality barn conversions and charming self-catering cottages. Properties **sleep from 2 to 22**. Tucked away at the quieter end of Wells-next-the-Sea, close to the water and **sleeping 4**,

The Lighthouse, Old Hunstanton – a super, most unusual holiday home!

Westwood is a charmer. We admired local pictures and the view of the sea from the double bed, deep and comfy armchairs and sofa. At Wighton, deep in timeless rural Norfolk, but only a few minutes' drive from Wells, *Old Barn Cottage* is very special – definitely one of our Norfolk favourites. There is a big conservatory, a well kept garden with playroom, an open fire, and use of a beach hut at Wells. **Sleeps 6.**

Pets welcome in many properties. Further details and brochure from Swallow Tail Holiday Homes, Carlton House, Market Place, Reepham, Norfolk NR10 4JJ. Telephone (01603) 308108. Fax (01603) 870304. **www.swallow-tail.com email: holidays@swallow-tail.com**

Ringstead, near Hunstanton   map 1/46
Pickles Patch/Tumblers

On our most recent revisit, on a hot August day, we happened upon an idyllic scene, with regular visitors to *Tumblers* sunning themselves outside their cottage. Both are delightful places, so we are not at all surprised that guests return year after year, sometimes two or three times a year.

Interiors are most welcoming, with deep sofas and armchairs, fine pictures, pretty curtains, good fitted carpets, all helping to make them

Exceptionally comfortable interiors, and welcoming and considerate owners...

real 'homes from home'. Specifically, Tumblers **sleeps 4 'plus 2'**, *Pickles Patch* **sleeps 6 'plus 2'**. The village itself is quiet, but with the traditional resort of Hunstanton and sandy beaches a short drive away.

TV and video; barbecue and garden furniture; linen and towels included, plus 'light and heat'. Dogs by arrangement. Guests can also enjoy a garden of about an acre. Cost: about £330 to £650. More details from Margaret Greer, Sedgeford Road Farm Holiday Cottages, Ringstead, Hunstanton, Norfolk PE36 5JZ. Telephone (01485) 525530 or 525316. **email: Ringstead.Gallery@btinternet.com**

Wells next the Sea
Chantry

'Wells' is a small family resort with real character and lots to do, plus easy access to some of the most beautiful parts of the North Norfolk coast. In the heart of the town, but tucked well away from sight and much bigger inside than one would imagine, as well as more imposing from the outside, we thought this delightful: not a show-house, but a practical and welcoming family home on three storeys. It has bags of character, and has been most sympathetically renovated and upgraded by the owners. We liked so many things: the small enclosed 'courtyard' garden, with many flow-

This was a lucky find, and it's notably quiet in the heart of such a busy little town.

ers and shrubs, the sense of history (it dates in part from the 17th century), the impressive amount of space – a lovely big landing, bathroom and dining room, for example – the original details, such as a rare brass *single* bed in one room, that have been retained, plus some old pine. Duvets or blankets available.

Sleeps up to 7. Not suitable for pets. Linen and towels available by arrangement. Cost: approximately £150 to £400. Details from Mrs V Jackson, 3a Brickendon Lane, Brickendon, near Hertford, Hertfordshire SG13 8NU. Telephone (01992) 511303. Fax (01992) 501627.

Sheringham   map 1/48
Sea Spray/The Flints/Shearwater Cottages

One of our readers, a train buff, took his family here on the strength of Sheringham being the terminus of the North Norfolk steam railway. Sheringham is full of character, and only yards from a Blue Flag beach. *Sea Spray* was once a fisherman's cottage, modernised and furnished to a good standard. Sea views from the master bedroom make binoculars a must! **Sleeps 4**. Electricity and bed-

The Flints: in the town and near the sea.

linen are included. TV, video, microwave. Pets welcome. Also in Sheringham, *The Flints* is a typical Norfolk brick and flint cottage just 300 yards from the beach. Comfortably furnished, it **sleeps 5**. Fuel, power and bed-linen included. TV, video, microwave. Small front garden. One pet welcome. *Shearwater Cottages* are two well maintained former fishermen's cottages 150 yards from the sea and Blue Flag beach. Shared courtyard. One **sleeps 4**, the other **6**. There are golf courses locally and good bird watching. **Brochure refs: B5161, B5164, B5162, B5163.**

Details: Blakes, Stoney Bank Road, Earby, Barnoldswick BB94 0AA. To book: (08700) 708090. Brochures: (08700) 708099. **Ref BMA 82. Live search and book: www.blakes-cottages.co.uk**

Edith Weston
Edith Weston Cottage Holidays

Having recently re-established its 'independence', Rutland is one of England's most characterful counties. Good holiday cottages are thin on the ground, but these would be winners in any company. Two are pretty stone cottages in the peaceful village of Edith Weston, one is in Morcott.

Of the two in Edith Weston, the smaller is a 19th century, two bedroomed cottage with a log burning stove and a big conservatory with cane furniture. It opens on to an exquisite garden full of flowers, baskets and tubs, and is rated Four Stars by the ETC. **Sleeps 4 plus 2** (a twin, a double and a sofa bed).

The second cottage, also 19th century and with four bedrooms, is the former home of owners Andrew and Jayne Barber, who still live in the village and know the area well. It has an excellent kitchen and a living/dining room with a central fireplace. Patio doors lead on to the large garden which has been featured in the Gardens 'Yellow Book'. It is ETC Three Stars but has been furnished and equipped to Four Star standards.

Edith Weston is near the south shore of Rutland Water, ideal for those who enjoy sailing, windsurfing, trout fishing, cycling or walking the 25 mile cyclepath, or birdwatching at the 350 acre Egleton Nature Reserve.

The third cottage is a 17th century period stone property in a quiet cul-de-sac in the conservation area in the much admired Rutland village of Morcott, about three miles from Rutland Water. It has been renovated to a very high standard and has three bedrooms. It also benefits from a large log burning stove in the oak-beamed living room and has a high quality fully fitted kitchen. The cottage also has a small conservatory and a private garden. **Sleeps 6 'plus 2'**. It is ETC Four Stars.

All the cottages have easy parking and are within enjoyable walking distance of the very good village pub. A bottle of wine awaits you on arrival. Costs: from £180 for a short break stay of three nights and from £385 per

This is one of the Edith Weston cottages, in a delightful, peaceful village setting...

About three miles from Rutland Water, the Morcott cottage is also quiet and cosy.

week. Prices include linen, towels, electricity, full heating, logs for the fire. TV/video. A cot and a highchair are available if pre-booked. Well behaved dogs are welcome.

Details from Mrs Jayne Barber, Brake Spinney, St Mary's Close, Edith Weston, Rutland LE15 8HF. Telephone (01780) 720081 or Mrs Oldershaw (0115) 937 3201. (Both telephones have an answer machine.)

Welton-le-Wold, near Louth
Stubbs Cottages

Foreman's Cottage, **sleeping 7**, is located on a high lying part of the family farm. It has fine views. We have stayed here: it has the warmest bathroom we have ever found outside Scandinavia, with underfloor heating. All the Stubbs cottages, in this guide without a break for 20 years, have a lasting reputation for being clean, nicely situated and *very reasonably priced*. They are in the hilly, wooded Lincolnshire Wolds (where good self-catering accommo-

Foreman's Cottage, deep in the Lincolnshire Wolds, is warm, comfortable and surprisingly spacious. And as with all the Stubbs cottages, it is very reasonably priced.

dation is thin on the ground). Among other properties there is, in the nearby off-the-beaten-track village of Welton-le-Wold, a 19th century schoolhouse, **sleeping 6**, with masses of character, and in the farmyard itself you will find semi-detached but cosy *Farmyard Cottage,* also **sleeping 6**. Dogs are welcome. Cost: about £210 to £305. A useful sketch map of Lincolnshire (so you don't miss the best beaches and holiday resorts) is incorporated in the details, available from Margaret Stubbs, C V Stubbs and Sons, Manor Warren Farm, Welton-le-Wold, near Louth, Lincolnshire LN11 0QX. Telephone/fax Louth (01507) 604207.

Little Steeping, near Boston map 1/57
Mill Hill Cottage (Vivat Trust Holidays)

We very much admire the work of the Vivat Trust – see Page 20 – and also like the county of Lincolnshire. So we were pleased to hear about this admirable building conservation charity's most recent holiday-property acquisition, on the edge of the Wolds in a lovely, rural part of the county, with the superb, sandy coast only about half an hour's drive. We will see it for ourselves during 2002. Originally a farmworker's cottage

Typical of the Vivat Trust: a prettily rural property of character and style...

built in about 1750, it was converted to holiday accommodation (without losing its character, and with a number of original features retained, by The Heritage Trust of Lincolnshire – who received a Civic Trust award for it in 2001. With a double and a twin reached by *very steep stairs*, there is also a single sofa bed in the sitting room. Among those 'original features' is a cast iron range and a brick floor.

Sleeps 4 'plus 1'. TV/video. No linen/towels. One pet welcome. Cost: about £475 to £595. Further details from The Vivat Trust, 61 Pall Mall, London SW1 5HZ. Telephone 020-7930 8030. Fax 020-7930 2295. **www.vivat.org.uk email: enquiries@vivat.org.uk**

Fulstow, near Louth
The Old Farmhouse

Lincolnshire is a beautiful county of vast skies, near-empty roads, green and rolling Wolds, antique shops, historic houses, way-marked walks, cycle routes, castles and a fine cathedral. These three lovingly cared for properties are charmers. *Bramble* and *Hawthorn* (both single-storeyed) overlook a paved, gravelled 'court-

The Old Farmhouse is one of our all-time favourite holiday homes: it's very special.

yard' with an unusual open-fronted barn. There are open plan sitting rooms, spacious bathrooms, and interestingly designed bedrooms (each has a double and twin). *The Old Farmhouse*, with a double and two twins, has long been a favourite of ours. Each is lovingly furnished, with good colour co-ordination and attention to detail. Fresh flowers and chilled wine complete the picture. The courtyard 'Information Centre' stocks maps, books and guides, with a regularly updated video library. Linen and towels included. Non smoking. Children over ten welcome. Not suitable for dogs. Cost: £198 to £450, according to occupancy. Details from Mac and Stephanie Smith, Waingrove Country Cottages, Fulstow, near Louth, Lincolnshire LN11 0XQ. Telephone/fax: 01507 363704.

www.lincolnshirecottages.com
email: macandstephanie@waingrove.demon.co.uk

Barnoldby-le-Beck, near Louth
Grange Farm Cottages and Riding School   map 1/59

With great views of the Lincolnshire Wolds and the surrounding country-side, just a few miles from the eerily beautiful coastal marshes, these newly available cottages have a lot going for them. A converted barn now incorporates three neat, spacious properties (not yet seen by us), which are notable for their original oak beams and archway entrances, terracotta floored and good sized

A good base in a fascinating county...

lounge/dining areas, private patios and gardens. An important feature here is the riding school on site with modern stables, spacious paddocks and grazing land, available to guests bringing their own horse or pony. The school has twelve horses of its own and offers tuition from qualified instructors for all levels from novices to experienced riders.

TV. Linen included, but not towels. Each **sleeps 4 'plus 2'** in a double and a twin, plus sofa bed. Cost: £175 to £275. Details: Mark Barford, Grange Farm Cottages and Riding School, Waltham Road, Barnoldby-le-Beck, Lincolnshire DN37 0AU. Telephone (07802) 310131. Fax (01472) 311101. **www.grangefarmcottages.com email: mbarford@msn.com**

Langwith, near Mansfield
Blue Barn Cottage

Featured in this guide for a number of years, this delightful family house on a mixed 450-acre farm near historic Sherwood Forest is a great favourite of ours. (We also know a family of nine who have holidayed here ten times.) It's close to the farmhouse at the end of a mile-long track from the village, yet very accessible, being only 15 minutes'

This quiet and spacious house is one of our personal long-term favourites...

drive from the M1 (junction 30). A cosy sitting room – all is very quiet here – with TV leads on to the dining room. Upstairs there is a double bedroom, a family room with a double and two singles, a twin room with cot and a small twin room, all opening off the landing.

English Tourism Council Three Stars. There is a large garden and barbecue. Cost: from £375, which includes all linen, towels, central heating and a 'welcome pack' of provisions. There is a big kitchen/breakfast room with Rayburn, electric cooker, microwave, fridge and freezer and an extra downstairs toilet/shower. Not suitable for dogs.

Further details, together with a colour leaflet, from June Ibbotson, Blue Barn Farm, Langwith, Nottinghamshire NG20 9JD. Telephone/fax Mansfield (01623) 742248.

Little Humby, near Grantham/Spilsby
Granary Cottage and Old Rectory Cottage

Granary Cottage (map 1/61) is a skilful conversion of an 18th century granary close to the owners' home and within extensive grounds that include a large south-facing garden and a wildflower meadow with summer house. With much original character retained (attic bedrooms, low beams and doorways, for example), it provides comfortable accommodation **for 2 plus 1** and is well placed for touring the Wolds. (Brochure ref:

Old Rectory Cottage: south facing views over the garden, and a private golf-course!

15320.) *Old Rectory Cottage,* within easy reach of Lincoln, Louth and Boston (map 1/62) , has an unusual feature: the use of the owner's Par 3 golf course! This well equipped single-storeyed cottage has an open plan kitchen/dining/sitting room and two ensuite bedrooms (thereby **sleeping 4**). Sorry, no children under 12, smokers or pets. (Brochure ref: 13826.)

Country Holidays, Spring Mill, Earby, Barnoldswick, Lancashire BB94 0AA. For bookings, telephone 08700 723723. Brochure line: 08700 725725. **Our reference: CMA 96**

Live search and book: **www.country-holidays.co.uk**

Yorkshire and The Peak District

In these days of regimentation and blandness, Yorkshire remains full of character and is marvellously varied. There is the comparatively unsung East Yorkshire, embracing such little known places as the quiet village of Lund and elegant Beverley, as well as one of our favourite cities – Hull. There are the renovated mills and industrial museums of West Yorkshire – whose rugged countryside has a charm of its own, and whose amazingly well preserved Keighley and Worth Valley railway competes with the Bronte Parsonage in Haworth as one of the county's greatest attractions.

And there are of course the better-known Yorkshire Dales and the North York Moors, as well as the North Yorkshire coast.

Among our Moors and Dales favourites are Helmsley, Hutton-le-Hole, Lastingham, West Witton and tucked-away Bainbridge, near Hawes. York itself is an impressive city best seen from the top of the medieval walls. You can walk right round to the Minster, York's magnificent cathedral. From the North York Moors, narrow roads lead down to secret seaside resorts such as Robin Hood's Bay. Nearby Whitby and Scarborough have their own character, but the real pleasure is seeking out little-known sandy coves and silent valleys among the dales and moors.

The best of Derbyshire and Staffordshire is contained within yet another National Park: the Peak District National Park is the longest-established in Britain, and attracts more visitors than any other, but its gritty but picturesque villages and great houses are little known among southerners.

We are keen on the market town of Ashbourne, the stately homes of Chatsworth and Haddon Hall, the fascinating Blue John Caverns (from '*bleu jaune*'), handsome Buxton, bustling Bakewell.

Sharp-eyed readers may notice some references in this edition to the English Tourist Board's 'National Accessible Scheme' for wheelchair users. Based on tourist board inspections, there are three categories. Category Three denotes that accommodation is accessible to a wheelchair user who is also able to walk short distances and up at least three steps; Category Two to a wheelchair user with assistance; Category One (rare and much prized) to a wheelchair user travelling alone.

Also: the national tourist boards, working with individual regions, have recently 'simplified' their grading schemes, moving for example from a two-tier format in which classifications such as 'Commended' and 'De Luxe' are coupled with a 'Key' grading from one to five. Critics say that having taken twelve years to get holidaymakers to understand that scheme, which came to work quite well, it was a shame to abandon it in favour of an 'oversimplified' star system from one to five. Five Stars speak for themselves – very good properties indeed, top notch in every way – and Four can come so close as to make almost no difference. But we have been interested to hear that some owners who have been granted Five Star status market themselves as Four Stars, thinking that Five sound too rarified and luxurious for some holidaymakers...

South Cave, near Beverley/Brough
Rudstone Walk Farm Cottages

Enhanced by vast skies and panoramic views of open country, these are excellent, professionally and painstakingly run properties – an outstandingly good base from which to explore East Yorkshire, one of England's more secret corners (good sandy beaches, traditional seaside resorts, and much else besides). Although entirely rural, they are only a few miles from the beautiful and inspiring Humber Bridge.

We came away from our most recent visit as keen as ever on the expensively appointed interiors, the peace and quiet, the professional way in which everything is run. Also impressive are the well tended gardens that set off the eleven farm building conversions attached to the handsome farmhouse (there is bed and breakfast too, and small upmarket conferences and seminars). Most recently available, and most 'top notch and pristine' of all, are the seven one-bedroomed cottages, each **sleeping 2**.

There are glorious walks and superb views from many cottage windows: you can even watch ships on the Humber estuary. Facing south west, most of the cottages also enjoy fabulous sunsets. Note too that the city of York is less than an hour by car.

There is an always-effective combination of bare-brick (or stone) and white or cream walls, enhanced by expensive lamps. There are deep armchairs, chintzy sofas, lots of pine. Several cottages have French windows and separate sitting-out areas. Internal doors close with a satisfying clunk, and although basically terraced, the cottages are quiet and self contained. Oak fitted kitchens are up-to-the-minute: microwaves, dishwashers etc, and excellent bathrooms have baths *and* showers. **Sleep 2 to 6.**

Highly praised home-cooked meals can be delivered right to your door. Or you can join fellow guests in the main house for dinner around a big candlelit table.

Well supervised dogs welcome by arrangement. TVs with Sky Sports. Cost: £190 to £480. Linen and towels included in the price, as are heating

Well tended, colourful gardens contribute greatly to the appeal of these cottages.

A typical bedroom, illustrating the style and good taste in evidence here...

and electricity. Details and a good brochure from Laura Greenwood, Rudstone Walk Farm, South Cave, near Brough, East Yorkshire HU15 2AH. Telephone Howden (01430) 422230. Fax 424552.

www.rudstone-walk.co.uk   email: office@rudstone-walk.co.uk

Dalby, near Malton
Field House

We really like the panoramic views from this welcoming, clean and well cared for cottage, and love the generous amount of internal space. Readers have called it a fine and reasonably priced base from which to explore the whole of Yorkshire (York itself is just over half an hour away, the North York Moors, the rolling Dales, the coast, the county's great country houses and gardens are eas-

This is excellent: reasonably priced, very comfortable and quietly situated. It is very well placed for exploring most of North Yorkshire.

ily accessible). The friendly owners live next door and there are horses to admire in the adjoining, tree-fringed fields (there were foals when we called one recent summer). We admired a spacious, beamed, light and bright sitting room with an open fire (fuel provided). The pleasant, good-sized kitchen/diner is well equipped with fridge, microwave and auto-washer. Despite being semi-detached, the cottage is quiet.

Sleeps 4 plus cot: a double and a twin. Dogs welcome. TV. Cost: about £230 to £360, including bedlinen and towels. Further details from Jane Appleton, Field House, Dalby, near York YO60 6PF. Telephone Brandsby (01347) 888389.

www.field-house.com   email: Jane@field-house.com

Green Hammerton, near York   map 3/66
Wasps Nest Cottages

These four most appealing properties are rare examples of traditional cottages that haven't been modernised into blandness. Within attractive gardens at the heart of the pleasant village, two of them, *Cobblers* and *Olgarth* (both **sleeping 2 plus 1**), are quaint, cosy and quite small, while two, *Forester's* (**sleeps 5**) and *The Old Manse* (**sleeps 4**), are bigger and

Superbly well situated properties for seeing almost the whole of Yorkshire...

rather stylish. Cobblers has an open fire and central heating, Olgarth has an all-night burning stove and open fire, Forester's has central heating and an oil-fired Aga cooker, and The Old Manse has central heating, woodburner and open fire. We liked the latter two's antique furniture, pictures, carpets, rugs, lamps and general comfort. TVs. Dogs welcome in three cottages. Linen, towels for hire. Laundry facilities on site. ETC Four Stars in three cottages, Three in Olgarth. Cost: about £180 to £405. Details from Mary Nixon, The Wasps Nest, Green Hammerton, North Yorkshire YO5 8AE. Telephone (01423) 330153. Fax (01423) 331204.

www.phnixon.demon.co.uk
email: waspsnest@phnixon.demon.co.uk

Scrayingham, near York
Sparrow Hall Cottages

These five first class conversions
stand on a farm, well away from the
main road but in easy reach of York.
They make a superb touring base for
the North York Moors and the sandy
beaches of Scarborough. Colleagues
have told us how much they enjoyed
the 'delightful' covered swimming
pool and the open fire (limitless
wood provided) in their cottage. We
Neat, warm and comfortable cottages,
plus a delightful pool.
have always liked the space and the feeling of good taste. *Stables,* **sleeping 4,** is the most traditional (suitable for the partially disabled) but all are
cottagey, with deep, comfy armchairs, *Jack's* is popular with honeymooners, being extremely private and secluded – though it actually **sleeps 3/4.**
Dairy and *Granary* each **sleep 6** in a double and two twins. *Orchard*
(**sleeping 4**) with its enclosed, wood-panelled staircase and window seat,
is maybe the cosiest of all.

TVs. Not suitable for pets. All are ETC Three Stars: Cost: about £200 to
£475. Details: Pam and Nick Gaunt, Sparrow Hall Cottages, Sparrow Hall,
Scrayingham, North Yorkshire Y041 1JD. Telephone (01759) 372917.

www.yorkcott-pool.freeuk.com email: holidays@yorkcott-pool.freeuk.com

York   map 3/69
York Lakeside Lodges

Many years in this guide, this is a
thoughtfully planned, tranquil place,
in which fourteen Scandinavian timber lodges stand (with a high degree
of privacy) on the fringes of a large
lake jumping with coarse fish. The
fishing is one of the charms of the
place: another is its location, with
coaches going to the York centre
every ten minutes, and a nearby 24-
You'd hardly believe you're two miles
from the historic heart of ancient York,
and not in the depths of the country...
hour Tesco's. Two lodges are ETC Five Stars (very private, with fine
views), the others are Four Stars. Winner of a recent Yorkshire White
Rose Award for tourism, and equipped to high standards, all are well insulated and double glazed: good for autumn and winter breaks. Options
include one, two and three bedroom detached lodges, one bedroom semi-
detached lodges, and one and three bedroom cottages at the rear of the
owners' house.

Sleep 2 to 7. Cost: £195 to £660 (just £90 for a two-night break in winter). Dogs are welcome. Colour brochure from Mr Manasir, York
Lakeside Lodges, Moor Lane, York YO24 2QU. Telephone (01904)
702346. Fax 701631.

www.yorklakesidelodges.co.uk email: neil@yorklakesidelodges.co uk

Burnt Yates (Nidderdale), near Harrogate
Dinmore Cottages

We stayed recently in the smallest of these three cottages, tucked away close to the owners' house at the end of a neatly maintained private lane.

Each (even the smallest) is spacious and well-cared-for, with many excellent details: wood burning stoves, peace, quiet and privacy without isolation, tidy flower borders, attractive pictures and old prints, and those always-useful Ordnance Survey

Many years in the guide, never anything but praise. Well off a main road, but conveniently located, these are excellent.

maps. Converted from 17th century farm buildings in the landscaped grounds of the owners' fine country house, they are handy for exploring North Yorkshire and its historic towns, houses gardens and abbeys.

Sleep 2 to 5. English Tourism Council Four Stars. One is ETC 'Category Two' for disabled people. Linen included. TVs, videos, microwaves. Not suitable for dogs. Cost: about £225 to £560; short breaks from £150. Details from Alan Bottomley, Dinmore House, Burnt Yates, Harrogate, North Yorkshire HG3 3ET. Telephone/fax (01423) 770860.

www.dinmore-house.co.uk

email: aib@dinmore-cottages.freeserve.co.uk

Brompton-by-Sawdon, nr Scarborough
Headon Farm Cottages

Down a no-through-road and off the beaten track, converted from 19th century farm buildings around a courtyard, Headon Farm Cottages (**map 3/76**) are handy for Scarborough and the North York Moors. *Byre* has a kitchen/diner and lounge/diner with plush sofa and chairs, from which open stairs lead up to a double and a twin bedroom with cot. *Barn* is

Big bathrooms, good beds, lots of books and pictures. Horse-riding a speciality...

similar, also with patio doors to the courtyard from the kitchen. *Stables* has space, a beamed lounge, an open staircase off the hall leading to a light landing, a double overlooking the courtyard, a large beamed twin. *Farm House Cottages* have beamed lounge/diner/kitchen (open fire if desired), a double, a twin and a bathroom. All **sleep 4**, plus Z-bed on request in Byre and Stables. Well-behaved dogs welcome: two per cottage. Short breaks from £70. TV/video. Linen and towels provided. Cost: about £180 to £380. Details: Clive and Denise Proctor, Headon Farm Cottages, Wydale, Brompton-by-Sawdon, North Yorkshire YO13 9DG. Telephone (01723) 859019.

www.headonholidaycottages.co.uk email: headonfarm@supanet.com

Harrogate, The Dales and around
Harrogate Holiday Cottages*

Harrogate is centrally placed for much of the best of Yorkshire, with easy access to York, the North York Moors, the Dales and fast roads to the splendid (and very varied) coast.

Thanks to Harrogate Holiday Cottages, a number of conveniently situated houses and apartments in and around the handsome town are available. We thought prices very reasonable, and noticed a good and flexible range of accommodation.

During a recent visit we saw a deceptively spacious, attractive stone-built house in a quiet residential location. **Sleeping 5**, it is most appealing and well-equipped, and close to the 200-acre 'Stray', carefully preserved grassland that helps give Harrogate so much character. Also overlooking a

There is a fine, spacious apartment in this elegant, listed Harrogate house...

This stone cottage has oak beams, an open fire and is bordered by a stream.

park, there is a roomy, light and quiet second floor flat, **sleeping 4**, in a handsome Edwardian house. Another, in a quiet street, overlooks the famous Old Swan Hotel. The company also operates beyond Harrogate, in and near such places as historic Knaresborough – known for its castle and Mother Shipton's Cave – in which several properties are offered overlooking the lovely River Nidd and Gorge, with many local walks. There are also properties at Bedale and Ripon (with its redeveloped market square and canal area) and some excellent properties with old world charm near Brimham Rocks and Fountains Abbey.

There is a 250-year-old semi-detached stone cottage, **sleeping 3 'plus 1'**, at Kettlesing, an unspoilt traditional village, so peaceful and quiet, about six miles from Harrogate. It has an open fire, as do about one in six properties. There are several properties in Nidderdale, an Area of Outstanding Natural Beauty, in the pretty Dales village of Darley, one of Yorkshire's 'best kept villages'. and Tockwith, near York.

A good number of properties are in villages and towns, which appeals to people without a car. About half accept pets and several encourage short breaks, particularly some of an extremely high standard near Thirsk. Details/excellent brochure from Harrogate Holiday Cottages, Crimple Head House, Beckwithshaw, Harrogate, North Yorkshire HG3 1QU. Telephone (01423) 772700. Fax (01423) 772359.

www.harrogateholidays.co.uk
email: bookings@harrogateholidays.co.uk

Wrelton, near Pickering
Beech Farm Cottages

If you're looking for a very high standard of comfort indeed, in a holiday house whose interiors are of five-star hotel quality, these should suit. The cottages are all ETC Five Stars, the highest quality rating possible, or Four Stars. Their excellence is reflected in the fact that they have won several awards, including the ETC's 'England for Excellence' award for self catering cottages and in 2001, *for the second time*, the Yorkshire Tourist Board's 'Self-Catering Holiday of the Year' award.

On the edge of the North York Moors, in a quiet little village at the entrance to Rosedale, Beech Farm Cottages are well positioned to give easy access to many attractions, including the North York Moors National Park, Pickering, Helmsley, the coast and even York itself. Within a courtyard backing on to open countryside there are eight sumptuous stone cottages **sleeping from 2 to 10**. This is effectively a hamlet in its own right, in which every house is a haven of comfort.

(In 2000 we met then new owners Pat and Rooney Massara just as they were putting the finishing touches to the properties for incoming visitors. You can be certain of a warm welcome.)

There is a good range of cottage sizes to choose from. Detached, single storeyed *Fat Hen* and *Dove Tree* **sleep 2 or 3** people. *Beech Royd* and *Tanglewood* (which is single storeyed) both **sleep 4**. *Columbine* and *Bracken Brow* **sleep 6**. For larger groups *The Farmhouse* (a listed building) and *Shepherd's Lodge* **sleep 9 and 10**. A cot (or cots) can be made available in every property.

Effectively a hamlet in its own right, in which every house is a haven of comfort.

Whatever the size of the cottage you choose, you will not find it cramped...

There's an excellent indoor pool, whirlpool spa and a sauna. Children also love the timber-framed play area, swings, animals, paddock and field. Included are electricity, linen, towels, heating (all have gas central heating and double glazing) and the use of the pool. All have TV and microwave and all, except the two small cottages, have dishwashers, videos and satellite TV. Cycles available.

Open all year, with short breaks outside the summer season. Cost: from about £250 per week. Details from Pat and Rooney Massara, Beech Farm, Wrelton, Pickering, North Yorkshire YO18 8PG. Telephone (01751) 476612, fax 475032.

www.beechfarm.com
email: holiday@beechfarm.com

Goathland
'The Camping Coach'

For many visitors the most memorable aspects of a visit to the North
York Moors National Park are the
steam-driven trains that ply between
Grosmont and Pickering, via, among
other places, Goathland. Uniquely
(though a second is on the cards) a
railway carriage that has been transformed into living accommodation is
a feature of very attractive, nostalgic
*The name does not do it justice: the
accommodation is rather special!*
Goathland station. It is set back quite privately behind fencing, though
naturally passengers are curious. **Sleeping 4**, it is hugely popular with
railway buffs, who do not balk at the price tag of £350 to £525, depending
on when they go. For as with the National Trust cottages, it is when
everyday tourists have gone home that such places come into their own,
when ghosts wreathe around the signal boxes and the railway tunnels. The
accommodation is comfortable (there are deep armchairs, for example)
and there is a bathroom, though with shower only rather than bath.

*Note: from the beautifully situated Hawthorn Cottage (Page 79) you can
see steam from the trains, but not quite the trains themselves.*

For details/brochure telephone (01751) 472508.

Beadlam, near Helmsley
Townend Cottage   map 3/86

Colour section A , Page 2

Less than an hour from Scarborough,
and on the edge of the North York
Moors (walking boots are recommended!), this is a deceptively spacious, well cared for cottage which
we have been pleased to feature *for
17 years!* A wing of the owner's 18th
century farmhouse, conveniently just
off the main road that runs through
the village, this is comfortable and
full of character. It is cosy in winter,
with its Baxi open fire, or those valu-
*Here you are very well placed for discov-
ering the invigorating North York Moors.
The cottage is deceptively roomy.*
able autumn breaks. There are good beds, a fine new kitchen, and all is
tastefully decorated and furnished, with double glazing, gas fired central
heating and even a log fire. Some internal stone walls are a feature, and
there are oak beams to add character. We like the wide staircase and the
big main bedroom.

ETC Four Stars. TV/video. **Sleeps 4**. Cost: about £175 to £330. Dogs and
other pets welcome. Details from Mrs Margaret Begg, Townend
Farmhouse, Beadlam, Nawton, York YO62 7SY. Telephone Helmsley
(01439) 770103.

www.visityorkshire.com email: margaret.begg@ukgateway.net

Cropton, near Pickering, and Rievaulx
The Green Cottage and Ashberry Cottage

The Green Cottage is a particularly attractive two-bedroomed cottage on the village green at Cropton. Dating from the 1800s, it is very special indeed. Original features such as oak beams and open fires in the sitting and dining rooms add to the character and romance of this delightful place, where furnishings are of a high standard throughout. With its own walled garden, it is just three miles from Pickering (take the North

Interior of Green Cottage: this is a real, 'roses round the door' charmer...

Yorkshire Steam Railway to explore the North York Moors) and ideally placed for discovering Ryedale. Scarborough and Whitby are about 20 miles away, York about 30.

Only a mile from Rievaulx Abbey, *Ashberry Cottage* is a romantic base for discovering the North York Moors. In a riverside setting, it has a beamed sitting room/diner with woodburner, two bedrooms (**sleeps 3 plus 1**), shared grounds and (fenced) riverside garden.

Hoseasons Holidays, Lowestoft NR32 2LW. For real-time availability and on-line booking: Telephone 0870 534 2342. Fax 0870 902 2090.

www.hoseasons.co.uk   email: mail@hoseasons.co.uk

Goathland, near Whitby   map 3/90
Hawthorn Cottage

This is a real beauty. When we first called we stopped to admire a steam train on the North York Moors Railway, then climbed up and over the moors looking down over the town to see *one of the most exquisitely situated cottages we feature in this guide*! We know the owners, who use the cottage themselves from time to time, and standards are very high. On the ground floor there is a

Quite beautifully situated, and sympathetically renovated. Very special!

large, fully equipped farmhouse kitchen, a spacious but cosy sitting room with an open stone fireplace, a double bedroom with a pine bed, a single room and a family bath/shower room. The first floor has a further two double bedrooms (one with four poster), another single, a twin, plus shower room. Two attic bedrooms, one twin, one single, are reached via a separate staircase from the kitchen.

Sleeps 2 to 10. Up to two dogs welcome. Linen and towels and logs included. Cost: £350 to £970. Details from Jan Hollingsbee, Fairacre Cottage, North Fambridge, Essex CM3 6NJ. Telephone (01621) 742100.
email: RHollingsb@aol.com
www.hawthorncottage.net

79

Ruswarp, near Whitby
Danby and Goathland Cottages

Cottages of reliable quality are hard to come by in this part of North Yorkshire where demand exceeds supply (Whitby is a still-authentic fishing port of great character, which manages a dual role as a family holiday resort). To reach the enclave of stone-built, handsomely tiled cottages, you climb two hundred yards, past a golf course, from the riverside village of Ruswarp (pronounced 'Russup'). Known as Heron Cottages, most are holiday homes,

These manage to combine a high degree of privacy and quiet without being uncomfortably isolated...

but private and nicely self contained, with a children's play area and attractive field and woodland surroundings. *Danby* and *Goathland* are adjacent, and are similar inside. We found the cottages roomy, with a spacious sitting room giving on to a back garden, a late afternoon sun trap.

We noticed comfortable sofas, a round dining table, big and deep cupboards, an attractive combination of stone and exposed beams, well fitted kitchens. Danby **sleeps 6** in two doubles and one single/bunk bedded room, Goathland **sleeps 5** in a double, a twin and a single.

TVs. Linen but not towels included. Not suitable for dogs or other pets. Cost: about £205 to £415. Weekend breaks. Further details from Mr and Mrs Greendale, Pond Farm, Brantingham, East Yorkshire HU15 1QG. Telephone (01482) 666966. Or from Mr and Mrs Holgate, Nunthorpe, Godmans Lane, Kirk-Ella HU10 7NX. Telephone (01482) 654917.

'Give us a break!'

Some readers have asked us over the years to identify cottages that are available for short breaks, not just in the winter months but in summer too. We rarely do this, because experience tells us that about four out of five owners and agents are able to oblige.

It is always worth enquiring about these very popular mini-holidays (doctors recommend them!) even at the height of the holiday season, as even the most sought after properties can have unexpected cancellations. You should expect to pay slightly more than the 'pro rata' daily price.

Ebberston (near Scarborough)
Cliff House

With immense style and energy Simon Morris, the owner of Cliff House, has turned what was a rather good cottage set-up into *one of the very best in the whole of Yorkshire*. And that's saying something!

Among much else he has turned its four acres of land, with the walled garden, an amazing pyramid-shaped treehouse, the secret wooded gardens and the trout pool, into a source of fascination for visitors. (Youngsters love the toddlers' play area and the animals.) There is a covered, heated pool with a jacuzzi, a hard tennis court and a big games room with table tennis, pool, and darts.

Cliff House stands conveniently on the A170 – though in several cottages you'd hardly know the road is there – and is only about ten miles inland from Scarborough, with the North York Moors on the doorstep.

Lilac **sleeps 4** in a downstairs twin with en-suite toilet and handbasin, and a first floor double room. There's a downstairs kitchen/diner with open fire; upstairs lounge with garden views, and bathroom. *Maple* with its own small courtyard, **sleeping 6** and suitable for people of limited mobility, has a downstairs en-suite twin, as well as two first floor bedrooms and bathroom. *Beech* (**sleeping 5**) has a downstairs twin room and bathroom, kitchen/diner and lounge with big picture windows enjoying excellent

A good-looking arrangement of houses, handy for the moors and the seaside.

We find a high standard of furnishing, comfort, and attention to detail.

views, a single and a double room upstairs. *Pine* and *Willow* (**sleep 4**) are 'upside down' cottages with bathroom, toilet and two bedrooms on the ground floor; beamed lounge/diner/kitchen (with open fire) taking advantage of first floor views. *Holly* **sleeps 6** in a double and two twins, and is quietly situated near the gardens. Its lounge has an open fire and picture windows; there is a dishwasher. *Apple* (**sleeps 2**) is converted from the laundry and apple store of Cliff House and has a beamed lounge and kitchen/diner, with double bedroom – overlooking gardens and apple trees – and bathroom upstairs. *Pear* also **sleeps 2** (**plus 1** in a pulldown bed) and we found it altogether individual and charming, light and interesting. A beamed kitchen/diner leads to the lounge and on into a beamed double bedroom with high sloping ceiling, overlooking the gardens.

ETC Three/Four Stars. TVs. Linen, towels and heating included. 'Sorry, no pets.' Cost: about £250 to £750. Colour brochure from Simon Morris, Cliff House, Ebberston, near Scarborough, North Yorkshire YO13 9PA. Telephone Scarborough (01723) 859440. Fax (01723) 850005.

email: cliffhouseebberston@btinternet.com

Scarborough/Scalby
Wrea Head Cottage Holidays

Down a quiet lane, yet only a short drive from Scarborough (its skeletal ruined castle on the headland is visible from some windows), these skilfully converted farm buildings alongside the owners' home are perfectly placed for enjoying both the seaside and the countryside.

The mainly south-facing, well cared-for cottages were national winners of the ETC's "England for Excellence" Award for Self-Catering Holiday of the Year. They were also winners *three times* of the much-coveted 'White Rose Award' as the Yorkshire Tourist Board's Self-Catering Cottages of

Children love to stay here, and to get to know the horses and the teddy bears!

A fine pool, sauna and jacuzzi bring something special to these cottages.

the Year. The high level of repeat business that they enjoy shows how readers too have taken them to their hearts.

There are nine in all, of differing sizes, with well-tended gardens. Most have sea views and are harmonious in red-brick and pantiled roofs. Set on the edge of the North York Moors National Park, only one hour from York, this is an ideal location to explore villages and market towns, the Heritage Coast and neighbouring forest drives. There's a sauna and an indoor heated swimming pool with a jacuzzi at one end. This sends small waves down the pool to the delight of young children who – joy of joys – also have their own Teddy Bears Cottage, a two-storey wooden playhouse complete with Father Bear, Mother Bear and Baby Bear upstairs in bed and its own fenced garden and picnic area. Older children will enjoy the unusually well-equipped adventure playground.

Hay Barn Cottage (**sleeps 9**) particularly impressed us with its clever design whereby sitting room, dining room and kitchen are separate but linked. There are well-chosen fabrics throughout (bedrooms in particular with their pretty duvets, curtains and table lamps are charming). Kitchens are modern, mostly with dishwashers, and overhead beams add character in the main rooms. All have full gas central heating, and are ETC Four Stars. Parking, linen, laundry, telephone and barbecues are included. TVs. No pets. Open all year. Cost: from £245 to £1150. Good value special breaks in winter, ie four nights for the price of three.

Further details from Chris and Andrea Wood, Wrea Head House, Barmoor Lane, Scalby, Scarborough, North Yorkshire YO13 0PG. Telephone Scarborough (01723) 375844; fax 500274.

www.wreaheadcotghols.demon.co.uk
email: ghcg@wreaheadcotghols.demon.co.uk

Cloughton, near Scarborough
Gowland Farm Cottages

On two sides of exceptional gardens, just off a quiet country lane, each of these four cottages is a gem. Both in the depths of the country and near the sea, they are lovely to come 'home' to after a day on the beach. Close to the owners' home, they are looked after with loving care and an eye for detail: we noticed deep, comfy sofas, attractive rugs on good carpets, pretty pictures and lamps.

Exquisite interiors, with an absolute commitment to comfort and warmth. Also, all the advantages of being both deeply rural and near the sea.

Sleep from 2 to 7. Formerly 'White Rose' Winners of the Self Catering Holiday of the Year in Yorkshire and Humberside, the cottages are English Tourism Council Four Stars. *Over Across* and *May* have a bath, while the other cottages have showers. 'Sorry, no pets'. TV/video. Central heating. Linen and towels. Cost: about £125 to £435. Details from Jeff and Angie Donnelly, Gowland Farm, Gowland Lane, Cloughton, Scarborough, North Yorkshire YO13 0DU. Telephone (01723) 870924.

www.gowlandfarm.co.uk
email: jeff@gfarm.fsworld.co.uk

Sleights, near Whitby   map 3/98
White Rose Holiday Cottages

Whitby is a fascinating, historic fishing port and resort, but reliable self catering properties are hard to come by. Less than three miles away, in Sleights, not yet seen by us but much praised by readers, are several properties: six cottages – three in a neatly arranged courtyard – and two bungalows. There's also a comfortably appointed flat in Whitby. This is a serious set-up, with high standards. Said a Mrs Walker from Nottinghamshire, 'We've stayed three times in *Primrose*, which is almost a home-from-home for us. We love the area, and the village'. A Mrs Allison, from Hertfordshire, also likes the village. She has stayed in *Rose Nook*: 'Just right for two adults and two children. It's right on the green, and it's lovely to have a coal fire.'

Pretty Primrose is one of three courtyard cottages.

TVs. Well behaved dogs welcome. Weekend breaks. Linen and towels included. Cost: about £210 to £470. ETC Three/Four Stars. Details from Mr and Mrs Roberts, Greenacres, 5 Brook Park, Sleights, near Whitby, North Yorkshire YO21 1RT. Telephone (01947) 810763.

www.whiterosecottages.com email: enquiries@whiterosecottages.com

Robin Hood's Bay
Farsyde Mews Cottages

Inside the North York Moors National Park, well away from main roads, these cottages (on a family-run stud farm) have easy access – across fields and with panoramic views of the sea and beach below – to the little fishing village of Robin Hood's Bay, one of the most loved and attractive places in North Yorkshire. As parking space in its steep narrow streets is almost non-existent, to be able to walk there in a few minutes from the cottages is a great advantage; the beach, partly sandy, is ideal for fossil hunting and has fascinating rock pools.

A private path through the wood leads past the old mill and its dam to the beach at Boggle Hole, and the Cleveland Way runs close.

The four original mews cottages, converted from a big stone barn, share a garden with fruit trees and a real well (with safety grid). They are small, modest but inexpensive, and we met guests who were very content. Space has been skilfully used with, for example, showers rather than baths. **Sleep 2 to 5**.

Mistal Cottage is outstanding and thoroughly deserves its ETC Four Stars. **Sleeping 4** in double and twin rooms (both have low sloping ceilings at the sides), it has a galleried landing and stairs (unsuitable for young children). A very big sitting-room/diner with coal/wood-burning stove, TV and video, looks on to the front garden and patio. Dishwasher and washer-dryer. Non smokers in Mistal Cottage only.

Unusually, private hire of the small, 82 degrees, swimming pool (20 by 8 feet, with an inflatable boat) within a log cabin can be arranged for guests in Mistal.

Visitors who are experienced riders have access to some fine horses for year-round hacking over beach, heather moors, fields or forest – or you can bring your own horse. There are cows, calves, donkeys, dogs, cats, ducks, hens, a cockerel and Paddington, a Newfoundland, who enchants visitors!. TV, video, books, games. Dogs welcome except in Mistal.

The excellent Mistal is outstanding. We stayed here ourselves recently...

The views are marvellous, and the whole atmosphere very much liked by readers.

Whitby is six miles, Scarborough 16. Cost: £150 to £365 (mews); Mistal: £300 to £565. Short breaks. Details/brochure from Angela and Victor Green, Farsyde House, Robin Hood's Bay, near Whitby, North Yorkshire YO22 4UG. Telephone (01947) 880249; fax (01947) 880877.

email: farsydestud@talk21.com

Kettlewell
Fold Farm Cottages

Kettlewell is one of the most photographed villages in Yorkshire, a delightfully well preserved, labyrinthine, stone built place right in the heart of the Yorkshire Dales. This is a quartet of traditional, very quiet, thick-walled, warm and comfortable cottages next to the friendly and hospitable owners' farm. We have met

Right in the heart of a famous village, with many successful years in this guide.

visitors revelling in the well cared for interiors, the deep carpets, the good quality lined curtains, the books, the table lamps, the antique or 'country' furniture. Beds are excellent, and original features have been retained. The location is super for exploring the Yorkshire Dales National Park, with Malham Cove and Tarn and Great Whernside nearby. **Sleep 2 to 5**. ETC Four Stars. TV. Linen and towels provided. Dishwashers in all but *Buttercup*.

Dogs welcome by arrangement, but one cottage is totally pet-(and smoking) free. Cost: approximately £160 to £330. Details from Mrs B Lambert, Fold Farm, Kettlewell, near Skipton, North Yorkshire BD23 5RH. Telephone (01756) 760886.

www.foldfarm.co.uk
email: info@foldfarm.co.uk

Kettlewell   map 3/101
Cam Beck Cottage

It's no surprise that Kettlewell is featured on many a calendar and picture postcard. And this idyllic 300 year old stone cottage – with even a trout stream running alongside – is tucked away in a corner at the top end of this exceptionally attractive small community, just six miles north of Grassington, at the foot of Great Whernside, deep in the Yorkshire

Kettlewell may be the most photogenic village around here. And Cam Beck is a haven from which to enjoy it.

Dales National Park This is marvellous walking country, with many walks starting from your front door. The comfortably renovated cottage, with beamed ceilings and an open fire in the lounge, **sleeps 4** in a double bedroom and a twin bedroom.

There is a bathroom with shower, a modern, fitted dining-kitchen, and a large, attractive and sunny garden next to the beck with garden furniture and barbecue. It is not suitable for pets or very young children. Parking is available for one car. Linen available.

Cost: about £195 to £395, including electric heating and coal for the open fire. Short breaks. Details from Mr and Mrs C Halliday, 3 Grange Drive, Horsforth, Leeds LS18 5EQ. Telephone Leeds (0113) 258 9833.

85

Buckden, near Skipton
Dalegarth and The Ghyll Cottages

Featured in this guide without a break since 1983, with never a single complaint and many, many glowing tributes, these are absolutely reliable. Not surprisingly, both Dalegarth and The Ghyll have Four Stars from the English Tourism Council. The latter are Disabled Category 2. But even those accolades do not tell the story of how the two groups of cottages in the same village have become synonymous with really comfortable living in the heart of one of the most beautiful parts of the Yorkshire Dales.

This tribute came from a reader a couple of years ago: '(It is)...the best self catering we have rented by far...a high standard of fittings and furnishings, extremely well maintained by the owner on site, for whom nothing is too much trouble...We are visiting in October for the sixth time...'

Lonely roads that go deep into wild country are pleasant enough for the

A neat cluster of purpose-built traditionally styled houses with superb facilities. The warm, covered pool, and the adjacent sauna, are irresistible, and the whole place is surrounded by the unspoilt beauty of Upper Wharfedale.

tourist, but when such roads combine scenic beauty with ease of access it is twice as nice! The B6160, which runs from near Skipton, through Upper Wharfedale, to the heart of the Dales, is one of those roads.

A few yards off it, on the south side of the small village of Buckden, in what was once the kitchen garden of a great house nearby, *Dalegarth* consists of a neat cluster of eleven purpose built, traditionally styled stone houses grouped around a dog-leg cul-de-sac. They are modern, neat and tidy, and fit very attractively into the landscape. Dalegarth is quiet, rural and, particularly inside each house, superbly designed to fit the needs of the holidaymaker. Spacious lounges are all on the first floor, to take advantage of woodland and hill views (this is fine walking and touring country), and seven of the cottages (there are basically two types) have small sauna rooms, so they are ideal for the outdoor type who appreciates all modern comforts.

The cottages, which are **ideal for 4 but can sleep 6** (two bedrooms, plus bed-settee in lounge), have excellent bathrooms, well-appointed kitchens and large, most comfortably furnished lounges with TV and individually designed natural stone fireplaces. They are classified as 'type A' and 'type B' and are identical except that 'type A' have a sauna in the bathroom, breakfast bar in the kitchen, patio-style windows leading out on to a balcony from the lounge and an en suite shower, toilet and vanity unit in the master bedroom. All the cottages have integral garages.

Dalegarth has an impressive indoor swimming pool, plus a solarium and games/exercise room and an exceptionally attractive terrace to sit on after your swim and admire the scenery. Also, there is a full linen service and a well-equipped laundry room that incorporates a large communal freezer.

Mr and Mrs Lusted, who live in one of the houses, keep these warmly carpeted, superbly-equipped properties as clean and efficiently run as any we have seen in our travels. They will be appreciated by people who are willing to pay a little extra for comfortable living in the midst of beautiful scenery, with hot baths and deep armchairs to come back to after long walks or scenic drives through the Dales National Park.

The three *Ghyll Cottages* were designed specifically for those with mobility problems. Built in natural stone, set in secluded landscaped grounds to the rear of the village of Buckden, in a quiet, sunny location, they share the leisure amenities of Dalegarth, less than two hundred yards away.

Susan and David Lusted have given considerable thought to the needs of

The Ghyll represents a considerable investment in thought and comfort. It enjoys a regular following.

View of The Ghyll's garden: how could you resist a ramble in the hills? Even on a Bank Holiday you can easily escape.

their guests and the well-planned accommodation is tastefully furnished and decorated to a very high standard. Each of the cottages has a covered loggia leading to an entrance porch which opens into a large lounge/dining room, off which is a fully-fitted and extremely well-equipped kitchen, including microwave, dishwasher etc. A double bedroom, thoughtfully provided with versatile 'zip link' beds, a spacious ensuite bathroom with spa bath, walk-in shower, etc, completes the downstairs, with another double bedroom and bathroom upstairs (one cottage has two upstairs bedrooms). The south-facing lounges offer direct access to sunny patios and every property has remote control TV and audio centre, video and video library, central heating and a full linen service. Main bedrooms have TV and radio. Wheelchair-bound people staying there have told us that The Ghyll has it 'just right' and could not be faulted for the facilities.

The Lusteds have a policy of welcoming inspection during changeover periods. No dogs at The Ghyll (except guide dogs) but a small dog at Dalegarth is possible by arrangement. Some cottages are 'non-smoking'. Cost: about £282 to £518. Special winter mini-breaks. Details and colour leaflet from Mr and Mrs D Lusted, 2 Dalegarth, Buckden, near Skipton, North Yorkshire BD23 5JU. Telephone/fax Skipton (01756) 760877.

Disabled readers should note that some while ago The Ghyll Cottages were chosen as national winners by the Holiday Care Service, at the World Travel Exhibition in Earls Court, London.

www.Dalegarth.com email: dalegarth@aol.com

Reeth and Healaugh

These very 'traditional' cottages have introduced hundreds of our readers to the special flavour of the Yorkshire Dales, where traffic jams are unheard of. Ably run by Robert and Janet Hughes, the cottages have featured in this guide *every year without a break since 1983*.

In many ways Swaledale represents the best of the Dales, its traditional limestone cottages set in an impressive, quiet but rugged landscape. Upper Swaledale, by the way, leads to Wensleydale via the exhilarating Buttertubs Pass: an unforgettable trip during which, even on the busiest weekend of the summer, you are unlikely to see many other cars.

Deep in Swaledale, at Healaugh, is Thiernswood Hall, where Robert and Janet Hughes and their family live. In the beautiful and tranquil grounds are two self catering properties which stand together (though with a high degree of privacy) away from the main house nestled on the edge of high-lying woodland.

The Bothy is a tucked away little eyrie, ideal for a couple who just want to close their door on the world. Cost: about £166 to £330. *Thiernswood*

Swale View is probably our personal favourite among those owned and run by Robert and Janet Hughes ...

Thiernswood Cottage is actually a substantial house in its own right – a very good place to 'come home to' ...

Cottage is particularly spacious, with a well equipped kitchen, dining room and sitting room, two charmingly co-ordinated bedrooms – one double with en-suite shower room, the other twin bedded with en-suite bathroom. It is very quiet, deep-carpeted and comfortable. **Sleeps 4**. Cost: approximately £235 to £510.

Linen and towels are included in Thiernswood Cottage and The Bothy; electricity is included in Thiernswood Cottage.

In the village of Healaugh there is a four bedroomed listed cottage called *Swale View*. Full of character, and with many old features retained, it has a particularly pleasant kitchen with an unusual vaulted dining alcove, a spacious dining room and beamed sitting room with a big Yorkshire stone fireplace. It is one of our own Yorkshire favourites. The main bedroom has a four poster double bed with ensuite bathroom. The cottage has a beautiful garden with spectacular views. **Sleeps 6**. Cost: approximately £240 to £545.

English Tourism Council Four Stars. There are televisions throughout. A dog is welcome in Swale View. Further details can be obtained from Mrs J T Hughes, Thiernswood Hall, Healaugh, Richmond, North Yorkshire DL11 6UJ. Telephone Richmond (01748) 884526, fax (01748) 884834.

Reeth, near Richmond
Wraycroft Cottages

Featured in this guide for 20 years, these neat, tidy and much liked cottages are at the heart of one of our all-time favourite North Yorkshire (large) villages. Surrounded by hills and bounded by the River Swale and the Arkle Beck, it is just eleven green, wooded miles from Richmond. Wraycroft Cottages are on the edge of the village, in two acres of land

We were not surprised that more than 80% of people who stay here come back.

bounded on the south side by the river. All the cottages face south and are enhanced by uninterrupted views of well kept gardens, panoramic views of the hills and glimpses of the river. They, together with their owners' bungalow, occupy one of the best sites in Swaledale. The three *Crofts* are two storeyed, linked but private, and built to a very high standard. *Wraycroft* is an exceptionally comfortable self contained bungalow and is suitable for visitors who have limited mobility. The properties, each one **sleeping 4**, are ETC Four Stars, and have a remarkably strong repeat business: *over 80%*! Cost: approximately £190 to £360, with reductions for couples. Not suitable for children, pets or smokers. A colour brochure is available from Mrs F Hodgson, Wraycroft, Reeth, Richmond, North Yorkshire DL11 6SU. Telephone Richmond (01748) 884497.

Coverdale and (near) Leyburn map 3/110/119

During a late spring 2000 visit to North Yorkshire to look at some of the properties on the books of Welcome Holidays (see our main feature on **Pages 10 and 11**) we discovered an exceptionally attractive, little frequented corner of the county where they have several properties. Coverdale is a delight (after several days on the road we hardly wanted to leave) and among other places Welcome have a 17th century cottage, **sleeping just 3**, in the hamlet

Full of history, and a great location in lovely, little known Coverdale...

of Gammersgill. Ref 1474. With a number of original features retained, an open fire, and immediate access to outstandingly good (and invigorating!) walks, this is rather special. Just an easy five minute drive from Leyburn, a small market town of great character, we loved a very privately situated but not isolated former farmhouse, set off by a tidy lawned garden, and **sleeping 7/8** people. There are two open fires, spacious rooms, fine views, a charming 'family house' atmosphere. Ref 4018.

Details from Welcome Holidays, Embsay Mills, Embsay, Skipton, North Yorkshire BD23 6QR. For brochures: (01756) 702200.
www.welcome.cottages.co.uk

Sedbusk, near Hawes, and West Burton
Clematis, Well and Shepherd's Cottages

We have had no hesitation in directing close friends to *Shepherd's Cottage*, **sleeping 6**, a real feather in the cap of Anne Fawcett, whose three stone built cottages are well suited for those hankering after individual properties located in picture postcard settings. We have had so many compliments about the Fawcetts over the years, and Canadian guests were full of praise as they showed us round this spacious Grade II listed Dales stone cottage (almost a misnomer if judged on size alone), around a quarter of a mile from Sedbusk itself. Renovated from one of the earliest farmhouses in the Yorkshire Dales (it was built in 1633), and standing back from the road in its own small field, the property impresses one with its spacious lounge and stone fireplace (coal supplied), the pine floor amply scattered with rugs, and a stylish original mullioned window.

Add lots of beams and exposed stonework, from the kitchen, kept cosy by the Rayburn which runs oil fired central heating throughout, to the three bedrooms (two doubles in the front, a twin in the back) with old stripped pine furniture and you quickly have the measure of the place.

Nor is it alone in providing a classic example of character with comfort. Of the original two cottages, *Clematis*, perched on a bank in the no-through traffic hamlet itself, enjoys spectacular views of the Dales, especially from the first floor front bedrooms. It has big rooms – notably the welcoming sitting room – lots of character, old pine, original stone flags, heavy oak beams, a wide staircase. **Sleeps up to 8.**

Set in a busier, though still tranquil, setting – West Burton is a filmset location, with cottages on both sides of a typical village green – the early 17th century *Well Cottage* **sleeps 4** (a twin and a double, both comfortable and sunny) with a pretty walled garden. As with the others, there is considerable space, beams and exposed interior stone with a fireplace in the generous sitting room.

Clematis has inspiring views, and is a house of great character and history.

Well Cottage is well placed in a completely unspoilt village.

Each cottage has Laura Ashley prints, TV/video, and is ETC Four Stars. Linen and towels for hire. Electricity on meter. Dogs are welcome, but must be controlled. Free trout fishing is available on the owners' farm.

Costs: from about £175 to £600. Detailed information from Anne Fawcett, Mile House Farm, Hawes in Wensleydale, North Yorkshire DL8 3PT. Telephone Wensleydale (01969) 667481. Fax 667425.

www.wensleydale.uk.com email: milehousefarm@hotmail.com

Rathmell, near Settle
Layhead Farm Cottages

One of the properties here sleeps 10: a great setting for a big family gathering.

If you like properties with character, always consider farm conversions. Layhead Farm Cottages have character in abundance! An old stone barn has been converted to create two cottages, *Cobblestones* and *Craggs Barn*. Both **sleep 5** in one double plus a single bed, and one twin bedded room. A bed settee can add **an extra 2**. Original oak beams and exposed stonework combine with contemporary comforts. Add a working farm with rural views, and setting, and you complete the most attractive picture. Additionally *The Stables*, **sleeping 6** in one double and one twin with a chair bed in each, is a newly converted barn with the same eye to detail and themed rooms. Doubling up as B&B accommodation, it benefits from a large kitchen, though space is generous all round.

All are ETC Four Stars. *The Farmhouse*, **sleeping 10**, has been renovated to provide comfortable accommodation. Pets by arrangement. Linen and towels; laundry facilities; payphone. Cost: from £200 to £600, including electricity. Details: Rosemary Hyslop, Field House, Rathmell, Settle, North Yorkshire BD24 0LD. Telephone (01729) 840234. Fax (01729) 840775. **www.layhead.co.uk email: rosehyslop@layhead.co.uk**

Giggleswick, near Settle
Close Cottage   map 3/116

A spacious house of great character...

There's something special about the traditional farmhouse, and this is a classic. Away from main roads, in an attractive part of North Yorkshire, near Skipton, it is part of a family-run farmstead. The very comfortable 17th/18th century detached house, set back behind a low stone wall and iron railings, is grander than a conventional cottage. We admired country antiques, high ceilings, a fireplace in the sitting room (there's central heating too), a family-style kitchen, table lamps, attractive pictures (framed portraits, local country scenes), a Victorian claw-foot bath in the spacious main bathroom. We met a family who liked the house so much they said they hurried 'home' after each day's sightseeing just to enjoy the atmosphere. The owners are kind and welcoming, as are the resident dalmations and Billy the cat.

Sleeps 6 in a double and two twins. ETC Four Stars. TV. Linen and towels included. Not suitable for pets. Cost: about £225 to £392. Details from Richard and Sue Hargreaves, Close House, Giggleswick, Settle, North Yorkshire BD24 0EA. Telephone/fax (01729) 822778.
email: info@close-house.co.uk

91

Stanbury, near Keighley
Sarah's Cottage

This is excellent: modestly priced, comfortable, located in a very interesting and attractive part of West Yorkshire – a really good find on a bright and breezy day. It has easy access to invigorating country walks, and among much else the Keighley and Worth Valley (Steam) Railway, ther Brontë Parsonage at Haworth. There is a well planned small garden, with a bird feeder that attracts 'all sorts' and a garden seat from which to enjoy the view, an exceptionally comfortable deep-carpeted ambience, absolute cleanliness

A Yorkshire gem: welcoming owners, masses of comfort, and inexpensive too...

We especially liked the table lamps, the main bedroom with its picture window, the neat kitchen/diner. There is a small second bedroom with adult-sized bunks and an upstairs bathroom with a power-shower over the bath. There is also a garage. Not surprisingly, this is English Tourism Council Four Stars. One well behaved dog is possible. Television and video. Linen and towels included.

Cost: about £120 to £250. Details from Eunice and Brian Fuller, Emmanuel Farm, 101 Stanbury, Keighley, West Yorkshire BD22 0HA. Telephone (01535) 643015.

email: brian.fuller2@btinternet.com

When we say 'dogs are welcome' it usually means most other animals are too. But do check...

Holestone Moor, near Matlock
Holestone Moor Barns

When we first visited these the Peak District was thronging with holiday-makers, especially around the fascinating town of Matlock, nearest place of any size to these most impressive conversions from original farm buildings. In contrast, high-lying Holestone was utterly peaceful, a seem-ingly away-from-it-all place, well away from main roads. (But it is not isolated, being next door to a dairy farm.)

Note: there is a demand among readers of this guide for big houses sleep-ing ten or more. One of Holestone's fits the bill: see below.

We looked first at *The Stables*, **sleeping 4** (ETC Four Stars) in a double and a twin bedroom. It has a particularly cosy sitting room with red sofa and armchair, well chosen and good quality fabrics, and the double bed has a truly unique feature: it is correctly known as 'the cannonball bed'!

The Barn is a *tour de force* – ETC Five Stars – with an imposing, even palatial, living room, and separate kitchen. It **sleeps up to 12** in five en-suite bedrooms, including a downstairs twin suitable for disabled users: ETC Category 2. (One bedroom has 2' 6" beds.) Note: for flexibility, all beds are singles. It even has its own games room, with a pool table.

The Barn is a fabulous conversion. Large groups should note: it sleeps up to 12...

Sitting room of The Stables: thoroughly cosy and inviting...

The landscaped gardens are a very important feature, and guests can explore all six acres. Children will love the newly planted woodland walks, the wildlife pond – home to rare water voles – the wildflower meadow and the paddock where there are barbecues and picnic tables.

The standard of finish and workmanship here is extraordinary. Renovat-ing the two properties was a labour of love for owners Vicki and Steve Clemerson. Our purple prose cannot sum up Holestone as well as actual guests: 'A truly wonderful place, full of character and energy'...'all sorts of interesting places to visit'...'we can honestly say we have never stayed anywhere as lovely as this'...

Both properties have woodburners as well as central heating. TVs. Not suitable for pets. Short breaks all year round: contact the owners for details. Wheelchair access in Barn. Linen and towels included. Cost: (Stables) about £331 to £554, (Barn) about £883 to £1470. Details from Vicki and Steve Clemerson, Holestone Moor Barns, Holestone Moor Farm, near Ashover, Derbyshire S45 0JS. Telephone (01246) 591263. Fax 591263.

www.hmbarns.co.uk   email: HMBarns@aol.com

Derbyshire
Peak Cottages*

It's no hardship to check out the properties on the books of this admirable agency. We have found ourselves (with cameras to hand!) in some extremely photogenic corners of the Peak District.

One silent, hot Sunday afternoon we saw *Church Farm Cottage*, deep in exquisite Dovedale. This is a joy: we want it for ourselves! It's Grade II listed, has stone flagged floors, beamed ceilings, rugs on polished floorboards, pretty bedrooms (it **sleeps 4 'plus 1'**). The owners have an 80-acre organic farm, and there are idyllic walks from the front door. Those owners have now completed their second holiday cottage – *Our Ancestral Barn*. It has three bedrooms and bathrooms to the same high standard.

Along an unmade track bordering the River Dove we came across *Ostlers End* and *Dovedale* (both **sleeping 6**). They are notable for superb pine and maple-wood interiors, and both have woodburners.

Dealing almost exclusively in Derbyshire, this organisation has a reputation for offering top quality cottages despite only having been around for seven years. Their well thought-out brochure is outstanding. Send for it even if you are not about to book a cottage, for it encapsulates the essence of the Peaks. It gives full details of each property together with the ETC

The Dairy at Hartington (not featured here) is an extraordinary conversion for 2.

Church Farm Cottage is a joy, but it's just one of this agency's super cottages.

gradings and useful information such as the distances to the nearest grocery shop, post office and railway station, the location of the nearest indoor swimming pool and the names of a recommended pub, take-away and restaurant within easy reach.

There are about 160 cottages altogether, ranging from converted barns to spacious country houses. Such as *Reuben's Roost*, *Bremen's Barn* and *Hopes Hideaway*, which have top-quality accommodation. For example, *Stubben Barn* (**sleeping 4**) at Handley, near Matlock, caught our eye, as it is suitable for anyone with mobility problems, being all on one level.

Also near Matlock, at Tansley, families looking for an indoor swimming pool would appreciate *Knabhall*, *Whitelee* and *Staley Cottage*. Such a pool is fairly unusual for this part of the country.

Cost: about £125 to £1000. For an outstanding colour brochure contact Colin MacQueen, Peak Cottages, Strawberry Lee Lane, Totley Bents, Sheffield S17 3BA. Telephone (0114) 262 0777. Fax (0114) 262 0666.

www. peakcottages.com email: enquiries@peakcottages.com

Hopton, near Matlock
Hopton Hall Cottages

We can hardly sum up the appeal of these cottages better than the reader who told us why she liked hers so much: 'It was great on an autumn visit to be out and about most of the day, sightseeing, walking and pubbing, then to come back to a cottage so full of warmth and comfort'.

The Derbyshire dales are all about crags, waterfalls, perfect stone villages, picture book farmhouses and barns, and as you turn into the imposing entrance to Hopton Hall, you are in for a treat. For this grand country house, whose front overlooks Carsington Water, embraces five sumptuous, expensively appointed cottages near the main house, mostly off a neat stable yard, private and self contained. The grounds include woodland, paddock with football and volley nets, barbecues.

Specifically, and most recently available, *The Granary* has seven bedrooms, six en-suite, all with TV except the bunk-bedded room; two are on the ground floor. **Sleeping 12 'plus 2'**, it has a good-sized, comfy sitting room with an open fire. A number of original features have been retained, and the dining area is big enough for 22. *Butler's Quarters* is almost as big, **sleeping up to 10**. There's a convivial sitting room with woodburner, an appealing kitchen-diner, and a rather 'private' arrangement of bedrooms: two doubles, two twins and a (children's) bunk room. One shower en suite, an additional shower room and two actual bathrooms.

We liked *Gardener's Cottage* immensely. **Sleeping 8** in two good sized rooms and two doubles (one, L-shaped, is especially charming), it is an 'upside down' house, with a pleasant first floor sitting room (open fire) with garden, woodland and countryside views, an attractive kitchen/diner.

Cottages 'full of warmth and comfort', in a lovely, very 'accessible' part of England.

All the cottages are every bit as well appointed as permanent homes.

Both doubles are en-suite (one with bath, one with shower), and there is an additional bathroom with over-bath shower. *Dove Cote* has a door on to the swimming pool, though the cottage (**sleeping 4** in a double and small twin) is entirely private.

Two of the larger cottages have their own gardens. There's an indoor heated swimming pool. Linen and towels are included. TVs/videos. Not suitable for dogs. Cost: about £300 to £2000. More details from Mr and Mrs Brogden, Hopton Hall, Carsington, Wirksworth DE4 4DF. Telephone (01629) 540458. Fax 540712.

email: H.E@saqnet.co.uk

Great Hucklow, near Castleton
The Hayloft

Just finding the place is a pleasure in itself! We enjoyed lunch in a fine pub in the award-winning Dales village of Tideswell, meandered across country (those cloud-scudding skies and rolling hills criss-crossed by dry stone walls), then turned off the A623 towards an attractive stone built farm.

There is comfortable accommodation in a first floor conversion (on one side it overlooks the neat farmyard and the valley beyond, on the other higher and wilder country: every room here has a good view). We liked the pleasant, good sized sitting room with open fire, noted well chosen rugs on a polished wood floor, a

At the end of a no-through-road, walkers will love this.

comfortable deep sofa, a grandfather clock and other antique pieces. There's a well appointed kitchen/diner, a spacious, warm bathroom, two twin rooms. The owners' pretty and safely enclosed garden is freely available to guests.

English Tourism Council Three Stars. **Sleeps 4.** TV. Linen and towels. Dogs are welcome. Cost: £130 to £295. Further details from Mrs M Darley, Stanley House Farm, Great Hucklow, Derbyshire SK17 8RL. Telephone (01298) 871044.

email: margot.darley1@btinternet.com

Most self catering holidays represent great value: compare the average weekly cost of a cottage with the actual value of the property.

Weston Underwood, near Ashbourne
Honeysuckle and Brook Cottages

We still remember a few days spent in the delightful, cosy *Honeysuckle*. It's a gem, tucked away down a lane, with no traffic to speak of, in a cottagey garden. With beams, antiques and a log burner, this 200-year-old cottage is a fine base from which to explore the Peak District and, say, Derbyshire's stately homes; also, golf in lovely surroundings is handy. Chintzy, warm *Brook* is more villagey, on the not-very-busy road.

Delightful 'hideaway' Honeysuckle has a four-poster bed in the main bedroom.

Honeysuckle **sleeps 6** in a double, a twin and a two-bunk room. Brook **sleeps 4** in a double-bedded room and a small bunk-bedded room. Stylish 'b and b' is available in the owners' handsome farmhouse nearby.

Not suitable for dogs. Linen and towels are included. TV and automatic washing machine in each. Cost: about £160 to £330 (Brook), £180 to £400 (Honeysuckle). Further details are available from Linda Adams, Park View Farm, Weston Underwood, near Ashbourne, Derbyshire DE6 4PA. Telephone/fax Ashbourne (01335) 360352.

www.parkviewfarm.co.uk   email: enquiries@parkviewfarm.co.uk

Cressbrook, near Bakewell
Cressbrook Hall Cottages

Readers have been impressed by Cressbrook Hall *(map 3/123)*, which lies half hidden away in an area known as 'Little Switzerland': lots of dramatic and craggy scenery close to the very heart of the Peak District National Park. We have visited *Courtyard Corner* (**sleeps 2**), *Hall Cottage* and *Garden Cottage* (each **sleeps 4 'plus 1'**, with the option of a reserve twin room). Courtyard

These cottages have great character and enjoy an excellent situation.

Corner is interesting and handy for the sauna. We liked even more the character of the cottages 200 yards away – especially the spectacular view of the Wye Valley enjoyed by *Lower Lodge, Rubicon Retreat* and the adjacent *Hidesaway*. **Sleeping 6**, this is suitable for wheelchairs. *Carriage Cottage* **sleeps 8/9**. Two bathrooms. Wheelchair-user-friendly. Bed and breakfast is available in The Hall.

Well behaved dogs welcome. TVs. Linen included. Cost: £115 to £875. Details: Mrs Hull-Bailey, Cressbrook Hall, Cressbrook, near Buxton. Telephone (01298) 871289; fax 871845. Freephone 0800 358 3003.

www.cressbrookhall.co.uk   email: stay@cressbrookhall.co.uk

Ilam, near Ashbourne
Slade House Farm

Under scudding skies, much enjoying the fresh air and the sense of freedom high up among the Derbyshire hills, we located these amazingly well situated cottages. Not only is the situation idyllic, but the standard of accommodation and, simply, the 'style' of the cottages are memorable.

Via narrow farm lanes above the handsome, partly National Trust owned village of Ilam, climbing ever higher up into the hills and with the views becoming more and more spectacular, we arrived at a small group of cottages converted from a Staffordshire farmhouse and barn. They are handsome enough from the outside, fitting harmoniously into their moorland surroundings, but it's the interiors that impress most.

We looked first at *Slade Tops*, **sleeping 2**, standing higher than the other two. Single storeyed, it is (for owner Alan Philp is an architect) charmingly on two levels – you walk down from the sitting room, with timber boarded ceiling and wood burner, to the well equipped kitchen/diner. The bedroom is spacious and (with a five-foot four poster) rather romantic. A bathroom with a power shower completes the cottage.

Then we looked at cosy *Slade Cottage*, **sleeping 4**, with a ground-floor kitchen-diner and a most attractive first floor sitting room, where we noticed velux windows, deep sofas and a small wood-burning stove set against a brick chimney. We also admired the set of collectible Denby pottery, which typifies the high standards that apply here.

Our favourite is *Slade House*, *perhaps one of the most appealing twenty or so properties in this guide*. It is a listed building dating back to 1642. Via the beautiful, expensively fitted kitchen, with a big round pine dining

Slade House (dating back to 1642) is a joy – one of our all-time northern favourites.

First floor sitting room of Slade Cottage – understated and extremely comfortable.

table, and a fine Vermont wood-burning stove, we walked through to the sitting room, features of which are a 19th century Irish dresser and a living flame gas fire. There are two first floor double bedrooms, both with king size beds (one a four poster), each en-suite, with antique furniture, heavy beams, and two twin bedrooms on the second floor, sharing a bathroom.

Each has a payphone and TV, is ETC Four Stars. Baby sitting and cycle hire are available. Not suitable for dogs or smokers. Logs are provided, heating is included. Cost: about £255 to £975. Details/colour brochure from Alan and Pat Philp, Slade House Farm, Ilam, Ashbourne, Derbyshire DE6 2BB. Telephone (01538) 308123.

www.sladehousefarm.co.uk email: alanphilp@sladehousefarm.co.uk

Eyam, near Bakewell
Dalehead Court

A private courtyard in the heart of one of the most historically famous and attractive Derbyshire villages, with ample private parking (unusual within Peak villages) is the setting. Three sympathetically converted stone properties, sumptuously comfortable, with antiques and fine pictures, are all finished expensively, with style. *Pinfold Barn*, **sleeping 6,**

Derbyshire has great appeal, and all these superbly maintained cottages make a fine base. This is the sitting room of The Captain's House...

is an 'upside-house' house with an inviting first floor sitting room, three cosy bedrooms, a stunning 'undersea' bathroom, a separate shower and the main bedroom en-suite. *The Captain's House*, **sleeping '4 plus 1'**, is a Victorian beauty, with a big sitting room, surround-sound cinema TV and a twin and a king-sized double bedroom. Attractive, stylish *Pinner Cottage* **sleeps 2**, also in a king-sized bed. Dogs welcome in Pinner only. ETC Four and Five Stars. Cost: about £190 to £440. Linen and towels available (free for two week stays). Details from Mr and Mrs D Neary, Laneside Farm, Hope, Derbyshire S33 6RR. Telephone (01433) 620214. **www.laneside.fsbusiness.co.uk**

Note: the owners also have three beautiful riverside cottages near the village of Hope, at the centre of Derbyshire's Peak Park.

Biggin-by-Hartington (High Peak)
Cotterill Farm Holiday Cottages — map 3/136

This is the most impressive part of the Peak District, and it was a pleasure to turn off a road on to a long private farm drive to see these three skilful conversions. *Dale View* is an 'upside down' cottage to take advantage of the views (it has a shower, not a bath), and the more conventional *Liff's Cottage* enjoys views of Liff's Hill, two miles away. Each **sleeps 4** in a double and a twin. *The*

A private lane, a memorable location...

Dairy is a **2-person** property of great charm, its one (double) bedroom within a gallery overlooking a big living room. A wood-burner is a feature in itself, and there is a spacious bathroom. All are ETC Four Stars. As well as the lovely dales, guests have immediate access to lawned gardens and meadows adjacent to a nature reserve and leading to the River Dove.

Linen, electricity and heating are included. Non-smoking. 'Sorry, no pets'. Cost: about £180 to £380, depending on which cottage and when. Details from Frances Skemp, Cotterill Farm, Biggin-by-Hartington, Buxton SK17 0DJ. Telephone (01298) 84447. Fax 84664.

www.skemp.u-net.com email: patrick@skemp.u-net.com

Darwin Lake, near Matlock
Darwin Lake Cottages

Matlock is one of the most interesting towns in Derbyshire. Just ten minutes' drive away, in a secluded but not remote location around a lake within a peaceful forest setting, is a group of houses of permanent home standard. The spacious interiors could be described as of *five star hotel* standard. (They are under the same management as the much-loved *Knockerdown Farm* properties

During 2000 we stayed in one of these brand new, spacious and expensively appointed properties...superb!

featured on Page 102.) We stayed briefly in the autumn of 2000, and met an extended family enjoying a reunion – *for Darwin Lake lends itself very well to large-group bookings*.) But there is flexibility here, and along with the large three bedroomed detached cottages there is an even more recent terrace of two-bedroomed cottages. Most bedrooms in each of the cottages are ensuite, decor is pristine, kitchen-diners 'have everything'. Pedestrian walkways allow for a good degree of contact with the lake, of which the holiday cottages have superb views. The 'Darwin Trail', a leisurely 15-minute stroll around the lake, is available to guests, and its wildlife and beauty can be enjoyed at any time of year.

Videos/TVs. Linen, towels included. Not suitable for dogs. ETC Four Stars. Cost: about £357 to £930; short breaks usually available. Open all year.

Further details and a brochure can be had from Nikki Manning, Darwin Lake, The Lodge, Jaggers Lane, Darley Moor, near Matlock, Derbyshire DE4 5LH. Telephone/fax (01629) 735859.

www.derbyshireholidaycottages.co.uk
email: cathy@knockerdown-cottages.co.uk

Hartington, near Buxton   map 3/125
Wolfscote Grange Cottages

A well signposted series of country lanes takes one higher and higher into the hills above Hartington, deep in the Dales, and, after two miles, to a picturesque cottage location. Walkers will love it. Poised above the Dove Valley, part of the farmstead (though delightful *Cruck Cottage* is separate and private), all four cottages are understated, full of comfort and character. (On the autumn day of our visit, all were warm, with efficient central heating.). We liked the rugs on wood floors, lovely views from most front windows, a brass bed in *Swallows Return,* a galleried double bed in Cruck, old pine. The three biggest have super spa baths. **Sleep 4 to 6.** Linen included, towels on request. Dogs welcome in Cruck. Cost: about £160 to £480. Details: Jane Gibbs, Wolfscote Grange Farm, Hartington, near Buxton, Derbyshire SK17 0AX. Telephone/fax (01298) 84342.

www.goodcottageguide.com/derbyshire
email: wolfscote@btinternet. com

Bamford (Hope Valley, near Bakewell)
Shatton Hall Farm Cottages

We've known Shatton Hall Farm for many years and never had anything but glowing reports. A mile from the main road, up a well surfaced lane, it is a haven of peace and tranquillity, with way-marked walks through new and ancient woodland. *Orchard Cottage* and *The Hayloft*, recent barn conversions, are next door to each other, have beamed living rooms furnished in old pine, and cosy coal-effect gas fires. *Paddock Cottage*,

Well converted properties, with extensive gardens, a tennis court and a trout lake.

down the yard and with a wood burning stove, is the perfect winter retreat. A well behaved dog is allowed there, as there is a fenced car park to this cottage. (Holly, the friendly resident labrador, understands!)

All the cottages **sleep 4** in two double bedrooms (one is a twin room) plus sofa-beds in Orchard and Hayloft. Recently renewed kitchens and bathrooms helped these thoughtfully planned cottages to achieve an ETC Four Stars rating. Cost: £200 to £400. Open all year. Details from Mrs Angela Kellie, Shatton Hall Farm, Bamford, Hope Valley S33 0BG. Telephone (01433) 620635. Fax (01433) 620689.

www.peakfarmholidays.co.uk
email: ahk@peakfarmholidays.co.uk

Ashbourne
Yeldersley Hall   map 3/121

Situated in twelve impressive acres three miles from the borders of the Peak National Park, this Georgian country house is special. (To help orientate you, the A52 runs close, and Ashbourne is two miles to the north west.) As well as two flats (Refs B4240/B4242), each **sleeping 2**, created from the original stable

Handy for much of the Peak District, and very comfortable in themselves...

block, there is the gorgeous *East Wing*, part of the main house. The latter **sleeps 4** and is a gem: its elegance, charm and comfort have secured it the ultimate accolade of ETC Five Stars. All the rooms face south over the gardens, original features have been retained and, among many good things, there is a Victorian half-tester bed in the main bedroom (Ref B4241). Though not so grand, the apartments are cosy and 'cottagey', and both are ETC Four Stars. Payphone and TV in each. Linen, towels and electricity are all included. There is an all-weather tennis court.

Details: Blakes, Stoney Bank Road, Earby, Barnoldswick BB94 0AA. To book: (08700) 708090. Brochures: (08700) 708099. **Quote ref BMA 82.**
Live search and book: www.blakes-cottages.co.uk

Knockerdown (Carsington), near Ashbourne
Knockerdown Farm Cottages

This is one of the most popular of the many cottage enclaves we feature. Knockerdown is an arrangement of former farm buildings, several with panoramic views, converted to high standards (maintained and indeed enhanced) and so it is not surprising that people return again and again.

During our most recent revisit we looked at the newly available *Farwell*, usefully **sleeping 6 'plus 2'** – the 2 in a comfortable and private ground floor bedroom. It is spacious, uncluttered, expensively fitted out: well recommended. And we've stayed in *Middleton*, a neat two storeyed cottage with a twin and a double bedroom and a good use of the available space.

Our main purpose was to visit nearby Chatsworth House and Haddon Hall, but we discovered what a useful touring base Knockerdown makes for other places, with the Dales on the doorstep. Carsington Water (all kinds of water sports, and cycle trails) is a few minutes away on foot. There are the eerie caverns of the High Peak to visit – in one, you can even take an underground boat trip – and Alton Towers.

Guests much appreciate the excellent indoor, very warm pool and leisure centre. It's a pleasant place to make new friends, but is also quiet and pri-

We have stayed here ourselves, and appreciated the tidy, unfussy interiors...

...as well as the excellent swimming pool: it was very warm on a chilly autumn day.

vate. There is an exceptional adventure playground, and three acres for children to romp in.

All the cottages, from one that **sleeps 2** to two that **sleep 10**, with fourteen others in between, **sleeping 4** plus cot **and 6** plus cot, are quite private. We noticed plain white walls, oak beams, pine fittings, good quality carpets, some exposed interior stone walls. Nearly all the cottages have an open plan arrangement of sitting room, dining room and kitchen. We applaud the 'instant heat' convector heater/storage radiators.

Videos, TVs. Video library. All linen and towels are included. Not suitable for dogs. English Tourism Council Four Stars. Cost: about £238 to £1341 weekly, with short breaks usually available (open all year) from about £150. Further details and a good brochure can be obtained from Cath Lambert, Knockerdown Farm, near Ashbourne, Derbyshire DE6 1NQ. Telephone/fax (01629) 540525.

www.derbyshireholidaycottages.co.uk
email: cathy@knockerdown-cottages.co.uk

Chinley, near Buxton
Cote Bank Farm Cottages

Pam and Nic Broadhurst, the owners of these three very special properties, really put themselves out for their guests (who return in droves). The cottages are full of comfort and character, with great attention to detail.

Cote Bank Cottage was first on the scene, then it was joined by *Cherry Tree Cottage* next door (both **sleep 6**). They are exceptional, lovingly cared for and skilfully adapted to modern living. Both overlook the children's-picturebook farmyard (little ones can feed the ducks and hens, and older ones are welcome to play more or less at will on the farm).

We remember Cherry Tree's big dining room, and Cote Bank's charming degree of 'chintziness'. Readers have written to say: 'The cottage was perfect – we felt at home and relaxed the moment we stepped through the door' and 'so sad to be leaving such great accommodation'.

Other factors in the cottages' favour are an open fire in both (plus central

Cote Bank and Cherry Tree quickly became firm favourites among our readers, being extremely well equipped, cosy and comfortable.

The Old House is full of history, a most unusual property just for 2 people, who'll love (as we did) the antique oak and the inglenook fireplace with its log burner.

heating throughout), fresh flowers, rugs, comfy armchairs and sofas, oak beams, antiques, lots of nooks and crannies, good paintings, excellent views, children's games and toys, comfortable bedrooms. Kitchens (with most attractive tiling) have dishwashers and microwaves. These are probably the best equipped farm-based cottages we know, with shaver points, electric blankets, rotary whisks, coffee filter machines, barbecues.

The most recent property is a historic and intriguing cottage dating from about 1560, **sleeping 2** and appropriately called *The Old House*. You descend most cosily from a bedroom with a five foot double bed and inspiring views of the Blackbrook Valley, into a lower-level sitting room with antique oak furniture and inglenook fireplace with log burner.

Situated as they are in the Peak District National Park (but only a mile from the village), the cottages make a fine base from which to explore the area. It is, by the way, easy to get here by train.

All are ETC Four Stars. Cost: about £200 to £580. Dogs welcome except in Cherry Tree. TVs/videos. Details from Mrs Broadhurst, Cote Bank Farm, Buxworth, via Whaley Bridge, High Peak, Derbyshire SK23 7NP. Telephone/fax Chinley (01663) 750566.

email: cotebank@btinternet.com

Northumberland and Durham

This is one of those regions of Britain holidaymakers don't know but fall for when they discover it. Some of them have only ever experienced Northumberland from the A1 trunk road, and although that offers tantalising glimpses of the fine coast, with possibly the best beaches in England, they should get further inland to experience the county at its best. This most northerly of all the English counties embraces a wide variety of countryside, much of it impressively 'wild and woolly', and some world-class castles: Alnwick, Warkworth, Lindisfarne, Dunstanburgh and Bamburgh. And if you venture into the Cheviot Hills, which beautifully straddle the English-Scottish border, you can be virtually alone except for curlews and skylarks even on an August Bank Holiday. Much further south, we are especially fond of the Tyne Valleys (North and South), and the Roman Wall country. That is well trodden, but little known are the beautiful windswept moors that characterise the three-way border between Northumberland and Durham and Northumberland and Cumbria. County Durham is in fact one of 'England's best kept secrets', not just for its deep, dark green river valleys, its stone villages set off so effectively by flowers, but its great castles (Barnard Castle is very impressive, as is the nearby Bowes Museum) and the historic city of Durham – a castle *and* a great, sombre cathedral. And one of the best family days out in the north of England is the Beamish Open Air Museum – full of nostalgia for mums and dads, full of things to amuse and educate children.

Weardale   map 3/132
The Stables/The Byre

Many years in our guide, only twelve miles from Durham City but in a peaceful and completely rural location on a farm (within An Area of Outstanding Natural Beauty) these lovingly cared for cottages are very highly recommended. *The Stables* is an 'upside down' cottage, **sleeping 6** in two en-suite bedrooms

Taken together, Gin Gan and The Granary can sleep up to 13 people.

– one with a four poster, the other with a double and two singles. The spacious sitting room has exposed stone walls and wooden beams. *The Byre* is a cosy, mainly open plan conversion (**sleeps 2** in a double **and 2** in an open twin galleried room). Suitable for wheelchairs. *Gin Gan,* **sleeping 5**, is a most attractive rounded building with a big sitting room and a big main bedroom (both bedrooms ensuite). Large family groups please note that this can be taken in conjunction with the adjacent *The Granary* (**sleeping 8**), making a rare property (known as *The Barn*) that **sleeps 13**.

TVs. Dogs welcome by arrangement. Linen and towels, electricity and gas are included. Cost: about £165 to £385 (The Byre and The Stables), £195 to £425 (Gin Gan). Otherwise, on application. Details from Linda Vickers, Greenwell Farm, near Wolsingham, Tow Law, Co Durham DL13 4PH. Telephone Weardale (01388) 527248. Fax (01388) 526735.

email: greenwell@farming.co.uk

Wycliffe, near Barnard Castle
Boot and Shoe Cottage

This is a super cottage. With the dark waters of the beautiful River Tees flowing a matter of feet from the cottage (trout fishing available by arrangement), and with access via a private lane alongside the river, this cottage – once used by a cobbler – is idyllic. With the considerate owners living next door, you won't feel isolated, but can unwind in privacy and

Full of style, beside a famous river...

quiet. Among memorable features we much approved of were deep sofas, an open fire, old beams and some antique furniture. There is a safely enclosed front garden, and French windows lead out to the back garden and a barbecue area, with steps right down to the river bank. TV. Not suitable for dogs (but kennels on site). Linen, towels, coal and logs provided. Welcome hamper, frozen meals to order.

English Tourism Council **Four Stars. Sleeps 4** (but, with one 2'6" bed, just three adults), plus an optional and charming double **for an extra 2.**

Cost: about £275 to £340. Details and an informative brochure from Rachel Peat, Waterside Cottage, Wycliffe, Barnard Castle, Co Durham DL12 9TR. Telephone (01833) 627200.

www.bootandshoecottage.co.uk
email: info@bootandshoecottage.co.uk

Bardon Mill, near Hexham
Gibbs Hill   map 3/131

These properties were badly hit by the foot and mouth fiasco of 2001, especially as the owner had just joined a marketing group promoting walking tours on and around the Roman Wall. That, of course, had to be put on ice. Most impressively in sight of 'The Wall', these are a good example of properties in one of the most scenically dramatic parts of Northumberland that *deserve* support from readers! They will not be

Bed and breakfast is also available in this quite memorable location – so friends and family might want to look in...

disappointed. There are three genuinely 'cottagey' properties, all with high tourist board gradings, **sleeping from 4 to 6.** Owner Val Gibson lives conveniently close at hand.

TVs. Linen and towels included. Natural spring water. Non-smokers preferred. Dogs possible by arrangement. Cost: about £150 to £575. Details from Val Gibson, Gibbs Hill Farm, Bardon Mill, near Hexham, Northumberland NE47 7AP. Telephone (01434) 344030.

Slaggyford
Bastle House

We love the South Tyne Valley, the hilly, cobbled small town of Alston (featured very recently in the BBC's 'Oliver Twist'), the walks along the route of the old Alston-Haltwhistle railway. Near one former station, Slaggyford, down a farm track and tucked away in a valley, Greenhaugh is part of a 16th century fortified

Nestling quietly among the hills close to the beautiful South Tyne valley...

house, or 'Bastle', nestling in 50 acres of private woodland and meadow. It is a real delight, with very friendly and welcoming owners. The Bastle House is one third of the Grade II listed farmhouse and incorporated buildings, adjoining the owners' part, but private. It has some memorable advantages, including panoramic views – appropriate when the house was vulnerable to Border raiders. There's a galleried landing, lots of exposed beams, a magnificent fireplace – the fire is complemented by central heating. There is even a (stocked) trout pond.

Sleeps 4 to 6 in two double bedrooms, both ensuite (one with shower), plus double sofabed downstairs. ETC Four Stars. Linen and towels included. Dogs by arrangement. Cost: about £225 to £350. More details from Keith and Deirdre Pepperdine, Greenhaugh Farm, Slaggyford, Northumberland CA8 7NW. Telephone (01434) 381123. Fax 381124.

Melkridge, near Hadrian's Wall
Common House Farm   map 3/138

Commanding spectacular views over the comparatively little-known South Tyne Valley, these stone cottages (along with the owners' farmhouse) are in an elevated position near Hadrian's Wall, on the edge of the beautiful Northumberland National Park. Surrounded by farmland, the cottages have been thoughtfully and sympathetically renovated from traditional farm buildings, and make an excellent base for both walking in and touring the North of England.

Neat and tidy, good views, peace and quiet. Better yet: handy for Hadrian's Wall.

English Tourism Council Three Stars. **Sleeping from 2 to 5**, the five cottages all face south, and have their own patio area. Well behaved pets are welcome. There are country pubs and a restaurant a mile and half away. Memorable walks start right at the front door.

Cost: about £140 to £340. Short breaks available. Details from Richard and Gloria Goodchild, Common House Farm, Melkridge, Haltwhistle, Northumberland NE49 9PF. Telephone (01434) 321680.

www.commonhousefarm.com email: stay@commonhousefarm.com

Akeld, near Wooler
Akeld Manor and Cottages

Here is a winning combination: great comfort and extensive facilities on the edge of the Cheviot Hills, which represent some of the least known stretches of wild countryside in England. Better still, some of the finest, cleanest, sandiest and least-crowded beaches in Britain are little more than half an hour's drive away.

The 'great comfort' involves interiors five-star hotels would be proud of, with deep carpets, subtle lighting that can add so much to the ambiance of holiday cottages, solid, handsome beds (five-feet wide in some cases), expensive fabrics, excellent insulation, last-word kitchens.

These are eight very sympathetic conversions of one-time farm buildings within 36 acres of the Northumbria National Park, and each one feels private and self contained. They range from a one bedroomed cottage **sleeping just 2, plus baby**, to four cottages that **sleep 4** and three that **sleep 6** (one of those actually **4 'plus 2'**). All have baths, and almost all have shower too.

We visited early on a Sunday evening and admired an indoor leisure centre being much appreciated by families who had been out and about during the day: a warm and inviting pool (which we could happily have plunged into after a day on the road), an antique full-sized snooker table (which might also have side-tracked us), a gym, solarium and games room. To round off the day for many visitors who want to take the self out of self-

Very sympathetic conversions, with sumptuously comfortable interiors...

...plus an up to the minute indoor leisure centre that is a huge attraction in itself.

catering there is a spacious restaurant and bistro, open all day and every day. Restaurant dishes include local monkfish and steak-and-ale pie.

There is huge demand among readers of this guide for larger properties, and the splendid *Akeld Manor* can certainly oblige. For the main house of the original estate, **sleeping up to 15**, is a real showpiece. We have too little space to detail all its charms, but there is for example a games room with pool table, a five-foot four poster in one bedroom, a private walled garden, two open fires. Short breaks. Not suitable for pets. Resident on-site staff. Linen included but not towels. Cost: about £269 to £891. Akeld Manor about £924 to £2109. Details from Pat and Sian Allan, Shoreston Hall, Shoreston, Seahouses, Northumberland NE68 7SX. Telephone (01665) 721035. Fax 720951.

email: allan.group@virginnet.co.uk

Rothbury
The Pele Tower

Full of history and 21st century comforts, this Grade II* listed, 14th century pele tower stands high above,
though because of trees out of sight
of, the unspoilt town of Rothbury.
It's a two-storeyed cottage of great
character (some cottage – it is actually a 19th century extension to the
original tower), lovingly cared for by

*High above unspoilt Rothbury and the
River Coquet, this is a real charmer. We
revisited in 2000, and found all was well.*

David and Agnes Malia. There are original stone flags in the excellent
modern kitchen, every labour saving device imaginable, video and digital
satellite television, CD/tape hi-fi, 'Play Station 2' entertainment system, a
woodstove, extra TVs in bedrooms, teasmade, whirlpool bath and shower,
mountain bikes and more. Unsurprisingly it was recently shortlisted in the
'England for Excellence' awards and is a former 'Winner of the Lionheart
Award: Most Popular Self Catering Accommodation'.

Sleeps 4 in a double room and a twin room. ETC Five Stars. Unsuitable
for pets or smokers. Cost: about £215 to £585. Details from David Malia,
The Pele Tower, Whitton, Rothbury, Northumberland NE65 7RL.
Telephone Rothbury (01669) 620410. Fax 621006.
www.thepeletower.com email: info@thepeletower.com

Glanton, near Alnwick   map 3/141
The Farmhouse

Geographically this is a very good
bet for seeing as much as possible of
Northumberland: the marvellous coast,
with its castles and sandy beaches,
the Cheviot Hills, the Scottish borders, historic Alnwick. Further afield
but within a day trip are the Roman
Wall and the Tyne Valley. Handy for
the A1, this is a spacious and uncluttered farmhouse. We liked the big
sitting room with its wood burning

*A good, very spacious find, well placed
for exploring all of Northumberland...*

stove and chinzty sofa and chairs, the big family kitchen, the sizeable
bathroom, the mainly lawned garden at the front, with wide views.

Attached to the owners' house (they have a small holding with animals
that visiting children will love) but very private, the house is approached
along a well tended private lane.

Sleeps 4 in a double and twin. TV/video. Linen and towels included. Not
suitable for pets. ETC Four Stars. Cost: about £180 to £360. Details from
Jackie Stothard, Northfield Farm, Glanton, Alnwick, Northumberland
NE66 4AG. Telephone (01665) 578203.

www.lowalwinton.co.uk email:jackie@lowalwinton.co.uk

Shilbottle, near Alnwick
Shilbottle Town Foot Farm and Village Farm

Outstandingly good cottages, in two separate locations: these are impressive. With glorious beaches on hand, easy access to the Northumbria National Park and the Scottish borders, and the Tyne Valley and Roman Wall about an hour, the location is (said one reader) 'fantastic'.

The properties have featured in this book since 1983 – *with never a problem or complaint*. There is a magnificent indoor heated swimming pool, sauna, steam room and 'sunshower'. Also a fully equipped, professionally manned fitness club, plus a games room with pool, table tennis and more, and a sports field with football goals, cricket net and golf net, an all-weather tennis court, adventure playground, pony riding and coarse fishing. A visit to the beauty therapist makes a rare treat.

On the working farm (Town Foot) there is a flat **for 2** and two two-bedroomed stone cottages, *Town Foot Cottage* and *Melrose Cottage*, looking over fields and hills. One **sleeps 5** and the other **sleeps 4**. They are delightful: quiet, clean and tidy, and we admired open fires, lots of books, five-foot wide double beds, and more.

At Village Farm, half a mile from Town Foot, *Wool Cottage* **sleeps 5** in two bedrooms: a true home from home, with beams and fireplaces. The 17th century stone farmhouse has been transformed into two homes, each **sleeping 4-6** (2 in a double or twin, 2 in bunks and 2 in the living rooms on sofa-convertibles). *Stableside* has a huge old stone fireplace with a wood stove, though *Churchside's* oil-fired Aga situated in a traditional farmhouse kitchen and an open fire in the living-room take some beating.

Major improvements to *Pantile Cottage* will provide an exceptionally comfortable, smoke-free, pet-free three bedroom and three bathroom property, **sleeping 6**. Two rooms are ensuite. Each of the three spacious Scandinavian chalets has a double, a twin and a bunk-bedded room. There is also a smaller chalet **sleeping 4** in a double and a bunk room.

ETC Three to Four Stars. TV/video. Dogs welcome, linen provided, electricity, logs and gas included. Cost: about £130 to £750. Further details from Mrs C M Stoker, Shilbottle Town Foot Farm, Shilbottle, Alnwick, Northumberland. Telephone/fax Shilbottle (01665) 575591.

www.villagefarmcottages.co.uk

email: crissy@villagefarmcottages.co.uk

Warm interiors, high ceilings, double glazing and excellent insulation make the chalets like comfortable family homes.

We recently had a letter from a ten-year-old boy who thought his holiday at Shilbottle was 'just great!'

Longhorsley
Beacon Hill Farm Cottages

Beacon Hill Farm Cottages are among that select band that show other cottage owners 'how it's done': superbly well situated, stylish and comfortable without being embarrassingly over the top, run with professional flair and good humour. It comes as no surprise to us that so many people return year after year, often coming to regard the owners as friends.

It also comes as no surprise that they won the English Tourism Council's *'England Self Catering Holiday of the Year' Award* for the year 2000. Having won this award in 1991, they are the only double winners ever!

The cottages are based on the 350-acre grass farm, which has some of the best views we have seen on our travels. This is a beautiful place with hedgerows full of birds and wild flowers. There are 40 acres of ancient beechwoods near the cottages and guests are free to wander in the woods, or anywhere on the estate, as if it were their own. It is difficult to imagine when here that the main road is only three miles away down quiet country lanes. Beacon Hill is perfectly situated for explorations of this fascinating county – Cragside, Wallington Hall, Alnwick Castle and Hadrian's Wall, and the superb coastline, are all within easy reach. You are also close to the mysterious Cheviot Hills, and Edinburgh is within a day trip.

Among the details that have impressed us over the years are the large quantity of books, the table lamps, the good quality pictures and prints and, above all, the superb views from many of the sitting rooms.

There is a beautiful 40' heated indoor pool, which is in a 75' long slate roofed building with large windows, giving excellent views across rolling countryside. There are also a sauna, solarium, spa room, changing rooms and large gymnasium: exceptional by any standards. Beyond the pool is an all-weather tennis court: both are available daily from 6 am to 10 pm. There are also 30 horses, on which to ride around the 350 acre estate, and beyond, in the quiet country lanes that are such an attractive feature of this area. Or try your hand at fly fishing for trout on a beautifully located two acre lake.

Cost: £235 to £1100. 'inclusive of everything'. **Sleep 2-6**. Linen is provided. English Tourism Council Four and Five Stars. Further details from Beacon Hill House, Longhorsley, Northumberland. Telephone/fax Longhorsley (01670) 780900. Fax 780901.

www.beaconhill.co.uk   email: alun@beaconhill.co.uk

Superbly comfortable interiors, but not overstated: nicely lit, with lots of books...

...well chosen rugs and pictures. Popular of course in summer, and cosy in winter.

Branton, near Wooler
Breamish Valley Cottages

This is a very good set-up indeed. Surrounded by countryside but only a short drive from the sea, Breamish is only half an hour or so from the spectacular coastline for which Northumberland is famous. Better yet, the lane running past the cottages is actually a dead-end, leading straight into the Cheviot foothills: no traffic disturbance here. (If you get through a week or a fortnight here without completing two or three full scale hikes into the hills we would be surprised!)

We have visited several times, and always found this very well run, very quiet and beautifully situated arrangement of cottages ticking over nicely. Standards are reliably high.

A lot of thought has gone into the layout, in particular in the two more recent cottages, *Honeymug* and *Daneshill*. These are upside down cottages with especially light and spacious sitting rooms and kitchens, with exposed roof timbers. We noticed lots of old and new pine, comfortable armchairs, wood burning stoves, table and/or standard lamps, attractive pictures and prints. All the cottages have dishwashers and washer dryers. Honeymug and Daneshill **sleep 6**, *The Old Mill* **sleeps 5**, *The Old Granary*, *Pottery Cottage*, *Southside*, *The Hayloft* and *East Hill* **sleep 4**, *Swallow Cottage* **sleeps 2**. *Cheviot Cottage* is another recent addition. **Sleeping 4**, it has two bathrooms.

A very private and harmonious enclave, many years in this guide and much liked.

Over the years, interiors have become yet more comfortable and stylish.

What really makes this lovely place into something worth a big detour is the indoor heated pool with hot spa, sauna, solarium and gymnasium – as smart as in an expensive health club. There is also a games room, as well as an all weather tennis court next to the football field (we have seldom seen tennis played with such a lovely backdrop!), putting and croquet.

There are free logs if you want them, oil-fired central heating throughout. Cost: about £210 to £865. Dogs are very welcome (the owners have a delightful Border terrier of their own, called Rusty, who is much loved by visiting children) except in Honeymug, Cheviot and The Old Granary. Satellite TVs, videos, CDs. Details and brochure from Peter and Michele Moralee, Breamish Valley Cottages, Branton, Powburn, Alnwick, Northumberland NE66 4LW. Telephone Alnwick (01665) 578263.

www.breamishvalley.co.uk

email: peter@breamishvalley.co.uk

Harehope Hall, near Alnwick
Cresswell Wing/Sawmill

Stylish Harehope Hall, deep in rolling farmland and with views of the
Cheviot Hills, is an imposing mansion, and guests in *The Cresswell
Wing* (it is on three floors) have a
substantial part of it to themselves,
so that anyone who appreciates high
ceilings, extra-big windows and
easy-going, traditional comfort will

Pleasant accommodation, a fine estate...

love it. We like the spacious drawing room with its deep sofas, the open
fire (lit when we last called), the big bedrooms – including two atticky
ones that would suit children – the 'country antiques'. **Sleeps 8** in two
twins and two doubles. (Extra beds available, if needed, plus cot). Central
heating. Most recently available is *Sawmill Cottage*, on a corner of the
estate. **Sleeps 4**. It is indeed next to a working sawmill. Linen and towels
included. Dogs *and horses* welcome. Note: a very special feature here are
carriage driving/riding holidays, using the lanes of the estate (but bring
your own horses/carriages!). TV. Cost: about £200 to £550. More details
from Alison Wrangham, Harehope Hall, Harehope, near Alnwick,
Northumberland NE66 2DP. Telephone Eglingham (01668) 217329.
email: john@wrangham.co.uk

Belford, near Bamburgh
map 3/146
Shepherd's Cottage

This cottage is so very well situated,
with an unimpaired view of Holy
Island (easy to visit), that it has been
known to turn holidaymakers into
photographers. The single storeyed
detached house, which is ETC Four
Stars, stands on a working farm on
the famous protected coastline, while
Bamburgh, with its castle and vast
beaches (plus golf course!) is also

*You will hardly find a better location in
which to absorb the romance of coastal
Northumberland. This is Holy Island...*

nearby. Pristinely clean and tidy, it is
reasonably priced (a bargain in
spring and autumn). Belford, which has a golf driving range, is just a mile
and a half away. There is access for the wheelchair bound, a large sitting
room, a separate dining room, a double and a twin bedroom, thus **sleeping 4** in comfort. There is a bathroom with over-bath shower, a fitted
kitchen with electric cooker, fridge-freezer, microwave, washing
machine, plus dishwasher. There is a Baxi fire in the spacious sitting
room, storage radiators and electric 'dual purpose' heaters in all the
rooms. Not suitable for pets. Linen included. TV and video. Cost: about
£150 to £375. Local car parking concessions (a big bonus). Details from
Mrs Iris Oates, Easington Farm, Belford, Northumberland NE70 7EG.
Telephone (01668) 213298.

Alnmouth, Bamburgh and around
Northumbria Coast and Country Cottages*

During one of our most recent revisits to Northumberland we detoured to one of the 'NCCC' properties that have an especially big following among readers. *Sandpiper* is just yards from the water's edge in the little known but most appealing seaside village of Low-Newton-by-the-Sea (it is also close to a charming, unpretentious pub). **Sleeping 8**, it is a listed 18th century, one-time fisherman's cottage of character, with a log-burning stove. Dogs are welcome. And at High-Newton-by-the-Sea, *Snook Point* is an extremely comfortable single-storeyed house with sea views. Among others by the coast, there are several properties in famous Bamburgh (best known for its castle and its beach), all of whose sitting room windows face the North Sea. And there are cottages of great character in Seahouses, Beadnell, Embleton and Craster.

This hugely respected agency covers one of the three or four most scenically impressive corners of England, and is based in pretty, unspoilt Alnmouth. We visited three of the cottages in the village itself: all three a delight! If you should book either of the two old 'smugglers' cottages' in Victoria Place (one is almost *on* the beach) or tucked away *Estuary View* (on three floors), you are in for a treat.

Most people will also love *High Linhope Cottage*, spectacularly situated on private land in the heart of the Cheviot Hills. Amid heather-clad hills, overlooking a tumbling burn along whose course is a pool ideal for bathing in on a hot day, it is reached by a gated road and **sleeps 6**.

The brochure for the agency's 200-or-so properties carries a colour photo of each. As well as such highly rural but not remote cottages mentioned above, they include town properties in famous and handsome Alnwick and several in Warkworth (as with Alnwick, the town embraces one of northern England's most famous castles).

And at Ingram, among the rolling Cheviot Hills, *Gardeners Cottage* and remote *Threestoneburn House* are recommended. At exquisite Alwinton, *Bridgend Cottage*, full of character, has an open range fireplace. But there are so many more good things we do not have space even to mention...

Details from Northumbria Coast and Country Cottages, Carpenters Court, Riverbank Road, Alnmouth, near Alnwick, Northumberland. Telephone Alnmouth (01665) 830783/830902. Fax 830071.

www.northumbriacottages.com email: cottages@nccc.demon.co.uk

High Linhope is quite a place, but move quickly to book it for a memorable time ...

Estuary View – and yes, the view from the house is as good as you'd hope!

Bamburgh, near Belford/Holy Island
Ross Farm Cottages

In this unforgettable location, a beautiful corner of an exceptional county, we are pleased to feature some of the most stylish properties (in three separate groups) we know anywhere in the north of England.

Firstly, the cottages at *Outchester Manor*. There are eight, on three sides of what was once a farmyard, and they are superb: each has its own character, but is part of a whole; each is reminiscent of five star hotel comfort (actually ETC Four Stars), but also has a 'cottagey' quality. All are spacious, easy on the eye, up to the minute in terms of facilities, *and we were not surprised that they won the self catering section of the Pride of Northumbria awards for 2001.* **Sleep from 2 to 6.** Cost: £183 to £535.

There are two groups of cottages at Ross, where the public road gives way to a lane (walkers only) that leads to sand dunes and the sea. One is within the peaceful hamlet, the other is down the lane towards the sea. The first we visited is one of a pair within a row of attractive cream-coloured cottages in the hamlet. Called *Sandpiper*, this was a delight in every way. We admired a welcoming sitting room, with well chosen lamps, a real sense of design and colour, lots of space. The cottage next door (*Oystercatcher*) is similar; also **sleeping 2 to 6**, it can be combined with Sandpiper to **sleep 12**. Each has a grassy garden big enough for ball games, and which children will love.

Then we continued along the lane to see, first, *West Coastguard Cottage*, **sleeping 2 to 4** in a double and a twin, both light and bright, with a cosy,

Outchester Manor: space and great comfort in rural splendour, near the sea.

Wagtail is one of 'the Ross cottages'. It sleeps up to six, and is ETC Three Stars.

smallish sitting room, a separate dining room, excellent upstairs views front and back: more a small house than a cottage, then the very comparable *East Coastguard Cottage* (all the last-mentioned properties are ETC Three Stars), and then *Coastguard Lodge,* which is Four Stars. This is a superb detached 1995 conversion, where we noted french windows on to a neat garden, a fine sitting room combined with an expensively appointed kitchen, a downstairs en suite double, a very attractive upstairs arrangement of two bedrooms, a twin and a single, and a good sized bathroom. In short, a real gem. The Ross Cottages cost about £198 to £535.

Not suitable for pets. Linen and towels included. Details and a good brochure from Mrs J B Sutherland, Ross Farm, Belford, Northumberland NE70 7EN. Telephone (01668) 213336. Fax 219385.

www.rosscottages.co.uk email: enquiry@rosscottages.co.uk

Bowsden, near Bamburgh/Holy Island
The Old Smithy

This very inviting detached cottage conversion, quiet but not isolated, is well placed for enjoying Northumberland. The fabulous coast is only five miles away (don't miss Holy Island) but when we first called we met a couple staying put: the wood burner was warming the cottage, and they were ensconced in the welcoming kitchen/diner. Adjacent to that there is a cosy sitting room (a former smithy) with a deep sofa/armchairs, attractive stripped pine, rugs, books, well chosen pictures, and other stylish things. This room overlooks the south facing walled garden and the Cheviot Hills. We

Warm and very well planned.

liked the skilful conversion, with two bedrooms downstairs and one upstairs, the bathroom with shower, a loo on each floor, the central heating that is complemented by the woodburning stove. This is a *traditional* farm: natural calf rearing, summer-grass-fed lambs, free range chickens. **Sleeps 6, plus cot.** TV. Dogs welcome. Cost: about £200 to £480. Details from John and Mary Barber, Brackenside, Bowsden, Berwick-on-Tweed, Northumberland TD15 2TQ. Telephone (01289) 388293.

web: http://business.virgin.net/john.barber/brackenside.htm
email: john.barber@virgin.net

Mindrum, near Cornhill-on-Tweed   map 3/150
Briar Cottage

Only a matter of yards inside Northumberland, so close to Scotland that you can almost hear bagpipes and smell haggis, this is a very well-cared-for cottage in exceptional countryside. We have stayed, and still remember such good things as a log and coal fire lit ahead of our arrival. There is a good-sized kitchen and sitting room/diner: from the window of that we watched cattle on the hills. Used from time to time by the owners, and thus with all the essentials, the cottage has a twin and a double, with new beds, a good sized bathroom with shower. Small front garden. Large enclosed lawned gardens to side and rear, including a paddock

A real winner amid quiet and beautiful countryside...

with picnic bench. Private parking. The area is good for touring, with the Scottish borders and the Cheviot Hills so close, and the coast half an hour away. Dogs welcome. TV/Video. Linen, fuel, electricity included. Cost: £185 to £335. Details from Northumbria Coast and Country Cottages, Carpenters Court, Riverbank Road, Alnmouth, Northumberland NE66 2RH. Telephone (01665) 830783/830902. Fax 830071.

www.northumbriacottages.com   email: cottages@nccc.demon.co.uk

Beal, near Holy Island
West Lodge/Stables/The Coach House/Bee Cottage

Holy Island is a 'don't miss' for visitors to Northumberland. So the location of *Bee Cottage* (**sleeping 4**) is all the more amazing: it has an extraordinary, uninterrupted, panoramic view from most rooms of Holy Island, accessible via the causeway at low tide. Close to the owners' farmhouse, it has a nicely lit sitting room with an open fire, a modern kitchen, a double and a twin. On a grander scale, *West Lodge, Stables* and *The*

Everything here is aimed at the highest possible standards. We revisited in 2001.

Coach House (**sleeping respectively up to 8, 6 and 6**) are recent additions to the Nesbitts' 'family' of cottages. They are beauties: masses of space, grand sitting rooms, sumptuous bedrooms, super ultra-modern kitchens. You'll not get lost (a complaint we've had about some parts of Northumberland!) as West Lodge, Stables and Coachhouse are in fairly close proximity to the A1. TVs. Dogs welcome. ETC Four/Five Stars. Linen/towels provided. Cost: £220 to £990. More details from Jackie Nesbitt, Bee Hill Properties, Beal, near Holy Island, Berwick-on-Tweed, Northumberland TD15 2PB. Telephone (01289) 381102. Fax 381418.

www.beehill.co.uk   email: info@beehill.co.uk

Belford, near Holy Island   map 3/156
Bluebell Farm Cottages

We are fans of the large village of Belford (and the excellent food at the Blue Bell Hotel there). Tucked away off one of the roads leading out of the village, we discovered this enclave of six stone and pantiled farm-building conversions. Neatly within what is effectively a hamet in its own right, and **sleeping from 2 to 7**, each is *admirably spacious*, with big windows, lots of light and a good

We really liked these unpretentious cottages, and their convenient location.

degree of privacy. We noted deep sofas and armchairs, properly fenced patios with picnic-benches and access to barbecues, in the case of *Farne*, *Lindisfarne* and *St Abbs*, backing on to a little burn. (There is a caravan park in the same ownership, out of sight of the cottages, though there is a shared reception office.)

TVs. Linen, towels, gas central heating and elecricity included. Short breaks available. Pets by prior arrangement. Cost: about £150 to £400. Details from Phyl Carruthers or Howard Wells, Bluebell Farm Cottages, Belford, Northumberland NE70 7QE. Telephone (01668) 213362.

email: phyl.carruthers@virgin.net

Scotland

Spectacular sunsets over the Atlantic, absolute peace and quiet on half inhabited islands, an old-fashioned courtesy and integrity among the people one meets: we envy people who have never been 'over the border', because they are in for such a treat when they do go. Scotland could be considered to be the most beautiful country in Europe. Many readers agree, reporting on idyllic cottages from where they have explored lochs, glens and burns, mountains, forests and hundreds of off-shore islands. Most memorable are the far west coast and the Hebrides, and a seascape peppered with islands from which ferries plough to and from the mainland. The north-east of the country has one of the greatest collections of castles in the world, and you can follow a 'whisky trail' to some well-known distilleries. World-famous too are some of the golf courses, such as the Open Championship course at Carnoustie, and the course at St Andrews. For skiers, Glenshee and Aviemore are Scotland's main resorts, but we would say the mountains and hills are even more impressive in spring, summer and autumn. It is invidious to pick out favourite routes or locations, but the road between Blairgowrie and Braemar, via Glenshee, takes a lot of beating, and even more dramatic is the journey from Tyndrum to the coast via Glencoe. We are keen on the strange 'lunar landscapes' of the wild country to the north of Lochinver, on the Trossachs, and the rolling brown moors of the Border country that is thick with ancient castles and abbeys

Duns   map 4/153
Wedderburn Castle Cottages

As you approach Wedderburn Castle via its long drive you could be 'miles from anywhere', though it is actually very accessible: the attractive and historic town of Duns is conveniently close. In sight of the magnificent castle we turned off to find two of the most cosily restored and decorated cottages we have found in many a mile. In *Grooms*, **sleeping 2** in a double-bedded room, we met an English couple on their umpteenth visit: they were so full of praise we

There are two cosy, quiet cottages within the grounds of this easily-accessible jewel of the Scottish borders...

could hardly get away! They showed us around. Here and in *Keeper's*, which **sleeps 4** in a double/twin and a twin that is effectively two separate singles, we noticed thoughtful lighting, good quality beds, comfortable easy chairs and sofas. *Note: in Paxton, just four miles from the ancient border town of Berwick on Tweed, there is another excellent cottage in the same ownership, not yet seen by us.* **Sleeps 3.**

TVs. Linen and towels included. Pets welcome. Cost: about £195 to £325. Details from David Home, Wedderburn Castle, Duns, Berwickshire TD11 3LT. Telephone/fax (01361) 882190.

www.wedderburn-castle.co.uk email: HomeMiller@compuserve.com

Duns
Duns Castle Cottages

We rate these very highly indeed. Most lovingly cared for, each has its own character, is very private but benefits greatly from the situation – either very close to the grand Gothic-fantasy of a castle (in the case of *Pavilion Lodge*), or on a slightly more distant corner of the great estate – to which guests have free-range access.

Partly because of the extremely hospitable owners you really do feel as if you belong. For example, we love the fact that it is possible to arrange to have dinner in the high ceilinged dining hall of the castle, in the company of the owners.

From a 2001 revisit we especially remember that charming *Pavilion Lodge,* a 'folly' gatehouse, is a cosy nest **for 2**, with a romantic turretted bedroom reached via a winding stair, and an open fire (the only one that has an open fire, though some of the other cottages have coal-effect gas fires). A good place for trainee Rapunzels.

The other delightful cottages are mostly half-hidden in the wooded grounds (complete with tranquil loch). We loved the quietness of each, the (in some cases) private gardens, the country antiques.

For example, *St Mary's,* which we also revisited in 2001, meeting very contented English guests, is a rambling family house **sleeping 11** that may be joined to *Coach House* (**sleeps 3**) behind. *The White House*, **sleeping 7**, is private, very comfy, and altogether charming. *Azalea Cottage* is elegantly furnished and sits up above the lake with its own drive and little paddock. This too was re-inspected, and we'd have been happy to move in there and then for a few days' 'R and R'.

Cottage guests can arrange to have dinner within the fabulous castle...

All the estate cottages are private, and more and more comfortable by the year.

(Elsewhere, in the same ownership, *Lindisfarne* is a substantial terraced stone house 30 yards from the beach at Berwick, with stunning sea and coastal views.)

TVs. Linen included, towels available at an extra charge. STB Three Stars. Cost: about £195 to £1180. More details and an intriguing map showing the cottages on the estate from Aline Hay, Duns Castle, Duns, Berwickshire TD11 3NW. Telephone (01361) 883211; fax 882015.

www.dunscastle.co.uk
email: aline_hay@lineone.net

Crosswoodhill, nr West Calder/Edinburgh
Wing/Midcrosswood/Steading Cottage

We weren't surprised to hear these three properties *(map 4/156)* won the Scottish Tourism Thistle Award for *Scottish Self Catering Operator of the Year 2001.* For they are outstanding, a fine base among the Pentland Hills for making visits to Edinburgh, Glasgow, Loch Lomond, the Trossachs and the Borders. Sheep graze right up to the doors of *Midcrosswood,* **sleeping 5,** a gem of a detached, single-storeyed cottage.

These are oustanding properties. This is the superb Midcrosswood: we have stayed...

Full of comfort and calm, it is STB Four Stars. At the hub of the working farm, *Steading Cottage,* also Four Stars, is stylish, detached and 'wheelchair friendly'. **Sleeps 6.** All, including the two-storeyed Three Star *Wing* of the handsome farmhouse *(sleeps up to 6),* have central heating, multi-fuel stoves, payphones, dishwashers, TVs, hi-fis and videos. Dogs by arrangement. Cost: £260 to £570. Linen, towels included. Credit cards. Brochure: Geraldine Hamilton, Crosswoodhill, by West Calder, West Lothian EH55 8LP. Telephone (01501) 785205. Fax 785308.

www.crosswoodhill.co.uk
email: ghcg@crosswoodhill.co.uk

Kelso and Westruther, by Lauder
Lyme Cottage/East Side Cottage   map 4/157/158

Conveniently located on the edge of the historic and attractive town of Kelso, and thus ideally situated for exploring the rolling landscape of the Borders, *Lyme Cottage* (Ref 80200) **sleeps 4** in a double and a twin room. It has its own quiet and enclosed garden, with summerhouse, and the bonus of a woodburner for slightly chillier times. Kelso, winner of many Britain in Bloom awards, has, *inter alia,* a racecourse, an

East Side is a former gamekeeper's cottage – lucky gamekeeper!

indoor pool, an abbey and Floors Castle. *East Side Cottage* (Ref 8580) is for people who enjoy being away from it all! Down a track, half a mile from the road, it is a handsome 19th century former gamekeeper's cottage in a quiet glade within 16 acres of its own mature woodland. **Sleeps 6** in a double and two twins (all with sloping ceilings). There's a woodburner, payphone, large garden and natural spring water supply.

Country Holidays, Spring Mill, Earby, Lancashire BB94 0AA. To book, telephone 08700 723723. Brochures: 08700 725725. **Quote ref CMA 96.**
Live search and book: www.country-holidays.co.uk

119

Straiton, near Maybole
Blairquhan

We have had so many enthusiastic reader reports of the cottages here. With panoramic views of mountains, lochs, rolling hills and tumbling rivers, the Blairquhan estate, in the wooded valley of the Water of Girvan, is, quite simply, a beautiful place. There are no rules about where, on the 2000 acre estate, you may go, and we understand those who have remarked 'The estate has more than enough to keep us busy for a whole fortnight'...'We felt no need to leave the castle grounds'...

Milton is outstanding by any yardstick, most usefully sleeping up to 21 people.

Cuninghame is a fairly recent conversion, with masses of character...

In the company of the charming James Hunter Blair we spent a sunny morning admiring each of the seven properties. *Cuninghame*, converted in 1995 from the original potting shed and bothy and situated on the wall of the glorious walled garden which was a riot of colour when we visited, has a living/dining room/kitchen with woodburner, French windows and a huge arch-to-floor window; downstairs are two twin bedrooms and bathroom; upstairs a further twin room and a spacious playroom. *McDowall*, also a former bothy and on the garden wall, has a kitchen/living room with sofa bed and a double bedroom downstairs; upstairs is a twin room overlooking the gardens. *Kennedy Cottage* forms one side of a courtyard which is part of Blairquhan Castle and has stone carvings dating to 1575. *McIntyre, Farrer* and *Wauchope* are apartments in the former coachman's house and stables; we especially liked the former, **sleeping 6**, with a large upstairs kitchen/living/dining room that has glorious views. *Bishopland Lodge*, tucked away on its own, has exceptional views towards the castle and of the Girvan Valley. The peace of it struck us – not a sound except for the sheep! Throughout we noted excellent carpets and rugs, pretty drapes and duvets, attractive pictures and posters, useful bedside and standard lamps. (Just twenty minutes away, high above the sea, is Culzean ['Cullane'], flagship property of the National Trust for Scotland.)

There is also a dower house, *Milton*, which we found enchanting. It **sleeps 21** in two doubles, eight twins and one single, has six bathrooms and is ideal for house parties, family reunions or fishing enthusiasts – with five miles of fishing on the estate (not included). £1500 per week.

Prices are from around £148 in winter to £392 in summer. Details from James Hunter Blair, Blairquhan Estate Office, Straiton, Maybole KA19 7LZ. Telephone Straiton (01655) 770239, fax 770278.

www.blairquhan.co.uk email: enquiries@blairquhan.co.uk

Dumfries & Galloway
G M Thomson & Co*

This extremely caring and efficient cottage letting agency has introduced many of our readers to an impressive, peaceful, green and rolling corner of Scotland. There is a case for calling Dumfries and Galloway 'the best kept secret' in the country. It can be a voyage of discovery for people who think they know Scotland but actually don't!

With an admirable new large-pocket size colour brochure featuring all the agency's 160 or so properties, this is a company that has gone from

This fine farmhouse (not featured) is north east of Castle Douglas. Sleeps 8.

This ancient fortified house, near Borgue, (not featured) sleeps up to 12.

strength to strength in just a few years. There are too many gems to detail here (*including a number right by the sea*), but outstanding places include the marvellously well situated *Almora*, near the sailing centre of Kippford (fabulous views from almost every room), **sleeping 7/8**. Also near Kippford, and right on the seafront at Rockcliffe Bay, *Colbeine House* is a family house of character. There's a recently restored 18th century beauty, *Glenharvie*, **sleeping up to 8**, and a similarly roomy farmhouse, with splendid views, called *Glen of Spottes*. And amid remote countryside that characterises much of Galloway, *High Mark Farmhouse* **sleeps 7**.

Extended families and groups of friends should note that there are several properties of the larger sort **sleeping 8, 9** and more – **in two cases 14**.

We have stayed in *Upper Double Cally Lodge*, **sleeping 2**, built around 1800, at the entrance to the Cally Estate at Gatehouse of Fleet. Full of charm and wonderfully romantic, it has a lounge with open fire (ash/oak logs provided), a dining room looking over the colourful, well laid out garden, and a kitchen with oak units, washing machine, microwave.

Colleagues also much enjoyed a summer holiday in *Auld Schoolhouse, Skyreburn*, **sleeping 7**. We loved its quiet position, the burn running through the well kept garden (fenced and safe for children). The sunny kitchen was the best equipped we had seen on our travels. There's loads of space, high ceilings, standard and table lamps, a separate 'no smoking, no dogs' lounge and even zip link single beds to make doubles.

The agency's well chosen properties range from small cottages, modern bungalows and town houses to small mansion houses and shooting lodges **sleeping 14**. Credit card bookings. Details from G M Thomson & Co, 27 King Street, Castle Douglas DG7 1AB. Telephone (01556) 504030. Fax (01556) 503277.

www.scothols.co.uk   email: lettings@scothols.co.uk

Blairgowrie, near Pitlochry
Ardblair Castle Cottages

There is a very special atmosphere here. With a good chance of seeing Highland cattle in the grounds, and two well maintained cottages in the lea of a picture-book castle, this is as 'Scottish' as you will get. Better yet, it is easily accessible, not remote.

There is indeed a magic about staying here – perhaps it's the location, perhaps the genuinely warm welcome – that gets so many of our readers waxing lyrical! The location is one of the best possible Scottish touring bases, three minutes' drive from the 'gateway-to-the-Highlands' town of Blairgowrie, but in rural surroundings rendered rather grand by those shaggy cattle.

The 19th century, white timbered coach house and stables that stand in the grounds of the castle have been converted by Mr and Mrs Blair Oliphant into two very well-equipped, extremely comfortable, painstak-

An unusual example of Scottish weather-boarding, behind which is an extremely comfortable and informal base from which to explore central Scotland.

A typical sitting room at Ardblair: neat, easy-to-look-after, unfussy and yet perfectly comfortable. 'Nice to come home to' after a day's touring...

ingly cared-for self-catering units. The open plan kitchen/living room, the tidy looks of the units, with their fitted neutral carpets (tiles in the bathrooms and kitchens) and simple pine furnishings, all lend a certain stamp of quality. *We have never, in over twelve years, had a reader-complaint.*

Among the good things we remember in the Ardblair properties are good books to read, a particularly attractive set of carved dining chairs in the *Coach House* and a delightful arrangement of dining table and benches in *The Stable*. The Stable has two bathrooms and **sleeps 9** in twin and triple-bedded attic rooms with sloping ceilings and Velux windows, plus four wee ones in an adult-sized bunk-bedded ground floor room. Though if all nine were in residence space might be tight. The Coach House **sleeps 5** in a double and triple-bedded room. Guests can enjoy the family's 800 acre farmlands, whose livestock includes those beautiful Highland cattle, geese and occasional visits from a local herd of deer. Another advantage here is the well recommended Recreation Centre in Blairgowrie.

Not suitable for dogs. Open all year (night storage heating, TV, double glazing). Cost: about £250 to £390. Linen provided. Details from Mr Blair Oliphant, Ardblair Castle, Blairgowrie, Perthshire PH10 6SA. Telephone/fax Blairgowrie (01250) 873155.

Scotland-wide
Country Cottages in Scotland*

Again and again readers tell us how much they associate Scotland with panoramic views and history. Happily we heard during 2001 from readers who had stayed in places that fit each bill perfectly.

One family stayed in *Macinnisfree Cottage*, on the Isle of Skye. **Sleeping 7**, this looks on to an extraordinary panorama that takes in some of western Scotland's most-loved coastal landmarks and seascapes. Ref SBC. And on the eastern side of the country, near Dornoch, a group of friends loved *Croick Farmhouse*. **Sleeping 8**, it stands on a great estate and has many antiques. Ref UNB.

Any of the cottages on the Ardmaddy Estate, about twelve miles south of Oban, brings together history (for the castle that is the focal point here is ancient and imposing) and fabulous views. There are four extremely well

Even in Scottish terms Macinnisfree Cottage enjoys a fabulous setting...

An unforgettable location, and three cosy cottages that are 'just for two'.

converted cottages, the biggest of which (in terms of accommodation) is *The Stables*, **sleeping 8**. Ref SBZ.

One of our favourite parts of Scotland is the Kintyre peninsula (beautiful, but little known among outsiders, with most of the charms of an island without any of the inconveniences of access) and we are very pleased to single out three extraordinary cottages, **each for 2**, that were once used by lighthouse keepers of the now-automated lighthouse on Davaar Island, off the mainland near Campbeltown. (Refs SEE/SED/UMG.)

Also surrounded by impressive (and for southerners more easily accessible) countryside, the cottages at Glenprosen, among the Glens of Angus, are traditional, private and tucked away but not remote – not far north of Dundee. We enjoyed our drive along lanes deep in the glen, appreciated the 6000 acre estate and especially liked *Tinkerbell*, **sleeping 2**. Ref SAL.

Further south, just ten minutes from the world-class city of Edinburgh and appropriately steeped in history, *Liberton Tower* is an amazing place, a 15th century castle keep that combines period features such as a refectory table, tapestry wall hangings, rugs on a stone slab floor and an open fire with modern comforts. It has spectacular views from a parapet walkway. **Sleeps 4**. Ref UKH.

Details and brochures from Country Cottages in Scotland, Stoney Bank, Earby, Colne, Lancashire BB94 0AA. Telephone (0870) 4441133. You can 'dial-a-brochure': (0870) 5851133.

Quote reference SMA 92

Balquhidder
Rhuveag

This is a beautifully situated house. Overlooking Loch Voil, near the village of Balquhidder, it is almost surrounded by a mass of trees, azaleas and rhododendrons. Having seen it, we know why it has such a following. Used frequently by the owners, it is warm and comfortable, with log fires, a Rayburn in the kitchen, and a

One of our all-time favourites in Scotland, both for character and location.

clothes drying room, as well as central heating. Though rural and 'traditional', there is nothing primitive about the cottage: in a splendid kitchen it has a dishwasher, washing machine, ceramic hob and more. It **sleeps 8**, and has three reception rooms (one of which, with TV, can double as a bedroom). The house gets water from a burn which flows through its six acres; there is splendid walking, as well as fishing, sailing and windsurfing. You can hire boats, and even learn to water ski on Loch Earn, at the end of the glen. There is a renowned farmhouse-pub, half a mile up the road, which has a superb restaurant and a full licence.

Dogs are welcome, but this is sheep country, and they must be well controlled. Linen and towels not available. TV. Cost: about £350 to £475. Details from John and Vanda Pelly, Spring Hill, East Malling, Kent ME19 6JW. Telephone (01732) 842204, fax 873506.

Kirkmichael, near Pitlochry   map 4/166
Balnakilly Highland Cottages/Log Cabins

During their years in this guide, we revisited to check on the ongoing upgrading of these well located but unpretentious properties. You could be 'miles from anywhere' in one of the seven traditional cottages/Norwegian log cabins on this 1500-acre family estate, but you're not in fact remote. We especially like *Loch Cottage*, which all but opens on to the water, and is just a short stroll from four cosy cabins. They **sleep 4, 5 or 6**. *Rowan Lodge* is rural but fin-

Loch Cottage has proved to be a popular choice. It is superbly well situated without being uncomfortably remote.

ished to a good standard, and *Strathview* has an Aga. Horse riding available on the estate itself. Skiing in the area in season. Walking, shooting and fishing are all readily available – on the estate and elsewhere. (The flora and fauna and the fishing are excellent: 'lots of salmon were caught in 1999'.) Dogs are welcome. Linen is provided, towels are available for hire. TV. Cost: £170 to £440. Details from Mr and Mrs Reid, Balnakilly Estates, Kirkmichael, Perthshire PH10 7NB. Telephone or fax Strathardle (01250) 881356.

www.balnakillyestate.co.uk   email: balnakilly@hotmail.com

Ecosse Unique*

Twenty years in this guide! This is an outstandingly good agency, run with great professionalism and a genuine concern that clients have a happy holiday. We have never had a whisper of a complaint.

It has about 300 properties spread all over Scotland, with a noticeable strength in the Borders, the West Coast, Skye and Mull.

In the Borders – a part of Scotland that can be as dramatically beautiful as the higher-profile north-west but is less crowded in the holiday season, and a lot nearer to England – there are many cottages in peaceful locations. Such as *Old Hyndhope* (**sleeping 6**), which stands alone in an exquisite hill-top location near Selkirk, and *Cringletie Cottage* (**sleeping**

The Old Schoolhouse (not featured) is a house of character near Jedburgh.

Lynaberack Cottage has a glorious, quiet location deep in the Highlands.

4), on a farm near Peebles, with Highland cattle, and elegant 17th century *Peffermill House* (**sleeping 6/7**) in Edinburgh. Romantically inclined people will – as we do– love the two houses on the Abbey St Bathans estate, near Duns: *The Retreat* (**sleeping 6/8**) and *Abbey Cottage* (**sleeping 5**), beautifully positioned near the River Whiteadder.

North of Edinburgh, among the Angus Glens, we saw, hidden away amid the rolling hills, the outstanding *East Kinclune* and *Strathmore Cottages* (both **sleeping 4**), and, in the hills of a private country estate near Dunkeld, the recently renovated, spectacularly-positioned *Keeper's House* (**sleeping 6/7**).

There are four idyllic cottages near Loch Tay and, in the foothills of the Cairngorms, ten minutes from Kingussie, we liked *Lynaberack Cottage* (**sleeping 6**) which lies in a 10,000-acre private country estate of hills, woods and moorlands, with good fishing nearby.

On the incomparable isles of Skye, Mull and Eilean Shona, there are another sixteen excellent shoreline cottages (of all sizes) in locations to die for, while in Inverness-shire and Sutherland, further north, there are traditional Highland cottages with log-fires that make very comfortable, always popular holiday homes.

Do request their brochure (stamp please) from Ecosse Unique Ltd, Lilliesleaf, Melrose, Roxburghshire TD6 9JD.

Telephone: (01835) 870779 (5 lines). Fax 870417.

www.uniquescotland.com

email: reservations@uniquescotland.com

Dunning, near Perth
Duncrub Holidays

We agree with one of our readers who wrote to say 'Perthshire's got the lot!'. She'd been staying in one of the much-admired, tourist-board highly graded Dalreoch Farm properties owned by Wilma Marshall, on the edge of the village of Dunning (easy to locate: just south of the A9 trunk road). *The Tower House* (STB Five Stars) was originally part of a

Chapel House incorporates orginal features (as does The Tower House)...

redundant church. On two levels, the main accommodation consists of an open plan kitchen/diner/sitting room on the ground floor and, via a narrow stone spiral staircase, an upper floor double bedroom (five foot bed) and bathroom. *The Chapel House* (STB Four Stars) has been added on to the original chapel, and in part is modern, incorporating parts of the original. It **sleeps 4** in a twin and a double. (Part of the chapel is a games room, with badminton and table tennis, available to all holiday tenants.)

Linen/towels included. TVs. Well behaved dogs welcome in Chapel House. STB Four/Five Stars. Cost: about £300 to £495. Switch/Solo/Access/-Visa/Mastercard. More details from Wilma Marshall, Duncrub Holidays, Dalreoch, Perth PH2 0QJ. Telephone (01764) 684368, fax 684633.

www.duncrub-holidays.com   email: ghc@duncrub-holidays.com

Camusericht, Rannoch   map 4/169
Tigh Na Vilt

This rare, traditional Victorian gamekeeper's cottage, in grounds of two acres, lies in one of the most wildly beautiful parts of Scotland, on a 13000 acre sporting estate. On the side of Loch Rannoch, looking south, it is idyllic for serious walkers and afternoon strollers, and for anyone wanting a week or two of absolute peace. It has been transformed without loss of the original

Absolute peace and quiet are virtually guaranteed in this very special place...

character, and is very comfortable, with central heating *and* an open fire (logs and coal, or possibly *peat,* included), a convivial kitchen-diner with a Stanley stove.

Mr and Mrs Baker of Chester have spoken rapturously of the space, the five foot wide main bed, the attention to detail, the visiting deer. Dogs possible by arrangement. Linen, towels included. TV. Cost: about £300 to £580. Details from Mrs L H Kerfoot, Camusericht Lodge, Bridge of Gaur, Rannoch, Perthshire PH17 2QP. Telephone (01882) 633207. Fax 633273. Or Pat Macdonald, telephone (01882) 633268.

email: sue@skerfoot.demon.co.uk

Tomich, near Cannich
Tomich Holidays

For many years, in this fabulous corner of the Highlands, we've featured
traditional stone and slate courtyard
cottages, a snug and cosy Victorian
dairy and six two-storeyed timber
cabins. *The cottages have extraordinary panoramic views*, among the
best in this guide, and are STB Four
Stars (the other properties are Three
Stars). The Victorian dairy is a stone built cottage, part of a Grade II listed
building. A two minute stroll away, among the trees, are the chalets, private but not remote, within 100 yards of another. Each is uncluttered and
surprisingly roomy, simple but comfortable, with balconies for wildlife
spotting, birch trees and grassy banks. Most are booked by guests returning to revel in the 'endless walks', the cycling, the wildlife, the quiet and
the lovely indoor pool. Tomich is a beautiful stone-built place, preserved
as a conservation village. Surrounded by imposing hills, it and the estate
are a tourist flagship. Dogs welcome. TV/video in every property. **Sleep 4
to 6**. Cost: £170 to £515. Details from Tomich Holidays, Guisachan
Farm, Tomich, By Beauly, Inverness-shire IV4 7LY. Telephone (01456)
415332 or fax 415499.

Even in Highland terms this is a beautiful location – quiet and not well known.

www.tomich-holidays.co.uk
email: admin@tomich-holidays.co.uk

Evanton, near Cromarty Firth
Foulis Castle   map 4/172

It's always a thrill to stay within or
right beside a historic house. And
they don't come more ancient (or
indeed romantic) than this. For 600
years Foulis Castle has been the
home of the Chiefs of Clan Munro,
and within the elegant *Pavilion*, very
much a part of the castle, there is a
spacious dining area linked to a well
equipped kitchen, a comfortable sit-
ting room – within what was the original fortified building – with an open
fire and deep, 'chintzy' armchairs and sofa. There are two large windows
in its thick walls looking out on to the castle's policies and fields. Said
one visitor we spoke to, a Mrs Monroe, of North Carolina (a clan connection!): 'It is all so stylish and full of character, with old pictures, carpets,
and so on, but facilities such as the kitchen and bathrooms are modern.'

Very much a part of the original castle: The Pavilion is in the centre, at the rear.

Sleeps 4 in a double and twin, both ensuite. TV and radio. Linen, towels
and central heating included. Not suitable for dogs. Short breaks. Cost:
about £287 to £430. Details from Mrs P Munro of Foulis, Foulis Castle,
Evanton, Ross-shire IV16 9UX. Telephone (01349) 830212.

Invershin, near Lairg
Linsidecroy Steading and Farmhouse

The journey to these properties is spectacular. Northwest of Lairg, en route for Ullapool, you travel across some of the most astonishing mountain and loch-scapes in northern Scotland before reaching this pair of absolutely pristine, neat and well furnished old-farm-building conversions. Each of them, **sleeping 2**, has a modern interior, with lots of pine, contemporary kitchen units, good beds and lots of comfort. A few

'Deeply rural' but not as remote as it might at first seem from the map.

yards away is the farmhouse itself: an absolute charmer, with hill and loch views: we were loathe to leave. It has character, light and spacious main rooms, an open fire in the sitting room, a pleasant round dining table at which many a foray into the most impressive scenery in Europe could be planned, attractive pictures and lamps. It **sleeps 5** (a double room, a twin room and a single room).

STB Three Stars (Farmhouse), Four Stars (Cottages). TV. Dogs welcome. Linen but not towels included. Cost: £210 to £300 (quite a bargain, we thought). Details from Robert Howden, The Factor's House, Berriedale, Caithness KW7 6HD. Telephone (01593) 751280; fax 751251.

Nethybridge
Speyside Cottages map 4/183

Fringed by dramatic scenery, ideally located for exploring the Highlands, Nethybridge is a village of character in its own right, wooded and secret. Golfers will love this location: there are six golf courses in easy reach, plus a 'nine hole shortie' that will appeal to beginners. Among all

A good selection of properties in a charming, unusual village setting.

Brian Patrick's properties (practical, convenient, clean and tidy) our favourite is *The Old Smithy*, **sleeping 9**. Full of character, it is warm and sunny with a wood-burning stove in the living room. Also for cosy out of season breaks either consider his smaller converted hay loft called *Stables Cottage*, **sleeping 2 to 4**, or tiny *Ben Studio* on the river bank, **sleeping 2**. There are other cottages **sleeping 6**, some on the riverbank. The cottages are STB Three and Four Stars. Dogs are welcome throughout. All properties have night storage heating, and include bedlinen and towels. Cost: from about £140 to £715 (for 9). Further details and an excellent colour leaflet available from Mr and Mrs B J Patrick, 1 Chapelton Place, Forres, Morayshire IV36 2NL. Telephone/fax (01309) 672505.

www.speysidecottages.co.uk
email: speyside@enterprise.net

Glen Strathfarrar, Struy, near Beauly
Culligran Cottages

Deep in the Highlands but not too remote, close to a salmon-rich river on a sporting estate, Frank and Juliet Spencer-Nairn have five properties. Better yet, guests have the delicious freedom of the metalled but private road leading up into the hills. Four are Scandinavian chalets, quite spacious, and with picture windows, **sleeping up to 7**; the other is a delightful, characterful, traditional

This is one of the best places in Scotland to observe wildlife in its natural habitat.

cottage with an attractive blend of 'antiquey', solid and modern furniture – including the obligatory stag's head! It has one double and two twin bedrooms, a good fitted kitchen, real character and is in a superb location (well off the Beauly to Tomich road) without seeming isolated.

Bikes available for hire. No TV. Trout and salmon fishing in the Rivers Farrar and Glass. Guided tours of Frank's deer farm. Dogs are welcome. Cost: about £129 to £429, depending on which property and when. Further details are available from Frank and Juliet Spencer-Nairn, Culligran Cottages, Glen Strathfarrar, Struy, near Beauly, Inverness-shire IV4 7JX. Telephone/fax (01463) 761285.

www.assc.co.uk/culligran   email: juliet@culligran.demon.co.uk

---

Nethybridge/Loch Lochy
Balnagowan/Ivy Cottage   map 4/186/187

We know both these well situated properties. *Balnagowan* is easy to find, tucked away quite near (but out of sight and earshot of) the A9 trunk road between Perth and Inverness, and is one of our favourites in Scotland (Ref B5620). The interior is sumptuous, with for example a woodburner in the well-appointed kitchen. There is superb, safe, interesting walking right from the front door, and there are lots of sporting

Ivy is by the water's edge on Loch Lochy, but is easy to get to and not isolated...

activities in the vicinity. **Sleeps up to 8** in four bedrooms. *Ivy Cottage* (Ref SD40) is right by the water's edge, at the northern end of Loch Lochy, very much on the tourist beat, with easy access to, for example, Ben Nevis, Loch Ness, Fort William and the Isle of Skye. There are loch fishing rights, and the cottage even comes with a 16-foot boat with outboard. **Sleeps 2** in a double.

Details: Blakes, Stoney Bank Road, Earby BB94 0AA. To book: (08700) 708090 Brochures: (08700) 708099. **Quote ref BMA82.**

Live search and book: www.blakes-cottages.co.uk

Scotland-wide
Large Holiday Houses*

What a combination: the romance of Scotland's great houses and castles, and their marvellous locations, plus the huge appeal of big properties in which two or more extended families or groups of friends can rendezvous. It's exactly what hundreds of our readers have been asking about for – yes! – 20 years!

Soon to expand over the border into England, Large Holiday Houses features (in a magnificent brochure – one of the two or three best we know) a number of historically important beauties. These include 14th century *Sundrum Castle*, in Ayrshire, one of the longest-inhabited in Scotland, *Craighall Castle*, in Perthshire, in the same family for almost a thousand years, and exquisite, formal but also charmingly intimate *Castle of Invercauld*, on Royal Deeside.

But it's not all castles. Also available are the architecturally exquisite *Dell House*, **sleeping up to 16**, on an estate that extends to the shores of Loch Ness, and the 1850s conversion of a mid-18th century house called *Big Barns*, at Golspie, in Sutherland. This **sleeps 11**. There are views of the Cairngorms across the sea, safe and sandy beaches nearby and – how's this for an after-lunch stroll? – Dunrobin Castle, open April to October, is within walking distance.

On a slightly smaller scale there is *Bragleen House*, near Kilninver, in Argyllshire. On a 4000 acre estate a few miles south of Oban, it has an absolutely idyllic situation overlooking Loch Scammadale. **Sleeps 7**.

On the other side of the country, on the Black Isle, *Poyntzfield House* is a most handsome Grade A listed Georgian mansion, also with snooker and two open fires. It has a library, a viewing tower and, for example, seven bathrooms. Very well situated for exploring the far north and west of Scotland, it **sleeps 16 'plus 4'** in the main house and the west wing.

The 'Large Holiday Houses' properties are geographically well spread: one could organise a journey of a lifetime around the properties featured.

Further details and a copy of the impressive brochure from Wynne Bentley, Large Holiday Houses, Poyntzfield House, Poyntzfield, Dingwall, Ross-shire IV7 8LX. Brochure line (01381) 610496. Bookings and enquiries (01381) 610496.

www.LHHScotland.com
email: LHH@LHHScotland.com

Bragleen House, on the west coast, is – typically – superbly well situated.

A bedroom in the Castle of Invercauld – elegant, and chic, not a museum piece.

Dalcross, East Inverness
Easter Dalziel

This is a most appealing trio of traditional, stone built cottages, which provides an exceptionally good base from which to explore the whole of the north, east and west of Scotland. Unpretentious but comfortably furnished, they are surrounded by a large grassy area, with a pretty heather garden to the front and panoramic views of the surrounding

Warm and very traditional cottages, well placed for touring. A kind welcome too...

countryside. On a working farm with beef cattle, sheep and grain, the jewel in this particular Scottish crown is *Birch*, at one end of the three adjoining properties. It is thickly carpeted, comfortably furnished, its pale green soft furnishings and deep-pile carpets easy on the eye. There's an appealing separate dining alcove. **Sleeps 6**. *Rowan* and *Pine* (**sleeping 4 and 6**) are a little more old fashioned but comfortable, warm and cottagey. They are reasonably priced, and open all year. STB Three/Four Stars. TV. Dogs welcome. Linen and towels included. Cost: about £130 to £415. Details from Mr and Mrs Pottie, Easter Dalziel Farm, Dalcross, Inverness IV2 7JL. Telephone and fax Ardersier (01667) 462213.
www.easterdalzielfarm.co.uk
email: ghcg@easterdalzielfarm.co.uk

Logie Newton, by Huntly
Logie Newton Holiday Cottages   map 4/190

We've had good reader reports of these, and like them immensely ourselves. Amid green and rolling farmland with easily climbable hills, these are very well cared for, single storeyed traditional cottages a hundred yards from the owners' working farm. Royal Deeside, with its castles, great fishing and even better golf, is just an hour away, and the little, old-fashioned North Coast resorts are less than that. We noted open fires,

A fine base for a part of Scotland all-too-many visitors overlook...

good beds, books, games and toys, comfortable sofas and armchairs of the traditional kind, clean, neat and tidy interiors, telephones, pictures and knick knacks, farm views. *Dykeside* **sleeps 6** in a double, a twin and a room with adult bunks (Z-bed available). *Tanaree* **sleeps 4** in a double and a twin. Both take a cot and are highly rated by the STB.

Dogs welcome. Small TV. Linen, towels and logs provided. Cost: £200 to £375. Details: Rhona Cruickshank, Logie Newton, Huntly, Aberdeenshire AB54 6BB. Telephone (01464) 841229, fax (01464) 841277.
www.logienewton.co.uk email: logienewton@aol.com

131

Ardgay, near Dornoch
Mid Fearn Cottages

There is a shortage of good quality accommodation in this north eastern corner of Scotland that is, however, a perfect point from which to explore the whole of the far north and north west (Gairloch and Ullapool, for example, are about an hour and a half by car, and one can easily arrange a day trip to Orkney).

Happily, these three side-by-side properties are among the very best there is in any part of the country: comfortable but not prissily so, warm, family-oriented, quiet, clean, private, and altogether a pleasant experience. They are all about deep sofas, attractive paintings, prints and antiques, but are nevertheless 'child-friendly'.

Charmingly, you cross a (gated) single track railway to get to the cottages. 'Peace, perfect peace' enthuses one entry in the visitors' book. Another (people from Worcestershire) mentions how idyllic the weather can be during autumn. Note here that the resident caretaker will supply logs, golf clubs and fishing rods. There is superb golf, fishing and hill walking for the more energetic, but you do not have to go far to see wildlife. Within the 14 acres of woodland, visitors include pine marten, otter and deer. Seals can often be seen in the Firths.

Rowan has three cosy bedrooms (**sleeps 6**), with an antique bed in one, full central heating by Rayburn gas-fired cooker, well equipped kitchen, spacious sitting room/diner. It also has a private walled garden. Cosy, low-ceilinged, two-storeyed *Struan Cottage* **sleeps 2,** and has quite a following of its own, with many repeat visitors. There is a beautiful view of the firth from the bedroom and bathroom.

Most recently available *Mid Fearn House,* **sleeping 10,** is a large property of great character, with for example two sitting rooms, a huge family

All three have access to a garden, plus character and loads of comfort...

Most unusually, precise plans of the different properties are available...

kitchen with Aga, long corridors, a good sized garden with sea views, and four large double bedrooms – one with a four poster – all of which, for this is a single-storeyed house, are on the ground floor. With fitted carpets, antique furniture and well chosen lamps, this is a very special place.

TV/video. Dogs are welcome. Linen, towels, microwave, electric fan oven, fridge-freezer, dishwasher and washing machine. Cost: about £95 to £1000. Further details are available from Jenifer Cooper, 17 Oakthorpe Road, Summertown, Oxford OX2 7BD. Telephone (01865) 439024.

email: jenifer.cooper@ntlworld.com

Leckmelm, near Loch Broom
Leckmelm Holiday Cottages

Ullapool is a splendid touring centre, a marvellous jumping off point for the Outer Hebrides and the far north. and a lively working community rather than 'a tourist destination', which does not by the way feel as distant as it looks on the map.

A few minutes' drive to the south of Ullapool, Leckmelm has appeared every year in this guide. And never a complaint!

If it's scenery you're seeking, the cottages that stand in the grounds of the 7,000 acre Leckmelm estate are well worth considering, and the bungalows that stand right by Loch Broom are quite exquisitely placed.

There are six *Campbeltown Cottages*, all with the advantage of being hidden from the main road (they are high above it), and all with a sitting room and kitchen on the ground floor, a twin or double bedroom and a bathroom and a smaller room with bunk beds on the first floor. They are very comfortable, solid and quiet, 'traditional', unpretentious but well cared for.

Quite close by, also with views from certain windows of the loch, *Farm Cottage* is a well preserved traditional stone and slate house. There is a

The most beautifully situated of the Leckmelm properties are, we'd say, Lochside Cottages (left), beside Loch Broom, in a peaceful location. One of its many advantages is its nicely walled-off picnic area. The views of the loch alone must be worth £100 a week, and we'd love to take a week here just to unwind and watch the water...

Farm Cottage is also close to the water, a substantial house of character...

The Campbeltown Cottages are well away from the main road, and very cosy.

particularly spacious dining room and a big, convivial dining table, the powerful combination of an open fire and central heating.

Sleep 4 to 6. Cost: about £160 to £320. Dogs are welcome. TVs, central heating.

Further details from Leckmelm Holiday Cottages, Loch Broom, Ullapool, Ross-shire IV23 2RL. Telephone/fax Ullapool (01854) 612471.

133

Isle of Skye/Plockton/Peebles
Rural Retreats*

This organisation is in a class of its own. It accepts only properties of a very high standard, and where quality is lacking it will apply its own criteria and bring them 'up to speed'.

We love the Scottish islands, though standards can vary, but we have had good reports of Rural Retreats' *Duisdale House*, on the Isle of Skye (map 193), and will see it for ourselves in 2002. It is a rare modern house on Isleornsay Bay, **sleeping up to 10.** There is a splendid, very spacious open-plan living room with deep, deep sofas and a cheery woodburning stove. This complements the underfloor heating.

Achnandarach Lodge is an unusual Swiss-chalet-style property, usefully **sleeping up to 9**, just two miles from the exceptionally attractive and well situated village of Plockton, with a most picturesque harbour and a fairy-tale castle on the headland, on the shores of an inlet of Loch Carron.

Achnandarach Lodge, at Plockton, sleeps nine, and is handy for the Isle of Skye...

Easter Knowe Farm is a highly desirable family house in lovely countryside...

Delightfully, there is a walk of just a few hundred yards through the forest behind the house that brings one to Loch Achnahinich.

The Scottish border country is one of Britain's best-kept secrets, and on the edge of the attractive village of Stobo, among rolling green hills, Rural Retreats feature a superb, rather rambling country house, **sleeping 8,** called *Easter Knowe Farm*. Unpretentious but comfortable, with lots of books and pictures, a particularly fine central staircase and a big family farmhouse kitchen, it is a very desirable place indeed.

The historic town of Peebles (try to see Traquair House) is just five miles away, Edinburgh under an hour. Closer to 'home', Stobo Castle is known for its health spa, and day visitors are welcome.

Details and a copy of the organisation's impressive brochure from Rural Retreats, Station Road, Blockley, Moreton-in-Marsh, Gloucestershire GL56 9DZ. Telephone (01386) 701177, fax 701178.

www.ruralretreats.co.uk
email: info@ruralretreats.co.uk

Attadale, near Lochcarron

This is the wild Highlands at its most scenically magnificent. But it is not remote or inaccessible. With panoramic views at every turn, the A890 is surely one of the most scenic routes in the Highlands, especially where it veers westwards from the Ullapool/Inverness road, and eventually arrives at Kyle of Lochalsh, across the bridge from Skye.

Half way along this route lies Lochcarron and, across the loch from the elongated, pretty, white-painted village, one of the most exquisite country estates we have found, with cared-for cottages to match. Railway enthusiasts should note that the famous Inverness to Kyle of Lochalsh railway runs past the entrance to the estate, and that there is a little station.

Along a private drive, with the single track railway and the loch behind us, we reached the owners' impressive mansion, and from there drove out into the estate, passing the beautiful gardens that are open to the public, and finally reached several of the cottages. Guests have complete access to the estate, famous for its wildlife and its natural beauty, except from 15th August to 15th October when they are asked to keep to the paths while deer are being culled. Loch fishing up in the hills is available, and there are boats for hire: one 40-acre loch is stocked with rainbow trout. During our visits we've met several people staying here, and envied them.

There is a double bonus of traditional cottages fitting beautifully into the landscape, and 21st century 'mod cons'.

Even in Scottish terms, Attadale is a spectacular place: do not forget your walking boots and binoculars.

The cottages offer that magic formula: complete harmony with their surroundings, and all the 21st century comforts that self-caterers increasingly demand. Prettily pale against the looming green hills, usually with just the sound of bleating sheep and perhaps a rushing burn to interrupt the blissful silence, they are most attractively and thoughtfully fitted out. We noticed open fires or wood stoves, good beds, lots of lamps, upholstered cane armchairs, many very attractive pictures (some by the owners' daughter, who is a painter). Here was a delightfully lit alcove in which to snuggle up with a book, there a cosy and congenial juxtaposition of dining room and kitchen. All are STB Four Stars.

Sleep 4 to 8. Well behaved, sheep-respecting dogs welcome. Linen and towels for hire. No TV reception. Cost: from £250 to £440. Colour brochure from Susan Watson, Attadale, Strathcarron, Wester Ross IV54 8YX. Telephone/fax (01520) 722862.

www.attadale.com
email: cottages@attadale.com

The National Trust for Scotland
Holiday Accommodation Programme

Readers who'd stayed in a couple of the National Trust properties we feature on Pages 18-19 spotted that for the first time in 2001 we also included properties in The National Trust for Scotland's programme. They went (from Buckinghamshire) to one of the apartments within romantic, fabulously situated *Mar Lodge*, on Royal Deeside.

We know the place and if we had to choose one great estate – there are over 77000 acres of it – that encapsulates the romance and beauty of mainland Scotland, this could be it. All five of the elegant apartments are graded Four Stars by the STB, and three of them have the advantage of access via the impressive main entrance and up the main stairs of the lodge. One of them, *Bynack* (on two levels), is notably roomy, and **can sleep up to 15** (though it is also available to smaller groups).

Also the stuff of which holiday dreams are made are Culzean Castle (pronounced 'cullane'), Brodick Castle, on the Isle of Arran, Castle Fraser, near Aberdeen, Craigievar Castle, Haddo House: all of these places are the high spots of many a Scottish touring holiday. But astonishingly, courtesy of The National Trust for Scotland, you can actually stay in them, *and at a very reasonable price.*

We can hardly think of a better way to tune into the history and romance of this beautiful country than to stay in, say, the spacious, high-ceilinged *Brewhouse Flat* in the west wing of Culzean Castle, on the Ayrshire coast (it has its own entrance) or in *Royal Artillery Cottage*, that forms part of the courtyard next to the castle. Being on the cliff edge, it has impressive sea views. Each **sleeps 4**. Or you can stay in one of the two most attractive detached cottages in the grounds of picturesque Craigievar Castle, near Royal Deeside. Both **sleeping 4**, *Kennels Cottage* and *Steading Cottage* are only about a hundred yards from the fabulous castle itself.

Try this on your friends: 'We'll be staying in Culzean Castle"...

Or Steading Cottage, in the grounds of (and facing) Craigievar Castle.

With only two properties available, one feels privileged enough. But at *Haddo House*, north of Aberdeen, there is just one, *Stables Flat*, **sleeping 4**. It is on the first floor in a handsome stable block dating from the 1820s. Guests have access (though not exclusively) to a tennis court.

For a copy of the irresistible brochure contact Holidays Department, The National Trust for Scotland, Wemyss House, 28 Charlotte Square, Edinburgh EH2 4ET. Telephone (0131) 243 9331. Fax (0131) 243 9594. **www.nts.org.uk email: holidays@nts.org.uk**

Glen Coe
Torren Cottages

Another marvellous location. Close to the mysterious and famous glen, these three neat, tucked away pebbledash bungalows stand in a leafy enclave close to the River Coe.

You first turn off a minor road that snakes uphill towards dramatic Glen Coe, then you cross a cattle grid and pause beside a mirror-like loch, then you continue along a track to the three cottages. *They have featured in this guide for nineteen years*, and we have never had a complaint. We have only ever seen them when they had people in (they are that popular!), and people were always delighted with them. They combine mod cons with just a hint of the outdoor life – the setting is beautiful and not remote and you do not have to have climbing boots to enjoy it. A high standard of comfort is achieved despite the comparatively small size and open plan nature of the single-storey buildings. All the cottages have underfloor heating, fired by an eco-friendly woodchip boiler, tumble dryer and dishwasher, and there is a shared laundry room useful for those damper Glen Coe days – for this is, after all, 'outward-bound country'.

The cottages are 'compact', but well planned and notably warm all year round.   *The river and the dramatic glen are close, but not overbearingly so...*

Better yet, there is a large drying room. There is a TV in each cottage, and a payphone in the laundry room.

All three cottages have a good degree of privacy, because they separately face the river through big picture windows and do not look directly at each other. The River Coe is very well fenced off from the properties and there is no danger to little ones, who will however, appreciate the opportunities for paddling and messing about should they be allowed to. There is a lot of pinewood, well fitted kitchens and sitting-cum-dining rooms.

This is an excellent base from which to tour not only the wild landscape of Glen Coe and Rannoch Moor (one of the most eerily remote parts of Scotland) but, being close to the Corran Ferry, it is also quickly accessible to the beautiful Morvern and Ardnamurchan peninsulas and, beyond them, the Isle of Mull.

Sleep 6 to 8. Highly rated by the STB. TVs. Dogs welcome. Discount for couples-only. Cost: up to a maximum of £575, weekend booking at £98 per night. Details from Victoria Sutherland, Torren, Glencoe, Argyll PH49 4HX. Telephone (01855) 811207. Fax 811338.

email: victoria@torrenglencoe.com

137

Strontian, by Acharacle
Seaview Grazings

We like the combination of Scotland at its most beautiful and comfortable places in which to holiday and enjoy the scenery. We recently re-visited Seaview Grazings after making the short crossing from the Isle of Mull – just one of many recommended excursions for visitors here – and found it as appealing as ever – an exceptional location.

The reactions of one of our readers is typical: 'We found Strontian an excellent centre for all grades of walking', she wrote...'wild glens, peaceful woodlands, beautiful coastal walks and stern mountain challenges...at the end of the week we felt that we had experienced only a fraction of what was on offer in Ardgour, Moidart and Morvern.

'Although we mostly cooked our own evening meals it was useful to know there were pubs nearby where we could have bar meals. In short, an excellent holiday.'

We have had other plaudits, and would certainly like to get away from it all ourselves in any of the fourteen Scandinavian real-log cabins – and we'd be happy to go at any time of year, for the houses are of permanent-home standard, with double glazing, fully fitted modern kitchens, full bath, linen and towels provided. They feel very private, but many readers also like the idea that there are neighbours (and the owners, who live in one of the cabins) on hand.

On a lightly wooded hillside above Loch Sunart, awarded Three Stars by the Scottish Tourist Board, *all* the cabins have lovely views of the loch and mountains. Built of real pine logs, they are warm, with large double-glazed picture windows. The fitted kitchens have four-ring electric cook-

Yet another extraordinary location on the west coast of Scotland! Quite amazing...

Each of the log houses feels private and self contained, but there's no isolation.

ers, washer/dryers, fridge/freezers, microwaves and roomy cupboards.

Boat hire can easily be arranged locally, as can loch fishing – for beginners as well as more experienced anglers – up in the hills.

Blankets/duvets, linen, towels and electricity are all included. Electric radiators. Iron and ironing-board. TVs. Well behaved dogs are welcome. Three properties have two bedrooms, **sleeping 4** (a double and a twin), the others have three **sleeping 6** (ie with an extra bunk bedroom), and all also have put-you-up beds for 2 more. Cost: from about £220 to £510, depending on when you go. Further details can be obtained from John Hanna, Seaview Grazings Holidays, Strontian, by Acharacle, Argyll PH36 4HZ. Telephone (01967) 402191.

Ratagan, near Kyle of Lochalsh
Kintail

This is a charming, well-cared-for semi-detached cottage on the shores of Loch Duich, which has fabulous sea-loch and mountain views and a coal fire. Tastefully refurbished by the owner as his highland retreat, nothing has been spared to make the house warm, welcoming and comfortable. All rooms enjoy mountain

Loch Duich, looking west over Kintail .

views, most overlook the loch. The spacious house has a well equipped kitchen (Stanley oil fired stove, microwave, dishwasher, automatic washing machine, etc), breakfast room, sitting room with open fire, dining room, drying room, bathroom with bath and shower, two bedrooms each with a double bed and a single bed. Small verandah and garden, and locked bicycle storage. Local wildlife includes eagles, buzzards, deer, otters, seals, porpoises. One dog or two toy dogs welcome. **Sleeps up to 6** plus cot/highchair. TV. STB Four Stars. Barbecue, payphone, bedlinen included; one bag of coal included, others at cost. Children's heated pool nearby. Details: Mr and Mrs Vyner Brooks, Middle Barrows Green, Kendal, Cumbria LA8 0JG, or 9c Altway, Old Roan, Liverpool L10 3JA. Telephone (015395) 60242 or 0151-526 9321/5451. Fax 0151-526 1331.

www.primecottages.co.uk

Three Mile Water (Fort William) map 4/200
Druimarbin Farmhouse

With great views of Loch Linnhe, three miles south of Fort William, this has always appealed to us. It remains one of our all-time favourites. We appreciate its home comforts, its 'atmosphere' and its location: excellent for touring. It is pleasantly rambling, very much a family home. Reached via its own drive, and on the edge of woodland, it

A house of great comfort and character...

sleeps up to 9 (in comfortable beds) – though the handsome dining table will actually seat 12. There is an open fire (logs are supplied) in the drawing room, which is graced by fine paintings, antique furniture, comfortable sofas, old fashioned armchairs. There are lots of good books, the odd bit of tartanry to remind you you're in the Highlands, a very well equipped kitchen, a payphone, Ordnance Survey maps.

TV. Linen by arrangement. Walk-in drying room. Dogs possible by arrangement. Cost: £650 to £800 per week. Further details are available from Mrs Anthony German-Ribon, 57 Napier Avenue, London SW6 3PS. Telephone/fax 020-7736 4684.

www.coruanan.co.uk email: germanribon@postmaster.co.uk

Isle of Mull
Glengorm Castle

You might think Glengorm Castle is too good to be true, but it *is* real. As you see it against the sea from the direction of Tobermory, four miles away, it is like a different world, something straight out of a children's fairytale book. Mull is one of Scotland's most romantic islands, and this corner of it, at its northern-most tip, is idyllic. On the estate

The Sorne Cottages are probably our favourites, but all the Glengorm properties appeal very much.

there are several cottages, but probably our personal favourites, the two semi-detached *Sorne Cottages* (**each sleeps 6**) feel well away from it all (though the castle is easily in strollable distance), with open fires and a lovely calm atmosphere. Not least, we love the local paintings done by the owner of the castle herself, Mrs Nelson. The smaller *Cnoc Fuar* (**sleeps 4**) lies between Glengorm and Tobermory (though nearer Glengorm). The two flats in the castle have beautiful views over the sea. Both are comfortable without being 'fussy'. Cost: about £170 to £600. Details from Mr and Mrs Nelson, Glengorm Castle, near Tobermory, Isle of Mull, Argyll PA75 6QE. Telephone Tobermory (01688) 302321.

www.glengormcastle.co.uk

email: enquiries@glengormcastle.co.uk

Isle of Seil, near Oban map 4/208
Achnacroish Cottage

Although nearly every square inch of Scotland's many islanded west coast between Oban and Kintyre is beauti-ful, there's something special about the 'Bridge Over The Atlantic' on to Seil Island: all crofts and yachts. Now bird watchers, walkers or 'away from it all' people can stay in one of these traditional homes, on a croft with sheep, but with all 'mod-cons'. They appreciate the log stove,

An exceptional property, used by the owners and very modestly priced...

the good quality double bed (there is also a 3ft. single bed and a futon), the easy chairs, the original stone flags, the inviting combined sitting room/dining room/kitchen. There are plenty of books, maps and walking suggestions. The owner has used the cottage for his own holidays for 25 years and is a member of the STB Quality Assurance Scheme, with Three Stars. **Sleeps 2, plus 2**. TV. Unsuitable for dogs. Linen, towels provided. Electricity by meter reading. Shower room. Cost: up to £270. Available March-October, or by arrangement. Details: Dr W Lindsay, 7 Shearwater Road, Cheam, Surrey SM1 2AR. Telephone and fax: 020-8661-1834.

email: walindsay@lindsaywa.freeserve.co.uk

Scotland-wide
Blakes Holidays in Britain (Scotland)*

Many of our readers, including some from overseas, have found Blakes's Scottish properties after trying their English ones.

An extended family from Germany stayed in two of the timber lodges in the delightfully situated *Ormsary Estate*, overlooking the beautiful Loch Caolisport, on the west coast. We know the place well: you can have hundreds of acres to yourself, soft sandy beaches that are never crowded, easy access to many miles of way-marked footpaths. All the properties **sleep 6**. Ref SH8201-SH8203.

We ourselves have stayed in one of the cottages on the *Delgatie Castle* estate, near Turriff, in the north east, and on a subsequent occasion visited friends staying in one of the sumptuous apartments in the castle itself. Ref B4267/4270/4272.

Delgatie is a bit off the beaten track, but Blakes are good at securing properties in famous places as Loch Lomond, Loch Ness, Loch Awe, Fort

Stay at Ormsary, and you have a 15000 acre estate virtually to yourselves.

Heatherbank, on the Dalhousie Estate, is a late-19th century classic, sleeping 6.

William, St Andrews, the rolling green Border country around Selkirk, as well as more remote spots that often capture the essence of Scotland's extraordinary history and romance.

We also know *Altamount Chalets*, near the lively town of Blairgowrie – usefully situated for touring. They are beautifully situated among trees and **sleep up to 6**. Ref SK5301/SK5401/SK57.

Usefully **sleeping up to 12** is *Isla Bank House*, on the outskirts of Keith – and thus well placed for people who want to experience the Speyside Whisky Trail. This is a splendid baronial-style mansion with many antiques, a library, a music room with a Bechstein grand piano. Ref SF12.

More rural are the *Dalhousie Estates Holiday Cottages*, three detached estate cottages nestling in the scenic and unspoilt Glenesk area. One of the cottages is spectacularly located in a remote part of Glen Mark: *Glenmark Cottage* (Ref SM16) is a 'back to basics' property dating from 1870 – no electricity, but there is gas and an open fire.

Further details are available from Blakes, Stoney Bank Road, Earby, Barnoldswick BB94 0AA. To book: (08700) 708090 Brochures: (08700) 708099. **Ref BMA82.**

Live search and book: www.blakes-cottages.co.uk

Stein (Isle of Skye)
The Captain's House

This is a winner, a well recommended base from which to enjoy the Isle of Skye.

This is rather special. Even in Skye terms, the waterside village of Stein is very pretty, with nothing out of place in the row of white houses that make up the village. They incorporate one of the best pubs and also one of the best seafood restaurants on the island. The handsomest house of all, which in turn is widely known for its ground floor art gallery and craft shop, is The Captain's House, and the first and second floors of this make up a charming and very spacious holiday house (self-contained, private and quiet). We really liked the big sitting room, the deep sofa and armchairs, the Victorian tiled open fire and a good sized TV with 'excellent reception'. This has a dining area or you can use the large kitchen/breakfast room that, as with all but one of the rooms in this most appealing property, overlooks the sea loch. There are three bedrooms.

Scottish Tourist Board Three Stars. **Sleeps up to 6** (ie four adults and two children). Non-smokers preferred. Linen but not towels included. Dogs possible by arrangement. Cost: about £195 to £335 per week. Details from Mrs Cathy Myhill, The Captain's House, Stein, Waternish, Isle of Skye IV55 8GA. Telephone (01470) 592223/592218.

Isle of Skye
The Old Mill/Tigh Anna

Tigh Anna enjoys fabulous sunsets, and is only a mile from a white coral beach.

Skye has long been a favourite among readers who like to escape the rat-race and get 'back to nature', especially for hill walking. We like to take trips into the Cuillin Mountains and to the Outer Isles. These two extremely comfortable, well equipped traditional properties **(map 4/202/204)** are ideal bases. Surrounded by mountain and coastal scenery, *The Old Mill* is a conversion of a former mill. At the northern end of Skye, ten miles from Uig (ferries to the Outer Isles), it **sleeps 6** in two doubles and two singles. Shops and a safe, sandy beach are six miles away. *Tigh Anna*, at Dunvegan, enjoys wonderful sunsets and spectacular views over the sea to the Outer Hebrides. It is a renovated, traditional croft cottage situated only a mile from the white beaches of Loch Dunvegan. There's an open fire in the sitting/dining room, a double, a twin and a single bedroom (thus **sleeping 5**), and a garden.

Details from Hoseasons Holidays Ltd, Sunway House, Lowestoft NR32 2LW. Telephone (0870) 534 2342. Fax (0870) 902 2090.

**On-line booking and 'real time' availability on the web:
www.hoseasons.co.uk   email: mail@hoseasons.co.uk**

Achahoish, near Lochgilphead
Ellary Estate Cottages

Accessible via one of the most beautiful lochside roads we know even in the west of Scotland (hardly any traffic) this is one of so many places that are 'worth the detour', where one is guaranteed 'peace, perfect peace'.

If it seems a long way on the map (it's about two and a half hours from Glasgow) we promise that the journey warrants the effort! The 15,000 acres on the very scenic promontory between Lochs Sween and Caolisport, in Argyll, belong to the Ellary estate, an ancient family property that is partly farmed (predominantly sheep) yet mostly left wild for recreation purposes. Guest are welcome to wander where they fancy.

An Ellary Estate holiday is for people who thrive on a day's tramping through woods and hills. Those seeking laid-on entertainment and nearby clubs should look elsewhere. Even the nearest shop is 20 minutes' drive.

No-one can guarantee that you'll see otter, deer, eagles, peregrines, wildcats or any other estate residents, but they will certainly tell you where and when to look. Apart from walking on the wild side you can take to the loch waters, though bathing does tend to be a chilling experience.

In any of these exquisitely situated cottages, you will feel a million miles from everyday anxieties.

The location is everything. It is a rare pleasure to take in the scenery from these wide verandahs.

There are several lovely beaches of white sand and Ellary has proved to be very popular with sailors who bring their own dinghies (the Ellary people will help you launch your vessel). There is also fishing – trout from the lochs and salmon and sea trout in Lochead Burn. Four of the self-catering units are ranch-type chalets, simply-built wooden structures with wide verandahs overlooking the loch. The cottages are mostly of stone, once the homes of estate workers, and each one has its own particular charms. *The Lodge*, most recently available, is a particular joy: we loved the spiral staircase! There is an open fire as well as night storage heaters, a double room and two twin rooms.

All this adds up to a peaceful retreat that is also suitable for energetic families, to which many of our readers return year after year.

Sleep 4 to 8. Cost: about £188 to £495. Pets usually possible by arrangement. Details from The Estate Office, Ellary, Lochgilphead, Argyll PA31 8PA. Telephone (01880) 770232. Fax (01880) 770386.

www.ellary.com

email: info@ellary.com

Machrie, near Port Ellen/Bowmore
Machrie Hotel Lodges

Islay is one of our all-time favourite Hebridean islands, and the *Machrie Lodges* are superbly positioned near the Machrie Golf Course and the Machrie Hotel. The hotel has a reputation for providing the best food on Islay: a huge bonus for self caterers, and there's an ongoing programme of improvements to its lodges. We visited two of three that have been

The Post House Cottage (above) and The Chalet both have unforgettable views...

upgraded – though they are all acceptable for a holiday base. We found these two delightful: closest of the group of fifteen to the golf links, and with extraordinary views of Laggan Bay (though every property has panoramic views). We admired a spacious triple aspect sitting room/-diner/kitchen, cosy bedrooms – two twins, one en suite – an excellent sense of colour co-ordination: we liked the deep-cushioned cane sofa and armchairs in dark green and tartan, the big reading lamps, the plain walls.

Sleep up to 6 (with sofa bed). TV. Dogs welcome in the 'standard' lodges. Linen/towels included. Cost: £180 to £750. Details: the Machrie Hotel, Port Ellen, Isle of Islay, Argyll PA42 7AN. (01496) 302310. Fax 302404.

www.machrie.com email: machrie@machrie.com

Appin   map 4/216
Appin Holiday Homes

With magnificent views from picture windows over Loch Creran, a beautiful arm of Loch Linnhe, this collection of warm, welcoming timber lodges enjoys one of the best locations (mid way between Oban and Fort William) on the idyllic west coast of Scotland. STB Three Stars, **sleeping 2 to 5,** all are self contained

More great views: photographers, day-dreamers and painters will like it here.

and easy to locate. Although several stand together, landscaping is sensitive, and within the grounds are good level, hill and beach walks. (*Note: a very comfortable mobile home is also available in a splendid setting right on the lochside: children often love these.*) Fishing is free; boats are available; there's a small launderette, a games room, a play area. Woods and burns are within the grounds where, too, an old railway station is being renovated. Nearby is a sealife centre, a licensed inn. TV. Bedlinen supplied. Cost: about £175 to £395; discounts for couples. A good colour brochure from Mr and Mrs I Weir, Dept GHGI, Appin Holiday Homes, Appin, Argyll PA38 4BQ. Telephone Appin (01631) 730287.

www.appinholidayhomes.co.uk
email: info@appinholidayhomes.co.uk

Port Charlotte, Islay
Lorgba Holiday Cottages

Almost all the Hebridean islands are a joy to visit, but Islay is extra-special. Among other reasons, we like to look in on Sarah Roy's much liked, white painted single storey cottage conversions in the village of Port Charlotte. They have been in our guide for many years, and we have only ever had very enthusiastic reports. We say 'in the village': in fact, they are effectively right on the beach, and one of the best beaches on the island at that: perfectly safe and sandy, and as pretty a place, often complete with fishing boats, as you will find this side of the Greek islands. But that is just one of many good things Lorgba has going for it. A reader commented recently on Sarah's 'friendly welcome and personal attention' and, in particular, 'the extra comforts provided for an elderly member of our party'.

The three original holiday units are neat and compact, and all three living-rooms have French windows opening right on to the beach. One **sleeps 2**, the other two **sleep up to 4**, and in those two cases, cleverly arranged kitchenettes are part of the living area.

The other two properties, *Carraig North* and *Carraig South,* are much larger, very well designed and **sleep up to 6**. Being on slightly higher ground, they have superb views across the loch to the Paps of Jura and, on a clear day, the North Antrim coast (the latter feature unique among the Scottish properties we include).

All the cottages have central heating and the two newer ones even have peat fires too: glorious! Among the details we picked up during our latest visit: triple aspect sitting rooms in Carraig North and South, framed Ordnance Survey maps, a message in one of the visitors' books that otters had been seen on the rocks outside the cottages.

Lorgba Cottages stand within a few yards of Islay's finest and safest beach.

Carraig North and South, slightly more recent, are also very well situated.

Among the many charms of Islay are other splendid beaches, and access to Jura from the attractive Port Askaig ferry point. Readers who have never heard of Islay should consult their maps. It is a delightful island, varied and full of interest. It also produces some of the finest malt whiskies in the world (several distilleries arrange tours).

Scottish Tourist Board Four Stars (Carraig), Three Stars (Lorgba). TV. Dogs welcome. Cost: about £115 to £395. Details: Mr and Mrs Roy, Lorgba Holiday Cottages, Isle of Islay, Argyll, Scotland. Telephone/fax Port Charlotte (01496) 850208.

Carradale, Kintyre
Torrisdale Castle Cottages and Apartments

The Kintyre peninsula has many fans. It has much of the character of the Hebridean islands without (some would say, though *we* love the ferry crossings) the 'hassle' of getting there. The peninsula has the advantages of an island, plus ease of access. In a sheltered, heavily wooded part of this quite exceptional, secret corner of Scotland, Torrisdale Castle is well down towards the Mull of Kintyre: it overlooks the Isle of Arran from its fine vantage point on Kintyre.

On the ground floor of the magnificent though not overpowering Torrisdale Castle itself, are the flats. We have visited and revisited them all, and always found a very high standard of finish. High ceilings, large rooms, very comfortable sofas, well equipped kitchens or kitchenettes, and just enough individual little details (like secret alcoves that actually form part of the turrets) to add a touch of character and individuality to each one. The flats all **sleep between 4 and 6**, with lots of space for an extra bed, and are STB Three Stars.

All the cottages, though on a leafy and exceptionally quiet estate, are well away from the others. *South Lodge*, which **sleeps 2**, is on the 'B' road that runs the length of the peninsula, but it is mainly used by local and holiday traffic. It has the advantage of overlooking a pretty and sandy bay which is, of course, readily available to all guests here. We particularly liked *Lephinbeag Cottage*, at the end of its own rough drive, overhung with tall trees and with a babbling burn rippling beside it. It is quite small (two bedrooms, **sleeping 4**) but one of those places that, with a peat or log fire burning, after a day tramping through the hills, must be a delight.

The recently upgraded *Lephincorrach Farmhouse,* with spacious kitchen and dining room, **sleeps 10** in five bedrooms. *Garden Cottage*, **sleeping 4** in two bedrooms – a downstairs double and, intriguingly, an attic room reached by ladder – is beautifully, peacefully situated among trees. *Glen House* is a converted croft house, **sleeping 7** in three bedrooms. Sky TV only here due to poor reception. All the cottages are STB Two Stars.

Televisions. Dogs are welcome. Cost: about £120 to £410. Further details are available from Mr and Mrs Macalister Hall, Torrisdale Castle, Carradale, Kintyre, Argyll PA28 6QT. Telephone/fax (01583) 431233.

www.torrisdalecastle.com
email: machall@torrisdalecastle.freeserve.co.uk

Lephincorrach Farmhouse has been recently upgraded and sleeps 10 in five bedrooms.

The castle itself, which dominates the estate and looks out to sea, contains several impressively roomy apartments.

Kilchrist Castle, near Campbeltown
Kilchrist Castle Cottages

Kilchrist Castle, close to the Mull of Kintyre, makes an imposing focal point for these white-painted cottages. Originally 17th century, they are named after Scottish Clans (*MacLeod, MacDonald, Campbell, MacGregor, Bruce, Angus*) and **sleep 2, 4, 4, 4, 2 and 6 respectively**. Charming Bruce Cottage is actually the original castle gatehouse. Behind the other cottages there's good hill walking, and there are two friendly Shetland ponies. The cottages (all electric) are clean and neat, with no wasted space and, though grouped (except for Bruce) around a courtyard, are quiet and private. Three golf courses are nearby, and the location is ideal for day trips to Northern Ireland and the Hebridean islands of Islay, Gigha, Davaar and Arran. STB Two Stars. Visitors' written comments include the following: 'One of the most beautiful places we have ever been to' ... 'when we leave, a little bit of our hearts will stay here'. Cost: about £130 to £298. Dogs allowed, but must (for this is a sheep-farming area) be well controlled. Details: William Angus, Kilchrist Castle, Campbeltown, Argyll PA28 6PH. Telephone (01586) 553210. Fax (01586) 551852. SAE appreciated.

www.oas.co.uk/ukcottages/kilchrist/index.htm
email: william.t.c.angus@btinternet.com

Do detour to the south of Kintyre to see these most unusual, unspoilt properties.

White painted, the windows picked out in yellow, they date from the 17th century.

One of the most important things about the owners and agents featured in this guide is that they are 'nice people to deal with'...

147

Cumbria and the Lake District

Don't take it for granted that the cottage that has a waiting list in August is available in November or January: the Lake District is popular all year round. You have to 'get in quick'. Especially among those idyllic places that are perched above or right beside famous lakes such as Windermere, Coniston, Derwentwater and Ullswater. But we are fond of less well known lakes such as Thirlmere, Bassenthwaite, Grasmere and Esthwaite, and of holiday cottages on the fringe of the Lakes-proper, such as the sleepy Eden Valley, or around the southernmost point of the region. Even there, places of character get booked up in the apparently unlikely months outside the main season. This does not surprise us: there is something special about striking off into the empty hills on one of those windswept, bright and showery days of early spring when clouds scudding across the ever-changing sky are reflected in the waters of a lake, or walking through the grounds of one of the region's country houses when winter is closing in. As for Christmas, any group bigger than a couple will have to secure their holiday cottage many months in advance. At any time of year there's lots going on: sheep dog trials, hound trailing on foot, ice skating in winter, fell racing, steam trains to ride, ballooning to try. Shops and restaurants remain open. Note that there is an especially good number of cottage letting agencies among the Lakes, the best of which are feaured in this section. The competition among agencies tends to make for high standards, and going through an agency can save disappointment and time consuming research, especially at popular times, when individually run cottages have been snapped up by regulars.

Kirkland, near Penrith
Kirkland Hall Cottages   map 8/220

This clutch of award-winning cottages is superbly situated at the foot of the highest peak on the Pennines, in an Area of Outstanding Natural Beauty. There are large gardens, and details such as the sandstone dovecote add to the charm. The four cottages have hand-built farmhouse kitchens, and all have dishwashers. Woodburners back up the central heating, fuel included. *The Haybarn* (**sleeps 6/7**) has a huge sit-in fire-

Beck is a perennial favourite, and very cosy for just two people...

place, a conservatory, two bathrooms and a minstrels' gallery. *Beck Cottage* is single-storeyed, in its own grounds. **Sleeps 2**. *Stables Cottage* has an especially welcoming interior and a south facing patio. **Sleeps 4**. *Shearers Cottage* (**sleeps 4**) has its own private garden. One dog by arrangement in Shearers. ETC Four Stars. Cost: from £195 to £495; short breaks in low season. Details from Lesley and Ian Howes, Kirkland Hall, Kirkland, Penrith, Cumbria CA10 1RN. Telephone/fax(01768) 88295.
www.kirkland-hall-cottages.co.uk
email: kirklandhallcottages@hotmail.com

Bewcastle, near Brampton
Bank End Farm Cottages

We've stayed here, and really like
the cottages and their situation.
Readers seem to agree! Just before
passing almost imperceptibly via
country lanes over the border into
Scotland, deep in glorious, rolling
but comparatively little-known countryside that is quite perfect for walkers, we found a delightful duo of
properties. For half an hour, en route
for them, we did not see another car.
There is *Barn Cottage* and *Old Farm*

*Much liked properties in an attractive
and quiet location. (ETC Three Stars)*

Cottage (the latter has a coal fire), overlooking a pretty, flower-filled garden and a river where brown trout fishing is available free. **Sleeping 2
and 6** respectively, both cottages are comfortable and warm. For those
who want to take the self out of self-catering, a good range of home-
cooked food is available. Each has a microwave, a dishwasher and electric blankets.

Well behaved dogs are welcome. Central heating. TVs and video players.
Cost: about £150 to £360, including bedlinen and all fuel. Details avail-
able from Mr and Mrs Liddle, Bank End Farm, Roadhead, near Carlisle,
Cumbria CA6 6NU. Telephone/fax Roadhead (016977) 48644.

Bailey, near Newcastleton
Bailey Mill Cottage

map 8/222

In an attractive corner of Cumbria,
only just inside the English border,
we have featured these courtyard
apartments for many years. Visiting
the Copelands' handsome horses, riding (and learning to ride) is very
much a part of Bailey Mill, and full-
day stable management courses are
available 10am to 4pm (£18 per day

Lots going on in a friendly place.

inc), also full board riding holidays. We know all five courtyard cottages in
the converted 18th century grain mill in an arrangement of single and two-
storeyed buildings – one of them, *The Folly*, **sleeping up to 8**. A bargain
for larger groups. Most **sleep 2 to 6**. A ground floor apartment called *The
Store* houses the original archway, dated 1767. Mountain bike hire on site,
also jacuzzi, sauna, toning table, and a meal service to your cottage or
served in the fully licensed bar. Dogs welcome. Baby sitting. TVs with
Sky; microwaves. ETC Two and Three Stars. Cost: about £98 to £498.
Short breaks – out of season – from £98 per cottage for two nights. Further
details from Pamela Copeland, Bailey Mill, Newcastleton, Roxburghshire
TD9 0TR. Telephone Roadhead (016977) 48617. Fax 48074.

www.holidaycottagescumbria.co.uk email: pam@baileymill.fsnet.co.uk

149

Lake District & Eden Valley
Clark Scott-Harden Holiday Cottages*

During 20 years in our guide, this much respected agency has become known among readers for the absolute reliability of its properties. There are no duds, and we have never once, in all this time, had anything but praise from holiday tenants.

In the autumn of 2000 we visited three properties we had not seen before, a delightful journey that took us firstly into one of our favourite (and least known) parts of 'the Lakes', north of the A66 near Greystoke. This was to see a most lovingly cared for and absolutely charming cottage **just for 2**, attached to the owners' house. With panoramic views, *Blencathra Stable*, in Mungrisdale, is 'small but perfectly formed', with however a spacious and notably warm bathroom and a most inviting double bedroom. We thought it would make rather a romantic hideaway.

Then we drove to the village of Whale, south of Penrith, to see *Whale Farm Cottage*. This is a rhapsody of style and good taste (whose owner is a professional interior designer) that seems to combine rural charm with rather sophisticated five star hotel comfort and facilities. **Sleeps 4**.

We also recently visited *The Barn,* at Edenhall, near Penrith, a spacious place **sleeping 8**, plus cot. There are two doubles on the ground floor, and one twin; a further twin is on the first floor. *Hayloft*, just six miles from Ullswater, **sleeps 4 'plus 2'**, plus cot. In both properties the kitchen is on the first floor, along with a vast lounge. The twin and double bedrooms are on the ground floor.

Totally in keeping with the tiny village of Reagill, south of Penrith, is *Dunkirk*. Along with a deceptively large lounge, with woodburner and a polished wooden floor, each room has an individual pastel theme and retains many original features. **Sleeps 8**, plus cot – two doubles, a twin and one with sofa bed and desk. A barn conversion and extension with a stream bordering the garden, this is a real retreat from the hustle and bustle of daily life. Prices for these range from £215 to £630.

Details and a good brochure from Shirley Thompson, Clark Scott-Harden, 1 Little Dockray, Penrith, Cumbria CA11 7HL. Telephone Penrith (01768) 868989; fax (01768) 865578.

www.csh.co.uk

email: Shirley.Thompson@csh.co.uk

We thought Blencathra Stable was an absolute charmer – understated and cosy.

Dunkirk, at Reagill (between Shap and Appleby) is a splendid barn conversion...

Talkin, near Brampton
Long Byres

We have, since our very first edition in 1983, admired these cottages for their use of space and for their wildly beautiful location. Close to the Cumbrian border and on the edge of the enchanting Eden Valley, in an area of Outstanding Natural Beauty, they prove that there is life after Carlisle, as you go towards Hadrian's Wall, north east of the Lake District. Some who come to Cumbria (and still include the Lakes in their plans) would not stay anywhere else. As well as enjoying forays to such famous places as Windermere, Keswick and Ullswater, they tend to be people who appreciate this 'serenely wild' corner of the Cumbria-Northumberland border country.

We revisited one recent autumn, and found that the character of the seven former farm buildings still comes over. With lots of pine and modern furniture (interiors have undergone a thorough overhaul over the last five years) the cottages look over the farm towards the fell. Such practical

Modest prices and a quiet location, with easy access to the Lakes, the Roman Wall country and the Scottish border...

Even inveterate lounge lizards might be tempted to invest in a pair of walking boots, and explore the fells...

items as washing machines, driers, etc have not been overlooked. There is also a small shop with essential provisions, and a speciality of home-made jams, marmalades and chutneys. Better yet is a tempting daily menu of freshly cooked and inexpensive dishes prepared by Harriet Sykes. All the houses are double-glazed – the only sound may be that of a passing curlew! – and have central heating and fridges. The houses are, except for size (**sleeping from 2 to 5**), fairly standard. All enjoy splendid views, and some of the sitting-rooms are upstairs to take full advantage of this. A charming beck ripples along within 50 yards of the property. Talkin Tarn, as pretty as any of the Lakes-proper, is within walking distance; Talkin village, half a mile away, offers the choice of two excellent pubs. Brampton, three miles away, is the nearest town. It has a railway station, and the Sykes will meet people.

Dogs are welcome, and children will enjoy the pets' corner. Cost: about £98 to £303, including electricity, hot water, heating, linen and towels. Excellent colour brochure available from Harriet Sykes at Long Byres, Talkin Head, near Brampton, Cumbria CA8 1LT. Telephone (016977) 3435. Fax (016977) 2228.

www. talkinhead.demon.co.uk
email: harriet@talkinhead.demon.co.uk

Windermere
The Heaning

One of our favourite views in the Lake District happens to be on the lane that one takes off the main Windermere to Kendal road (the A591) towards a collection of cottages that have featured in this guide for fifteen years. It is a secret valley, a rhapsody of green, with hills and a vast sky, completely belying its proximity to busy Windermere, an important Lakeland focal point. (A five minute taxi ride from Windermere railway station, The Heaning could well be a place to holiday without a car.)

As well as being so well situated, the place has an interesting history, having once been a stud for first class carriage horses. In 2000 we called again in our horseless carriage to meet the welcoming new owners, looking first at *Stable Cottages*, a terrace of four cottages converted from 16th and 17th century buildings, their exteriors partly unchanged: a remarkable historical survival. They are neat and cosy, and on an autumn day were warm. We admired the skilful use of space and noted much upgrading, with stylish new electric heaters (plus oil-fired central heating), deep sofas, new carpets. They are '**just for 2**', with a spacious first floor bedroom (one has twins, three have a double). Each has a shower room. Glazed doors open on to a shared garden area at the front, exclusively for Stable Cottages' guests' use.

Across a landscaped water-garden, with flowers and shrubs, we looked again at *Heaning Barn Cottages*, also in a row of four. They are a fairly recent conversion of a 19th century barn. The end two each have three storeys, the middle two have two; the larger cottages **sleep 6**, the smaller ones **sleep 4**, but all are spacious, with sitting rooms at first floor level. On the lower floor there are two bedrooms with double or twin beds, and a large bathroom (full bath). The two larger cottages have an attic bedroom with handsome four poster beds and en suite shower rooms, and impressive rural views. Here too there is an effective programme of

Close to Windermere, but utterly peaceful – and full of history too...

The Heaning Barn properties, a recent conversion, are notably spacious...

upgrading, also with new heaters to enhance the storage radiators.

Dogs by arrangement in some properties. Linen included, towels available; some have dishwashers. TVs/videos, plus radio cassettes or stereos. Cost: £200 to £480. Details from Mr and Mrs Moulding, The Heaning, Windermere, Cumbria LA23 1JW. Telephone/fax (015394) 43453.

www.theheaning.co.uk

email: info@theheaning.co.uk

Kirkoswald, near Penrith
Howscales

We are big fans of Cumbria's Eden Valley (quiet sandstone villages, an easy drive to the popular Lakes, the meandering River Eden, access to Hadrian's Wall and the Pennines), and these five most lovingly cared for cottages grouped appealingly round a cobbled courtyard make for a very good touring base. We've

Very comfortable, very well situated...

stayed here ourselves, in one of the three two-storeyed cottages that have their open plan sitting room/dining-room and kitchen areas on the first floor to make the most of the splendid views. The other two are single-storeyed, one of them (*Hazelrigg*) a former milking parlour that is suitable for wheelchair-bound guests. This **sleeps 2** in one of our favourite cottage features – a zip-link double. The gardens are charming, and there are well-planned sitting-out areas. TVs. No smoking. Dogs possible by arrangement. ETC Four Stars. Linen and towels included. Cost: about £155 to £420. Details from Liz Webster, Kirkoswald, Penrith, Cumbria CA10 1JG. Telephone (01768) 898666. Fax 898710.

www. eden-in-cumbria.co.uk/howscales
email: liz@howscales.fsbusiness.co.uk

Crosby Garrett, near Kirkby Stephen
Mossgill Loft

Crosby Garrett (**map 8/233**) is a most appealing conservation village in the Upper Eden Valley, distinguished by a viaduct on the Settle to Carlisle railway: a car-free holiday is possible. The Victorian schoolroom has been cosily converted into a holiday property: a large living/kitchen area, a most welcoming double bedroom and bathroom. There are lattice windows, original beams, an open fire,

New for 2002 is an adjoining converted chapel sleeping 4. It can be joined with Mosgill Loft to sleep 6.

rugs on wooden floors. Stone steps lead up to the entrance; there is a sitting out area and off-road parking. Walkers should note: this is only two miles from the Coast to Coast Walk and the Pennine Way. The Yorkshire Dales National Park is eight miles, the Lake District 45 minutes. Use of the owners' tennis court on request. We heard from readers about 'a warm welcome, lovely fell walking, fresh flowers, peace and quiet'. Cost: a modest £155 to £210. Short breaks, low season, £40 per night. Electricity. fuel, linen and towels included. TV. One dog possible by arrangement. Details from Mrs Clare Hallam, Mossgill House, Crosby Garrett, Kirkby Stephen, Cumbria CA17 4PW. Telephone (017683) 71149.

email: clarehallam@yahoo.com

Ambleside and Central Lakeland
Cottage Life and Heart of the Lakes*

This miraculously unspoilt corner of Britain is well served by cottage letting agencies, and this is one of the very best. Featured in this guide for seventeen years, it has some real gems on its books. Sadly, we only have room to mention a handful.

Most of the 'Cottage Life/Heart of the Lakes' cottages are open all year round: winter has a big following, when people tend to ask for open fires – about half the agency's properties have them.

During a recent tour of inspection we much admired *Huntingstile South*, one of the finest properties we have seen. (Wordsworth is said to have visited the house for social occasions.) Among much else, we admired a huge drawing room, high ceilings, deep sofas and deep pile carpeting. A little palace, in fact! **Sleeps 8**.

Just a short stroll from Grasmere village (and thus well placed for one to

'Huntingstile South is one of the finest properties we have seen.'

Goody Bridge is neat, single storeyed, cosy and ideal for 2.

enjoy this much-loved village when the day tourists have gone), *Goody Bridge Cottage*, a very neat, rather cosy single storeyed cottage, **sleeps just 2** in a double. It has its own garden – rare around here for a small cottage – and a coal effect gas fire. A few yards away, adjacent to the owners' house, two-storeyed *Goody Bridge Barn* is a delight, a very sympathetic conversion of a 300 year old building, with fine country views from the rear. **Sleeps 4**, in a five foot double and a twin.

In Ambleside – always an option for people holidaying without a car – we visited two very sought-after, characterful cottages. One, *Baddeley Cottage*, is actually owned by a retired antique dealer, so you can imagine the knick knacks and the fine furniture. **Sleeps 2**. Just round the corner, 17th century *Bakestones Cottage,* **sleeping just 4**, is also a gem.

The Bield (Little Langdale) is thought to date from 1610, and we would say it is *one of the top dozen houses we have seen on our travels*. With its big family kitchen, stone flags on the floor, comfortable living room with open range fire, and oak panelling retained with sculptural and painted detail, it is an exceptional place. **Sleeps 10**.

The properties range from ETC Two to Five Stars, and all include free leisure club membership. Details from 'Heart of the Lakes'/'Cottage Life', Fisherbeck Mill, Old Lake Road, Ambleside, Cumbria LA22 0DH. Telephone (015394) 32321. Fax (015394) 33251.
www.heartofthelakes.co.uk email: info@heartofthelakes.co.uk

Chapel Stile, near Ambleside
Oakdene

This is very special indeed. At a very central point within the National Park, in the heart of the Langdale Valley, this superbly situated, large and modern house contains two extremely well equipped units which **sleep 6 and 8** respectively. For example, you'll find waste disposal, full size microwave-circulaire oven, halogen hob, to name but a few. We

Many years in this guide: spotlessly clean, 'ship-shape', and superbly situated.

liked the first floor living room of the three bedroomed unit, with its 'ergonomic' layout of the kitchen (oak fitted), dining and lounge areas. The spacious ground floor living room of the four-bedroomed house is 'U' shaped, round a fireplace made of local greenstone. There are charming views, big screen TVs with teletext and video recorder, drying cabinet, large garden. Payphone. Full oil-fired central heating included. Electricity by meter reading. No pets. Cost: the three bedroomed house from £300 to £690, the four bedroomed from £360 to £890. Out of season breaks from £145 or £165 (two nights).

Further details available from Mrs P Locke, Frank Locke Ltd, 17 Shay Lane, Hale Barns, Altrincham, Cheshire WA15 8NZ. Telephone Altrincham 0161-904 9445.

Borrowdale, near Keswick   map 8/244
Rockery Cottage and Maiden Moor Cottage

Amazingly well situated, these cottages are in the heart of the north Lakeland walking country, with fine mountain views and a panoply of well-known fells all around; yet the 'bright lights' of Keswick are only about three miles away. These attractive modern cottages are warm and inviting, with glowing visitor book entries, such as 'a truly comfortable home-from-home in all weathers'.

Absolutely at 'the heart of the Lakes'...

They stand in the well kept private grounds of the Greenbank Countryhouse Hotel, where dinners can be enjoyed. The hotel and cottages are a quarter of a mile off the main road, approached from a private driveway: a quiet location. The cottages can **sleep 3/4** in two bedrooms, and among other good things have well-fitted kitchens.

TV. Linen, towels, electricity and heating (panel/storage heating) are all included. Dogs are possible by arrangement. Cost: around £200 to £450, and are especially good value for an autumn break. Further details from Mrs Jean Wood, Greenbank Countryhouse Hotel, Borrowdale, Keswick, Cumbria CA12 5UY. Telephone (017687) 77215.

Loweswater, near Cockermouth
Loweswater Holiday Cottages

Twenty years in this guide, and never a complaint. These most appealing properties have attracted nothing but whole-hearted praise from our readers. Michael Thompson once owned and ran one of the best known hotels in the region, but some years ago this was transformed into quite irresistible self catering cottages. (With echoes of their original incarnation as part of the hotel, all are serviced daily, which is a great rarity in self catering terms.)

All the cottages are very comfortable, attractively lit, and altogether welcoming. Each one has memorable views from the windows which, considering the location, is a huge bonus.

We especially recall *Hannah's*, with its open fire, a big kitchen/diner (we even spotted a fondue set in the kitchen!), three double bedrooms and some antique furniture, including a four-poster bed.

At the far end of the building, *Sheila's* is more open plan, with a triple aspect sitting room and French windows on to a private garden. When we last called, a cheerful fire was burning in the grate. These two properties **sleep 6 and 4** respectively, and all the bedrooms have private bathrooms.

Opposite the former hotel is the converted Coach House, which contains four cottages. Low key in decor, and tasteful, they are kept up to a high standard of decoration with good quality wallpaper and carpets common to all. They are *Lanthwaite, Shell, Brackenthwaite* and *Howe*. A detailed and very well produced colour brochure provides a good impression of all the properties.

ETC ratings are Four to Five Stars. Winter breaks are available. Dogs are welcome. There are televisions and central heating throughout. Cots, highchairs and all heating, lighting and linen are included in the rates. Cost: approximately £140 to £725 per cottage per week, depending – as always – on which cottage you choose and when you go.

Scale Hill (arrowed): how is this for a cottage location? It is quite outstanding even compared with other parts of the Lake District, and our readers have come to love it. Michael Thompson is a particularly kind and welcoming host...

For further details and a quite exceptional loose leaf brochure contact Michael Thompson, Scale Hill, Loweswater, near Cockermouth, Cumbria CA13 9UX. Telephone/fax Lorton (01900) 85232.

www.loweswaterholidaycottages.co.uk

Borrowdale, Keswick and around
Lakeland Cottage Holidays*

New owners have recently taken over this very long established agency of 50 or so properties within an eight mile radius of Keswick, and look set to keep to a tradition of matching our readers with suitable properties.

The majority of properties are managed (bookings, cleaning, spring cleaning and maintenance) by the agency, and those that aren't have owners close by to maintain standards. Historically, Lakeland Cottage Holidays refuse far more properties than they take on.

The brochure is full of practical advice and understated cottage descriptions – the superlatives are saved for the landscape! If you want more illustrations than the watercolour drawings in the brochure, see their website (details below).

During an autumn 2000 visit to the Lakes we picked out a good handful of properties that we had not seen before: big houses with fine views, stone cottages, white-walled cottages, farmhouses and town-house terraces. Serious walkers would love *Townhead Barn,* **sleeping 6/8**. With a casserole in the Rayburn while one walked the surrounding fells – bliss!

A real lakeland classic in the quiet village of Rosthwaite...   *The agency reports a strong following for modern houses in popular locations. This is near Keswick...*

Situated in the quiet village of Threlkeld, it is off the beaten tourist track yet, amazingly, less than five miles from Keswick.

In the tiny hamlet of Seatoller, in the Borrowdale Valley, (most of the surrounding countryside is National Trust owned) is a former quarryman's cottage called *Bell Crags*, where we really liked the open fire in the sitting room and the patio by the stream plunging down from Honister Pass, with views across to the magnificent old High Stile oakwood. **Sleeps 4/5**.

The agency has several properties in Keswick, and we were impressed by *Underne*, a very comfortable, surprisingly spacious terraced cottage in a peaceful corner of Keswick. **Sleeps 4/5**.

Further details and a copy of an informative brochure are available from Lakeland Cottage Holidays, Keswick, Cumbria CA12 5ES. Telephone Keswick (017687) 71071. Fax 75036.

www.lakelandcottages.co.uk info@lakelandcottages.co.uk

Windermere, Ambleside and beyond
Lakelovers*

This is one of the four or five best regional cottage letting agencies we know. The staff all know 'every stick and stone' of the Lake District, and have on their books some of the most characterful properties in this much-loved part of England. It is run as a very tight ship, in many cases on a full property management basis, with correspondingly high standards and big advantages to holiday tenants.

We stayed recently in *Rigges Wood*, virtually on the shores of Esthwaite Water, with partial views of that, and just two minutes' drive from the fascinating and historic village of Hawkshead. It is a warm and very comfortable family house, **sleeping 6** in a double and two twins, with a most efficient coal-effect gas fire, a pleasant family dining room, lots of irresistible books and a good-sized back garden in which children can let off steam. (They should also be able to spot red squirrels.)

On the shores of Lake Windermere, *Beech Howe,* **sleeping 6**, is very sought after. On a steep bank, separated from Windermere only by lush

Waingap is private, quiet and very stylish indeed: a memorable cottage for seven...

Swallows Cottage (not featured) offers a rare chance to be based at Grasmere.

tree filled gardens, with no less than 200 yards of private lake frontage, there are views of England's biggest lake from virtually every window. The smallish sitting room is especially charming and cosy and this, at one end of this extremely comfortable, carefully colour co-ordinated cottage has a double aspect, so it is always light, bright and inviting.

About ten minutes' drive to the east, in the direction of Kendal, but well away from the main road up a long, narrow lane, *Waingap* **sleeps 7**. Extremely private, this is really stylish and exceptionally comfortable. Blissfully quiet, with a huge open fire in the fabulous sitting room, deep sofas, exceptional pictures and prints and loads of readable books, this is an outstanding place to stay, with wide-ranging rural views.

Among so many outstanding properties we like (and have stayed in) *Curdle Dub*, at Coniston, a listed building in a pretty row within walking distance of the village and the lake. There is an open fire. **Sleeps 4**.

For a copy of an outstandingly well written and seductive brochure, which exudes a pride in the area and dedication to the cottage business, contact Lakelovers, Belmont House, Lake Road, Bowness-on-Windermere LA23 3BJ. Telephone (015394) 88855. Fax 88857. Brochures: 88858.

www.Lakelovers.co.uk email: bookings@Lakelovers.co.uk

Applethwaite, near Keswick
Croftside/Croft Corner at Croft House Holidays

These have stunning views: the panorama of the north-western fells to the south, Skiddaw to the north. The location is rural but not remote: just over a mile fom Keswick and its facilities. We know the location well. Three properties (one occupied by the owners) are dovetailed within a handsome Victorian country house. *Croftside* is a substantial part of the main house, **sleeping 5**, while *Croft*

A superb setting even in Cumbrian terms.

Corner is a ground floor apartment **sleeping 2 to 3**. There are restful gardens and a separate children's play area. Previous visitors are full of praise. Said one: 'Apart from the well planned rooms, we appreciate such details as the tea tray, with shortbread, awaiting our arrival.' Said another: 'It is such a peaceful spot, with Skiddaw behind, and the owners are so kind and welcoming.' ETC Four Stars. TVs/videos. 'Sorry, no pets'. Linen, towels, cancellation insurance, cot/high-chair included. Short breaks. Cost: about £260 to £495 (Croftside), about £190 to £340 (Croft Corner). Details from Mrs J L Boniface, Croft House, Applethwaite, Keswick, Cumbria CA12 4PN. Telephone (017687) 73693.

www: crofthouselakes.co.uk email: holidays@crofthouselakes.co.uk

Grasmere map 8/253
Hollens Farm Cottage

Within a short walk of Grasmere village, Hollens Farm Cottage is a holiday home of character that should appeal greatly to our readers. Restored by local owners Andy and Chrissy Hill, it dates from the 1800s, when it was the dairyman's cottage,

ETC Four Stars, pets by arrangement...

the farm supplying milk to Grasmere. It offers warmth and comfort, with exposed beams, stripped pine and flag floors. A natural-gas Rayburn cooker, central heating and an open fire combine to warm this cosy place! Upstairs, there are two pretty bedrooms with good views, brass and iron bedsteads, deep set windows and fitted carpets. Outside, there is a quiet courtyard with a picnic table and walks from the door to Silver How, Loughrigg and the Fairfield Horseshoe, with Wordsworth's Dove Cottage a stroll away. The cottage is well equipped, with microwave, dishwasher, washer/dryer, fridge, TV and payphone. There is ample parking. **Sleeps 4**. Non-smokers preferred. Linen and towels are provided. Cost: about £310 to £495. Details: Andy and Chrissy Hill, Esthwaite Old Hall, Hawkshead, Ambleside, Cumbria LA22 0QF. Telephone (015394) 36088 or 35188.

www.grasmereholidaycottage.co.uk
The owners' restaurant: www.thejumbleroom.co.uk

Skelwith Bridge, near Ambleside
Riverside and Garden Cottages

Overlooking the bubbling River Brathay, quite near the Ambleside to Coniston road, in the heart of 'the Lakes', these exceptional cottages are ETC Four Stars. *Riverside* has a sitting/dining room with exposed beams and inglenook fireplace with open fire, kitchen and separate pantry. We noticed a rocking chair, old china and books. The main bed-room has a canopied four poster and, with two twin-bedded rooms the cot-

Garden Cottage (on the right) is a little gem, fitting perfectly into its setting.

tage **sleeps 6** (plus cot and high chair); Victorian style bathroom. Non-smokers preferred. *Garden Cottage* has a bedroom with draped double bed, bathroom and kitchen with dining area, sitting room. Electric fire. **Sleeps 2**. Non-smokers only. In neither cottage are pets welcome. TV. Payphone. Barbecue. Well equipped kitchen: dishwasher, automatic washing machine and tumble dryers, microwave etc. Night storage heaters. Details: Mr and Mrs Vyner-Brooks, Middle Barrows Green, Kendal, Cumbria LA8 0JG, or 9c Altway, Old Roan, Liverpool L10 3JA. Telephone (015395) 60242 or 0151-526 9321/5451. Fax 0151-526 1331.
www.primecottages.co.uk

Clappersgate, near Ambleside   map 8/256
The Old Coach House

Dating from about 1704, this cottage has been imaginatively and artisti-cally refurbished to a high standard without losing its 'bijou' charm. There is a skilful use of the available space (a good sized bathroom, for example). The property nestles at the foot of Loughrigg, one of the most picturesque fells. Guests enjoy fell and lake views and the shared, secluded riverside garden, with moor-

A sumptuous interior. The road beyond the house is not really obtrusive. This is English Tourism Council Four Stars.

ing and fishing rights and river access to Windermere. The sitting/dining room features a pine and marble chimney piece and a dresser and corner cupboard, handmade in antique pine. The small but well equipped kitchen has a microwave and dishwasher, and the bathroom bath *and* shower. A four poster bed graces the double bedroom. Dogs not welcome. Non-smokers preferred. **Sleeps up to 4 (or 3 plus cot)**. TV. Barbecue. Payphone. Details: Mr and Mrs Vyner-Brooks, Middle Barrows Green, Kendal, Cumbria LA8 0JG, or 9c Altway, Old Roan, Liverpool L10 3JA. Telephone (015395) 60242 or 0151-526 9321/5451. Fax 0151-526 1331.
www.primecottages.co.uk

Elterwater, near Ambleside
Wheelwrights

Featured in this guide for eleven years, Wheelwrights has introduced hundreds of our readers to the delights of the Lake District.

Said one of them, from Norfolk: 'We are "Wheelwrights people". We have stayed in several of their cottages, and never been disappointed.'

All the properties are located in the heart of South Lakeland, amid some of the most magnificent mountain scenery in England, mostly in the villages of Elterwater, Chapel Stile, Skelwith Bridge, Grasmere, Outgate (as well as the surrounding areas). All these are ideal bases for exploring this extraordinary, marvellously unspoilt part of the country.

Places to see include the village of Elterwater itself, where Wheelwrights is based (there's a pub of character on the village green). As well as the winding main road, there is a narrow, helter-skelter 'back road' from here to Grasmere, and – one of our favourite routes in the whole of the lakes – a memorable stretch from Elterwater via Chapel Stile to Little Langdale.

Most of the farms around here are rented from The National Trust, so hardly a blade of grass or a boulder is out of place. Do note especially that this part of 'the Lakes' is less busy in the autumn, winter and spring, when the high proportion of Wheelwrights properties with open fires or woodburners really come into their own.

Grasmere is a tourist honeypot, and Grasmere lake is one of the most accessible of all in the area. There are some very good restaurants and traditional tea-shops in the village itself.

Cost: about £245 to £1400. Well behaved dogs are welcome in most properties. All have English Tourism Council gradings, from Two to Four Stars. Discounted leisure facilities are available at the smart Langdale Country Club, close to Elterwater.

Details and a well written, loose-leaf style brochure are available from Wheelwrights, Elterwater, near Ambleside, Cumbria LA22 9HS. Or phone and speak to Anne, Ian, Emma, Heather or Ben on (015394) 37635/37571. Fax (015394) 37618.

www.wheelwrights.com
email: enquiries@wheelwrights.com

Buttermere, within an easy and scenic drive of all the Wheelwrights properties, is probably our own favourite lake.

Elterwater in winter. This is the time the many Wheelwrights properties that have woodburners or open fires really score.

161

Bassenthwaite
Bassenthwaite Lakeside Lodges

These properties give holidaymakers a rare chance to get close to the shores of Bassenthwaite Lake, one of the least known of all the Lakes. They are 'eco-friendly' too: the properties have recently undergone a change in colour to make them blend in even better with the heavily wooded shores that make Bassenthwaite Lakeside Lodges, tucked away down a leafy lane, so attractive. It is a gregarious mini-community made up of about 60 log cabins/lodges, fifteen of them for holiday let, among mature trees and built to exceptionally high standards. Even during an early Sunday morning recent visit, the place was humming.

While obviously not for those who want to be lonely as a cloud, this remains the sort of location where visiting children – and adults – will enjoy making new friends, though they can be private too. We noted, once again, the care taken in choosing top-notch kitchen and bathroom ranges, likewise comfy sofas more usually associated with up-market traditional holiday houses. This is graphically illustrated with *Thornthwaite*, where, as the newest of the Lakeview Lodges (**sleeping 6** in either two or three bedrooms), great care has been taken to provide contemporary touches. This was the latest we have seen of five that are of holiday cottage proportions. Previously we have seen a *Woodland Lodge*, **sleeps 6**, and a *Parkland Lodge* and *Lakeland Lodge*, both **sleeping 4 to 6**, also a *Lakeside Lodge*, **sleeps 6**. Visitors have by the way always singled out the quality of the reception staff.

Right by the shore of one of Cumbria's least known but pleasantest lakes.

Interiors are sumptuous, and we were not surprised by all the repeat bookings.

As well as generous balconies with gas barbecues and outdoor furniture, the lodges have picture windows, TVs and videos. There is a free video, books and games library. Nearby you can hire mountain bikes, play tennis and golf, and go horse-riding. Keswick is just ten minutes' drive.

Dogs are permitted only in the category of the smaller Parkland, Lakeview and Woodland Lodges. Linen and towels are, as you would expect here, included. Cost: about £295 to £810, depending on which property and when. Short breaks are available. Details available from Bassenthwaite Lakeside Lodges, Scarness, Bassenthwaite, near Keswick, Cumbria CA12 4QZ. Telephone (017687) 76641. Fax 76919.

www.bll.ac
email: enquiries@bll.ac

Ireby, near Bassenthwaite
Daleside Farm Cottages

The light was fading over the fells as we arrived to see these three comfortable, warm, clean-as-a-whistle cottages. With great attention to detail (for example, owner Isabel Teasdale had just lit the woodburning stove in *Rose Cottage*, **sleeping 2 'plus 1'**, for visitors who were due at any minute – but note that all three have woodburners) each, in its

These are very special indeed – real gems that are a tribute to the owners...

way, is a little palace. We liked the deep sofas, the expensive china, the good carpets, the pretty, feminine, rather chintzy style and envied the couple in *Primrose*, regular visitors, relaxing over tea and cakes in the plush sitting room. This **sleeps 4** in a twin and a double (four poster). On a 500-acre working farm in an Area of Outstanding Natural Beauty, the cottages are quiet, and *Rambling Rose,* **sleeping 4,** has panoramic views from its first floor living room/balcony. But actually they all have good views. Not surprisingly, the cottages have received awards, including Keswick in Bloom, A Certificate of Merit from the Keswick Tourism Association. Not suitable for dogs. Linen and towels included. Cost: about £230 to £440. Details from Mr and Mrs Teasdale, Daleside Farm, Ireby, Carlisle, Cumbria CA7 1EW. Telephone (016973) 71268.

Welton, near Carlisle
Well Cottage and Green View Lodges   map 8/262

These are among the best properties of their kind that we know. People love to sit on the balconies of the three Scandinavian chalets (triple glazing, electric central heating, lots of comfort, cosy bedrooms, surprisingly big sitting rooms, views of the Caldbeck Fells). One **sleeps 4**, two **sleep 6**. Under the same friendly and welcoming ownership are *Well Cottage, Well House* and *Chapel Cottage*, genuinely 'cottagey' alter-

These are among the best Scandinavian chalets we have ever come across...

natives to the chalets. The first is roomy and sunny and the second, among other good things, has a wood burner. The last has an impressive pine staircase and a 'hideaway' double bedroom. Several famous lakes are just a short drive away. The cottages **sleep 6/7, 4** and **2** respectively. Cost: from about £159 low season up to £488 for 6. ETC Four Stars. Dogs possible by arrangement in three. Linen and towels included. Radios and TVs. Details from Anne Ivinson, Green View, Welton, near Dalston, Cumbria. Telephone (016974) 76230, fax 76523.

www.green-view-lodges.com email: ghcg@green-view-lodges.com

Buttermere
Bowderbeck

This is an idyllic, classic, picture-book Lake District cottage, and we weren't surprised that it has doubled up as Wordsworth's 'Dove Cottage' in a recent film about 'the Lakeland poets'. Though there is a timber extension at the end of the white-washed-stone 17th century cottage of

Lake District cottages don't come much more authentic or well located than this.

a kind Wordsworth would not have known, he'd have appreciated its view of Buttermere, which for many visitors is the most romantic and beautiful of all. The cottage interior is a blend of modern comforts and original character with, for example, cushioned cane furniture, rugs on slate floors and an attractive (and original) stone staircase up to a roomy first floor, where there is a spacious main bedroom, a roomy twin, a single, a separate wc, shower and bathroom, plus WC. The lake shore is only half a mile away, and children will love the little beck that runs alongside the cottage. But this makes Bowderbeck unsuitable for children under five. **Sleeps 7 'plus 1'**. Not suitable for pets. No smoking. Payphone. Linen supplied, not towels. Cost: about £290 to £425. No TV reception. Details from Michael and Anne Bell, New House, Colby, Appleby-in-Westmorland, Cumbria CA16 6BD. Telephone (017683) 53548.
email: k.bell@twentyfirst.co.uk

Great Broughton, near Cockermouth
The Manse   map 8/266

Only about five minutes' drive from Cockermouth (Wordsworth's birth-place there is open to the public), and with Bassenthwaite, Buttermere, Loweswater and Crummock Water easily accessible, Great Broughton is a village of real character: a 'proper' community and not a self conscious tourist honeypot. (Being only a short distance from the Solway coast is another bonus.) At the heart of the

On the western side of the Lake District, a very comfortable holiday base...

village, which has several shops and a good pub, The Manse is a fine partly Georgian house, the middle part of a former vicarage that is the owners' second home – always a reliable indicator of good standards and facilities – and available for holiday letting. It is thoughtfully lit, with deep sofa/armchairs, expensive fabrics, exposed beams, some modern pine furniture. We liked the pictures, all of them watercolours or antique engravings of the Lake District. There is a small garden at the front. **Sleeps 4** in a double and a twin bedroom. Not suitable for dogs. No smoking. Guests to provide own linen and towels. Cost: about £225 to £290. Further details from Mr and Mrs Taylor, Wedgwood, 12 Heathfield Drive, Redhill, Surrey RH1 5HH. Telephone (01737) 780191.

Burton-in-Kendal, near Kendal   map 8/268
4 Green Cross Cottages

Full of character and comfort, this cottage dates from 1637, has lots of old beams and is an ideal base for the Lakes, South Cumbria and the Yorkshire Dales. One can also enjoy local walks on fells, across limestone pavements, and by the canal. In a short, pleasant terrace of cottages, with the rear on the main street, it has a charming living room with an attractive dining alcove and lime-

A lovingly cared-for cottage, well situated for visiting the Yorkshire Dales and the whole of Cumbria...

stone fireplace. We admired the 'cottagey' interior with its matching fabrics, the well equipped kitchen. There is a wide, easy staircase to the first floor, two bedrooms and a good bathroom with large airing cupboard. Parking for one car, small courtyard garden with furniture; payphone, TV. The village is a busy, charming mix, with Georgian and Queen Anne houses, two shops, and pubs with restaurants.

Sleeps 4. Cost: £150 to £270, including gas central heating. Short breaks from £90. No smoking, pets possible by arrangement. Linen included. Maps, videos, books and games. We'd expect ETC Four Stars. Contact Mrs Frances Roberts, 32 Sevenoaks Avenue, Heaton Moor, Stockport, Cheshire SK4 4AW. Telephone (0161) 432 3408.

Watermillock, near Ullswater
Land Ends   map 8/270

Just a mile from Lake Ullswater, these four log cabins are in 25 peaceful acres of gardens and natural woodland, with streams and exceptional birdlife, on the slopes of Little Mell Fell. Opposite the cabins is "guests' own" lake, with ducks and moorhens and areas of mown grass with seating for walking or relaxing. (Look out for red squirrels in the trees behind the cabins, tawny owls

At the end of a busy day's travelling we'd have liked to stay here ourselves...

and woodpeckers.) Dogs are 'very welcome', and can have plenty of exercise on the doorstep, with no main road to worry about. There is a second lake further down the grounds, and an 18-acre field for strolling in. One is surrounded by dramatic scenery, many attractions and superb hillwalking. The nearest village is Pooley Bridge (three miles away), but there is a pub serving good food just a mile down the road.

Sleep 2 to 5. TVs. ETC Three Stars. Linen included, but not towels. Cost: about £210 to £415. Open all year. Details/brochures from Land Ends, Watermillock, Cumbria CA11 0NB. Telephone (017684) 86438.

www.landends@btinternet.com   email: infolandends@btinternet.com

165

Sebergham, near Caldbeck
Monkhouse Hill Cottages

Nineteen years in this guide, the Monkhouse Hill cottages are a jewel of the more northerly part of the Lake District. They are, as we confirmed on a recent revisit during a golden late afternoon in autumn, very well located: Keswick for example (via lovely Mungrisdale), Bassenthwaite Lake, Cockermouth, the coast, the Eden Valley and the Northumberland border are all within a comfortable and, incidentally, very pleasant drive. Set back from a not especially busy B-road, they are easy to find but also completely rural.

Regular upgrading over the years has made these into some of the best properties in the whole of Cumbria. They form a most attractive, exceptionally neat, clean and tidy enclave round a former farmyard, with impressive panoramic views, and they are run with understandable pride and great professionalism by the resident owners, who have three young children and are therefore tuned in to the needs of families on holiday.

We were keen to see the latest addition, which is *Great Calva*. Most usefully **sleeping 12 'plus 2'** in seven bedrooms, it has the always-desirable feature of an upstairs sitting room, a sauna and spa, and an ETC grading of Five Stars. We met an extended family staying, coming to the end of their holiday and not wanting to leave.

Also new on the scene, also with Five Stars, is *Cloven Stone*, designed for two couples. This too has an upstairs sitting room, which we loved, to make the most of the views, and two downstairs doubles – one of which can be reorganised as a twin. There are seven other cottages, each with its own particular endearing features. There are two **sleeping 2**, three **sleeping 4**, one **sleeping 6**, and one **sleeping 8**. Most will take at least one cot.

Cottages of a very high standard indeed, professionally and painstakingly run, in a very good touring area...

We visited again in 2000, and met a number of holidaymakers revelling in the warm and very comfy accommodation...

Cost: about £230 to £1555 (including electricity, linen and towels). Home cooked meals; welcome tea-tray, with home-made cakes. Dogs welcome in every cottage except *Fisher Gill*, which is for 2 and geared especially to honeymooners. Free use of hotel leisure club with indoor pool. TV/video, CD/radio. Laundry room. Games room, children's playground.

Colour brochure from Jennifer Collard, Monkhouse Hill, Sebergham, near Caldbeck CA5 7HW. Telephone/fax (016974) 76254.

www.monkhousehill.co.uk   email: cottages@monkhousehill.co.uk

Cartmel
Longlands at Cartmel

Lat autumn we met the enthusiastic new owner of Longlands. (Could it really be twenty years since we visited these cottages for the very first edition of this guide?) In the lee of a fine Georgian mansion, the nine cottages are grouped on two and a half sides of a grassy court, on the edge of substantial grounds that contain a rare walled garden that's being restored to a productive fruit and vegetable garden and which is worth a visit in itself. Beyond that, pastureland leads to a line of low hills that invite exploration.

Only a mile north of Cartmel, in the southern Lake District, Longlands is just a short drive from one of our favourite parts of 'the Lakes': the western side of Lake Windermere and, not far beyond that, Esthwaite Water and Hawkshead.

We admired work in progress on the walled garden, on several of the cottages that, while certainly full of individual character and comfort, are being substantially upgraded with, for example, revamped kitchens, antique furniture and gas coal-effect stoves where practicable.

Although the cottages stand 'cheek by jowl' you still have a high degree of privacy and independence. All the furnishings and decor are of a very good quality, and bedding and furniture are of a high standard; there is double glazing, good quality carpets and a real sense of style and good taste...

We looked particularly at *The Old Nursery*, **sleeping 6**, which, like most of the cottages, has an open fire and a dishwasher. It was very warm, spacious and quiet. We also liked *The Laundrymaid's Cottage*, **sleeping just 2**, quiet and cosy and with good views, and *Groom's Quarters*, also **sleeping 2**. This has both a king sized bed and a zip-link option, which we much approve of, that can make for a six foot wide bed.

The cost (for most units) is in the region of £190 to £820 (including linen and towels) depending on season, and from November to March weekend and mid-week breaks are available. Dogs by arrangement. Also, visitors may use the excellent pool and leisure facilities nearby. English Tourism Council Four Stars. Details from Martin Ainscough, Longlands at Cartmel, Cartmel, Cumbria LA11 6HG. Telephone (015395) 36475. Fax (015395) 36172.

www.cartmel.com

email:longlands@cartmel.com

Patton, near Kendal
Field End Barns/Shaw End Mansion

While visiting properties on the Kendal side of Cumbria we stayed here briefly in the spring of 2000, delightedly dropping down from a little used country road to the farmstead and its nest of barn conversions: as private as you want them to be, but fairly neighbourly too. (On our travels we had met a group of young professionals from the neighbouring county of North Yorkshire who had taken over the biggest property here for a week-end at a very advantageous price indeed, and had a great time.)

Just three miles north of Kendal, in this secluded, quiet rural setting, *Field End* has the River Mint running nearby. There are good views of the Howgill Fells, and some very popular lakes, including Grasmere and Windermere, are only about half an hour's drive. The five fine barn conversions are well away from any traffic noise and offer spacious accommodation for **between 2 and 10**. They enjoy full oil-fired central heating *plus* open fires in local-stone hearths, spacious kitchen/dining rooms and sitting rooms. We were not surprised to hear that they have a Country Landowners' Association Farm Building Award Commendation.

Award-winning barn conversions in a peaceful, rural but not remote location.

Shaw End Mansion: a degree of grandeur, with great views from each apartment.

Up on the hill, only about half a mile away, we also visited (for the first time) a most impressive, major restoration of a Georgian mansion called *Shaw End*, with its original facade intact. So it has a lot of history but the advantages of being what is effectively a new building.

There are four high ceilinged apartments, all accessed via the impressive main entrance, two on the ground floor, two – reached via a fine, sweeping pine staircase – on the first floor, all with superb interiors, including large sitting rooms with open fires, and exquisite views of the River Mint, in which children love to play. As with the Field End properties, Shaw End guests have the run of the 200 acre estate. Three apartments **sleep 4**, one **sleeps 6**.

Trout and salmon fishing (one rod) is available on the Mint. TV, washing machine, telephone, microwave, linen included, towels available for a small extra charge. Dogs welcome by arrangement. Cost: about £155 to £410. Details from Mr and Mrs E D Robinson, 1 Field End, Patton, near Kendal, Cumbria LA8 9DU. Telephone (01539) 824220, fax 824464.

www.diva-web.co.uk/fsendhols
email: fshawend@globalnet.co.uk

Windermere and Ullswater
Matson Ground Estate Cottages

Just a mile from Windermere and its lake, but enjoying an exceptionally peaceful and quiet situation above and away from through traffic, we found *Helm Farm* to be a top-quality conversion of traditional farm buildings. **Sleeping 2 to 5** in four units, each enjoys privacy and has been craftsman designed to a very good standard. *Helm Lune* **sleeps 5** in a double and a triple (three single beds – two of which can form a second double). The Habitat style (lots of pine) is set off by a high ceiling, beams in the spacious living room, and an open fire. *Helm Eden* **sleeps 4** in a double and two full size bunks, *Kent* **sleeps 4** in a double, with two in children's bunks. *Helm Mint*, **sleeping 2**, is on the ground floor only, and has a cosy L-shaped living room/kitchen. It is the only one that does not have a fireplace. (Helm Mint is available at a reduced rate if taken with Lune, Eden or Kent.) All include linen and towels, TV, video/CD player. Microwaves and washer/driers in all except Mint. Outside payphone, barbecue and shared garden with furniture. Fuel is provided for open fires, effective night storage heating is included. Cost: about £110 to £440, with short breaks available. Not suitable for dogs. There is a wide choice of attractions, with footpath walks from the door. ETC Three Stars.

We then drove towards the lovely countryside around Ullswater and, in the beautiful Grisedale Valley, close to Helvellyn and many other mountains, found the spacious, modernised 17th century farmhouse called *Elm How* and the smaller, quaintly beamed *Cruck Barn* – adjoining properties **sleeping 10 and 2** respectively. A hint of remoteness, among stunning mountain scenery, makes these really attractive 'away from it all' places. No TV reception due to the hills, but videos and CD players are available.

Eagle Cottage's location is absolutely superb even in Lake District terms...

Cruck Barn adjoins Elm How, and is an out-and-out charmer, sleeping 2.

Linen/towels provided. Dishwasher in *Elm How*. Microwaves, washer/driers. Open fire (fuel provided) in Elm How. Electric storage heating included. Barbecues. Not suitable for dogs. ETC Three/Four Stars.

Popular *Eagle Cottage* perches just above Glenridding village and **sleeps 4**, with lovely views all round, including the lake. Steep approach track. TV, video and CD player. Linen, dishwasher, microwave, open fire, storage heating, as in Elm How. Cost: £230 to £800. Not suitable for pets. ETC Four Stars.

Colour brochure from Matson Ground Estate Company, 3 Lambrigg Terrace, Kendal, Cumbria LA9 4BB. Telephone (01539) 726995. Fax 741611. **www.matsonground.co.uk   email: matsong@compuserve.com**

Wales

Wales's intricate and varied terrain seems to belie its size. Every few miles, every turn in the road seems to promise new things to see, more history to reach out and touch. Almost as soon as you're over the border (say via Ross on Wye, or Ludlow) the magic, the sense of past and the scenic beauty envelop one. We'd say: 'The total is greater than the sum of its parts'. A noticeable number of readers have taken to the Pembrokeshire Coast and, for example, the Llyn Peninsula, in the north. In Pembrokeshire, Tenby is much-loved, while people who discover smaller resorts such as Broad Haven and Newport tend to rave about them. There are lofty peaks and magnificent beaches, and although the most dramatic scenery is around Snowdonia, almost every corner of the Principality is holiday country. There are the soft, rolling, lightly wooded English-Welsh borders, the brown moors of the Brecon Beacons National Park, our own favourite coastline around Barmouth, the rather proud, rather self contained town of Dolgellau, the ever-bustling inland resort of Porthmadog and nearby Portmeirion, the architectural fantasy that's like a cross between Portofino and Munchkin-land. There are castles to storm, ponies to trek with, salmon and trout to catch, steam trains to travel on. Or consider the superbly scenic British Rail line that runs from Shrewsbury across to Welshpool, goes over the Mawddach estuary and then via Barmouth up to Harlech Castle and beyond. And we don't want to forget the Isle of Anglesey: one of our favourite towns in the whole of Britain is Beaumaris, just over the Menai Straits, and the hinterland is as Welsh as anywhere we know.

St David's   map 5/276
Derwen and Beth Ruach

These are among the best cottages we've found in the west of Wales. Delightful! First, on a sunny morning on the westerly outskirts of prettily preserved St David's, we saw *Derwen*. Quite plain from the street, it is a joy inside: a fine elongated kitchen/ diner leading through to a light, sunny sitting room with spectacular westerly views: imagine the

Beth Ruach is a very stylish, comfortable and spacious family house...

sunsets. There's a grassy garden too. With an excellent arrangement of bedrooms on two floors (it's a three-storeyed house) we rate this highly.

Close to the heart of the town, *Beth Ruach* is on a grander scale, up a private drive, spacious (and cool on a hot day) with a particularly comfortable sitting room. It too has a skilful layout of bedrooms and **sleeps (yes!) up to 18**. This also has sea and country views from upstairs: but, of course, you would want to explore this fabulous part of Wales, not just look at it! Dogs welcome in one cottage. Linen and towels included. TVs. Payphone. Cost: about £100 to £1750. Details (excellent brochures) from Thelma Hardman, 'High View', Catherine Street, St David's, Pembrokeshire SA62 6RJ. Telephone (01437) 720616.

Welsh Country Cottages*
(A part of English Country Cottages)

Just three miles from the sort of sandy beach for which Pembrokeshire is famous, there are two good-sized cottages on a Grade II listed 16th century farm. Colleagues working on this guide have stayed in, and praised, one of them. This is *East Jordeston Cottage*, a handsome mid-18th century extension to the main farmhouse. **Sleeps 7**. Ref OKG.

Tyn Y Ddol is on the edge of the Snowdonia National Park. **Sleeping 10 'plus 2'**, it even has the River Dee flowing through the farmland that surrounds the house. Dating from the 18th century, it has a woodburner, original oak panelling, a games room, a piano and much more. Ref JAZ.

Deep in some of the most spectacular country in Snowdonia, which is really saying something, *Aber Cottages* (near Beddgelert) are just six miles from the sort of sandy beaches that are the essence of happy family holidays. Dutch readers of this guide stayed two years ago, and reported 'lots of things to do, lots of comfort – a place to remember for a long time'. They also told us that, having discovered English Country Cottages (and their Welsh and Scottish sections) they will probably stay with the organisation. Ref JBM/JBN.

There are many properties on the island of Anglesey – a chance for people who think they know Wales to explore a corner of it that can easily be overlooked. Several are close to one or more of the island's spectacular sandy beaches. *The Old Rectory*, **sleeping 10** (Ref OLB), has fabulous views of Snowdonia and is calm and relaxing. It has an open fire, and dogs are welcome by arrangement. We have also visited a fine and spacious farmhouse called *Cwrt*, **sleeping 7**, on the owners' estate near Llanerchymedd. Ref JMB.

Near Dolgellau, *Hermon Mawr* is a conversion of a former chapel. **Sleeping up to 8** (always remember, you do not *have* to be 8!), it is deep in the national park but only a short drive from the seaside. Ref JYM.

For further information about any of the properties featured here, write to English Country Cottages, Stoney Bank Road, Earby, Barnoldswick BB94 0EE. For bookings telephone (0870) 5851155. You can also 'dial-a-brochure': (0870) 5851111.

Quote reference EMA 94
www.english-country-cottages.co.uk

Cwrt, on Anglesey, is one of our own Welsh favourites. Sleeping up to 7, it dates partly from the 16th century...

East Jordeston Cottage, sleeping 7, is full of character, with many historical features lovingly retained...

171

Saundersfoot, near Tenby
Blackmoor Farm Holiday Cottages

Despite the impression of being deep in the countryside, Blackmoor Farm is only two miles from the glorious Pembrokeshire coast at Amroth and, tucked away at the end of winding country lanes, just a short drive from Saundersfoot's glorious sands and much loved Tenby.

Young children were playing happily among the trees near these beautifully cared for cottages when we last visited. Families with children have always praised these cottages. They also appeal to people who appreciate purpose-built accommodation in an attractive courtyard location. Resident owners Len and Eve Cornthwaite ensure that families enjoy a warm and friendly atmosphere. Blackmoor Farm has cattle grazing peacefully, and the old stables in the spacious gravelled farmyard contain a resident donkey called Dusty: children can enjoy rides on Dusty outdoors most days. There is also a huge barn which has become a covered riding arena and impromptu play area in wet weather. Those children are also well away from any traffic, for Blackmoor Farm is surrounded by its own 36 acres of pastureland and is accessible only by a private drive. (But be warned: more than one adventurous child has asked if next time the family can book one of the expensively appointed and discreetly situated mobile homes!)

There are just three cottages, south facing, side by side in a courtyard setting. Accommodation is two-tiered. Downstairs there are two bedrooms (each with full size twin beds, which can convert to bunk beds) and a well fitted out bathroom with bath *and* shower. Upstairs there is a large open-plan room containing the kitchen/dining section and comfortable living area leading on to a small patio balcony. A sofa bed allows the cottage to **sleep a maximum of 6**. The single-storeyed *Stable Cottage*, a converted farm building, **sleeps 2,** and has an appealing triple aspect living room. The decor and furniture are modern, comfortable, simple but attractive. Each cottage is well equipped, heated by storage heaters and, with double glazing and good insulation, cosy in the early and late seasons.

Cost: £188 to £428 (less than this for Stable Cottage). Televisions. Linen is provided but not towels. Laundry facilities. Games room. Not suitable for dogs and other pets. More details from Len and Eve Cornthwaite, Blackmoor Farm, Amroth Road, Ludchurch, near Saundersfoot, Pembrokeshire SA67 8PG. Telephone/fax Llanteg (01834) 831242.

www.infozone.com.hk/blackmoorfarm/ email: ltecornth@aol.com

South-facing balconies, each with a table and two chairs for alfresco meals.

Stable Cottage – just right for 2, and a modestly-priced introduction to Wales.

Walwyn's Castle, near Little Haven
Rosemoor

Even in terms of rural west Wales, this is one of the most attractively situated cottage set-ups we know. And since new owners (from Holland) took over, Rosemoor has been quietly upgraded to even higher standards.

Quietly tucked well away from any main roads, it is very family-orientated: indeed, although the cottages are very private and self contained, it is a lovely place for children to make new friends. The whole of the Pembrokeshire Coast National Park is very easily at your disposal, as are the county's magnificent beaches, of which Marloes is perhaps the best known. The Rosemoor Nature Reserve has a path through a bluebell wood on the western side of the lake which enables a visitor to walk round the Reserve in less than an hour.

The holiday homes were created from the red sandstone outbuildings of the large Victorian house in which they have their home. One group, *Rose, First, Peace, Apple, Spring Cottage* and *Orchard*, look inwards on to a large open courtyard with a raised round central lawn and shrub-bed and outwards over open rolling and wooded countryside. *The Coach House*, distinctively capped by a small belfry and with a patio on to the walled garden, *Gardeners Cottage* and *Holly Tree* (a superbly upgraded unit in what were the servants' quarters to the main house) are detached from the main group of six that form the U-shape round the courtyard. All are different in size, character and decor, ranging from the single bedroomed Rose Cottage to the very spacious five-bedroomed combination (with internal connection) of Peace and Apple. Apple has three bedrooms and two bathrooms, one of which is en-suite to a ground floor bedroom, professionally designed for disabled use. All are very well equipped, not only with the essential needs of the holidaymaker in mind, but with those thoughtful extras such as night-lights for children.

The three-bedroomed Coach House is distinctively capped by a small belfry. It is of course just one of Rosemoor's several 'characterful' properties here in rural West Wales. It is handy for beaches and lovely countryside, but not at all remote.

Cost: about £110 to £650. Dogs welcome. TVs, microwaves, conventional ovens, crockpots, fridge-freezers. Home-cooked meals. Linen supplied. Laundry facilities. All have central heating, some also have woodburners. Games room. Attractive playground. For an exceptional brochure contact John M and Jacqui Janssen, Rosemoor, Walwyn's Castle, Haverfordwest, Pembrokeshire SA62 3ED. Telephone (01437) 781326/fax 781080.

www.rosemoor.co.uk email: rosemoor@walwynscastle.com

173

Llanfallteg, near Whitland
Gwarmacwydd Farm Cottages

At the centre of a working farm that children will love (lambs, calves, rabbits to meet, and ancient wood-lands to explore) this is an attractive, quiet and spacious arrangement of cottages. Conveniently, the focal point here is the owners' handsome Georgian home. Adjacent to the main house are *The Coach House* (**sleeps 4/6**) and *Butler's Cottage* (**sleeps 2/3**), which can be linked to make one bigger property. Across

A reliably warm welcome at this very quiet, spacious and comfortable set-up.

grassy open ground, but still part of the original farm, stand *The Old Barn* and *Tower Cottage*, **sleeping 6** and **2/3** respectively, and also combinable. Our favourite has always been the roomy, stylish Coach House, with a triple-aspect sitting room/diner and central heating. Wales Tourist Board Four Stars. No smoking. TV. Well behaved dogs by arrangement. Linen (not towels) and heating included. Cost: £125 to £450. Details and brochure from Angela Colledge, Gwarmacwydd Farm, Llanfallteg, Whitland, Carmarthenshire. Telephone (01437) 563260; fax 563839.

www.a-farm-holiday.org

email: info@a-farm-holiday.org

Newgale, near St David's   map 5/284
Bryn-y-Mor

High up on the cliffs above Newgale Sands, in a glorious position with a quarter of an acre of fenced ground, is *Bryn-y-Mor*. With superb views sweeping out across St Brides Bay, wide sandy beaches are directly below the cottage – reached by cliff path (or car). St David's is seven miles away, Haverfordwest ten; the cottage is a quarter of a mile off the

Idyllically situated on cliffs overlooking St Brides Bay and sandy beaches.

coast road. It is simply furnished and not for those expecting every labour-saving device, but rather for those who appreciate the seclusion, the spectacular sea views, the cliff-path conservation area, walking, bird-watching and studying wild flowers – in short, the opportunity to get away from it all and revel in nature at its best. The sitting room has an open fire and leads on to a verandah overlooking the sea. **Sleeps 9** in four bedrooms. Linen and towels are not included. Dogs welcome. Cost: about £200 to £300. Details from Nicholas and Vanessa Arbuthnott, The Tallet, Calmsden, Cirencester GL7 5ET. Telephone/fax (01285) 831437.

Coastal Wales
Quality Cottages Cerbid*

A number of holiday letting agencies are run by people who have made a great success of renting out properties they actually own. One of the best examples is Leonard Rees, whose own 'Cerbid Cottages' *have appeared here every year since the guide's inception in 1983.*

We revisited the Cerbid properties, down a sleepy lane in an idyllically quiet backwater of deeply rural Pembrokeshire, during a recent summer, and were reminded of what little jewels (well, not all so little) they are.

The high standards here tend to be reflected by the quality of Leonard Rees's agency properties, ninety per cent of which are within five miles from the sea – a huge selling point.

For example, just a few minutes from Newgale beach, which consists of over a mile of golden sands, is *The Red Hen House*. A superb barn conversion with sweet-smelling honeysuckle over the door, it is idyllically set in a secret valley conservation area complete with a private south-facing garden and a nearby trout lake. The feature stone fireplace makes it a good bet for the shoulder season.

If you want a dramatic coastal location, you will be impressed, as we were, by *Craig Yr Awel*, on Whitesands Bay, just a few yards above the beach. We could enjoy a week here just watching the ever-changing sea below. During a most enjoyable visit we noticed lots of books to read, comfortable leather armchairs. There's an open fire which is an absolute

Bridge View, in the hamlet of Middle Mill (not featured), is a real charmer. It is located just over a mile from the delightful harbour village of Solva.

The Red Hen House is an admirable barn conversion, and is marvellously well situated. It has 'honeysuckle round the door', and an impressive open fireplace.

delight when the sea mist comes down or autumn nights close in, and a glazed patio with, as you would imagine, spectacular views. **Sleeps 10**. Dogs are welcome here.

Valley Cottage, seven miles from Tenby, lies within an acre of grounds overlooking the 'secret waterway' of the Haven at Milford. **Sleeps 5**, pets welcome. And *Pontfaen*, in the beautiful lush and wooded Gwaun Valley between Fishguard and Newport, is a most impressive Victorian country house which **sleeps 11**.

A handsome full colour brochure, which also contains details of the Cerbid properties, can be obtained from Leonard Rees, Cerbid (GHCG), Solva, Pembrokeshire. Telephone Croesgoch (01348) 837871.

Newport, Pembrokeshire
Carreg Coetan

We have long known this location, memorable for its backdrop of wooded hills and its fine, safe, child-friendly beaches. The original group of four cottages – very private, quiet, nicely arranged within well tended lawns – that we first knew under a single ownership are now owned separately, and Carreg Coetan (owned by local people) remains available for self-catering holidays.

Nearby there are two spectacular beaches, a nine hole golf course and riding stables...

Since we first visited, it has become partly creeper-covered and attractively fenced. We especially like the big picture window on to the patio, gardens and the hills, which helps to make the neat, practical, easy-to-maintain interior bright and welcoming. The combined sitting room/diner is cosy, with a clever use of space, is fully carpeted and there is a comfy three piece suite.

Sleeps 4 in a double and a twin, There is a car port and room for two other cars. Linen is included, but not towels. Pets are welcome by arrangement. Cost: about £181 to £442. Further details are available from Mr and Mrs Carey, Waunwhiod, Newport, Pembrokeshire SA42 0QG. Telephone (01239) 820822.

www.scarey.clara.net
email: susan.carey@btinternet.com

---

*The editors of *The Good Holiday Cottage Guide* welcome calls from readers needing more information about properties than we can easily give in these pages. Perhaps when the location is more important than the cottage itself – say for a wedding or a reunion – or when a big group of friends or colleagues wants to take over a whole complex. (A number of owners welcome extended families but will actually refuse non-family groups.) There are no charges for this, no fancy premium rate phone calls. Telephone (01438) 869489 or email: frank@cottageguide.co.uk*

Please note: while by definition we approve of all the letting agencies featured in this guide, we cannot possibly vouch for every single property on their books. Several agencies, for example, include in their portfolio a couple of properties that are slightly 'out of synch' with the rest, perhaps simpler places geared to the requirements of walkers or fishermen, or in some cases properties that are really only suitable as annexes or for accommodation overflows.

Llanafan, near Aberystwyth
Pen y bont Bungalow

We have discovered over the years just how many of our readers enjoy a rural base that is only a few miles from the sea. In a peaceful green but not isolated spot, Pen y bont should fit the bill: well insulated and therefore warm, with the useful combination of an open fire and storage radiators, with superb views from patio picture windows, carefully tended

Peace, perfect peace, deep in the country but only a few miles from the sea...

gardens and miles of good walking through woods and along river banks, this is indeed rather special. (Good focal points for strollers are the two Forestry Commission picnic sites within two miles.) Buzzards and red kites are regularly seen from the grounds, and the trout fishing is very good in local rivers and lakes. And the seaside? Aberystwyth is only about ten miles away, and there are less well known beaches and harbours to discover, such as Aberaeron and Ynyslas. Ample parking. **Sleeps 5** in two twins and single (new divans). Linen, not towels included. Not suitable for dogs. Non-smokers preferred. Cost: about £250 to £400. Very full details, and a map, from Brenda and Norman Jones, Fernlea, Blakeley, Stanton, Shrewsbury SY4 4ND. Telephone/fax (01939) 250754. **email: blakeleygr@aol.com**

Boncath
Fron Fawr   map 5/288

Though we have featured them since 1985, we recently revisited to check out these three established cottages (deceptively spacious and as clean as the proverbial whistle), and a new property. This **sleeps 8** and is double glazed and centrally heated, with a large wood-beamed lounge and a

A short drive from good beaches that are one of West Wales's 'best-kept secrets'.

wood-burning stove. All the cottages are equipped, as one of our readers put it, with 'virtually everything': TV, hairdryer, microwave, dishwasher and enough kitchen equipment to keep any cook happy. Fron Fawr is a short drive from some delightful seaside places (good beaches, views and never any crowds). You will find a rolling lawn with swings where children can play, and enticing paths into woodlands inhabited by badgers, rabbits and a resident pair of buzzards.

Cost: approximately £210 to £795 per week. Linen, towels, gas, electricity, and wood are provided. The cottages have three or four bedrooms, and **sleep between 5 and 8**. Details and brochures from Jackie Tayler, Fron Fawr, Boncath, Pembrokeshire SA37 0HS. Telephone (01239) 841285. Fax (0870) 1209175.

www.fronfawr.co.uk   email: ghcg.cottages@fronfawr.co.uk

Taliaris, nr Llandeilo
Maerdy Cottages

These are impressive. In a peaceful valley surrounded by woods and farmland, a 300 year old farmhouse and its original stone buildings have been converted into seven cottages. Two are 'wheelchair accessible', all are in natural wooded gardens. With

Comfy cottages in a fine rural location...

its own secluded garden, *Stable Cottage*, on one level, has original 15th century windows and lofted ceiling. **Sleeps 7**. *The Granary* **sleeps 5** on the ground floor and enjoys views from the upstairs living room and kitchen. *The Farmhouse* oozes character with oak panelling and a huge inglenook fireplace. **Sleeps up to 10**. *Barn Cottage* (once a barn!) **sleeps up to 8**. *The Cottage,* the smallest, tucked away on its own, is popular with couples, but can **accommodate 4**. *Dan y Cefn*, on a hill and well off the road, is a traditional stone built cottage with breathtaking views. **Sleeps 5**. *Valley View* **sleeps 8** in four double bedrooms (two upstairs and two downstairs), it also has a spacious first floor open-plan kitchen-dining-living room that allows up to 20 to dine together. Home baking/meals service; pets welcome; bedlinen provided, towels on request (as are cots, highchair, barbecue and bicycles). WTB Grade 4. Cost: £205 to £780. Some credit cards accepted. Details: Mrs Margaret Jones, The Annex, Dan y Cefn, Manordeilo, Llandeilo, Carmarthenshire SA19 7BD. Telephone (01550) 777448, fax 777067.

www.maerdycottageswales.co.uk email: danycefn@netscapeonline.co.uk

---

Nannerth Fawr, near Rhayader   map 5/291
Showman's Trailer

Amid hilly countryside in deepest mid-Wales, though not far from the English border, we came across a most unusual and intriguing holiday property. In the grounds of a farmhouse that is the focal point of holiday cottages featured on the opposite page, we much admired this carefully restored vehicle of the 1930s. It

We thought this would make a very romantic spot for honeymooners...

is the kind of thing you see at a historic-vehicle fair, but will rarely get the chance to stay in. It **sleeps 2** in a small double, with the added possibility of a sofa bed for one extra person (made up from upholstered benches in the living area). There is a small woodburning stove, a TV and a kitchenette. There is a WC and shower adjacent, even a small verandah, garden furniture and, usefully, an adjacent barn suitable for barbecues. Linen included. Tent space available.

Cost: £120 to £170. Details from Alison and André Gallagher, Nannerth Fawr, Rhayader, Powys LD6 5HA. Telephone/fax (01597) 811121. **www.nannerth.co.uk email: info@nannerth.co.uk**

Wales
Wales Holidays*

This is just a taste of what's on offer from this very highly regarded agency: two quietly situated WTB Five Star cottages in exquisite country-side at the foot of Cader Idris, near Dolgellau; a Victorian house (semi-detached, **sleeping 8**) right on the River Ystwyth – good fishing literally from the doorstep – and only five miles from the seaside resort of Aberystwyth; an apartment in a handsome listed Georgian mansion liter-ally next door to fascinating Beaumaris Castle. (Brochure references for the above are respectively H357/H427, N336 and I111.)

A number of readers have praised Wales Holidays over several years, and we were pleased (in the summer of 2001) to make contact.

Based in Newtown, in mid-Wales and not far from the English border, it has a very good geographical spread. Unusually – though not uniquely – the agency welcomes callers at its premises. But you don't need to make the trek! There is a user-friendly brochure with an astonishing range of holiday possibilities, and a most effective and appealing website.

During our 2001 visit we especially liked a spacious and quiet farmhouse overlooking the village of Llangurig (good walking, two pubs that serve above-average food). Fronting on to pastureland – we met new-born foals – it is due to become the owners' retirement home. **Sleeping 7 'plus 2'**, brochure ref A246, it has a woodburner in the sitting room, an Aga in the

This beautifully maintained house, close to Llangurig, is private and quiet...

This Five Star beauty below Cader Idris will turn lounge lizards into walkers!

dining room and a downstairs four-poster. It is in fact one of the pleasan-test family-orientated houses we have encountered in many a long mile.

In deeply rural countryside, after a meandering drive along narrow lanes from the small town of Rhayader, we came across a quite delightful set-up. Close to the house of the charming owners, we admired a pristine and most impressive barn conversion, **sleeping up to 7**, two fine traditional cottages each **sleeping 4** and then, unforgettably, a superbly restored, award-winning traditional Welsh longhouse.We do not have enough space to describe it, but for starters: **sleeping up to 10**, it dates from the mid 16th century, and retains its original oak beams, a spiral stone staircase, a huge open fireplace. Refs K176-179.

All this and more is to be found within this most impressive agency, whose inspiring brochure is available from Wales Holidays, Bear Lanes, Newtown, Powys SY16 2QZ. Telephone (01686) 628200. Fax 622465.

www.wales-holidays.co.uk   email: info@wales-holidays.co.uk

Rhyd-Yr-Eirin, near Harlech

For its sheer character and its unforgettable location this certainly comes
into our Top Twenty. We love it, and
colleagues (with two young children) thoroughly enjoyed an 'away
from it all' holiday here. When we
say it is isolated, we mean *isolated*!
It oozes atmosphere. You're 900-feet
up, sheltered by hills to the north and
east, in an oak-beamed, three-bedroomed, 17th century farmhouse with

Splendid isolation, lots of atmosphere.

an unusual stone staircase, original sitting-room window, antique furniture and a wide-ranging Welsh-holiday library. There is an open fire in the
inglenook (coal/wood provided) and each room has a storage or wall
heater. The all-electric kitchen, bathroom and shower-room are up to a
very high standard. It takes fifteen minutes by car, allowing for gate-
opening, to get to Harlech and the glorious, sandy beaches. Concealed
TV, radio-cassette player, telephone, double-oven cooker, microwave,
fridge-freezer, dishwasher, washing machine, spin-dryer. **Sleeps up to 7**.
Cost: £150 to £500 (discounts for early booking/fortnights). Well-trained
dogs welcome. Details with map and plans of the house and garden
(including the bog-garden) from Mr Chris Ledger, 7 Chelmer Road,
London E9 6AY. Telephone 020-8985 1853.

www.rhydyreirin.com   email: info@rhydyreirin.com

Llanbedr, near Harlech
Nantcol   map 5/313

Unforgettable! From this 14th century stone built Welsh longhouse,
five miles from Llanbedr village up
a narrow valley road, you can walk
straight up the hills. It is perfection
for walkers, bird watchers and lovers
of the countryside. From the last
farmhouse where you collect the key,
you drive up a grassy track to the
spectacular location and the view.
You can explore Snowdonia, relax

*What should we show – the house itself
or the fabulous view? We love them both,
and readers do too ...*

on a long sandy beach or play golf at Royal St David's, Harlech, a championship course. As we walked in, it was a joy to see real log fires burning at both ends of the living room. This oak beamed cottage is filled with
many interesting pieces of old Welsh furniture. The spacious farmhouse
kitchen was just as welcoming, with a large oak table and, yes, an oil-
fired Rayburn stove. Another bonus: no TV! **Sleeps 6/7**. Linen not provided. Open all year, Christmas by arrangement. Short breaks possible.
Dogs by arrangement. Cost: from about £300. Details from Stephanie
Grant, Bollingham House, Eardisley, Herefordshire HR5 3LE. Telephone
(01544) 327326. Fax (01544) 327880. **email: bollhouse@bigfoot.com**

180

Llanfrothen, near Penrhyndeudraeth
Felin Parc (Millhouse)/Tan-y-Clogwen (Cottage)

Readers love these cottages, and it's a pleasure to detour along a little lane accompanying a bubbling river towards them. Their owner, Owen Williams-Ellis, is a nephew of Sir Clough, the famous architect of Portmeirion: see below. Rooms are characterised by many interesting antique pieces and curious bygones, much solid old-fashioned comfort and wood-burners. Bedrooms invite lazy lie-ins while you listen to the

Houses full of character in a superb, but not isolated, riverside location.

river. In *Felin Parc* (**sleeping 8**, though there is a detached 'annexe' that **sleeps 2** more) we noted lots of beams, a big leather chesterfield, gleaming horse-brasses. In *Tan-y-Clogwen* (**sleeping 4 plus 2 extra** on a ground floor sofa bed) there is a cottagey sitting room and a 'step down' dining room with superb views. TV. Well-behaved dogs welcome. Felin Parc is WTB Grade Four; Tan-y-Clogwen is Grade Three. Cost: (Felin Parc) £300 to £650; with the annexe, £400 to £800; (Tan-y-Clogwen) £200 to £450. Details: Owen and Veronica Williams-Ellis, San Giovanni, 4 Sylvan Road, London SE19 2RX. Telephone/fax 020-8653-3118.

www. northwales-cottages.co.uk email: rupert.williams-ellis@talk21.com

---

Portmeirion, near Porthmadog
Portmeirion Cottages

map 5/315

Colour section A, Page 5

The young daughter of one of our readers compared this amazing place with Munchkinland, in 'The Wizard of Oz'. And the architect, Clough Williams-Ellis, would surely be delighted to think that many of those pastel coloured, higgledy-piggledy, cottages that characterise his life's work are so often occupied by people enjoying Portmeirion's atmosphere. It's like nowhere else in Britain.

It is like a picture-postcard come to life!

Better yet, the various cottage interiors are cosy and lived-in, and surprisingly spacious considering how 'neat' they seem from outside. We spotted many antiques, good beds, well equipped kitchens, often superb views from upper windows. We saw cottages at the very centre of the sometimes bustling, sometimes silent village. NB: at certain times most cottages can double up as hotel accommodation, depending on demand. **Sleep 2/8.** TVs (Satellite). Heating, towels, linen included. Direct-dial phones. Cost: £450 to £920. Details: Portmeirion Cottages, Portmeirion, nr Porthmadog, Gwynedd LL48 6ET. Tel (01766) 770000. Fax 771331.

www.portmeirion-village.com email: hotel@portmeirion-village.com

St Dogmaels, near Cardigan
Trenewydd Farm Cottages

Spacious, comfortable and scrupulously clean cottages, whose location is one of the most desirable on the whole of the coast of Wales: not surprisingly, there is a high percentage of repeats among readers who have stayed here. (We too have stayed.)

We have featured the Trenewydd cottages in this guide for eighteen years now without a break, and never heard anything but praise.

A warm welcome is always extended to the visitor to the skilfully converted and most assiduously run group of *Wales Tourist Board Five Star* rated cottages. New owners are continuing a tradition of warm hospitality, and the cottages have received a number of awards for the overall quality of their product.

The cottages score highly with young families and pensioners alike, all appreciating the reliable attention to detail. *They are also a big hit with those seeking tranquillity in the quieter months of the year, with weekend and midweek breaks available.*

Although you would never guess, the cottages were in fact converted from what used to be a series of cowsheds and other outbuildings! There are pretty gardens and lawns around them, a children's play area, barbecues and tables for eating outdoors, all within view of some very tame farm animals: a lovable donkey and pony, a rabbit, guinea pigs, pet sheep, and lambs in spring.

Amenities guests enjoy include a beautiful heated swimming pool of generous proportions sunk into a glorious stone-walled garden. (This makes a perfect natural sun-trap.)

The farm is on a quiet country lane well away from the main road, surrounded by a pastoral landscape with large hedgerows that contain an abundance of wild flowers. Poppit Sands and the pretty seaside village of St Dogmaels, on the Teifi estuary, are only two miles away, and there you can pick up the northern tip of the Pembrokeshire Coastal Path, offering miles of spectacular walking. Trenewydd is situated on the very edge of the Pembrokeshire National Park, the nearest town, Cardigan, being just three miles away.

All five cottages at Trenewydd are very impressive, **sleeping between 2 and 9** in a choice of two, three and four bedrooms. *Bwthyn Derw* and

We have never had anything other than glowing praise for the warmth of the welcome and the top notch interiors.

The cottages are notably spacious and uncluttered, and they enjoy a good degree of privacy.

Bwthyn Onnen have the facility of linking their lounges for those families wishing to holiday together. We have actually stayed briefly in Bwthyn Onnen and would have happily settled down for a fortnight.

Needless to say, the cottages are equipped with every amenity, including dishwashers, washer-dryers and fridge-freezers, as well as traditional furnishings in Welsh pine, wood beams and Welsh-orientated knick-knacks.

A heated pool fits harmoniously into the carefully landscaped grounds of this well-run arrangement of cottages: they are among our all-time favourites in Wales.

There are plenty of the little touches that make a holiday home memorable, such as a Welsh tea served on arrival, a complimentary food hamper of milk and local produce like cheese, butter and eggs, lots of local information, a shopping service (no charge) that will fill your fridge and freezer to order before arrival. There is now a range of home-cooked dishes for guests to purchase.

Bedlinen is provided, with beds made up before you arrive, and towels can be provided for overseas visitors. Cots, highchairs and stairgates are also available at no extra charge, and all the cottages have televisions.

The kind of feedback we have had from readers of *The Good Holiday Cottage Guide* sums up the appeal of such cottages. Speaking from the heart, they put it better than we ever could:

Wrote a family from Maidenhead, in Berkshire: 'We never thought when we first came to Trenewydd in 1994 that we would still be coming four years later. Apart from the beautiful countryside, lovely beaches and the many attractions in the area, we also feel very relaxed here due to the pleasant surroundings and your excellent hospitality.'

Wrote a young couple from Highgate, in North London, who first stayed at Trenewydd while attending a big family wedding in Cardigan: 'What started off as just a convenient place to stay became somewhere to go back to for a proper holiday. We have been back three times, and recommended the cottages to others.'

Cost: about £180 to £825 weekly, depending on which cottage you choose and when. Short breaks (available from mid September through to the end of June, excluding Spring Bank Holiday week) from £70 for 2 people for two nights, low season. Well behaved dogs are welcome by arrangement, but not during the school holidays. Further details and a good brochure are available from Cheryl Hyde, Trenewydd Farm Cottages, St Dogmaels, Cardigan, Dyfed SA43 2BJ. Telephone (01239) 612370. Fax (01239) 621040.

www.trenewyddfarm.fsnet.co.uk
cherylhyde@trenewyddfarm.fsnet.co.uk

Llwyndafydd, near New Quay
Neuadd Farm Cottages

These are very special indeed. In a delightful corner of rural Wales, within exceptional gardens, these cottages are run with great skill and care by Malcolm and Karina Headley, outstandingly welcoming, efficient and thoroughly professional owners, whose entire operation seems to us to be faultless. We have stayed in the smallest of the cottages (an 'upside-down' cottage), and we were delighted to be part of an altogether admirable mini-hamlet to which people return time and again.

Featured in this guide since its very beginning, these lovingly cared for, award-winning cottages are constantly improved and have received enormous praise from readers and professionals in the travel industry. The Headleys, who live in the farmhouse nearby, have created an idyllic setting with peaceful gardens and grounds; privacy is easily attained.

Deservedly, the outstanding gardens have earned many awards.

It is a harmonious arrangement, and not at all cramped.

And as for those immaculately maintained gardens! Enormous work and care have helped to create prolific 'cottage gardens' with abundant flower beds, roses and wistaria-covered old stone walls, mangers full of trailing plants of every kind, wooden tubs of begonias and fuschias, woodland paths through camellia- and hydrangea-filled glades, herb gardens and water gardens around the ponds, not forgetting the lake in the valley with waterlilies and iris. *Winners of a CPRW Living Landscape Award and Wales in Bloom in 1998, 1999, 2000 and 2001.*

This historic estate of 35 acres in a corner of rural mid Wales was built overlooking what is said to have been the site of a country house where the future Henry VII lodged shortly before the Battle of Bosworth Field in 1485. Llwyndafydd is a lovely green, wooded, secret place, only a mile and a half from a beautiful stretch of National Trust owned coast. The nearest beach, Cwm Tudu Cove, is sandy and delightful.

Each cottage is a little different from its neighbour: these are, after all, conversions of farm buildings that Malcolm and Karina have skilfully transformed into cottages. Top grading awards from the tourist board are almost superfluous, and serve merely to reassure. Neuadd Farm Cottages (ten in all) range in size, **sleeping from 2 to 6** in comfort and style. One is particularly versatile in that it can be linked by means of a door to another, larger property. Particularly noticeable are the original paintings on the walls, the handmade doors with wooden latches, and the delightful furnishings: we especially admired the handmade lampshades and the matching lined curtains, the tasteful soft furnishings and comfortable sofas. The atmosphere is one of quiet, country comfort. The kitchens are very well equipped with dishwashers and microwaves, and there is a laundry room and a telephone for visitors' use. There is backup heating for chilly summer evenings, and nightstore heating for all-year-round comfort; six cottages have woodburners, each with its own wood supply: all included in the price. All cottages have videos, and there is a video library.

For the ultimate in holiday facilities there is a magnificent heated outdoor swimming pool set in a walled garden overlooking the valley. Neuadd Farm, which covers rolling green hills above the picturesque hamlet and the village inn, is the territory of the people staying here, so that at various times of the day you will see a family pottering off to feed the rabbits or visit William and Mr Nibbles, the pigmy goats, and the little pigs. Children can make new friends with other cottage dwellers or maybe experience baby chicks and a mother hen for the first time. There are

Not everyone knows about the superb beaches in this part of west Wales.

Cottage interiors are, without exception, of a reliably high standard.

ducks, a pony and donkeys, sheep in the meadows and a lake in the valley, with fishing. Nearby there are sandy beaches and tiny coves where you might see seals and dolphins.

A mile away, in the same ownership, is the outstanding *Pen Cwm*, ten minutes' walk from the secret little cove at Cwm Tudu. It has sea views, direct access to a network of National Trust paths, is very well situated, very quiet and private and is a delight inside. While retaining original features such as beamed ceilings, it enjoys a high level of comfort: a big woodburner, furniture the Headleys charmingly describe as 'squishy', an antique dining table and chairs, TV/video, good carpets throughout. **Sleeps 4**. Visitors are welcome to use the Neuadd facilities. One dog is welcome. Cost: about £300 to £650. Linen and towels included.

From the coastal footpaths there are spectacular views across Cardigan Bay to the distant mountains. The harbour village of New Quay has pubs and restaurants overlooking the bay, several specialising in local seafood, trout and salmon. It is a haven for small boats, and temporary membership of New Quay Yacht Club has been arranged for Neuadd visitors.

Cost: about £275 to £880, including bedlinen, towels, electricity and logs. Dogs accepted in three cottages. Details and colour brochure from Malcolm and Karina Headley, Neuadd Farm, Llwyndafydd, Llandysul, Cardiganshire SA44 6BT. Telephone/fax New Quay (01545) 560324.

www.neuadd-farm-cottages.co.uk   email: mheadley@btconnect.com

Aberdovey
Aberdovey Hillside Village

High above the Dovey Estuary, with the small seaside town of Aberdovey nestling below, a well landscaped site is the setting for recently refurbished accommodation of a high standard. Many readers have enthused, and some go back for family holidays year after year.

Part of the charm of the 'village' is its gradual development over 18 years from one or two holiday houses to a sculptured sprawl of terraces, gardens and paths – all in Welsh slate – with later apartments seemingly built into the hillside.

Whatever the weather, Aberdovey is the sort of place in which a family could happily spend a fortnight, and it's worth noting that it is served by one of the most scenic of all British Rail's routes, and is a splendid point from which to explore North Wales.

A huge bonus here is that all guests receive complimentary membership of a local Country Club for the duration of their stay. This entitles them to use the swimming pools, saunas, steam room, fitness room and spa baths without charge.

The village is much appreciated for its siesta-like peace. All the accommodation is light and airy, with panoramic views and a terrace or balcony big enough for eating alfresco as well as sunbathing. The leisure area has a well equipped fitness room with a choice of a comprehensive range of keep fit equipment, plus a pool table and table tennis. Children will enjoy

For eighteen years this arrangement of holiday properties has proved exceptionally popular among readers of our guide. There is a very high percentage of repeat visitors.

the play area with soft forest bark underfoot, and a picnic bench. There is a special 'Little Tikes' area for younger ones.

The whole complex occupies just one corner of a thirty-acre site that is yours to wander. The sandy beach is just five minutes away. Aberdovey itself has tennis courts, a bowling green and a links golf course.

Short breaks out of peak times. Dogs welcome at £11.75 per week. Costs are inclusive of VAT, all electricity charges, heating costs and bedlinen. Details/colour brochure from Aberdovey Hillside Village, Aberdovey, Gwynedd LL35 0ND. Telephone (01654) 767522; fax 767069.

www.hillsidevillage.co.uk
email: info@hillsidevillage.co.uk

Criccieth
Rhos Country Cottages

The open sea and good, safe beaches are close to these three popular properties amid peaceful farmland in this rural corner of North Wales. *Rhos-Wen* is an extremely well equipped purpose-built bungalow in the same grounds as one of the original cottages, *Rhos Dhu*. **Sleeps 6** in three bedrooms, one with a four poster.

Peacefully rural, yet close to the sea and good beaches, the new bungalow complements the other two houses.

There are two bathrooms, one with an excellent sauna. WTB Five Dragons. Rhos Dhu is light, airy and well equipped with a Neff kitchen, microwave, coffee machine and a dining area. The comfortable sitting room has an open fire. Upstairs are two bedrooms, **sleeping 5**, and a fully carpeted bathroom with jacuzzi. Cost: about £180 to £600. The two properties have spacious lawned gardens and garden chairs. Half a mile away is *Betws-Bach*, a large farmhouse from about 1675, **sleeping 6**, and Grade ll listed. We admired old stone walls, ancient beams, a huge fireplace, a snooker table. There's a garden with patio. Cost: £160 to £600. Small dogs welcome. Private fishing for brown trout. Electric storage heating. Details from Mrs A Jones, Rhandir, Boduan, Pwllheli, Gwynedd LL53 8UA. Telephone/fax: (01758) 720047 or telephone: (01766) 810295.

www.rhos-cottages.co.uk

Hafod Elwy (Betwys Y Coed) & Criccieth
Tyn Y Craig and Isfryn

You'll have no neighbours to worry about: *Tyn Y Craig* (**map 5/323**) is a mid-17th century house reached via a long private track. It is very much a family house, **sleeping 9**, with a woodburner, in an elevated position (great views) on a 500-acre working farm. Up to two dogs are welcome. In an exceptional location for tour-

Tyn Y Craig offers privacy and good views.

ing, the Snowdonia National Park and attractive Betwys Y Coed are just ten miles away. You can try your hand (or your foot) at watersports on the nearby Lake Brenig. Ref 11189. *Isfryn*, just two miles from Criccieth, also very usefully **sleeps 9**. Once a gamekeeper's house, it has a garden and barbecue. As with Tyn Y Craig: the house makes a good touring base, with excellent access to the Lleyn Peninsula, just a bit off the main tourist beat, with its super family beaches. Ref 1223 **(map 5/324)**.

Details from Country Holidays, Spring Mill, Barnoldswick, Lancashire BB94 0AA. To book, telephone 08700 723723. Brochure line: 08700 725725. Quote reference **CM091**

Live search and book: **www.country-holidays.co.uk**

Llanrug, near Llanberis
Bryn Bras Castle

We've had lots of encouraging reports from readers and have visited this quite remarkable, early 19th century mock 'castle' several times ourselves. (It has much more to do with stylish but unpretentious country house living than gazing from medieval castle battlements.) The castle certainly offers an unusual holiday, and for one of our readers it was 'a dream come true'. They rang us a while ago and said, 'We had always fancied the idea of living in a castle, and Bryn Bras made our dream possible.' It is important to note that people staying in one of Mrs Gray-Parry's castle apartments, every one of which has bags of character, have special access to the castle's main rooms.

Bryn Bras, designed by Thomas Hopper and a Grade II* Listed Building, often features in guides to Britain's outstanding houses and castles. It is a splendid point from which to tour North Wales: the summit of Snowdon is only six miles away. But shops, inns and restaurants are all near.

All the apartments have the highest grade with the Wales Tourist Board. They feel lived in and are always comfortable: there are antiques and bygones, but these are not museum pieces. Most recently, after walking through the elaborately decorated and furnished rooms and corridors and also enjoying the 32 acres of grounds and garden and country views, we looked at, among others, *Gerddi* (Garden), which has glorious views of the garden and its statuary. This apartment has a big sitting room and lots of space, peace and quiet. The bedroom furniture is particularly elegant, while the Art Deco bathroom has a mirrored ceiling! **Sleeps just 2**. We particularly enjoyed the easy-going ambience of *North Tower* (**sleeps 2**),

A rare chance to stay in an unusual Regency-period Romanesque-style castle.

Several of the Bryn Bras bedrooms are full of style and interest.

which has a most spacious sitting room and an almost circular tower bedroom with a delightful late-Victorian carved bed. We think the romantic atmosphere will definitely appeal to discriminating couples.

West Wing is different in character, with fairly small, cosy, rather private and convenient rooms leading off from its main corridor. It has two bathrooms and **sleeps 4**. A particularly appealing feature is the view of castle turrets and, in the distance, the Isle of Anglesey.

All Bryn Bras kitchens, by the way, include dishwasher and microwave and there are many other items provided for guests' comfort, such as hairdryers, toiletries and fresh flowers.

There is simply too little space here to characterise all the Bryn Bras properties – a study of the colour brochure is highly recommended in this instance because each apartment has its own very distinctive style.

In each you cannot fail to appreciate the historic surroundings, the beautiful grounds and the degree of care which Mrs Gray-Parry and her staff put into the castle. *Tan-y-twr* **sleeps just 2** (a honeymoon hideaway, perhaps) and has a charming staircase, as well as a snug living room with sloping, beamed ceiling. *Simdda Fawr*, with huge chimney, good carpets, comfy armchairs, two pleasantly old-fashioned bedrooms, and a pretty kitchen, **sleeps 4**. *Muriau* has a most attractive dresser, a huge ornately carved wardrobe. Also **sleeps 4** in two bedrooms and is, by the way, tucked away in the oldest part of the castle, beside a courtyard complete with fig tree.

In many ways the most appealing of all is *Flag Tower*. It's a Rapunzel-tower, a favourite among honeymooners. Working your way upwards you reach the circular 23' diameter lounge, kitchen and dining area on the first floor by a wide winding staircase. The room is surrounded by ornate panelling and Romanesque pillars, adorned with delicately carved woodwork. Carry on up to the second floor and you come to a white-tiled bathroom, with a round window, and on up to the large romantic circular bedroom, with an elegantly draped half-tester double bed. **Sleeps 2**.

Hot water and central heating are supplied free to all apartments: one reason why Bryn Bras is an excellent place for spring, autumn and winter breaks. Another reason is the beauty of the Welsh countryside – mountains, lakes and forests, heritage buildings, exceptional sandy beaches and a wide range of recreational facilities. In the Reception Hall there is comprehensive information, including details of the excellent variety of restaurants, inns and cafes in the locality.

Guests have the full run of the gardens, which are as remarkable as the castle.   *There's nothing 'twee' in the interiors, which are comfy and well cared for.*

Dogs are not allowed, nor, regrettably, to preserve the tranquillity of Bryn Bras, are young children. Duvets, bedlinen and electric blankets supplied with beds made up ready. Flexible start and departure days, as preferred, for any stay, at any time of the year. Short breaks all year round. Cost: about £350 to £620; short breaks, for example, from £160 for 2 persons for 2 nights. Details and an excellent brochure from Mrs Gray-Parry, Bryn Bras Castle, Llanrug, near Caernarfon, North Wales LL55 4RE. Telephone/fax Llanberis (01286) 870210.

www.brynbrascastle.co.uk
email: holidays@brynbrascastle.co.uk

Uwchmynydd, near Aberdaron
Penbryn Bach Cottage

This two hundred year old one-time farmhouse has its own small garden, and is surrounded by four acres of pasture. Adjacent to it is a small and seasonal licensed restaurant known for its seafood (but it's still quiet and self contained). Peacefully situated above Aberdaron Bay, en route for Wales's own 'end of the world' and also for Bardsey Island, this is a cosy retreat with vast, tranquil rural

Good views, an open fire, peace and quiet. Having a restaurant next door is a bonus, not a disadvantage.

views. The house has a glazed entrance porch, an old ship's door entry to a hallway, a small comfortable lounge with beamed ceiling and open fire, a ground floor double bedroom, a snug dining room, a well fitted kitchen and bathroom. A narrow, steep stairway leads to two 'crogloft' bedrooms, a double and a single. This property is not suitable for young children and less agile adults, but ideal for two couples. Available all year. **Sleeps 4 to 5**. TV. Not suitable for dogs. Cost: £195 to £325. Details: Roger Jones, The Golden Fleece Inn, Tremadog, Porthmadog, Gwynedd LL49 9RB. Telephone (01766) 512421. Fax (01766) 513421.

Note: the properties featured on this and the opposite page have featured in The Good Holiday Cottage Guide for sixteen years without a break...

Aberdaron   map 5/328
Sanctuary Cottage (Bryn Du Farm)

Tucked away along narrow lanes on the Llyn Peninsula, this has sandy beaches within a mile and a half and a network of footpaths leading to the sea. The large lounge has an ingle-nook fireplace with multi-fuel stove, an old dresser with Willow Pattern plates, TV and video, dining table and piano. Open stairs lead to the first floor, with one double bedroom, one twin bedded room and a third

A sanctuary indeed, warm and stylish.

bedroom with bunk beds. All the rooms are small and cottagey, with rural views. The bathroom has an electric shower over the bath. There's a small, stone-floored dining room and a well-modernised kitchen with double oven and microwave. A utility room off the kitchen houses the fridge/freezer, washing machine/dryer, and dishwasher. Fronting the length of the cottage is a large, sunny conservatory with cane furniture and dining table and chairs – well recommended by guests! Windows are double-glazed. **Sleeps 6**. Cost: £195 to £425. Available all year. Not suitable for dogs. Further details from Roger Jones, The Golden Fleece Inn, Tremadog, Porthmadog, Gwynedd LL49 9RB. Telephone (01766) 512421. Fax 513421.

Tal-y-Bont, near Conwy
Pant Farm

One of the most popular Welsh properties we feature, well away from the main road and along a private, gated track, this has charming views. The main part of the farmhouse dates back to the 16th century, but its fairly recent restoration includes just about every 21st century creature comfort. It has a good-sized 'farmhouse' kitchen/breakfast room with

Standing in ten acres of pastureland, this property really is 'one in a hundred'.

dishwasher, microwave, and pine furniture. There's a utility room with washing machine, a dining room with massive inglenook fireplace and a sitting room which again features inglenook, bread oven, TV and video and has been sympathetically extended with French windows to the garden. Upstairs there's an elegant master bedroom, a twin-bedded room with washbasin and a third bedroom with two single beds. The bathroom has a bidet, and a second bathroom comprises shower, toilet and washbasin. (There's also a downstairs loo and washroom.) The house has double glazing, gas fired central heating, a woodburner. Not suitable for dogs. **Sleeps 6**. Cost: £225 to £425. Available all year.

Details: Roger Jones. The Golden Fleece Inn, Tremadog, Porthmadog, Gwynedd LL49 9RB. Telephone (01766) 512421. Fax 513421.

Tal-y-Bont, near Conwy
Robyn's Nest   map 5/331

Over the drive from Pant Farm, though self contained, *Robyn's Nest* shares a remarkable situation in ten acres of land, overlooking the River Conwy and positioned perfectly for the coast (ten miles) and the heart of Snowdonia (Betws-y-Coed's just six miles). Although it can be used to augment the Pant Farm accommodation for larger groups by 2/4, it can,

Full of warmth and character, yet with all mod cons and a secluded patio.

of course, be rented separately. Among many excellent features the house offers split level accommodation (that always appeals to us), with a king sized bed in the main (ensuite) bedroom and a dining area and big sitting room on the first floor, with a picture window overlooking the valley. Delightful! Better yet, there is a woodburning stove, as well as central heating. The ground floor contains a modern fitted kitchen, separate bathroom and toilet and a twin bedroom. There's an old stable door out on to a private paved patio area. TV/video. **Sleeps 4**. Not suitable for dogs.

Cost: £225 to £395. Available main season and bank holiday weeks only. Details: Roger Jones, The Golden Fleece Inn, Tremadog, Porthmadog, Gwynedd LL49 9RB. Telephone (01766) 512421. Fax 513421.

Uwchmynydd, near Aberdaron
Talcen Foel

This old Welsh farmstead cottage is situated below the summit of Mt Anelog, two miles from the seaside village of Aberdaron and one from the Seafood Restaurant at Penbryn Bach, mid-way between Sanctuary Cottage and Penbryn Bach Cottage (see Page 190).

In a remote position approached by a rough track from the hamlet of Uwchmynydd, it is not suitable for anxious car owners! At the end of the gated track flanked by heather and gorse, the old Welsh farmstead comes into view, surrounded by ten acres of hillside pasture. There is ample parking in front of the cottage, with glorious sea and mountain views over the Irish coastline towards the Wicklow Hills, with Bardsey Island round the corner, Mt Anelog towering above, and far reaching views to Cader Idris, Aberdaron Bay and the mid-Wales coastline.

The cottage was completely re-built and modernised in 2001 in the 'Roger Jones' fashion', combining an 'olde worlde' atmosphere with all mod cons!

Specifically, the entrance hall leads into a flagged dining area with a large inglenook housing an oil fired range, a fully fitted galley kitchen with microwave, automatic washing machine. A double bedroom with wood floor and a large fitted wardrobe looks out across the Irish Sea. A second bedroom, also with sea views, has two single beds. Above the kitchen/dining room area is an open, raised 'crog loft den' approached by

A super new addition to the 'cottage guide' family, with fabulous views...

It is comfortable but not 'prissy', combining modern needs and history.

a wooden ladder. Internal steps lead down into the spacious lounge (formerly the cowshed): there are spectacular views from four windows, cosy lounge seating, a feature fireplace with woodburner, TV and video.

This property is only available July/August, the first week of September, Christmas and New Year. Ideal for honeymooners, 'stressed out' couples, walkers and birdwatchers. The main coastal path (the Pilgrims Way) skirts the cottage en route to the end of the peninsula. No other vehicles are allowed up the track, adding to the privacy. Aberdaron (shops, pub and beach) is two miles away, Whistling Sands beach three miles, Pwllheli main town and marina 17 miles. Cost: £425 per week inclusive of electric and storage heaters (winter), reductions on fortnightly bookings. Linen not provided. 'Sorry no pets'. **Sleeps 2 to 4.**

Contact: Roger Jones, Golden Fleece Inn, Tremadog, Porthmadog, Gwynedd LL49 9RB. Telephone: 01766 512421. Fax: 01766 513421.

ladwins Farm, Suffolk. A great location, an exceptional pool and sauna. Page 39.

Jane Good's Holiday Cottages, Suffolk. Many real beauties within this agency. Pages 40/41.

ere Lodge, Norfolk. In a quiet part of Norfolk, but not remote, these are all attractive cottages ithin exceptional grounds and with the bonus of a most impressive leisure centre. Pages 52/53.

lagstaff, Norfolk (arrowed). Our favourite 'orfolk views, masses of character. Page 62.

Poppyland Holiday Cottages, Norfolk. Reliable quality and lots of style. Page 60.

lippesby Cottages, Norfolk. 'Deeply rural' harm, but not far from the sea. Page 56.

Norfolk Holiday Homes. This is just one of the many gems on their books. Page 58/59.

Edith Weston Cottage Holidays, Rutland. A cosy retreat in 'so English' gardens. Page 67.

Townend Cottage, North Yorkshire. The M[?] are almost on your doorstep. Page 78.

Fold Farm Cottages, North Yorkshire. Really 'cottagey', in a charming village. Page 85.

Dalegarth/The Ghyll, North Yorkshire. Rig[?] at the heart of the Dales. Pages 86/87.

Thiernswood, North Yorkshire. One can stay by 'the big house' or in the village. Page 88.

Shepherd's Cottage, North Yorkshire. Gra[?] II listed, dating from 1633. Page 90.

Peak Cottages, Derbyshire. Very reliable cottages in a much-loved region. Page 94.

Honeysuckle Cottage, Derbyshire. Tucked away, cosy, warm, full of character. Page [?]

...de House, Derbyshire. One of our 'top 1' places in the north of England. Page 98.

Shatton Hall Farm, Derbyshire. Welcoming owners, and there's tennis too. Page 101.

...eacon Hill, Northumberland. Absolutely ...p-drawer, with many awards. Page 110.

Even for Northumberland, Ross Farm Cottages are spectacularly placed. Page 114.

...airquhan, Ayrshire. Located within one of ...otland's 'best kept secrets'. Page 120.

Culligran Cottages, Inverness-shire. A classic Highland setting, good fishing. Page 129.

...ne of our greatest finds last year was the ...spiring Large Holiday Houses in Scotland...

...whose idyllic properties include Auchinroath House (left) and Achinduich (above). Page 130.

Colour section A, Page 3

195

Mid Fearn. On Scotland's north east coast, well placed for northward touring. Page 132.

Attadale, Wester Ross. A fabulous setting for these comfortable, traditional cottages...

... with rare, complete access to a beautiful estate. Just imagine the great walking...

...and, being so unusually close to nature, wildlife you will see.... Page 135...

Torren Cottages, Argyll. In a memorably dramatic situation, close to brooding Glen Coe. Page 137.

Glengorm Castle, Isle of Mull. A real story book castle, super accommodation. Page

Torrisdale, Kintyre. Comfy apartments and cottages on this 'secret' peninsula. Page 146.

Bank End Farm, Cumbria. Here's how to stay in both England and Scotland. Page

Colour section A, Page 4

Long Byres, Cumbria. Twenty years in this guide, a 'serenely wild' location. Page 151.

The Heaning, Cumbria. Very rural, but still handy for focal-point Windermere. Page 152.

Daleside Farm, Cumbria. 'Little gems', a pleasant, easy drive from Keswick. Page 163.

Longlands at Cartmel, Cumbria. Inviting interiors, a neat courtyard setting. Page 167.

Rosemoor, West Wales. Family-orientated, near beaches, deep in the country. Page 173.

Aberdovey Hillside Village, mid Wales. Superb views over the Dovey estuary. Page 186.

Trenewydd, Mid Wales. One of our readers' all-time Welsh favourites. Spotless interiors, a sought-after location near the coast, an inviting swimming pool. This is special! Pages 182/183.

Colour section A, Page 5

Neuadd Farm Cottages, Mid Wales. Featured in this guide since it first appeared in 1983, the outstanding: they are run with great professionalism and 'tender loving care'. Pages 184/185

Bryn Bras Castle, North Wales. Castle apartments, each with its own character, with access to acres of fine gardens and grounds. The summit of Snowdon is just six miles. Pages 188/189.

Trallwm Forest Cottages, Mid Wales. Quiet, unpretentious, 'deeply rural'. Page 206.

Portmeirion, North Wales. A magical Munchkin-land, but it's 'for real'. Page 181

Pant Farm, North Wales. In ten acres of land, these quite outstanding cottages, featured by us many years, have the big advantage of woodburning stoves <u>and</u> central heating. Page 191.

recon Beacons Holiday Cottages, Mid Wales. Quite simply, we consider this one of the very
est regional cottage agencies in Britain – and it's a fascinating region. Page 207.

arno. Mid Wales. Choc-full of comfort and charm, and well placed for touring. There are many
nusual features, and a great attention to detail on the part of the welcoming owners. Page 206.

r Johns Hill, Carmarthenshire. Children
lore it, especially for the animals. Page 211.

Bosinver, Cornwall. New owners and huge
improvements; near the sea. Page 225.

refanny Hill, Cornwall. Guests effectively have their own inn when they stay in one of these well
paced, highly individual properties. The place is like a hamlet in its own right. Pages 220/221.

Boak Edge, Cornwall. Bring your binoculars – the views from here are terrific. Page 226.

Coverack, Cornwall. A picture-postcard cottage in a very popular place. Page 226.

Sea Meads, Cornwall. Perennial favourites among readers, right by the sea. Page 231.

Trevathan Farm, Cornwall. A warm welcome these fine, one-time farm cottages. Page 230.

Classic Cottages, Cornwall. This outstandingly good West Country cottage agency really does 'set the standards'. We have never had anything but praise from readers. Page 236-238.

Cornish Collection, Cornwall. Near Looe, consistently reliable properties. Page 224.

Treworgey Coach House, Cornwall. Lots to great style, in a hundred acres. Page 214.

Quality Cottages*
(North Wales)

Snowdonia, the glorious beaches of North Wales, and the increasingly popular Isle of Anglesey are high on people's lists of favourite holiday destinations, and are becoming better and better known among overseas visitors. (Dutch travellers especially love the terrain!) Finding good quality self catering accommodation in such popular tourist destinations can be fraught with difficulties, but we find Quality Cottages both painstaking and reliable.

One reader from Southend, in Essex, who found Quality Cottages through the pages of *The Good Holiday Cottage Guide* said of Leonard Rees, the energetic genius behind it, 'You do feel that you are in safe hands'. *And at the cottage guide we have never, in nineteen years, had any kind of complaint.* (Leonard Rees's own holiday cottages at Cerbid and his other agency properties in Wales are dealt with on Page 175.) He is well represented in the Snowdonia National Park, the Llyn Peninsula and Anglesey

Cefn Old Farmhouse is outstanding, and is featured on the cover of our guide...

This fine 'House near Abersoch' overlooks Cardigan Bay and golf links.

where, among other properties, he has a charming, traditional, white-washed stone cottage tucked into the hillside above the village of Nefyn, with panoramic views of *three* bays: Nefyn (within walking distance), Morfa Nefyn, and Porthdinllean National Trust Village and beach. The property is surrounded by three acres of land grazed by Jacob sheep.

Cefn Old Farmhouse is a classic of its kind. Near Caernarfon, it has distant views of Snowdonia and the Menai Straits. If we wanted to introduce overseas friends, for example, to a memorable and authentic Welsh property this might be the one. It has a big inglenook fireplace, a conservatory with a foldaway snooker table, and an inviting dining room with a dining table that takes 12 (the house's five charming bedrooms sleep the same number in total). There is even an old chapel pew on the landing on which to gaze through a picture window at the view of Snowdonia.

At Abersoch, on the Llyn Peninsula, we were attracted by the 'House near Abersoch', which has panoramic views across Cardigan Bay towards Snowdon. A stone-built Welsh cottage (**sleeping 8**), it is ideal for families, water-sports enthusiasts or anybody just wanting a peaceful retreat.

Details of these and more from the Quality Cottages brochure, with many interior photographs: Quality Cottages, Cerbid, Solva, Haverfordwest, Pembrokeshire SA62 6YE. Telephone Croesgoch (01348) 837871.

Snowdonia/Anglesey/Llyn Peninsula/Pwllheli
Shaw's Holidays*

Shaw's Holidays have around 150 properties on their books, covering Snowdonia, the Llyn Peninsula, Anglesey and the North Wales coast. Among others one can choose from properties close to sandy beaches, bustling seaside towns or tucked away in the heart of majestic Snowdonia.

During a recent visit we were pleased to see, for example, three contrasting properties on 'the Llyn', a town house on Pwllheli's promenade, a delightful country cottage, and one we especially admired – *Trefaes*, at Abersoch. An imposing detached house built by a sea captain (it has a number of port-hole windows to prove it!) in the early 1900s, it is still owned by the same family. The property is in an elevated position overlooking the beach, yet only minutes away on foot from the village centre. (Abersoch is a popular sailing, fishing and golfing destination.) Trefaes is in about an acre of mature grounds, a haven for those who like to wallow in lovely surroundings. It is beautifully furnished and extremely spacious, with five bedrooms and two bathrooms. The sitting room, with an open fire, has spectacular views. **Sleeps up to 8**. Linen not provided. No pets. Open all year, breaks out of the main season. Cost: from £320 to £800.

Tan-Yr-Orsedd, 'the delightful cottage' that we visited, is outside Llanengan hamlet, a mile or so from Abersoch: a perfect rural setting. It is a whitewashed semi-detached cottage with a cosy sitting room with open fire, dining room and four bedrooms. The lawned front garden is well-maintained. **Sleeps up to 7**. Pets welcome. Linen not provided. Open all year, short breaks outside main season. Cost: from £180 to £520.

28 Min-Y-Mor is a three storeyed townhouse on the sea front at Pwllheli, built in the 1970s. The agency has a few similar promenade properties which enjoy uninterrupted views of Cardigan Bay. Within a short walk of the town centre and leisure centre, these properties are ideal for family holidays. Pwllheli has excellent sailing facilities and an 18 hole golf course. The property we visited had three bedrooms and a first floor sitting room with a balcony from which to enjoy the best of the views. **Sleeps up to 5**. Pets welcome. No linen. Open all year. Breaks available outside main season. Cost: from £150 to £420 per week.

Details from Shaw's Holidays (01758) 612854 – fax 613384 – or write to Shaw's Holidays, Y Maes, Pwllheli, Gwynedd LL53 5HA.

www.shaws-holidays.com email: all@shaws-holidays.com

Tan-Yr-Orsedd is deep in the country on the Llyn Peninsula, close to Abersoch.

Salt in your veins? Try a Shaw's property on Porthmadog harbour.

North and Mid Wales
Snowdonia Tourist Services*

Geographically very appealing: all the properties on the books of Snowdonia Tourist Services are within the Snowdonia National Park, on the Llyn Peninsula, the Isle of Anglesey or the North Wales Coast, and all are graded by the agency itself, from 'excellent' down to 'plain'.

This well established holiday letting agency offers about 130 properties, ranging from traditional country cottages, farmhouses and bungalows to town houses and holiday chalets.

Among several we have looked at is *Bryn Heulog*, a detached villa in the Portmeirion conservation area which commands uninterrupted views of the spectacular estuary and the mountains. A footpath leads down to the foreshore, a haven of tranquillity. The four bedroomed property has a well

Bryn Heulog is 'an artist's delight', and we love the footpath to the foreshore...

Captain's Beach House is in a marvellous location right on a beach...

equipped kitchen, dining room and sitting room with open fire, TV and video. **Sleeps up to 7**. No pets. Central heating throughout. Cost: about £40 per person to £700.

One could fall asleep to the sound of the gently rolling sea when staying at the *Captain's Beach House*, in a private location right on Aberdesach beach. It is surrounded by dramatic sea and mountain scenery. Glorious sunsets can be enjoyed from the lounge, sundeck and patios. The three bedrooms will **accommodate 6** (and one dog). Cost: about £185 to £460. Weekend breaks available.

Driving down towards the harbour at Porthmadog we came across one of a number of townhouses overlooking the estuary, with panoramic views of the Snowdonia Mountains. (If you listen carefully you might hear the Ffestiniog Narrow Gauge Railway.) To take advantage of the best views, in each case the lounge is located on the first floor. **Sleeps up to 5,** plus cot. Cost: from £110 to £375 per week.

Short breaks are available in these and many others; most are open all year. Details and brochures can be obtained from Snowdonia Tourist Services, High Street, Porthmadog, Gwynedd. Telephone (01766) 513829. Fax (01766) 513837.

www.snowdoniatourist.com

email: all@snowdoniatourist.demon.co.uk

Menai Bridge/Anglesey/Snowdonia/The Llyn
Menai Holiday Cottages*

All the 100-plus properties of this highly regarded agency are on Anglesey, the Llyn Peninsula and Snowdonia. None are far from good beaches and magnificent mountain scenery. They range from one bed-roomed cottages to rambling farmhouses, as well as an impressive manor house on a country estate. Some are simply furnished, reflected in a modest rent, others are 'last word' in comfort. Many, such as *Capel y Waun*, a converted chapel near Llanberis, are houses of great character and charm.

We really liked *Plas Cadnant Lodge*, a delightful Gothic cottage with a summerhouse painted with golden pheasants, from where views of the Menai Strait and Snowdonia can be enjoyed. On the Cadnant estate *The Old Dairy* and *The Brewhouse* have been lovingly converted and fur-

Aber Farmhouse (not featured) is close to the beach. Coastal views, an open fire...

Afternoon tea laid at cosy, convivial Ty Poeth, which accommodates up to ten...

nished to a high standard, as has *The Coach House*, **sleeping 12**, the heart of this award-winning courtyard restoration. Almost thirty people can be accommodated in Cadnant's gracious surroundings, with a magnificent reception room in *The Coach House* big enough to entertain all 30.

Near Criccieth, its castle above the beach, is attractive *Cefn Treflaeth*, a house with fine views to sea and mountains.

For larger parties Menai Holiday Cottages offers a surprising number of houses well beyond cottage size. The largest, *Presaddfed*, a 17th century manor house, has ten bedrooms and nine bathrooms, and here riding or clay pigeon shooting can be arranged for beginners or experts. A new addition is *Druidsmoor*, **sleeping 10**, which is spacious and comfortable, with views across the bay at Trearddur. Other spacious houses that accommodate larger families or groups of friends are *Crecrist Bach*, in a commanding headland position at Trearddur Bay, and *Ty Poeth*, looking across the Menai Strait to Snowdonia. *All welcome weekend house parties*, except in high season.

Cost: £120 to £2100 per week. Short breaks available in most properties. Delicious home-made meals. Local produce 'starter packs'. Nursery hire and activity booking. For a most readable brochure, with good line drawings and lots of detail, contact Menai Holiday Cottages, 1 Greenfield Terrace, Hill Street, Menai Bridge, Anglesey LL59 5AY. Telephone: (01248) 717135.

www.menaiholidays.co.uk
email:ghc@menaiholidays.co.uk

St Asaph's and Menai Bridge
Oakleigh House/Maid's Parlour/Butler's Pantry

Just over two miles from the pint-sized cathedral at St Asaph's and under six miles from Rhyl, *Oakleigh House* **(map 5/335)** is also well placed for touring Snowdonia. Notably, it has its own indoor heated swimming pool and games room, and **sleeps up to 9** in a king-sized double, a double, a family room with twin beds and bunk beds, and a Z-bed. Up to two dogs are welcome.

At Menai Bridge, in the grounds of the owner's house, *The Maid's Parlour* and *The Butler's Pantry* **(map 5/336)** have the shared use of a covered swimming pool, and have their own garden and patio. This is a good jumping-off point for Anglesey – with some of the best beaches in Britain – and Snowdonia. (We strongly recommend a short local trip to Beaumaris.) One dog is welcome in The Butler's Pantry. There is direct access to the Menai Straits, and two Blue Flag beaches are just 20 minutes' drive away.

Details from Hoseasons Holidays Ltd, Sunway House, Lowestoft NR32 2LW. Telephone (0870) 534 2342. Fax (0870) 902 2090.

On-line booking and 'real time' availability on the web:
www.hoseasons.co.uk
email: mail@hoseasons.co.uk

Oakleigh House is handy both for Snowdonia and the coast...

The Maid's Parlour and The Butler's Pantry are suites within this fine house...

A number of readers have asked why our 'special categories' listings at the end of this book makes no mention of short breaks, as these are an important part of the self catering scene. It can however be assumed that nine cottages out of ten that we feature are available for short breaks. Mostly these are for a minimum of two nights. The short breaks season is generally taken to be autumn through to spring, with some tremendous bargains to be had by the increasing numbers of people who appreciate rural Britain in the quieter months of, say, November and February (except for the famous 'February half term'!). Some owners say 'We just like to have the cottages lived in then rather than left empty.' A surprising number of properties are available for short breaks at any time of the year, including the height of the season...

Abergwesyn
Trallwm Forest Cottages

At the heart of a working forest, in a
deeply rural part of mid Wales and
well away from any crowds, is a
clutch of cottages converted from
former farm buildings, most of
which are beside mountain streams.

*Peace, perfect peace, deep in the forest
and well away from any main roads. The
cottages are unpretentious but comfy,
well cared for, reasonably priced...*

Siskin, a detached stone cottage, is
for a couple (non-smokers). *Nant-
Garreg* is full of character, has oak
beams, an inglenook fireplace and
sleeps 4. Two cottages, *Kestrel* and *Red Kite,* are two-bedroomed and
very comfortable. *Trallwm Farmhouse* **sleeps 7**, has a large lounge/diner
and a blend of rustic and modern, with one of the three bedrooms downstairs. *Magpie* is a cosy cottage for a non smoking couple. *Trawsgyrch,* a
large, traditional Welsh stone farmhouse overlooking hayfields, is well
equipped for the **9/10 it sleeps**. Cost: from about £200, fully inclusive, for
2 people. One well-behaved dog is welcome by arrangement (in Nant-
Garreg, Siskin and Trawsgyrch). TVs and phone in Nant-Garreg, Siskin
and Trawsgyrch only, plus payphone for general use. Details from George
and Christine Johnson, Trallwm Forest Lodge, Abergwesyn, Llanwrtyd
Wells, Powys LD5 4TS. Telephone/fax Llanwrtyd Wells (01591) 610229.
www.forestcottages.co.uk email: trallwm@aol.com

Libanus, near Brecon
Carno   Colour section A, Page 6

These are delightful: among the best
we've seen in Wales, the product of
years of dedication by the owners.
Not surprisingly, all have Five Wales
Tourist Board Stars. In a high valley
along a track off a no-through-road,
there is a renovated 17th century
farmhouse, barn and apartment **(map**

*Among the best in Wales...and they have
'Walkers and Cyclists Approved' status!*

5/338). *The Farmhouse* has an inglenook fireplace, bread oven and original stone staircase, while *The Barn* has a beautiful conservatory overlooking the gardens and the mountains. All three have lounge/diner, beamed
double/twin bedrooms, two bathrooms, very well equipped kitchens, dishwasher, washing machines, fridge freezers, full central heating. TV, video,
music centre, classical music collection, videos, books, games for all
ages, barbecue, garden furniture, an indoor heated swimming pool and a
drying room. Linen, towels, heating included, swimming extra. Well controlled pets welcome. The Barn and Apartment are classified Disabled 2.
Cost: individual properties from £240 to £420. Barn plus Apartment £500
to £800. Details from Mrs June Scarbrough, 'Carno', Libanus, Brecon,
Powys LD3 8NF. Telephone (01874) 625630, fax 610345.
www.carnfarm.co.uk email: june.scarbrough@lineone.net

Brecon Beacons and around
Brecon Beacons Holiday Cottages*

Over a couple of very warm summer days during 2001 we were pleased to visit and re-visit some of the properties handled by this much-loved agency. It is a remarkable organisation, with over 250 cottages and farmhouses in and around the Brecon Beacons National Park.

It is run by the energetic Liz Daniel, who recently won the accolade of 'Best Small Business in Wales', and has figured in the the finals of 'Welshwoman of the Year'. Her properties range from a tiny cottage **for 2** opposite Llanfrynach Church to spacious, rambling farmhouses **sleeping up to 50**, and ideal for large families and reunions.

Among others we visited two of the larger properties. Firstly, the remotely-situated (but by no means bleakly lonely) *Crofftau,* whose long, beautifully-furnished lounge/dining room upstairs has a steep beamed ceiling, wood burning stove and spectacular mountain views on both sides. Hard to believe that it was once a barn. **Sleeps 8**. Cost: £700. We don't have the space to convey why it is so very special, but as an example

The Smithy is a fabulous house which, not surprisingly, has won awards. It incorporates several original features.

Lwyn Cor enjoys splendid (and we mean 'splendid'!) isolation. It has loads of character, also with original features.

we were much impressed by the panoramic views, the space, the antiques, the pictures, the huge first floor living room and its extraordinary 1950s Wurlitzer juke box. If ever there was an excuse for a party...

We also loved *Lwyn Cor*, the wing of a spacious former farmhouse and chapel **sleeping up to 10**. We remember the big woodburner in an inglenook in the impressive living room, many books, original features such as a circular oak staircase. There is a lovely atmosphere. Cost: £800.

Bullens Bank, 1000 feet above sea level, has impressive views across the Wye Valley. This secluded three-bedroomed cottage has two comfortable living rooms, a wood-burning stove and a pretty garden. **Sleeps 6/8**. Cost: £435. We also recommend *The Smithy*, in tiny Llanthony. **Sleeping 6**, it has beamed pitched ceilings, antique polished floors, a large open hearth and an attractive garden skirted by the River Honddu. Cost: £445.

Details from Elizabeth Daniel, Brecon Beacons Holiday Cottages and Farm Houses, Brynoyre, Talybont-on-Usk, Brecon, Powys LD3 7YS. Telephone Talybont-on-Usk (01874) 676446. Fax (01874) 676416. **www.breconcottages.com email: enquiries@breconcottages.com**

Sennybridge, near Brecon
Cnewr Estate

The Cnewr Estate is a great location from which to enjoy the Brecon Beacons National Park, a carefully preserved and much treasured corner of rural South Wales, to the full. You can choose between a big 1890 farmhouse, a waterman's house and two shepherd's cottages, all of them on the 12,000-acre Cnewr Estate (owned and farmed by the same family since 1856), and all much praised by readers over the years.

The whole area is ideal for walking, and you could spend a day on the mountains without leaving the estate. There is fly-fishing on the estate's Cray Reservoir, *one of only four in Wales with wild trout*, as well as the hill streams.

We revisited them all in the late summer of of 2001. Probably our favourite is *Cnewr Farmhouse*, which **sleeps 12** in six twin bedrooms and has a long dining table big enough to seat everyone comfortably in the huge well-equipped kitchen. The main sitting room has unspoilt views down the valley and there is also a TV-lounge/children's room, two bathrooms and shower room. The owner's private dining room is available by arrangement for special occasions. There's lots of warmth and a good number of 'country antiques'.

The other three properties are all beside the Sennybridge to Ystradgynlais road but the windows facing it are double-glazed, though there is little traffic. *Nantyrwydd House*, alone in a valley setting, was built to provide accommodation for the nearby (abandoned) waterworks. It **sleeps 8** in two twins and two doubles (one on the ground floor) and has a good sized sitting room with open fire, dining room with oil-fired cooker and fitted kitchen with electric cooker, microwave, washing machine. Small fenced garden. *Fan* and *Gelli* cottages overlook Cray Reservoir, having been built as shepherds' cottages to replace two houses lost when the reservoir was built. They are identical in layout, with three twin bedrooms, bathroom, sitting room, dining room and large kitchen. Both **sleep 5/6**.

Each cottage has an open fire (logs provided free), payphone and TV. Well-behaved dogs welcome. Linen and towels provided. Cost, including heating and electricity, from about £125 to about £525. Short-breaks are available at less busy times of the year. Detailed brochures are available from the Cnewr Estate Ltd, Sennybridge, Brecon, Powys LD3 8SP. Telephone (01874) 636207. Fax (01874) 638061.

www.cnewrestate.co.uk   email: cottages@cnewrestate.co.uk

You don't have to be twelve, but Cnewr Farmhouse can take that many people...

Calmed by watery views? Fan Cottage overlooks peaceful Cray Reservoir...

Wales
Blakes*

Colleagues booked one of this agency's biggest properties for a reunion and a big party during 2001. This is *Park Hall*, in two and half acres just 500 yards from a sand and single beach (in a location we know well, rather a well-kept local secret) near Llwyndafydd, in Cardiganshire. It **sleeps up to 18 adults and 2 children**, and has a licence to perform marriages. Ref B4932.

One of our American readers tries where possible to stay in self catering accommodation that has a full-sized billiard table. He would like *The East Wing*, a self contained part of a fine, mainly Georgian country house, **sleeping 5**, that dates back originally to the 16th century. In one of our favourite parts of Wales, the Lleyn Peninsula, the Grade 11 listed house is on a working farm. Ref WN50.

We have noticed how many people are looking for (so to speak!) panoramic views, and Blakes have one of the most spectacularly situated properties we know. This is *Glyn Garth*, a seventh floor apartment overlooking the Menai Straits and, beyond, the mountains of Snowdonia. It is between Menai Bridge, linking Anglesey and the mainland, and one of our favourite Welsh towns – Beaumaris. We have visited colleagues staying in this property, and did not want to leave! **Sleeps 6**. Ref WA13.

A long-time favourite of *Good Holiday Cottage Guide* readers, and featured on the cover of this edition, *Erbistock Mill*, near Llangollen, is a converted water mill in a spectacular setting on the banks of the River Dee. Retaining many original working parts and with spiral staircases and partly enclosed balcony overlooking the river and weir, it **sleeps 10**. Electricity and bedlinen included. 'Sorry, no pets'; it is not suitable for unsupervised children, the elderly or infirm. Ref WN76.

Just a stroll from the pseudo-Mediterranean village of Portmeirion, and with sea and mountain views, *Plas Penrhyn* is well placed for exploring the Snowdonia National Park and has the Ffestiniog Railway and excellent sandy beaches nearby. Once owned by Bertrand Russell and used by the novelist Elizabeth Gaskell for her honeymoon, it now offers two properties **sleeping 3/4 to 8/9**. TVs. Sorry, no pets. Refs WN27, WN74.

Details from Blakes, Stoney Bank Road, Earby, Barnoldswick BB94 0AA. To book, telephone (08700) 708090. Brochures: (08700) 708099. **Live search and book: www.blakes-cottages.co.uk Quote Ref BMA82.**

Park Hall, sleeping 17, is just yards from a little-known sand and shingle beach...

The East Wing is Grade II listed, sleeps 5, and has a full sized billiard table...

Powis Castle, near Welshpool
The Garden House

Originally the home of the Dowager Lady Powis, this spacious and airy cottage is quite delightfully located in its own grounds beside one of the English/Welsh border country's most famous National Trust properties. Just below the castle itself, the substantial, partly creeper-clad stone-built property **sleeps 6**. During a 2001 visit we especially liked the farmhouse-styled kitchen (well-equipped, however, to modern standards), the unpretentious but comfortable sitting room/dining room, with an open fire and an appealing family-style dining table. There are three good-sized bedrooms (one double and two twins), with memorable views of the castle gardens, and hills beyond. There is also a games room, and even a garage.

Full of history and comfort, almost a part of a famous castle, and so well placed for touring the Welsh borders...

Details/brochures from The National Trust (Enterprises) Ltd, Holiday Booking Office, PO Box 536, Melksham, Wiltshire SN12 8SX. Telephone (0870) 4584422. Fax 4584400. (A card suggesting a voluntary £2 contribution towards production, postage and packing is included.)

www.nationaltrustcottages.co.uk email: Cottages@ntrust.org.uk

Llanrhaeadr, near Oswestry map 5/345
Tom's Cottage

Originally the servants' quarters to the main house, Bron Heulog, this Victorian cottage has been modernised, and now **accommodates 2**. Adjacent to the big house, which is now a B & B establishment run by the owners, it has a compact kitchen with a Victorian range and a lounge area cheered by a log-burner. French windows give character to the double-bedded room upstairs, which lead to a good-sized bathroom and a south-facing cosy conservatory with views over the quiet village of Llanrhaeadr. There is a walled garden, and guests can enjoy daily visits from two fostered, genteel donkeys. No-smoking.

Sleeps just 2, but the owners also offer bed and breakfast...

Details from Hoseasons Holidays Ltd, Sunway House, Lowestoft NR322 2LW. Telephone (0870) 534 2342. Fax (0870) 902 2090.

On-line booking and 'real time' availability on the web:

www.hoseasons.co.uk

email: mail@hoseasons.co.uk

Laugharne
Sir Johns Hill Farm

In ten acres and surrounded by woodland dropping gently down to the sea, Sir Johns Hill Farm is rural indeed, yet only half a mile from the village of Laugharne (famous as the one-time home of Dylan Thomas) with restaurants, pubs, shops and a children's park. In this fabulous location, with *outstanding* sea and rural views, four holiday properties are available. *Merlin,* a stone and slate conversion of a period barn with exposed stone and timbers and a log fire, **sleeps 5** in a ground floor double and a gallery bedroom with three single beds; *The Old Stables* (yes, they were!) which is all on one level, **sleeps 4** in a double and a twin; *Wren Cottage,* **sleeping 2**, has excellent views across the estuary to the Gower Peninsula. The largest property, *Sir Johns Hill Farmhouse*, **sleeps 6** in an ensuite double, a twin and a bunk room, and has amazing views of the estuary, Pendine Sands and – on a clear evening – the coast of North Devon.

New owners Liz and Philip Handford have been extremely energetic since taking over, upgrading the cottages and embarking on a programme of continuous improvement.With the energy comes enthusiasm to make holidays here happy and memorable, so, for example, kitchens are comprehensively fitted and equipped; log burners, TVs/ videos are throughout; a supply of videos and books is available; bedding, towels and logs are provided; there is free use of a washing machine and tumble drier. Meals can also be provided by arrangement. Attractions on site include pony rides, grooming ponies and donkeys and the opportunity to help on the farm. There is also a chance to go flying at Haverfordwest with Philip or to take the dogs down to the beach with Liz.

Dogs welcome (£15 per week per dog). Short breaks. Cost per week: about £160 to £580. Further details from Liz and Philip Handford, Sir Johns Hill Farm Holiday Cottages, Gosport Street, Laugharne, Carmarthenshire SA33 4TD. Telephone (01994) 427667 or 427780.

email: liz.philip@lineone.net

Rear of Sir Johns Hill Farmhouse and Wren's Cottage: both have great views...

An aerial view of the cottages, as taken by the owners themselves...

Do note that we cannot vouch for all the properties on the books of the generally excellent letting agencies we feature, but only those we have visited or have had strong recommendations of. When booking through an agency, it is always worth spending time discussing your requirements in detail.

The West Country

Marvellous sunsets, which can be enjoyed from carefully chosen cottages, luscious crabs, clotted cream and Cornish pasties, coastal footpaths, ancient castles: for more than a century, the West Country has been the most sought-after holiday destination in Britain. The proximity of the sea, wild moors, two national parks, great stately homes: these are just a few of the characteristics of the region. And the climate *is* a few degrees warmer than elsewhere. On the eastern side of the River Tamar from Cornwall is Devon, with dramatic tors and moorlands fringed by charming villages. On the borders of Devon and Somerset, Exmoor is pony trekking and walking country, where wild ponies and deer roam freely. Exmoor has a stretch of coast it can almost call its own, and some spectacular views. In Somerset, Cheddar Gorge and Wookey Hole are memorable. Over the border in Dorset, it is easy to find country houses that are off the tourist beat. (Lyme Regis is a delight.) There's elegant and not-quite-spoiled Bath, and the best of Wiltshire is the essence of rural England, unchanged for hundreds of years. It is dotted with ancient pubs, and half its holiday cottages seem to be thatched!

Botelet, near Herodsfoot
Manor Cottage   map 6/348

With its oak beams, flagstone floors and open fireplaces, Manor Cottage, a 17th century listed longhouse, with origins mentioned in the Domesday Book, is certainly rather special. The dining room doors open to a private walled garden created from earlier ruins, and the kitchen features a covered floodlit well (a first for us!). Coupled with this is a flair for design

A spacious traditional farmhouse, suitable for family groups and couples.

for which Richard Tamblyn has been featured in Elle Decoration. The cottage has been furnished with rare simplicity to a standard that makes guests instantly feel at ease: they often choose to stay twice a year. Brass beds are made up with beautiful antique linen, the fire is lit and table laid with flowers, tea and biscuits. There are books, magazines and a piano for your enjoyment. In 230 acres, with a neolithic hill fort, there is plenty to explore. The Tamblyn family have lived on the farm since 1860 and the present generation now offers 'b and b' in the Georgian farmhouse across the cobbled courtyard. The home cooking is excellent, and you can order freshly baked bread, dinner and even breakfast. Helen is a trained aromatherapist and reflexologist and treatments are available. **Sleeps 5** in three bedrooms (double, twin, single); one bathroom, one shower room. Linen supplied. Dishwasher, fridge/freezer, washing machine, dryer, microwave, TV, video, CD/tuner. Woodburning stove. Babysitting. Dogs by arrangement. Cost: £195 to £850. *NB. A further cottage, not yet seen by us, is available.* Details from Julie Tamblyn, Botelet, Herodsfoot, Liskeard, Cornwall PL14 4RD. Telephone/fax (01503) 220225.

www.botelet.co.uk   email: stay@botelet.co.uk

Polperro
Marigold and Penny

These two fishermen's terraced cottages are tucked away down one of the narrow streets of this quaint fishing village. Each has a small, square, low-ceilinged room on each of the three floors – a kitchen/dining-area at the bottom, sitting room with TV on the first floor and a bedroom at the top. Whole families once squee-

Cosy, unpretentious, very reasonably priced for such a famous location...

zed in, but now they have been comfortably adapted **for 2 to 4** people each. *Penny* is one terrace back from the harbour in 'The Warren' at the most desirable end of Polperro. *Marigold* is a couple of streets back, but that's still no distance, as everything seems miniature in this classic Cornish fishing village. At Penny you'll be tempted to spend time in the bedroom as it has a harbour view. At Marigold, where the rooms are slightly bigger, steep steps outside the back door lead up to a sloping garden and seat from which to enjoy the view over the village rooftops. Cost: about £160 to £300. Not suitable for dogs. Fully equipped. Linen provided but not towels. Details and colour photos from Martin Friend, The Maltings, Malting Green Road, Layer de la Haye, Essex CO2 0JJ. Telephone (01206) 734555. Fax (01206) 734900.

email: martinfriend@rmrestorations.freeserve.co.uk

Polperro
Kirk House   map 6/350

Situated in the famously picturesque fishing village of Polperro, Kirk House is a beautifully converted 19th century chapel, the only self-catering property in the village to accommodate **up to 10 people** *in serious comfort.* The house is just five minutes' walk from the working harbour from where there are boat trips, stunning cliff walks, access to the beach and a natural rock swimming pool. Kirk House has a vast open plan loft style living/dining area with exposed chapel-roof timbers, a log burner and stripped pine floors, seating up to 10 with ease.

A powerful combination: sleeping 10, in Polperro...

There are five individually furnished bedrooms; one king-size, one double and three twin, a fully equipped kitchen and utility room, bathroom, shower room and a private walled courtyard with barbecue, patio heater and furniture. The Eden Project is only 30 minutes' drive. Baby/toddler items provided free. Linen, towels, central heating, electricity included. Dogs welcome. Cost: £599 to £1800. Special 'Lifestyle Breaks' available. Contact Richard or Corinne Lewis: Telephone/fax (01789) 730486.

www.kirkhouseholidays.co.uk
email: enquiries@kirkhouseholidays.co.uk

Treworgey Manor, Liskeard
Coach House Cottages

A reader recommendation from Hampshire led us to this delightful place: 'a fabulous conversion, beautifully and imaginatively done'. Not only does it feel welcoming, but it also has that happy knack of creating a high degree of comfort without losing the character of the Manor – itself in the same family for over 400 years and now under the ownership of Jeremy and Jane Hall. Even the large heated outdoor pool looks no more out of place than the ancient clocktower, the symbol of this architecturally pleasing group of 16th century courtyard cottages, each neatly decorated with hanging baskets of flowers. An all-weather tennis court, games room and boules pit complete the outdoor attractions.

You could even hold a small dance in *The Coach House* which, **sleeping 8**, has a half size snooker table in the sitting room. There is one double bedroom with en suite bathroom, two twin-bedded rooms, a bunk-bedded

Discovering this beautifully cared for Cornish oasis of comfort and style on a warm summer afternoon raised our morale considerably!

one and a bathroom, making it ideal for two families, or for those bringing grandparents. *Paddock View* and *Deer Park* both **sleep 6**, but vary in the distribution of bedrooms and also in decor, each being delightfully distinctive with good use made of original beams, paintings, ornaments and objects of interest from the old manor buildings.

Middle Barn **sleeps 4** in a double bedroom and a twin, and has an upstairs bathroom. Pets are accepted in this property. Dogs will certainly appreciate the walks, the Manor being tucked into 100 acres of pasture and woodland. Children will also have fun exploring the nooks and crannies around the courtyard, not least the mysterious priest's hole, next to the laundry room, which Jeremy recalls climbing into as a child.

With the rare chance of having a cook prepare a meal when you wish there is every temptation to stay put in your own little world. Which is where short breaks, weekend parties – renting all four cottages – come into their own. Each garden has a table and chairs, plus barbecue.

Electricity and calor gas are included, and also an initial basket of logs (each property has a open log fire); linen is supplied, except beach towels; there is a laundry room, payphone and TVs. Cost: about £190 to £940. Details are available from Jeremy or Jane Hall, Coach House Cottages, Treworgey Manor, Liskeard, Cornwall PL14 6RN. Telephone (01579) 347755. Fax (01579) 345441.

www.cottages@treworgey.co.uk

Looe
Trenant Park Cottages

We'd put these in our 'top twenty'. They have such a lot going for them: well located for touring or just closing the door on the world and staying put, lovingly cared-for by owners living nearby, spacious and very comfortable indeed without being twee.

We recently revisited all four cottages, which have featured in this guide for many years. Each looks over lush lawns, with lovely valley views beyond that. Meeting two German families, we saw their cottages through their eyes: absolute havens of comfort, with an eye for detail.

It's surely the Trenant cottages' location that brings people back again and again, plus the way the owners pamper their guests with little extras such as clotted cream teas and fresh flowers on arrival, the plentiful wildlife: many guests feed badgers from their cottages, children feed ducks and other waterfowl on the ponds, and woodpeckers, barn owls, birds of prey, foxes and rabbits are all regular sights. It is because the environment is safe for children. It is probably also the gardens: sweeping lawns and cottage garden flowers, plus a dovecote complete with – yes! – doves.

Trenant is just a five minute drive north of Looe, so you are perfectly placed for visiting the beaches of the south Cornwall coast, the wilder north via Bodmin, and even crossing the Tamar into Devon. Or you might prefer to go on some of the wonderful walks or laze on the beach at Looe.

You are close to the fine lodge house where the owners live. The cottages all have views over parkland with fine oak and chestnut trees. Each is notably spacious, and the interiors are among the most welcoming we have seen, with traditional country furnishings, sofas and armchairs you can sink into, acres of carpet. The well equipped kitchens have dishwashers,

As harmonious a grouping of cottages as we've seen in Cornwall...

We especially remember the manicured gardens that set the cottages off so well.

washer/driers, microwaves and coffee makers. All have antique and brass bedsteads, antique pieces, lots of books. One **sleeps 2**, two **sleep 4** and one **sleeps 5**. There is a payphone in each cottage, and a home-cooked meals service with 'delicious meals brought to your door'.

Open all year. Central heating as well as log fires. Dogs welcome. Linen provided. TVs, videos. Cost: about £195 to £645. Further details are available from Elizabeth Chapman, Trenant Lodge, Sandplace, Looe, Cornwall PL13 1PH. Telephone (01503) 263639/262241.

www.holiday-cottage.com   email: Liz@holiday-cottage.com

Duloe, near Looe
Treworgey Cottages

This is, quite simply, an absolutely oustanding arrangement of cottages. (We called last year, and for a few moments just stood mesmerized by the view.) We were also there to visit a property we had not seen before, which turned out to be a real beauty.

Where is this idyllic place? It is high above the valley of the tidal River Looe, with south-facing views over patchwork fields, wooded slopes, and the river itself. Better yet, owners Lynda and Bevis Wright have land-scaped the prettiest of private gardens for each cottage, with flower borders, masses of roses, and clematis climbing the mellow stone walls, individually tailored to bring both colour and a good degree of privacy to each and every one of the cottages.

The cottage we had not seen before, and fell in love with, is *The Barn*. Every bit of permanent-home quality, it exudes good taste, is well planned and spacious, and has a most appealing garden. It **sleeps 8**.

The Barn is a delight, but each cottage is individually and beautifully

We love the fact that, unusually, every cottage has its own private garden...

... and particularly remember bedrooms that are both romantic and comfortable.

styled, mostly with family antique furniture, original paintings, wool carpets and oriental rugs – and plenty of books.

All the cottages have TVs, videos, dishwashers, microwaves, washer-driers and fridge-freezers, while most have fan ovens and ceramic hobs.

The Wrights specialise in holidays for romantics. This is reflected in the bedrooms, with their antiques, old lace, and fresh flowers. The master bedrooms either have beautiful brass beds with really comfortable mattresses, or exceptionally attractive four poster beds draped in Laura Ashley fabrics.

All the cosy sitting rooms have open log fires or log burners, with polished slate hearths, comfortable sofas and armchairs, mostly covered with Laura Ashley prints or Sanderson fabrics.

Some cottages are **just for 2**: *Orchard* is particularly bright and attractive. And the prettiest of all the cottage bedrooms, we thought, is surely *Well Cottage's*. As for other individual cottages, we were pleased by single storeyed *Secret Garden*, where we met a young couple with a baby who had stayed in several Treworgey cottages but liked Secret Garden best. And what did they like most? Well, the garden, of course!

The Wrights offer a very popular and comprehensive menu of homemade 'ready to heat and eat' meals, from simple pies for a light lunch to a three course dinner, with a good choice of delicious starters, main courses, and mouth watering desserts. You can enjoy, too, some homemade cakes for tea. The outdoor heated swimming pool, just for the few cottages at

A pool-with-a-view is just one of Treworgey's many charms.

We are not surprised that so many readers' children don't want to leave.

Treworgey and Coombe, is beautifully landscaped and 'gardened', and designed not to intrude on the tranquillity of the cottages. The pool and the delightful summerhouse-cum-changing room's sheltered position is a suntrap, yet enjoys the view too. The crystal blue water, weather permitting, is maintained at 84 deg F.

Short breaks and flexible dates are welcome between November and April. With each cottage having log fires and ample central heating, Treworgey accommodates many happy guests in winter – Christmas and New Year are very popular. (By the way, Treworgey is easy to get to by train – there's even a tiny, toytown station at Sandplace, down the road.)

Treworgey is a licensed riding establishment, and riding is available on high quality horses and ponies. You can hack through beautiful woodland or take qualified instruction from novice to advanced standard.

For those who enjoy the comfort of a quality hotel but prefer the freedom of a cottage, Treworgey is ideal. Cost ranges from £195 to £1250, according to cottage and season. (They have one, two, three and four bedrooms, and **sleep from 2, plus baby, to 8**.) Children and pets welcome.

Further details are available from Lynda and Bevis Wright, Treworgey Cottages, Duloe, Liskeard, Cornwall PL14 4PP. Telephone (01503) 262730. Fax (call first) 263757.

www.cornishdream.co.uk email: treworgey@enterprise.net

With lots of animals and a new playground, Treworgey is 'child-friendly'!

Interiors are well planned, comfortable and always clean and warm.

Polperro
Jews Bank Cottage

Almost every nook and cranny of Polperro, surely one of the most photographed seaside villages in Britain, is worth a second glance. But *Jews Bank Cottage* is worth a third or a fourth: not only is it pic-ture-postcard-pretty, and one of the oldest houses in the village (with some fascinating architectural det-

A romantic cottage in a very famous place, best of all when day-visitors leave.

ails), it also enjoys one of the most enviable situations in the whole of Polperro. It is virtually on the seagull-haunted inner harbour – all fishing boats, dinghies and whitewashed houses – where nothing is out of place, nothing jars. The cottage will appeal greatly to visitors wanting some-thing romantic to remember and, while comfortable, retains a number of original features such as beamed ceilings, an open fire and exposed floor-boards in the kitchen and bathroom.

Sleeps just 2 in a double. TV. Car parking space. Not suitable for pets. Electricity by coin meter. Linen is included (and beds made up), but not towels. Cost: about £175 to £300, depending mainly on the time of year you go. Further details from Jackie Ruscoe, Oversteps, Mill Lane, Polperro, Cornwall PL13 2RP. Telephone (014388) 6948.

Fowey   map 6/356
Fowey Harbour Cottages*

This small agency specialises in 'value-for-money' properties – three in Fowey and six in Polruan. It is run with style and care, and has a good following. Our inspector particularly remembers her first 'recce': 'We looked down on the RAF's Red Arrows in flight as they raced over the estuary that divides Fowey from Polruan during carnival week, and

No 2 Chapel Lane, Polruan, is nothing special from the outside, but is most appealing inside – not least for the view!

you can do this from several of the houses on the hillsides above the water.' But at *any* time the views of the busy little harbour are magnifi-cent, so take your binoculars! In Fowey we have seen *17a St Fimbarrus Road*, a well-converted apartment (ETC Two Stars) in a tall Victorian ter-race house with large lounge and two bedrooms (**sleeping 4**), and readers have recommended an ETC Two Star semi-detached bungalow known as *Palm Trees*, near Fowey. Most **sleep from 4 to 6**. Dogs are welcome in the majority, and all have TV. Linen is available for hire. Cost: about £100 to £750. Short breaks are available. Details can be had from David Hill, 3 Fore Street, Fowey, Cornwall PL23 1AH. Telephone (01726) 832211. Fax 832901.

email: hillandson@talk21.com

Classy Cottages

Polperro – Lanlawren – Lansallos
(Three very different locations)

Willy Wilcox and Quay Cottages (Polperro)

We know why over the years so many of our readers have chosen these. Where else could you lean out of the window for a chat with the fishermen on the quayside, listen to the swish of the sea or, in winter, curl up in front of a cosy open fire while the spray from winter storms lashes the heavy wooden shutters? And there is no question about the quality of the Nicolles' cottages: they are graded up to ETC Five Stars.

Willy Wilcox and Quay: surely among the most fabulous locations we know...

Lanlawren Farm (three miles west of Polperro)

One reader told us that all the children could think about while the family was out and about during the day was getting back to the swimming pool...

Lanlawren, which means 'Valley of the Foxes', is another coastal, deeply rural, off-the-road location of two small clusters of stone walled cottages (4) and apartments (6) in what were the former barns of the 13th century monastery farm. The Nicolles have a private indoor swimming pool here for all their guests to enjoy, with sauna, spa, games room and children's corner, and they invite people to 'come and enjoy those wonderful mornings bottle-feeding lambs and collecting hens' eggs'....

Blanches Windsor and Blanches Meadow (two miles west of Polperro)

These beautiful, classic coastal properties, with panoramic sea views and three acres of gardens, are just off the coastal footpath, minutes from an almost-private cove. This was the Nicolles' own home. It is divided, and **sleeps 2 to 16**. Few cottages we know could boast a sitting room as large as this entrance hall!

The Nicolles have 14 cottages, and their hallmark is quality: see their website for the whole story. Dogs welcome by arrangement. A nice touch: you are offered a maid service and a final cleaning service. A Cornish cream tea completes the welcome. Cost: about £95 to £1860. Details: Fiona and Martin Nicolle, Blanches Windsor, Looe, Cornwall PL13 2PT. Telephone (07000) 423000.

Hallway, Blanches Windsor.

www.classycottages.co.uk   email: nicolle@classycottages.co.uk

Duloe, near Liskeard
Trefanny Hill

Scores of our readers have stayed here on our recommendation (we first wrote about it in 1983), and it is probably the most popular Cornish set-up we feature. Indeed, during the last thirty or so years, excluding one two-day period, the Slaughter family have never been without people who have stayed here before, and on some occasions they have been completely full of regular visitors.

It's hard to believe that over 40 years ago, when the Slaughter family first discovered Trefanny Hill, it was a desolate ruin. Nestling above a tributary of the West Looe River, this ancient farming settlement was at one time a thriving, medieval smugglers' hamlet which in the last century was granted its own school, smithy and chapel. Even today, Trefanny Hill retains a village atmosphere. The cottages are lovely, their grey stone or

There is a village atmosphere at Trefanny Hill. The cottages are well spread out and enjoy a feeling of independence.

Each cottage has its own individual character. They range in size from those for 6 to mini cottages just for couples.

white walls draped with ivy, roses and other climbers and looking just like everybody's idea of what a country cottage should be. Each has bags of character, and reveals the Slaughters' amazing eye for detail. There are seventeen cottages in all—well spread out, each with its own garden.

There are five different sizes of cottage, appropriate to the size of your family, ranging from a cosy cottage just for **2** (either with an antique brass double bed or four poster, or king-size/twin beds) to a three-bedroom for **6** (7 with a cot). Among the little extras you will find are plenty of books (including a set of coffee table items on wild flowers, trees, birds). There are video recorders, hairdryers, electric blankets, hot water bottles, alarm clocks. The kitchens are fully equipped with filter coffee makers, spice jars, wine coolers, microwaves, dishwashers and extras galore. All the cottages for 3 or more also have a washing machine/tumble dryer installed, while the smaller ones without this have access to washing machines and dryers in a traditional Cornish building nearby.

Each garden has chairs, a table, a parasol and a good barbecue so you can enjoy fine weather to the full. Standing in 75 acres, Trefanny Hill is surrounded by rolling greenery and commands a wide panorama over the Looe Valley. Among the permanent residents are the ducks on their pond, the chickens, doves, cats, Jacob's sheep and shire horses. The wild flowers in springtime are particularly magical. There are no half-hidden eyesores that detract from the peaceful atmosphere. The interiors of the cottages are like private homes. The furniture is good, old and varied. Each cottage is distinctly different; some have Laura Ashley and Sanderson wallpaper and fabrics, most have oak beams that are up to 400 years old, and log fires.

Perhaps the most memorable part of our most recent visit was strolling downhill past the heated outdoor pool that is accessible to all Trefanny's guests – it is amazingly scenically situated, and always warm – and then through fields towards a wooded stream where we discovered *Tregarrick Millhouse*, another of those substantial family houses that make these journeys so worthwhile. We do not have the space to convey all its delights, but noted most appealing reds and greens in the decor and, outside, large grounds with a stream and a mill pond. **Sleeps 6**.

A tea and coffee tray greets every arriving guest, and all linen – crispy white, generous in size – is provided. Shared amenities include that beautiful heated swimming pool, a children's play area, a grass lawn with badminton net, a golf net for driving practice and more. There is an attractive

Most unusually, cottage guests at Trefanny Hill have their own cosy little inn, which is much enjoyed for drinks, snacks and full meals.

In this attractive setting, people staying at Trefanny Hill have ready access to one of the most impressively situated outdoor pools in Cornwall!

lake, a full size tennis court, trout and salmon fishing rights on a river that flows within the estate, and an enchanting bluebell wood.

The tiny inn within the hamlet is also a popular feature, where you can relax in a cosy, informal atmosphere for drinks or candlelit dinners. Dishes are cooked to order using fresh local produce (freshly caught local fish is the chief speciality of the house), or alternatively you can eat in the privacy of your own cottage by choosing from the full and varied menu offered by a home cooked meals service.

More fishing (lake, river and sea), windsurfing, including hire and instruction, riding, golf, sailing and many more activities are all available in the area. Each cottage has an information folder and relevant Ordnance Survey maps. We wish this was universal!

A typical comment culled from the visitors' books in the cottages reads 'For a long time we have looked for a holiday that offers top class hotel accommodation with the freedom of self-catering – at last we have found it'. Said one visitor from Lancashire, 'it's the most honest brochure I have seen in many years'. And a Surrey couple have been to stay 41 times!

Cost: about £190 to £1250. Children and well behaved pets are welcome. Details from Don, Eileen and John Slaughter, Trefanny Hill, Duloe, Liskeard, Cornwall PL14 4QF. Telephone Lanreath (01503) 220622.

www.trefanny.co.uk enq@trefanny.co.uk

Pelynt, near Looe
Tremaine Green

The cottages most loved by readers of *The Good Holiday Cottage Guide* are often the ones that are part of a little hamlet in its own right. There's the sense of belonging to a community, and such places are popular with children, who are able to make new friends.

At Tremaine Green especially, the whole family will appreciate the on-site games room – table tennis, pool, darts and other games. Also, there's a hard tennis court, putting green, swingball, pigmy goats, rabbits and miniature ponies to feed, good beaches and restaurants a short drive away.

Featured by us some years ago, Tremaine Green now has new owners who are devoting time and money to bringing the cottages 'up to speed' with 21st century comforts. Every building is unique in its way: and even the old road sign at the heart of this hamlet helps to give the place its special character.

Among so many good things, in *Dairymaid's* we particularly liked the antique half-tester bed, the pretty fabrics, the open fire. (All the kitchens have microwave, dishwasher and fridge-freezer in cottages sleeping 4 or

We love the fact that Tremaine Green's cottages are private and self-contained...   *...but are at the same time part of a tucked away hamlet, 'part of a whole'.*

more.) Other details we liked: *Ploughman's* very comfortable settee/deep armchairs, its Ordnance Survey map on the landing.

Many cottages have a genuine, old four poster or half tester at least in the main bedroom, most have some exposed stonework to add to the character, all have a special individual charm.

There are eleven cottages all told, **sleeping 2 to 6,** and there are cots and occasional single beds available in most.

New for 2002, all cottages are now double-glazed, and the open fires in *The Farmhouse* and Ploughman's have now been re-instated. Videos are available for rent, and tickets for the Eden Project (fourteen miles away) are for sale to save you queueing. Tremaine Green has the makings of a memorable holiday – as repeat business confirms – and with the new, all-inclusive oil-fired central heating it makes a cosy winter retreat too.

Dogs and other pets are welcome. Linen is provided. TVs and videos. Cost: about £100 to £700. An excellent colour brochure is available from Justin and Penny Spreckley, Tremaine Green, Pelynt, Looe, Cornwall PL13 2LS. Telephone Lanreath (01503) 220333. Fax 220633.

www.tremainegreen.co.uk   email: stay@tremainegreen.co.uk

Tredethick, near Lostwithiel
Tredethick Farm Cottages

Not only did Tredethick win the ETC's 'Best Self Catering Holiday of the Year' a couple of years ago, but it has picked up *seven other awards* in the last eight. This track-record says a lot about these exceptional cottages, situated on the edge of the Fowey valley between the small town of Lostwithiel and the pretty creek-side village of Lerryn (inspiration for Kenneth Grahame's

Great care has been taken here to retain original features...

'Wind in the Willows'). Grouped around a pleasant landscaped courtyard, all the cottages have been tastefully and thoughtfully decorated. Facilities outside the cottages include a games room, barbecue area, children's outside adventure playground and indoor playroom, pets' corner with goats, lambs, chickens and a pony to ride. All children's facilities have been sensitively located to allow couples to appreciate the rural peace undisturbed. In fact a third of the bookings still come from couples only. **Sleep 2 to 6**. ETC Four Stars. Dogs possible by arrangement. Cost: about £150 to £880. Further details available from Tim and Nicky Reed, Tredethick Farm Cottages, Lostwithiel, Cornwall PL22 0LE. Telephone/fax (01208) 873618. **www.tredethick.co.uk   email: holidays@tredethick.co.uk**

Scorrier, near Truro
The Butler's Cottage   map 6/362

Thoroughbred horses were grazing in the park that fronts the elegant main house when we arrived at this delightful cottage. Butler's is a very comfortable, spacious, recently renovated wing of 'the big house'. We admired the terraced garden at first floor level, the super and well equipped flagstoned kitchen, the antiques, the excellent paintings and prints, the first floor sitting room with beautifully chosen sunflower yellow sofa and armchairs, the long bath in the excellent bathroom. All is stylish and elegant, but not uncomfortably so: you can put your

A real charmer, very well located for seeing Cornwall.

feet up here and unwind completely. All in all, this is a gem: the only thing lacking is the original butler to wait on you. With an open fire in the sitting room, central heating, and lots of books and board games, we thought this would make a good base in the autumn, winter or spring.

Sleeps 4. TV/video; payphone. Pets are possible by arrangement. Linen and towels are included. Breakfast pack. Cost: about £250 to £360. Weekend breaks. Details from Richard and Caroline Williams, Scorrier House, Scorrier, Redruth, Cornwall TR16 5AU. Telephone (01209) 820264. Fax 820677. Mobile (0370) 618595.

Looe
Cornish Collection*

Featured in every edition of *The Good Holiday Cottage Guide* since the first one appeared back in 1983, Clive Dixon's properties have been enjoyed by literally hundreds of our readers. 'Cornish Collection' is an individually run Looe-based agency which presents very comfortable cottage and apartment accommodation – providing a level of facilities and style equal to the best in Cornwall. In every case the sea is minutes away and the wide range of activities available nearby extends from parascending and jet-skiing to golf, fishing, tennis and riding. 2002 sees the introduction of many new properties, some with swimming pools and one or two much larger holiday homes sleeping up to 13 people.

The picturesque cottages Clive Dixon looks after at *Kellow* are as spick and span outside as they are cosy inside. Originally converted from a Cornish farmstead, they accommodate from **2 to 6**. While each has certain distinctive features they all share such agreeable characteristics as fitted carpets, Cornish stone fireplaces with cheery log effect fires, reading lamps and very well equipped kitchens. *Thrift Cottage*, **sleeping 4**, is particularly attractive with its gleaming brass and handsome four poster bed. The views from the patio/barbecue area to the sea are an added bonus.

Orchard and *Rosemary* cottages, **sleeping 4 and 6**, are both very pleasing, as are *Little Oaks* and *Bay*, **sleeping 4 and 5**. About half a mile away is *Seadrift*, an immaculate bungalow **sleeping 4** with 180° sea and coastal views. (There are ample supplies of books, magazines and games.)

Occupying a commanding position right on the sea front, the *Rock Towers Apartments* at West Looe are really special. The views are stunning (with the waterfront only 40 feet away) and take in the town, harbour, river estuary, main beach and coastline. Accommodating **from 4 to 8**, all ten apartments offer sea views, beautiful furnishings, washing machines, microwaves, inclusive electricity and gas central heating, private parking. Most have patios or balconies, en-suite bathrooms, whirlpool baths and dishwashers. Cottages *and* apartments have remote control TV and video and there is a full linen service, including towels.

Cost: about £165 to £1645. Dogs and other pets not accepted. Details from Clive Dixon, Cornish Collection, 73 Bodrigan Road, East Looe, Cornwall PL13 1EH. Telephone and fax (01503) 262736.

www.cornishcollection.co.uk email: cornishhol@aol.com

This is the memorable view from the Rock Towers Apartments.

Inside one of the apartments: readers have praised their style and comfort.

St Austell
Bosinver Cottages/Lodges

This attractively-situated estate of six timber lodges, eleven stone cottages and a fine thatched farmhouse seems to go from strength to strength. It has been much-upgraded and improved by the new owners.

Tucked away in a valley just three miles from the sea, and a short walk to the village shop and the good local pub, the properties are scattered among trees, gardens and meadows in 30 acres of farm and parkland, close to the Eden Project and Heligan Gardens. There are woodland walks, a lake for coarse fishing, a solar-heated pool (three to seven feet deep), a tennis court, pony rides, a games room and an impressive adventure playground.

Each of the properties is different in style, with facilities such as woodburners, storage heaters, microwaves, videos and fridge-freezers; some have central heating. *Rose*, for instance, **sleeping 3**, is a romantic hideaway (we loved its *trompe l'oeil* mural of an old-fashioned kitchen) while *The Barn*, **sleeping 8**, is a spacious conversion of a 150-year old building with glorious views. It is suitable for two families, with two bedrooms and a bathroom on each of the two floors.

Hillside and *Valley View* are newly-built, each with a double and twin bedroom, both en-suite. The purpose-built timber lodges, **sleeping 2 to 4**, are smaller and plainer, but each is privately situated. The 400-year old thatched farmhouse, with six bedrooms (**sleeping 11** plus cot), and two bathrooms (plus an en-suite master bedroom), is very much in a category of its own, being a listed longhouse. Its living-room is 36 foot long and

Harmonious and peaceful, though still a place for children to make new friends.

The swimming pool is a huge bonus...just that 'little bit extra' that visitors love...

has a massive granite fireplace, underfloor heating, a wood-burning stove and an Aga. A smaller living room (with a sofa-bed that **sleeps 2 extra**) has French windows leading on to a private garden.

Sauna (up to four people); pay-phone; laundry; individual barbecues; bikes for hire; linen (not towels) included; cots and high-chairs available where there is suitable space. Some properties available Friday-Friday, some Saturday-Saturday. Short breaks (minimum three nights) available. Cost: from about £120 to £900 (Farmhouse £500 to £1400). Dogs by arrangement, no smoking. Details from Mrs Pat Smith, Bosinver Farm, St Austell, Cornwall PL26 7DT. Telephone/fax (01726) 72128.

www.bosinver.co.uk   email: bosinver@holidays2000.freeserve.co.uk

225

Coverack, near Helston
Sea Front Holiday Cottages

Coverack is the kind of Cornish fishing village publishers of pictorial calendars drool over. We were captivated by *Puffin* because of its uninterrupted views across the bay. A neat little house for **2 to 5**, it is tucked away along a lane at the north end of this pretty fishing village. Recently renovated, it has stripped woodwork and a brick fireplace. The garden is across the lane and drops down from a grassy terrace (with seats) to a low cliff above the beach. As for *Trevarrow*, we'd vote it the prettiest cottage in the village because of its pastel-pink walls

The village is a huge draw, and Trevarrow is a joy...

and thatched roof. It was once a smuggler's hideaway. Though comfortably modernised, it still has its original shipwreck beams and inglenook fireplace. **Sleeps 6.** Excellent kitchens; microwaves, washing machines/tumble dryers. Short breaks. Linen included, as is electricity at cost, though not towels. Bookings Friday to Friday. Cost: approximately £215 to £675. Further details from Raymond and Iris White, Little Pengwedna Farm, Helston, Cornwall TR13 0AY. Telephone (01736) 850649, fax 850489.

www.good-holidays.demon.co.uk
email: ray@good-holidays.demon.co.uk

Coverack, near Helston
Boak Cottages   map 6/367

Any property with fantastic views over a classic Cornish fishing village is bound to be a winner. In this case, two stylish apartments, the ground and first floor of a well renovated house. With a pair of binoculars and a tube of suntan oil you don't really need to move, except that the village is surrounded by lovely walks and has two good sandy beaches. *The Top Flat* **sleeps 5** in three attractive bedrooms with good beds. We noted also

The apartments are great, but with one photo to choose, it had to be the view...

a handsome pine grandfather clock in the hall, a pine kitchen/dining room opening into a well proportioned sitting room with superb views, plain white walls and really comfortable furniture. *The Lower Flat* **sleeps 2** in one charming bedroom (a great view of the beach from the bed!). There's a space-saving kitchen/diner/sitting room. Both flats have night-store heating, TV, microwave oven, shared washing machine in outside shed. Cost: £100 to £480, depending on when you go. Well behaved dogs welcome. Linen can be provided for both flats if required. Details from Jake Roskilly, Tregallast Barton, St Keverne, near Helston, Cornwall TR12 6NX. Telephone (01326) 280479. Fax (01326) 280320.

Maenporth, Falmouth, and around
Cornish Holiday Cottages*

With just 50 or so very much 'hand-picked' properties (owners really do compete to get on her books) Ruth Austen's agency is *one of the best we know*. In 2001 we revisited some old favourites and saw some properties that were new to us.

Tregullow, near where Mrs Austen lives, is a modern bungalow, **sleeping 4**. It occupies a memorable cliff-top position overlooking Falmouth Bay. The sumptuously comfortable L-shaped lounge, with French windows and an open fireplace of Cornish slate, makes the most of the view. An archway leads from the neat dining-room with pine dresser into the kitchen, fitted with oak cupboards, electric oven, hob and microwave.

Not far away is the more family-orientated, comfy but not 'fussy' *La Paz*. **Sleeping up to 8**, and very quiet, it has the advantages of a good sized garden and an open fire. Also in the same leafy residential area is *Helford Point,* a new acquisition of high quality **sleeping up to 6**. It is a three-bedroomed bungalow in a large garden, with stunning views of the mouth of the Helford River and Falmouth Bay.

Closer to Falmouth – in fact, just two minutes' walk from the High Street – *6 Jane's Court*, **sleeping 4/6**, is in Packet Quays, with views from the two bedroomed apartments over Falmouth Harbour. Built in 1985, it is part of an architect's award winning complex. So expect high standards.

Helford Point has fabulous views out to sea, and lies in an Area of Outstanding Natural Beauty. It sleeps 6...

Though close to Falmouth town centre, 6 Jane's Court is quiet. It too has amazing views: in this case of Falmouth harbour.

Different in character is *Sail Loft* (**sleeps 5** plus cot), part of the group of holiday cottages at Calamansac, in the wooded western headland of Port Navas Creek overlooking the Helford River. Designed to maximise the views of the river, the first floor living accommodation is entered via a bridge and balcony from private car parking. It is well equipped, with bedroom one, with double bed and window seat, enjoying river views. The second has twin beds, the third a single bed with space for a cot.

We also loved *Clare Cottage*, in the so-picturesque waterside village of Durgan. It is a beautifully modernised old fisherman's cottage with a particularly irresistible sitting room with a piano and lots of books. **Sleeps 6**.

Cost: from about £153 to £1325. Several of the organisation's properties welcome dogs and most welcome young children. Details from Mrs Ruth Austen, Killibrae, Maenporth, Falmouth, Cornwall TR11 5HP. Telephone/fax (01326) 250339.

Portscatho, near Truro
Jacaranda

This is a strong combination: a modern, spacious and very comfortable bungalow situated in a much-sought-after place. Featured here for many years, it is situated in a peaceful cul-de-sac and both the sitting room and dining room have a spectacular view of St Gerrans Bay. Year after year it continues to be a particular favourite with our readers. It has fitted carpets throughout, and a particularly roomy

Modern houses in superb seaside locations have a big following among our readers, and Jacaranda certainly does...

sitting room. The bungalow has been joined by two bedroomed ground floor accommodation: neat, tidy and cosy, and the sitting room there also has sea views. There are open fires in both properties. The nearest beach is a pleasant ten-minute walk away. You are also close to safe bathing (of particular relevance to families with small children), fishing and good pubs. **Sleep 6 and 4** respectively.

Cost: approximately £120 to £450 per week – a bargain for those spring and autumn holidays. TV. Dogs are welcome by arrangement. There is a covered garage. Further details are available from Mrs Radford, Nchanga, Treventon Close, Portscatho, Truro, Cornwall TR2 5UP. Telephone/fax (01872) 580517.

Portscatho, near Truro   map 6/370
Pettigrew Cottage

We know exactly why this is the sort of seaside hideaway that artists and writers dream of – yet it equally well suits a family. Rich in history, tucked away only 150 yards from the harbour, it was once the home of sailmaker Edward Peters, great-great-grandfather of present owner Hilary Thompson, who has written a book about him. It still feels like a family home, which is much of its

A lucky find in sought-after Portscatho (cottage on the right, with side entrance).

charm: the kitchen/diner is equipped with electric cooker, microwave and more. **Sleeps 4**, in a first floor front double bedroom, with sea view, and a back twin bedroom with a view over the small back garden with a cobbled yard. The living-room has an open fireplace made of local stone, handy for early or late holidays to which this cosy property is suited. Linen on request; electricity by meter; cot on request; TV.

Car parking (one vehicle). Dogs by request. Cost: from £150 to £350. Details from Hilary and Philip Thompson, Chenoweth, 1 The Quay, Portscatho, Truro, Cornwall TR2 5HF. Telephone (01872) 580573.

email: hilnphil@aol.com

Ruan Lanihorne
Watersmeet

On our first visit to this deceptively spacious 200 year old (but modernised) cottage one hot, sunny day, when rural and coastal Cornwall were at their best, the owners were enjoying the cottage and the garden for themselves. The situation is delightfully rural, down a little used country lane on the outskirts of an

Good beaches ten minutes' drive away, on the edge of a small rural village...

attractive small village (a pleasant pub, paths leading down to a beautiful, wood-fringed, partly silted up creek known mainly to bird watchers). Sandy beaches are only about ten minutes away, and St Mawes, with its ferry to Falmouth, is also close. We admired a triple aspect sitting room with an open fire, noticed a good sized TV, a separate dining room, and a well appointed kichen with washing machine, dishwasher and microwave. Stairs to the first floor bedrooms are quite steep.

The cottage **sleeps up to 9**, in a double, a twin, a small single, a room with two three-foot bunk beds, plus a sofa bed in the sitting room. There is gas central heating: this, as well as electricity and bedlinen, is included. Dogs by arrangement. Cost: approximately £250 to £600. Further details are available from Mr and Mrs Denham, 27 The Drive, Northwood, Middlesex HA6 1HW. Telephone (01923) 826614.

St Martin, near Helston   map 6/372
Mudgeon Vean Farm Holiday Cottages

Owner Sarah Trewhella puts it well in her informative leaflet: 'Leave the city life and come and share the peace and tranquillity of our small farm near the Helford River'. Two cottages, *Swallow* and *Swift*, are identical, **sleeping 4/5**. Thoughtfully converted from the former dairy, they have a cosy open-plan sitting/dining/kitchen around an open fire. The third, *Badger*, **sleeping 4/6**, is

Another marvellous Cornish location.

attached to the farmhouse. In addition to having beautiful valley views the farm, in 'organic conversion', with various livestock, is a delight for children. The farm is bordered by a beautiful National Trust walk to the Helford River at Tremayne Quay, where a canopy of ancient trees will shade you from the heat of the summer or shelter you in winter. If parents can drag children away, they"ll find the coves of the Lizard and the beaches of North Cornwall are in easy driving distance. Cost: £100 to £340. Dogs welcome by arrangement (£10 pw). Linen is included. Further details from Mr and Mrs J Trewhella, Mudgeon Vean, St Martin, near Helston, Cornwall TR12 6DB. Telephone/fax (01326) 231341. **email: mudgeonvean@aol.com**

St Endellion, Port Isaac
Trevathan Farm

On a hot summer afternoon in 2001 we revisited these farm-based cottages and found them as quiet and relaxing as ever. Although they are very much part of a farmstead, each cottage is very private, and has bags of individual character.

We remembered from our first visit being followed around by Polly and Honey (goats) and William and Blackie (sheep) as we inspected old farm buildings transformed into holiday homes over the past fifteen years. The Symons family has farmed here since 1850 and this is still a busy 250-acre working farm keeping them fully occupied. They have about 100 sheep and about 200 cattle and calves, fields of corn, pick-your-own

Original farm buildings have been turned into excellent holiday houses.

A busy working farm, and each pet animal has its own name.

strawberries and a tribe of pet farm animals – all of them with names. And the Symons's daughter runs a tea-room/farm shop.

Wherever you go, there are panoramic views over miles of unspoilt countryside. Another bonus is that visitors can become as involved as they like. There are are eggs to hunt for and usually lambs or calves that need hand-feeding. The dogs, cats, ducks, rabbits, Shetland ponies and pot-bellied pigs also like attention. There's a well-equipped games room, a tennis court, a play area and (in the same ownership) a one-acre fishing lake.

The nine cottages here are well spread out. Each has its individual character, and its own garden with chairs and barbecue. **Sleeping 2 to 8**, the cottages are extremely well equipped. Kitchens, for example, even have food processors, deep-fat fryers and slow-cook pots. Two have dishwashers. *Fuschia* and *Cherry* both have their bedrooms on the ground floor. *Bramble*, *Clover* and *Damson* cottages are single-storeyed.

At Tregoodwell Farm, near Camelford, the Symons also rent out *Polmear House,* which overlooks a sheltered wooded valley. With five large bedrooms (**sleeping 12** plus cots), two lounges, dining-room, kitchen, conservatory, utility room and games room, it is perfect for a big family group.

All are English Tourism Council Three Stars except for one that has Four. Cost: approximately £140 to £1000 for the cottages; from £300 to £1200 for Polmear House. Dogs are welcome in two of the cottages. Linen is included, and towel hire is available. TVs and videos. Further details can be obtained from Henry and Shirley Symons, St Endellion, Port Isaac, Cornwall PL29 3TT. Telephone/fax (01208) 880248.

www.trevathanfarm.com   email: Symons@trevathanfarm.com

Praa Sands
Sea Meads Holiday Homes

This amazing place has so much to offer: the mile-long sandy beach, facing due south into the broad sweep of Mounts Bay, the nine-hole golf centre, riding stables within easy reach, not to mention the charm of the properties themselves! And one of the greatest draws, especially for families, is that glorious beach which is only a five minute walk; you can not only see and hear the waves, you can almost touch them!

On our last revisit we were delighted to rediscover the properties on a private road almost hidden from the little cluster of buildings above the beach. Sea Meads is a group of five detached houses, each with its own private garden facing the sea, spacious lounges with large sliding patio windows through which to enjoy those views, dining areas with serving hatch from modern kitchens equipped with dishwashers, fridge-freezers, cookers with extractor hoods, microwaves, washing machines, clothes driers, bathrooms with heated towel rails and wall heaters – everything to permanent-home standards.

Solmer, Sunwave, Sea Horses and *Sunraker* are all similar. On the ground floor there is a twin-bedded room with en-suite bathroom and toilet, and a small room with double bunk beds. Upstairs are two large bedrooms (one double, one twin) – each has a small balcony with magnificent sea views, and a second bathroom with shower unit. The ambience is one of brightness and light, with comfortable furniture and charming domestic touches. There is plenty of space, a private garage to each house, room in the garden for ball games, all-in-all a recipe for the most exacting family who just want to laze about or go in for strenuous activity. **Sleep up to 8**.

This is a typical bedroom-balcony view!   *Semi-tropical gardens, superb interiors.*

The fifth house, *Four Winds*, **sleeping 5**, is lower lying and separate from the others. We loved the big, very comfortable sitting room and the linked sun lounge on to the sea side; we also liked the different-level dining area and the ensuite bedroom with impressive sea views. The other bedrooms are a twin and a single.

Cost: approximately £195 to £910, depending on which property and when you go. TVs/videos. Dogs are welcome. Linen is included, towels are available on request. There is a games room, with table tennis, pool and darts.

Further details from Wendy Amos-Yeo, Best Leisure, North Hill, Shirwell, Barnstaple, Devon. Telephone (01271) 850611. Fax 850693.

Padstow
Harbour View

Sometimes it's nice to let the world go by and just sit in the window here...

The location is amazing. Right at the heart of one of Cornwall's favourite small resorts, this attractive, three-storeyed Grade II listed building on the quayside allows you to keep an eye on what's going on! It was built as the Harbour Master's office about 400 years ago when sailing boats brought cargoes from around the world. Now yachts and fishing boats keep the harbour busy, and during the summer the quay is one of the liveliest spots in North Cornwall.

The building has been converted successfully into four apartments. *Stepper* and *Gulland,* on the first floor, and *Pentire*, occupying the whole of the second, have superb views over the harbour, so we were not surprised to learn that artist visitors like to settle down with a brush in their sitting-room window-seats. Stepper and Pentire have two bedrooms, Gulland has one. *Daymer*, at the back, has one bedroom and is more suitable for people simply wanting a handy base at a reasonable price.

All are ETC Three Stars. Washing machine, tumble dryers; dishwasher in Pentire. TVs. Linen included. Car parking, dogs extra. Cost: about £150 to £575 per week. Details: Mrs Tereen Oliver, telephone/fax (0707) 120 2105.

Launceston map 6/380
Bamham Farm Cottages

Very good conversions, with the bonus of an indoor pool, sauna and solarium...

Retaining the authentic character of a 200 year old farmhouse and former farm buildings, while keeping ahead with facilities, has played a big part in satisfying the demands of discriminating self-catering visitors to this top-notch complex. This is due mostly to the enthusiasm with which Richard and Jackie Chapman, both locals, have tackled the conversion over 20 years. The ultimate attraction for many must be the huge 36ft by 15ft indoor swimming pool, heated year-round, with adjoining paddling pool, plus sauna and solarium. Add a children's play area, games room, boules and private fishing, and the family appeal becomes obvious. Bamham is also well suited to out of season short breaks.

The cottages (four have Three ETC Stars, four have Four) are individually designed, carpeted and tiled throughout, with extensive gardens and ample parking. Linen and and towels available. No pets. Laundry room, TVs, video recorders, cots and highchairs. Cost: from £195 to £870. Details from Jackie Chapman, Higher Bamham Farm, Launceston, Cornwall, PL15 9LD. Telephone (01566) 772141 Fax 775266.

www.cottages-cornwall.co.uk   email: jackie@bamhamfarm.co.uk

South West Cornwall
St Aubyn Estates

In four separate and highly desirable coastal locations in the south of Cornwall, James and Mary St Aubyn run their family business in 'faraway' west Cornwall, offering high quality holiday cottages in stunning coastal locations. Three of the cottages are near the slightly-off-the-beaten-track historic town of Marazion (very near Penzance) and six are near the dream-holiday picture-postcard village of Porthgwarra.

Better yet, they are outstandingly good in their own right. *Venton Farmhouse*, at Marazion, is a joy. We took our time to enjoy the space, the quiet, the upgrading to an extremely high standard with no loss of the character of this substantial farmhouse. Among so many good things is the view across the water to St Michael's Mount, the spacious walled garden (unusual for a seaside location) and a private path to the rocky beach below. We admired some excellent local pictures, mirrors, six foot double beds in several instances, a superb big dining table, a top notch kitchen, stylish and understated colours. With Five ETC Stars (no surprise there), it **sleeps 10**, and is not overpriced at a maximum of £1695.

Within a few minutes' drive of Land's End, making our way cautiously along narrow high hedged lanes towards the sea at Porthgwarra, we looked out for picturesque *Corner Cottage* and *Cove Cottage*. Literally yards from the cove, each cottage was occupied when visited by people delighted by their find. In Cove we admired a well planned combined

Venton Farmhouse is a superb property, overlooking St Michael's Mount...

We looked at two super properties in picture-postcard Porthgwarra Cove...

kitchen/dining room and sitting room, and an unusual basement with a glassed-over stream below. **Sleeps 4** in a double (ensuite) and a twin. In Corner we liked the double brass bedstead, the expensive pine floor. **Sleeps 2**. Each has central heating. No TV in either (inadequate reception).

Not yet seen by us are, also at Porthgwarra, *Lower Roskestal Farmhouse*, a substantial granite farmhouse **sleeping 11**, and *Three Chimneys*, a recent complete renovation of two hill-top cottages, **sleeping 8**. More remote than these is *Faraway Cottage* at Nanjizal, **sleeping 4**. At Marazion, *Trevarthian Farmhouse* is an attractive period home **sleeping 12** and at Relubbus is *Relubbus Vene,* **sleeping 4 'plus 2'**.

Details and brochure from Clare Sandry, St Aubyn Estates, Manor Office, Marazion, Cornwall TR17 0EF. Telephone: (01736) 710507 or 710233 (office hours). Fax 711544.

www.staubynestates.co.uk   email: godolphin@manor-office.co.uk

Cornwall – countywide
Forgotten Houses

We've seen some inspiring country houses – many in the West Country. But visiting a handful of the properties on the books of this unusual organisation, devoted to restoring and preserving mainly-tucked-away country houses (occasionally 'just in time') made for a memorable day in 2001.

At Bosvarren, up a tree lined drive (seemingly remote, though just ten minutes' drive from Falmouth), we looked at three of the five houses in the hamlet, each with garden, parking and countryside access. There are two Elizabethan farmhouses, a larger Georgian house and a 1990 renovation of a 16th century cottage adjoining a later stone barn. There's ample safe parking and each house has a safely enclosed lawned garden.

Lower Bosvarren is a listed Elizabethan farmhouse that retains original features, including the roof of small 'scantle' slates and two huge stone fireplaces (one with two old bread ovens). It has two sitting rooms and two woodburners. It **sleeps 8** in four bedrooms.

Higher Bosvarren is another old farmhouse, which **sleeps 7** in three bedrooms. It also has two sitting rooms with a woodburning stove within each huge fireplace, and a sheltered south-facing garden. *Little Bosvarren*, the renovated 16th century cottage/barn, **sleeps 4** in two bedrooms with room for a **possible 2 extra**. There is a vast first floor sitting room with woodburner and direct access to the walled garden.

We also looked briefly at attractive *Bosvathick Lodge,* near Falmouth, a cosy traditional gate lodge with a good-sized garden, **sleeping 4.** The Lodge is the smallest of all the properties, which range upwards to include the truly magnificent, such as the renovated Georgian mansion at *Tresillian*, near Newquay, which can provide the highest standards of comfort for two or three families in an astonishing house and gardens.

Both Higher Bosvarren (above)...   *...and Lower Bosvarren are delightful.*

Also under the Forgotten Houses umbrella are *Trenethick Barton*, an important early medieval Grade I house that was *modernised* (!) in around 1550, and *Mellinzeath*, close to the Helford river. Thought to have been rebuilt after a fire in 1665, it lies in what has been described as 'a quite extraordinarily lovely valley'. Both **sleep 4/5.**

It's fascinating, but we can only scratch the surface here. Best to send for a copy of a functional, not glossy but intriguing, detailed brochure, which includes floorplans, from Forgotten Houses, Bosvathick, Constantine, Falmouth, Cornwall TR11 5RD. Telephone (01326) 340153. Fax 340426. Or see the well regarded website: **www.forgottenhouses.co.uk**

St Tudy, near Wadebridge
Chapel Cottages

Full of character, with original stable front doors, beamed ceilings, polished slate floors, window seats and, in three, large granite fireplaces with cloam ovens, *Chapel Cottages* are a group of four listed stone-built cottages on the edge of the quiet village of St Tudy (a shop and an inn are a short walk away). Each cottage is individual and pleasant, with good

Lots of character in a very convenient small-village location.

bedrooms, one with a double and single bed, the other with twin beds – and everything on hand for comfort and convenience. The pine kitchens are attractive, with individual washing machines. This is a good touring base, for within easy reach are Bodmin Moor, the Camel Trail and the beaches of Trebarwith, Polzeath and Daymer Bay, while craggy Tintagel and Boscastle are also encouragingly close.

Cost: approximately £110 to £368 per week. TV. Linen, cots and high chairs are included. Private parking. Not suitable for pets. Further details are available from Clifford and Margaret Pestell, 'Hockadays', Tregenna, near Blisland, Cornwall PL30 4QJ. Telephone/fax (01208) 850146.

www.hockadaysholidaycottages.co.uk

Lezant, near Newquay
East Penrest   map 6/386

The striking 70-foot long lounge/-dining-area/kitchen, with its hefty old wooden beams, leaves you in no doubt as to the building's origins as a barn. 'When we converted it, we wanted to maintain its character,' Jo Rider told us. She and her husband organically farm the 90 or so acres around, which feel blissfully remote, though are only five minutes from the A30. Rather than dividing it up, they left the upper floor as it was and

Children can watch the farm at work, and adults will appreciate that this excellent conversion can sleep up to ten.

installed four double bedrooms below (**sleeping 8 to 10**). The 'longroom' has radiators, wood-burner and Aga in the kitchen area. French windows lead on to a patio and a south-facing floor-length window provides a grandstand view of the farmyard. There are three bathrooms.

Bedlinen (but not towels) is included. Piano, books, home-cooked meals, baby-sitting available. Wheelchair access to both floors. No smoking indoors. Cost: about £350 to £1000.

Details from Stephen Joyce, P O Box 21, Hertford, Hertfordshire SG14 2DD. Telephone (014388) 69489.

The West Country
Classic Cottages*

'Classic', as they are widely known, have an outstanding reputation among our very many readers who have used them over the past 20 years. They offer a wide range of possibilities – a seaside cottage just for 2 here, something inland for an extended family there – and their catchment area of Cornwall, Devon, Dorset and Somerset does yield some of the most interesting family holiday homes – every one different in its own right – in the country. Extremely well known in the West Country and among the many thousands of people who travel to that eternally popular corner of Britain for their holidays, Classic are uncompromising: it is almost unheard-of for a cottage to be accepted on to their books without some improvements being required.

In ten acres of woodland and paddock, Maenporth is very special. We would rate it among our top ten in Cornwall...

We love its big rooms and the sea views several of them have. But it is not remote: Falmouth is only three miles away...

Our visits and revisits to Classic properties over several seasons have yielded many gems. First on our list was *Maenporth Cottage*, a very impressive and superbly situated house by Maenporth beach, that looks out to sea. We saw it just as it was being spruced up for incoming tenants, and we really envied them their stay, for the huge sitting room – handsome white leather sofas, among other good things – and the main bedroom look directly out to sea (and the rising sun). Everything is expensively appointed, and there is lots of space. **Sleeps 10**.

We loved *Man O'War,* in the sea-buffetted village of Cadgwith. It is the archetypal seaside cottage, full of character but also exuding the loving care with which Classic Cottages is associated. The sitting-room enjoys romantic views of the waves and of fishing boats tucked in for the night. Approached by a short, steep drive, it has its own parking space – rare in the village – and a short walk brings you to the cottage itself. The footpath continues all along the cliffs to one side, giving some spectacular sea views, but if a lazy stroll to the village pub is more to your liking, walk the other way and you will be in the centre of the village within a minute or two. The ivy clad cottage is Grade II listed and has been furnished with every comfort. A combination of old pine, an open fire, Laura Ashley fabrics and dried flowers add up to a most charming home. **Sleeps 8**.

Overlooking the harbour in Falmouth, there are several flats available in purpose-built 'town' properties finished to an extremely high standard. Among them are *Admiral's Quay* and *The Anchorage,* which have balconies overlooking the water and are quite exceptionally comfortable, with big windows, deep sofas and armchairs. Both are admirable, but the latter is a memorable property by any standards, especially for its combined sitting/dining room, which has floor to ceiling picture windows to set off the view. These two apartments **sleep 4 and 6** respectively.

Among other cottages we were taken with *Corlan*, in Mullion, a very skilful conversion indeed that is on the edge of Mullion village (with panoramic views from the rear) and yet only three quarters of a mile from the beach. **Sleeping 4**, it has a charming gallery with a ladder and low headroom that is just made for children.

More views and, better yet, the waterfront apartments at Falmouth are extremely well appointed...

As with many of the Classic properties they are certainly of permanent-home standard...

Originally an alehouse, *Ivy Cottage* in the delightful north Cornwall village of St Tudy (named the Best Kept Village in Cornwall in 2000) lies close to the start of the Camel Trail. Bursting with character with, for example, original slate flagstones throughout the ground floor, beamed ceilings and the occasional low lintel, it features *three* inglenook fireplaces and period furnishings. It **sleeps 6** and has an enclosed garden.

In the Teign Valley, which borders the edges of Dartmoor National Park, Leigh Farm is tucked away in a small and very pretty valley of its own. Here, in 60 acres of fields and woodland (wonderful wildlife, particularly less common species of birds), and with a pretty water course running

A record for us: Ivy Cottage has no fewer than three inglenook fireplaces!

Corlan is one of our favourites, not least for the sleeping gallery children love.

through the courtyard down to a wildlife pond, are three completely refurbished cottages. *The Cob* was virtually totally rebuilt to extremely high standards using, for example, slate flagstones, wooden floors and, on the landing, an unusual feature of glass bricks. Furnishings are particularly comfortable and the large sitting room has an always-welcoming woodburner. As you would expect in a property of this calibre, the kitchen has

The Cob's exposed stone, original beams and 'country furniture' appeal to us...

And bedrooms are pretty and well lit (the cottage sleeps 6).

cooker, microwave, fridge/freezer, washing machine and dishwasher. **Sleeps 6** plus cot. *The Forge*, next door, **sleeps 4** in a double and a twin and is similarly appealing with exposed stonework and a beamed ceiling. It can be opened up with The Cob to provide accommodation for 10. Tucked away *Granary Cottage* makes a romantic and relaxing retreat for **just 2**. The large living area is upstairs, facing over the garden and to the fields beyond. A particular joy of these three properties is the owner's passion for collecting unusual and fine pieces, pictures, prints and *objets d'art*, which is clearly seen throughout.

In one of the most distinctive locations in England, very close to the picturesque National Trust owned Corfe Castle, *Brook Cottage* is itself full of character, and is Grade II listed. The sitting/dining room, in yellow and blue, and with a number of original features sympathetically retained, is especially appealing. **Sleeping 6**, this makes a good point from which to explore the charms of a county that tends to hide its light under a bushel.

Visitors to Corfe Castle tend to gaze admiringly at Brook Cottage...

And that is without even getting to see the especially charming interior...

To obtain further information and a copy of the impressive and extremely readable and detailed Classic Cottages brochure, please contact Classic Cottages, Leslie House, Lady Street, Helston, Cornwall TR13 8NA. Telephone (01326) 555555. Fax (01326) 555544.

www.classic.co.uk

classic
cottages

Port Gaverne, near Wadebridge
Gullrock

We revisited these historically interesting cottages, just two minutes' stroll from Port Gaverne's sandy beach, in the summer of 2001.

They are tucked nicely away down a narrow lane, a convivial arrangement of cottages on three sides of a grassy courtyard with flower borders and historical associations. The building was originally constructed about 200 years ago to cure and store the fish catches landed in the cove, and was used for this until the turn of the century.

These are sensibly priced (particularly good value outside the main holiday season), unpretentious and 'practical' units in what can sometimes be an expensive corner of the West Country. We particularly liked the bigger, *Seaways*, **sleeping 6** in three double or twin rooms, with a spacious sitting room and a pleasant outlook on to the courtyard at the front and trees at the rear. The charming and cosy flat called *Creekside*, looking in part over the courtyard, is cleverly arranged to **sleep 6** in four bedrooms.

Each unit has a dishwasher, microwave, fridge-freezer, TV and video, CD/radio cassette and full central heating. An outbuilding houses washing/drying machines, a payphone and an assortment of garden furniture. The grounds include not only the courtyard, but an outer garden with barbecue and picnic area, and there is a parking space for each cottage. The beach, just 75 yards from Gullrock, is very sheltered, providing safe bathing and fascinating rock pools. The coast path crosses the head of the

Even by coastal Cornish standards, this is an irresistible little village.

And the cottages themselves are in a tidy, well kept and rather historic courtyard.

beach, leading over the westward headland to the village of Port Isaac, and east along wild and remote clifflands to Trebarwith.

Visitors' pets are very welcome, and Gullrock's resident pets are all friendly. Sample prices including electricity and heating: £160 February, £350 May, £640 August (open all year). Discounts are available to parties of three people or fewer from April to October, except during the summer school holidays. Off season short breaks (which is some people's favourite time by the sea in Cornwall) may be booked at a daily rate.

Linen not provided, but towel hire available. TVs. Full details are available from Malcolm Lee, Gullrock, Port Gaverne, Port Isaac, Cornwall PL29 3SQ. Telephone (01208) 880106.

www.goodcottageguide.com/cornwall/gullrock.html
email: gullrock@ukonline.co.uk

St Agnes/Perrancoombe
Rosemundy Cottages

In the summer of 2001 we visited these lovingly cared-for cottages, whose owners have married historical character with 21st century standards of comfort, and have a huge following among readers as a result.

We looked again (while it was being spruced up for new arrivals) at *Jasmine Cottage*. This is one of three cottages, each with its own garden, just two minutes' drive from a large sandy surfing beach at Perranporth, with its cliff and cave formations, rock pools and natural arches.

Here, as in all the other cottages, there are deep dralon suites and smart pine kitchens. For those with young families, the two-bedroom cottages have been well equipped with cots, high chairs, a laundry room and a small children's play area.

Couples and families with older children (12 years plus) will find that *Rose Cottages*, in a small conservation area in the village of St Agnes, are in a special place with beautiful old trees, rich in wild life, bounded by a stream. Close by, the natural coves of Trevaunance and Chapel Porth (National Trust) are linked by the Cornish Coastal Path which takes you past restored engine houses – relics of Cornwall's tin mining history.

In all the cottages we like the marriage of exposed stone, white walls and sturdy beams. Some have woodburning stoves in inglenook fireplaces, while all have night storage heaters. You can choose from either a one or two bedroom cottage **sleeping up to 5**. All are equipped to a high standard with TVs, microwave ovens etc. Bedlinen (not towels) is included.

We've wondered whether the owners here (there are two locations) invented the term 'tender loving care'...

All the cottages are warm and comfortable – but not pretentiously so – and very well situated for the seaside.

All are well situated for touring, walking, leisure facilities, including golf/driving ranges, horse riding and fishing (sea and coarse). One dog allowed in some cottages only by arrangement. Private parking. Colour brochure from Martin and Jenny Butterworth, Deep Dene, Rosemundy, St Agnes, Cornwall TR5 0UF. Telephone (01872) 552293.
www.rosemundy.clara.net email: jenny@rosemundy.clara.co.uk

Treneglos, near Launceston/Tintagel
Higher Scarsick

This most beautifully situated property (it comes highly recommended, and we'll see it for ourselves in the spring of 2002) is a substantial part of the owners' farmhouse. It is a place for absolute peace and quiet, to experience 'the sound of silence'. With the distant views of Dartmoor on the horizon, and such irresistible places as picture-postcard Boscastle

Here one can experience that rare commodity, 'the sound of silence'...

and Tintagel a short drive away, this has lots going for it. A Mrs Walker of Enfield has been many times, and says 'The owners are so friendly, the cottage is very clean and warm, and the children love helping on the farm, and even bottle-feeding lambs in spring. On a warm day it's nice to eat outside in the garden (table and chairs provided), which is quite a suntrap.' A nice touch here, which seems to typify the caring owners' attitude, is the Cornish cream tea offered on arrival.

TV/video. Open fire. **Sleeps up to 6** in two doubles and a twin. Not suitable for pets. Babysitting. Linen and tea towels included (plus personal towels for overseas guests). Cost: about £120 to £350, with discounts for couples. Details from Heather French, Higher Scarsick, Treneglos, Launceston, North Cornwall PL15 8UH. Telephone/fax (01566) 781372.

Poughill, near Bude   map 6/392
Honeysuckle/Valley View

Not yet seen by us but well recommended, these two well equipped cottages are part of the Trevalgas Farm complex, which lies within its own spacious grounds, and has wide-ranging rural views. *Honeysuckle* **sleeps just 2**, *Valley View* **sleeps up to 7**. Trevalgas is less than a mile from the village of Poughill, which has a pub serving good food and a

Lots to do in a super, popular location...

shop. The cottages are just a mile and a half from the coast, known far and wide for its miles of golden sandy beaches and bracing cliff walks. The ever-popular, never-crowded seaside resort of Bude, one of our own favourites, is also quick and easy to get to.

Hugely appealing is of course the 40-feet long indoor swimming pool, along with a games room containing a pool table and table tennis. TVs. Dogs are possible by arrangement. Linen included but not personal towels. Cost: about £200 to £850.

Further details available from Rosemary Lauder, 2 Blackgate Cottages, Westleigh, Bideford, North Devon EX39 4NS. Telephone (01271) 860232.

Tintagel
Tregeath

Featured *in every single edition* of this guide since its beginning, this one-time farmworker's cottage appeals as strongly as ever. It is tucked quietly away in what some people call 'the middle of nowhere', and is none the worse for that. Its popularity is easy to understand, at least for those simply wanting an unpretentious character cottage which has

Not far from Tintagel, this does not claim to be a show-house, but we like it, and have always had good reports.

been enhanced by a small rear patio area in matching slate and stone. The result is a sort of snug-bar feeling, ideal for an off-season retreat or for lazing in the summer sun, listening to very little except the sound of sheep from the 50 acres of adjoining farmland. About a mile from Tintagel, and one and a half from the surfing beach at Trebarwith Strand, this is no showhouse, more a sensible family home with a very convenient galley-kitchen, a combined sitting/dining room and stairs up to two double bedrooms. There's a roomy single bedroom adjacent to the sitting room and a pleasant enclosed and safe garden. **Sleeps 5** plus cot.

Cost: £100 to £400. TV/video. Payphone. Single dogs welcome. Further details from Mrs E M Broad, 'Davina', Trevillett, Tintagel, Cornwall PL34 0HL. Telephone/fax Camelford (01840) 770217.

Bossiney, near Tintagel map 6/394
'Newlands'

Many of our readers like comfortable, modern properties that are handy for famous tourist destinations. Here is one, a stone's throw from Tintagel Castle and some of the most spectacular, rocky coastal scenery in Cornwall. It is a very well maintained bungalow offering spacious accommodation with all the 'mod cons' one appreciates so much: big bedrooms, big windows, constant hot water. But, more traditionally, it

A spacious family house with a most inviting garden, very close to a famous coastline along which such substantial houses are hard to find.

has an open fire. It is set back even from the quiet road it's on, and we can see why it has a following with big families (and, say, two smallish families travelling together), for among other good things there is a handsome front garden with hydrangeas and a sheltered back garden with a lawn and shrubs. In short, we thought this an excellent base, especially as it can accommodate **up to 7** people.

TV. One dog only welcome. Bedlinen provided, towels an optional extra. Cost: £290 to £510. Details from Mr Wickett, Bossiney Farm, Tintagel, Cornwall PL34 0AY. Telephone (01840) 770481.

St Genny's, Crackington Haven
Mineshop Holiday Cottages

This is an exceptional location: as you go from one tiny, hidden lane into another, shortly after you turn west off the A39 Camelford-Bude road and come, finally, to leafy Mineshop, you feel a thousand miles from the workaday world and have some of the most dramatic coastal scenery in Cornwall just a short stroll down the lane. (We do enjoy finding corners of Britain we would not normally discover when putting together *The Good Holiday Cottage Guide*.)

During our most recent revisit, Mineshop's wandering ducks were being fed by guests sitting contentedly on the verandah of *The Old Shippon*; in the cool of the evening. They (the guests, not the ducks, although the latter may have tried to accompany them!) planned to walk down the green and tranquil footpath to the beach, which they would probably have to themselves. In one of the lodges, in the same green and sunny location, a couple were brewing up and simply enjoying the view of the garden.

Mineshop has a strong following among people who like getting 'away from it all' without feeling isolated: the owners of the Mineshop cottages live in the centre of what is effectively a private hamlet. More than half of each year's visitors have been before, and one family has been 20 times!

Effectively under the same ownership, but scattered elsewhere in this dramatically striking corner of North Cornwall, are three quite excellent cottages, each one beautifully located – one high on a headland, and very private. The other two are adjacent to each other, close to one of the coves near Widemouth Bay. The first, *Cancleave*, has dramatic views of the

Marvellously well situated: Millook House and Little Millook.

One of the Mineshop properties: lots of greenery and peace and quiet.

famous bay. The Cornish coastal footpath runs close to the house. There's lots of pine, good table lamps. *Millook House* and *Little Millook* are down in the valley below, and we thought the former a real gem: very much a traditional farmhouse. Both have deep sofas, low ceilings, some antique furniture. These two **sleep 8 and 6** respectively.

Cost: approximately £106 to £750 per week, according, as usual, to size and season. Bed linen is supplied in most cottages. (Cots provided.) TVs, laundry room. Obedient dogs are allowed. Registered with the Cornish Tourist Board.

For further details please contact Mr and Mrs Cummins and Mr and Mrs Tippett, Ref: GH, Mineshop, Crackington Haven, Bude, Cornwall EX23 0NR. Telephone St Genny's (01840) 230338.

Trengale, near St Neot
Lower Trengale Farm

This thirteen-acre smallholding seems to us as well suited for a spring or autumn break as for a full-scale summer holiday. We've always thought what an excellent base this is for exploring Cornwall: though deep in the country, you are only about half an hour's drive from some of the best beaches in the West Country, and the Eden Project. Converted *Many years in this guide, ideal for large groups. Super beaches half an hour away.* from a stone barn, the three cottages offer quality accommodation for **2 to 6**, attractively furnished and at a sensible price. There are good facilities for children, with a playground and games room. A large artist's studio on site makes this a marvellous place for groups to holiday together, and a series of excellent residential craft holidays is on offer.

ETC Four Stars. Dogs welcome by arrangement. TVs/videos, woodburning stoves and dishwashers. Linen and towels provided; laundry service. Cost: from about £180 to £530. Details from Mrs Louise Kidd, Lower Trengale Farm, Liskeard, Cornwall PL14 6HF. Telephone Liskeard (01579) 321019. Fax 321432.

www.trengaleholidaycottages.co.uk email: lkidd@eurobell.co.uk

Looe Valley   map 6/399
Badham Farm Holiday Cottages

If you alight from the single-car train at Causeland Halt, on the picturesque Looe Valley Line, you'll find yourself just beyond the peaceful picnic area which makes the setting for Badham, three miles from Looe, that little bit different. As do a delightful animal/bird paddock for children, a coarse fishing lake and a big games room with small bar. *The Farmhouse* **sleeps 10** and *The Stable*, **sleeping 6**, *Deeply rural, but also near the sea...* has its open beam sitting room upstairs. These and *The Coach House* (**sleeps 2**) have patios with garden. *The Dairy* has three bedrooms, **sleeping 7**, one on the ground floor, sitting room, with original flag stone floor, dining room, kitchen, small patio and garden. *The Byre* and *The Hayloft* (**sleep 4**) are self-contained, with pretty sitting rooms.

Linen, towels, electricity included; central heating. TV, radio/cassette players, hairdryers, electric blankets and electric fires. Video players for hire. ETC Three Stars. Dogs welcome. Cost: about £105 to £785. Details from Joyce and Robert Brown, Badham Farm, St Keyne, Liskeard, Cornwall PL14 4RW. Telephone/fax (01579) 343572.

Chapel Amble, near Wadebridge
Rooke Country Cottages

Standards are very high here. We revisited in the summer of 2001, and found everything humming along beautifully. We didn't meet any guests, as they were all out and about, and we envied them such fine cottages to 'come home to'.

Less than a mile from Chapel Amble, but deep, deep in the country, you turn into an enclave of stone-built farm buildings no longer needed for farmworkers which has been turned, with skill and an impeccable sense of taste, into top-notch holiday accommodation.

The Forge **sleeps 5**, both *Walnut Cottage* and *Jasmine Cottage* **sleep 4**, and each bears the unmistakable Rooke Farm stamp of quality. For example, among so many of the details that set these easily into a 'best of Cornwall' bracket, you will find king-size beds in the main bedrooms (most of which are en-suite), an inglenook open fire in Forge, and wood-burning stoves in the other two; each has a private garden area, of course with garden furniture, and each has a really extensively equipped kitchen. In these latest three we like the light, modern pine look, the patterned rugs on expensive pine floors, the beams and the pretty touches such as well chosen table lamps, attractive pictures and curtains.

In all six cottages there is an eye for detail with, for example, hanging baskets, plain white walls and exposed stone, beams, old stripped pine, good quality deep pile carpets, thoughtful lighting.

To recap on the existing properties, there is *The Farmhouse,* a fine, spacious family home **sleeping 7**, *Honeysuckle* **sleeping 2 'plus 4'** and

We are absolutely full of admiration for what has been achieved here.

Forge is 'cottagey', but very up to date in terms of comfort and facilities...

Meadow **sleeping 6**. These have now been refurbished in order to keep standards high and in line with the newer cottages. All have a wood-burner, and kitchens are of show-house quality, bathrooms with baths *and* showers, main bedrooms that are en-suite. Digital TV, DVD, videos, hi-fis, phones with modem connection.

Sleep 2 to 7. ETC Five Stars. Dogs possible by arrangement. Cost: £350 to £1150, including linen, towels, electricity, heating, logs/coal and mid-week maid service. Details from Rob and Gill Reskelly, Rooke Country Cottages, Chapel Amble, Wadebridge, Cornwall PL27 6ES. Telephone (01208) 880368. Fax 880600.

www. rookecottages.com   email: info@rookecottages.com

Cornwall – countywide
Cornish Traditional Cottages*

Forty years ago, the original directors of Cornish Traditional Cottages bought a derelict cottage in Padstow and renovated it for their family use. It was the first of many such ventures and the start of a hobby which developed into a business. By the early 1970s other owners wanted their cottages to be let by the company and so Cornish Traditional Cottages, the first holiday letting agency in Cornwall, and one of the first in the country, was born.

Since its early beginnings, the agency has always prided itself on the personal and friendly nature of the service offered – as true today as ever. You can speak to a real person (not a machine) between 9 am and 9 pm seven days a week ('answering machines cannot answer questions and personal response is so much more helpful'). Then there is the 'smiles'

Contrary to appearances, handsome Hawkstor Farmhouse is modern ...

Leaze Farmhouse, in contrast, dates partly from the 13th century...

system of rating properties – generated entirely by customers from the grading the company asks them to give a cottage's fittings, furnishings and equipment, after their holiday, on the questionnaire sent to them.

Peregrine Hall, on a hill overlooking Lostwithiel, is in a quiet location only fifteen minutes' drive from the Eden Project. In ten acres of gardens, meadow and woodland, this magnificent Gothic style hall built by George Edmund Street, designer of London's Law Courts, is far from being imposing, but a relaxing retreat into a historical context with modern day facilities to match. This includes a 26 ft by 15 ft solar heated swimming pool in the colourful garden, and keep-fit room, with multi gym, table tennis, sauna and hot tub.

There are eight cottages available here (**sleeping 2 to 6**), seven of which have the top, three-smiles grading. *Wing Cottage* (**sleeps 4**, three-smiles) provides light and spacious accommodation, with a delightful south facing sitting room heated by a multi fuel stove set into the old local stone hearth. It has two bedrooms, one with a double bed and splendid views, the other with single beds; there is also a small nursery. *Rose* (**sleeps 2**), another three-smile grading, has a distinctive gallery bedroom with double bed and shower compartment/wc.

Tinkers is a fine example of the pretty little 17th century fisherman's cottages that line the main street of Boscastle. With slate floors, beamed ceilings and an inglenook fireplace, it **sleeps 4 to 6** in comfort, and has its own attractive garden.

Leaze Farmhouse is one of the oldest (13th century), one of the most isolated and one of the most popular properties on this agency's books (so get in quickly for a booking). A holiday cottage since the first world war, it is delightful for an away-from-it-all holiday, being at the end of a moorland road in an area of Bodmin Moor that enjoys wide open views. The moorland village of St Breward is a five minute drive. **Sleeps 2 to 4**, one-smile, plenty of character. Also on Bodmin Moor, equally isolated, yet in contrast to Leaze, entirely modern "traditional" (built in 1991) is *Hawkstor Farmhouse*, **sleeping 6 to 8**, three-smiles.

Virtually sitting in the water at Polruan is *Folly Cottage*, **sleeping 4 to 6**, one-smile, an ex coastguard boat shed!

We have, among our readers, an increasing number of garden fans, who would love the cottages at Tregrehan and its famous collection of camellias, rhododendrons and conifers. The walls of the estate's old grain mill enclose a secret garden at the entrance to *The Coach House*, which has a

Pilot's Lookout, only a few feet from harbour and beach, is Grade II listed...

Pentire Cottage, on Pentire Farm, has an open fire and memorable views...

twin room and a king size bedroom with an additional single bed. *Sprys Cottage* is tucked away from main courtyard and **sleeps 2** in a double room. *Gamekeepers Cottage* is the end cottage in the old carriage house and **sleeps 4** in a king size double and a twin room. There is a spacious walled garden, entered through a glazed door from the rear twin bedroom. The cottages here are two-smiles. The Eden Project and Carlyon Bay's sandy beach and golf course are less than ten minutes' drive, and the area abounds with coves, beaches and delightful walks.

Coastguards and *Porth Lystry*, **sleeping 6 and 4/6** respectively, and both with three smiles, are quality conversions of coastguard cottages with fabulous views across Falmouth Bay. And as its name implies, *Pilots Lookout*, at Mousehole, offers a good vantage point from which to enjoy the buzz of the harbour and the sea in all its differing moods.

At the end of a rough track – but enjoying spectacular views over the Camel Estuary – is Pentire Farm, with two-smile properties. These include the *Farm Wing* (**sleeps 6 to 8**), with four bedrooms, one with substantial bunk beds, and *Pentire Cottage* (**sleeps 4 to 6**) with a working open fire. Beamed farm-style kitchen. One bunk room downstairs, a double and a room with two pine singles upstairs.

Pets are welcome in about a third of the agency's properties. For further details and an excellent brochure, with a clear and attractive illustration of each property, contact Cornish Traditional Cottages, Blisland, Bodmin, Cornwall PL30 4HS. Telephone (01208) 821666, fax (01208) 821766.

www.corncott.com email: info@corncott.com

St Breward, near Bodmin
Penrose Burden Cottages

Twenty years in this guide, *and never a whisper of a complaint* about these traditional stone buildings and their kind, hospitable and thoroughly professional owners. The cottages have appeared on television and in the national press, and those owners have received a 'Highly Commended' Award in the Holiday Care Awards.

The views are typically Cornish, offering wide, lush countryside not far removed from the beaches, which are some 20 minutes' drive away.

Walkers and ramblers should take note that Bodmin Moor is about a mile away, and for the less energetic there are superb walks down through the woods to the river meadows below the cottages. Free trout and salmon fishing is available on the farm's own mile-long beat of the River Camel. In addition visitors have the opportunity to fish all the local Anglers' Association water in the vicinity (extending to nearly seventeen miles). Keen salmon fishermen should note that the Camel is the latest river in Britain – closing in mid-December.

It is not easy to believe you are on a busy farm here: all is tranquil and the working centre of the farm is at a respectful distance from the cottages. While the majority of farm building conversions are grouped around a central courtyard, those at Penrose Burden are sited in a much more spacious and random way. The cottages each enjoy an individual garden and

Butterwell has long been one of our personal Penrose Burden favourites.

The layout of cottages and gardens is very sensitive and very attractive.

panoramic views over the wooded Camel valley, rolling pastures, and the moors beyond. Riding is available nearby, and arrangements have been made with the country hotel (just over half a mile away) for guests to use their indoor heated swimming pool, sauna, bar and tennis courts.

Imagine you have just arrived: it is evening: you are tired from your journey, but there is a meal on order for you to look forward to. As you drive in, there, as promised, is resident housekeeper Jennifer to welcome you (who will already have made up your beds, as all linen and continental quilts are provided). There are fresh flowers on the tables and your meal is ready – delivered and cooked by a neighbour. You stroll round your cottage – perhaps it is *Otterbridge* with its pine four poster bed, a woodburner in the large open plan living area, and fine views from the low level windows, or maybe *Wenford* (of which more later) with its thoughtful and subtle lighting, its original oil paintings by a well known artist. Indoors you will find locally made pinewood furniture, and outdoors a picnic table and benches with a portable barbecue. Penrose Burden extends to about 500 acres. The traditional stone cottages by the farmhouse are, respectively, *Butterwell,* Otterbridge, *Goosehill* and *Snappers*, each **sleeping 5**, *The Linney*, **sleeping 4**, and *Jingles*, which **takes 2 plus 1** little one. They all have woodburners (free logs provided), TVs, lovely farmhouse russet tiled floors (fitted carpets in bedrooms) and pine fittings of a high standard, good pictures. Well behaved dogs are welcome here.

Most recently available here is the impressive, mainly open-plan *Toad Hall*, **sleeping 6 'plus 2'**. It has three en-suite bedrooms (wheel-in showers) and a gallery room that can be used as sleeping accommodation or, for example, a separate TV room.

Half a mile down the hill are another two charming cottages. More recently restored and converted, Wenford and *Troutstream* lie by a small bridge over the Camel. Wenford is the largest of the cottages here, **sleeping 6** in three bedrooms. Built 200 years ago for the local toll-keeper, it has two bathrooms (one ensuite) and is fully insulated with ceiling heating, imaginative lighting (dimmer switches controlling hanging lamps or sunken fittings), the original exposed oak beams, good storage space, and those fine tiled floors with attractive rugs, pine furniture ... just as in the other cottages. Troutstream Cottage (just beyond Wenford, and built to the same standards) **sleeps 5** in two bedrooms, and a sofa unit makes the fifth bed. All nine cottages have electric night store heating – free between October and April inclusive. Menus of ten home-made dishes (plus desserts) are sent prior to arrival. Orders are taken daily thereafter.

The cottages relate prettily to each other, but are also as private as you would like.   *All is easy on the eye, with a skilful use of local stone and slate.*

Rodney Hall is disabled himself, and all Penrose Burden's cottages are sympathetically designed to suit the needs of wheelchair users. It is important to say, however, that such features are unobtrusive. All the accommodation is of a high standard and provides comfort and relaxation for every holidaymaker. The cottages are open all year round.

Glancing through the visitors' book it was evident that the same families return year after year throughout a long booking season. Nancy and Rodney Hall live in the farmhouse and are always available to assist.

NB Should readers have friends who are disabled, they should send for a copy of the special Penrose Burden leaflet for disabled guests.

Cost: about £180 to £550 per week. Brochures from Nancy and Rodney Hall, Penrose Burden, St Breward, Bodmin, Cornwall PL30 4LZ. Telephone Bodmin (01208) 850277 or 850617.

www.penroseburden.co.uk

Rock
Cant Cove Cottages

This is where we reach for our book of superlatives. Cant Cove is the sort of place that gives tourism in Britain a good name. All the interiors, as well as the splendid setting, are worthy of five star hotels. (But if we had our own stars to award, these properties would get ten.)

The location alone, overlooking the wide, ever-changing Camel estuary, has always left us wide eyed. The Mediterranean-style gardens glow with colour in summer, while the accommodation itself is close to perfection.

Orchard House (not featured) has exceptional views of the estuary and farmland, and sleeps 6.

Stylish, open-plan Isabella has a certain Scandinavian ambiance about it, but is still very much 'in keeping'...

In the hands of Colin and Sue Sleeman, who were cheerfully sorting out guest queries when we called in the summer of 2001, cottage tenants never really need to wander far from this exclusive 'hamlet' of six properties. In 70 acres of private farmland, with uninterrupted views, it offers wildlife walks, complimentary tennis, croquet and a golf practice area.

Built to an executive standard, they are generously spaced out to attract large families as well as those seeking an intimate off-season hideaway. Each has its own private garden, patio area and barbecue.

Particularly impressive is *The Farmhouse*, **sleeping 6**, a wistaria swathed replica of an original 18th century farmhouse that stood here previously. Original stone flags are used in the hallway while the ultra-modern kitchen is effectively a modern recreation of the original; in the sitting room there is a log burning fireplace. The main bedroom has a four-poster bed with en-suite bathroom, another has twin beds with en-suite shower room. A third has a twin. There is a Victorian style bathroom. All properties have 'whirly baths', and The Farmhouse and *Old Granary* (**sleeps 8**) even have saunas. The Farmhouse is close, though not obtrusively so, to the excellent astraturf tennis court.

We admired *Kate* (**sleeping 5**), with a separate lounge and kitchen. Unlike its sister house, *Isabella,* which **sleeps 5,** it is not open plan. Both typify the standard that's earned all the properties Five ETC Stars.

Open all year (out of season the open fires for which logs are provided free really score). No pets. Cost: about £335 to £1905, including gas, electricity, linen and central heating. Details from Colin and Sue Sleeman, Cant Cove, Cant Farm, Rock, Wadebridge, Cornwall PL27 6RL. Telephone (01208) 862841. Fax (01208) 862142.

www.cantcove.co.uk   email: info@cantcove.co.uk

Blisland
Hockadays Cottages

A lovely, quiet location and kind and conscientious owners: though this is deep in the country it's just fifteen minutes' drive from the spectacular coast (and handy for Bodmin Moor and the Camel Trail). After negotiat-

Private, self-contained, and modestly priced. Each is a perfect hideaway, but the owners are conveniently close by.

ing some of North Cornwall's leafiest lanes, we recently turned up a private one to rediscover two small, totally charming, well looked after cottages called *Demelza* and *Rowella*. Each is within a converted stone and slate building that feels very private, and each is a wonderful hideaway **for 2** plus a baby. Among the details within the 17th century converted barn are white painted walls setting off oak beams, wall lamps, some original features retained such as wooden lintels, small paned windows, cottage doors. Each has a living room, a separate well equipped kitchen, bedroom and bathroom. One is an 'upside down' house, with the bedroom downstairs. There is a big garden, parking, and excellent views.

TV. Linen is included. Regrettably they are not suitable for pets. Cost: about £100 to £268. Details: Margaret Pestell, 'Hockadays', Tregenna, near Blisland, Cornwall PL30 4QJ. Telephone/fax (01208) 850146. **www.hockadaysholidaycottages.co.uk**

St Issey, near Padstow   map 6/405
Trevorrick Cottages

What a lovely atmosphere! We revisited in 2001, and met several very contented people staying. These six cottages (converted from old buildings beside the owners' farmhouse) have the attractions of a heated swimming pool (Easter to October) and a games room in a large barn. *Lily Pad Cottage*, which has a four-poster, and the *Old Round House* are

Easy access to some of North Cornwall's many sandy beaches is a bonus here...

cosy hideaways **for 2**; the latter has an attractive semi-circular living room with an open fire and a vaulted ceiling. Single-storeyed *Serendipity* (**sleeps 4 or 5**) is suitable for people with limited mobility. Two further cottages (*Owl's Roost* and *Curlew Cottage*) are two storeyed; *Badger's Way* (single storeyed) is the largest of all, with a log fire and a garden. These **sleep 4 or 5**. TVs. ETC Three Stars. Cost: £179 to £699. Out of season short breaks. Dogs welcome, linen included; towels, night storage heating available. Baby-sitting and B& B available. Details: Mr and Mrs Benwell, Trevorrick Farm Cottages, St Issey, Wadebridge, Cornwall PL27 7QH. Telephone/fax (01841) 540574.

www.trevorrick.co.uk   email: info@trevorrick.co.uk

Widemouth Bay, near Bude
Kennacott Court

This impressive development, on a 75 acre former farm just off the A39, is the creation of Howard and Maureen Davis, following his retirement from international banking. In under ten years Mr and Mrs Davis have planted 9000 trees, created a five-hole golf course and two nature trails, and built two all-weather tennis courts and a leisure centre. From the grounds, as well as from many of the cottages, you get magnificent views over rolling farmland to the sea. Indeed, Widemouth Bay, one of the best beaches on the North Cornwall coast, is only a mile to the west. For shop-

The Farmhouse, where the owners once lived, is (as they all are) ETC Five Stars.

The leisure centre is one of the best we have come across in our travels.

ping, the busy little town of Bude is less than three miles away, and a supermarket is even nearer.

The accommodation is in eighteen smartly furnished cottages, with mod cons that must surpass those in many a home. No surprise then to hear that the Davis's are past winners of an ETB 'England for Excellence' Silver Award. Each of the eighteen is graded Five Stars by the English Tourism Council – *the highest grading.* The cottages, **sleeping 2 to10**, are mostly in converted farm buildings (though the Old Orchard cottages are purpose-built and quite special). They have dishwasher, washer/dryer, microwave, fridge/freezer, remote control TV, video, CD/cassette player and direct dial telephone; some have a second TV.

We thought *The Farmhouse* would be ideal for a really convivial family gathering. Everyone would be able to eat together around the huge pine table in the big cosy kitchen. To help the catering run smoothly, it has two toasters, two kettles, a heated trolley and a mountain of large pots and utensils. All the bedrooms, fitted in pine, are a good size, including a double with shower/WC on the ground floor. The larger of the two sitting rooms has a stone fireplace (fuel provided free), and is well stocked with books and games. The other leads to the conservatory, which overlooks a large secluded garden with croquet lawn and gas fired barbecue.

Adjoining it, *Granary* (**sleeping 6**) has its own walled garden and huge windows which make it very light and airy. A feature we particularly like is the open gallery upstairs, with the three bedrooms (a double and two twins) leading directly off it.

Eight of the cottages are around a courtyard and have an 'upside down' layout – bedrooms down, living rooms up to take advantage of the outstanding views. *Sandymouth* (**for 2**) is popular with honeymooners, is very spacious and has a four-poster bed and en-suite bathroom with sunken corner bath. The upstairs living area has lovely views. Similarly, *Millook*, **sleeping 6** in three downstairs bedrooms, has a large living/dining area on the first floor, ideally positioned for watching the golfers.

Children love *Foxhole*, because the twin bedroom with dressing room is up in the roof space, reached by a spiral staircase. Another unusual feature is its sunken living room with a 'living-flame' electric fireplace for chilly days; indeed we noticed this cheering accessory in several cottages. *Salthouse* (**for 4**) is on one level, so is suitable for wheelchairs.

We were particularly impressed by the wide range of activities available

A most impressive restoration of properties on a 75 acre former farm.

The adventure course is a challenge for adults as well as children!

on site. The superb indoor leisure centre, purpose-built, with wheelchair access throughout, includes a 38-foot swimming pool and – for adults only – sauna, solarium, fitness room and full-sized snooker table. The games room – for all ages – has a pool table, table-tennis and table-football. The library is well stocked with books as well as 300 videos, including plenty for children, and games: all are available on free loan.

Outside, an adventure 'assault' course provides as much fun for adults as their offspring. Parents can let their children wander around the nature trails on their own and a three-quarter-mile path is suitable for prams and wheelchairs.

The par-18 golf course is playable in under an hour – useful, as Mr Davis points out, if you have impatient non-playing companions awaiting your return. It's popular too for introducing children to the game – and pushchairs are welcome around the edge. A practice net and nine-hole putting green are nearby. Picnic tables, gas barbecues and a dog walking area complete the scene.

Cost: approximately £220 to £1780; electricity and central heating are included. Bedlinen (apart from cot sheets) and towels are provided. Cot, highchair and stairgate available free. Dogs are welcome in The Farmhouse and The Granary – though only between October and May in some of the other cottages, and not at any time in others. Open all year (golf April-October, £25 per week). Further details from Mr and Mrs H Davis, Kennacott Court, Widemouth Bay, Bude, Cornwall EX23 0ND. Telephone (01288) 361766.

www.kennacottcourt.co.uk

email: maureen@kennacottcourt.co.uk

Bridgerule, near Bude
Glebe House Cottages

Standing on the hilly outskirts of the village of Bridgerule, Glebe House, a lovely late Georgian stone built house in five acres of formal gardens, lawns and woodland, commands beautiful uninterrupted views. Having featured here for eighteen years without a break, it holds a special place in our hearts, and so we were particularly pleased to revisit recently and see how, during the last few years, the new owners have upgraded the cottages and put their own stylish stamp on them. And what they have done to the *gardens* is amazing.

All of the seven spacious, warm and comfortable cottages have exposed beams and mellow stone walls, and are ETC Four Stars. **Sleep 2 to 6**. We admired the carefully chosen fabrics, comfortable chairs and sofas, the discreet pictures, old farm implements and saddlery items on the walls.

The Old Stables and *The Mews* are similar in layout, built on two floors with open-plan staircases. Old Stables has the original uprights for the stalls in the middle of the lounge. Both have canopied beds and whirlpool baths (Old Stables's is a double!). *Little Barn*, *Granary* and *Coach House* have their living rooms upstairs with fine exposed roof timbers. At ground level each master bedroom now has an ensuite shower room as well as the recently refurbished main bathrooms. Granary and Little Barn

A stone-built Georgian house, with cottages of a very high standard and considerable character nestling close by.

Living rooms are very spacious and comfortable, and the owners have a particularly good eye for detail.

have had 'minstrels' galleries' created to provide additional sleeping accommodation. These two can be linked to take larger family groups. *Gamekeepers* and *Poachers* provide accommodation to an extremely high standard while maintaining their old world charm, with exposed beams and other period features. Both cottages have four-posters in the main bedrooms and double whirlpool spa baths: ideal for 2 people or families.

All are welcome: honeymooners, 'senior citizens', families with young children. Cots, highchairs and baby listeners are free, and there is a children's play area and games room. There is a bar and a good restaurant for guests' exclusive use. Central heating, electricity and bedlinen included. TV. Cost: from £220 to £765. Pets not allowed. Details and an excellent brochure from James and Margaret Varley, Glebe House, Bridgerule, Holsworthy, Devon EX22 7EW. Telephone Bridgerule (01288) 381272.

www.glebehousecottages.co.uk
email: holidays@glebehousecottages.co.uk

Shirwell, near Barnstaple
North Hill Cottages

Our latest visit to these 'tucked away' (in the nicest sense of the word!) cottages turned into a most enjoyable journey of rediscovery. By the time we'd travelled the last mile along a private lane up a wooded valley, sharing peaceful views with none other than a few grazing sheep, we remembered it would be hard to find a more rural spot. Indeed North Hill's tranquillity seems to be disturbed by nothing more than the occasional sound of a distant tractor.

This is the sitting room of Harvest (sleeps 6): light, bright, beamy and spacious. *We were not surprised to find that a place of such excellence has a fine pool.*

Around the 17th-century stone farmhouse, several old barns, pig-sties and shippens (cow-sheds) were turned into exceptionally comfortable cottages with exposed beams and timbers and log-burning stoves. South-facing, they nestle at the top of the valley enjoying glorious views back to the Taw Estuary from their living areas, bedrooms and gardens.

There are eight cottages altogether, with appropriate country names such as *Harvest* and *Orchard*. Each varies slightly in design and size but all have pine furniture, fitted carpets and kitchen areas equipped with microwaves and fridge-freezers. We particularly recommend *Rye* as a special, romantic hideaway **for 2**, as it has a four-poster bed in an alcove, or *Ivy*, whose four-poster room has an en-suite bathroom. The larger cottages, **sleeping 4 or 6**, make this a haven for families too.

With no traffic to worry about, even the youngest children can enjoy the freedom of the countryside. As well as the surrounding fields and woodland, there is a duck pond and plenty of lawn to play on, with swings, Wendy house and climbing frame. Also, everyone can enjoy the indoor heated pool as it has a shallow toddlers' pool beside it – so important for young non-swimmers. Solarium, whirlpool, sauna, fitness room (multigym, rowing machine and exercise bike) and games room complete the impressive indoor leisure facilities. Outdoors there are picnic tables, barbecue, areas for badminton and volleyball and an all-weather tennis court.

For those wishing to brave the outside world, Barnstaple, Ilfracombe, Woolacombe, Lynton and the sandy beaches of North Devon are all just a short drive away. ETC Three Stars. Not suitable for dogs. Linen and towels included. Cost: about £210 to £828. Details from Wendy Amos-Yeo, Best Leisure, North Hill Cottages, Shirwell, near Barnstaple, Devon EX31 4LG. Telephone (01271) 850611. Fax 850693.

www.bestleisure.co.uk.

Lee Bay, near Croyde
Mill Field Cottage

We love revisiting this property for
the guide (as we did in 2001), and
hope to stay here ourselves one day.
The location is stunning: one of the
most beautiful parts of the North
Devon coast, overlooking Lee Bay,
surrounded by National Trust land.
The cottage stands in its own garden
and fields and there is a fabulous

A charming base with spectacular views.

view over the bay. It has been upgraded over the years to a high standard.
We like the large sitting/dining room, with its many books, leading into
the sun room in which one could spend a fortnight just watching the tides.
Local features and pleasures include excellent surfing at Woolacombe,
Croyde and Saunton, golf courses, horse riding, sea trips from Ilfracombe
to Lundy and for anglers and naturalists, plus walking on coastal paths
and beaches. It's much recommended for spring or autumn breaks.

Television, payphone. **Sleeps 7** in three single rooms and two doubles
plus cot. There are two bathrooms, a garage and parking space. Well
behaved dogs by arrangement. Cost: £300 to £575. Further details from
Michael and Sally Wilkins, 47 St John's Avenue, Putney, London SW15
6AL. Telephone 0208-788 6438, fax 0208-780 0188.

email: mw@channel-marine.ndo.co.uk

Langtree, near Great Torrington
Stowford Lodge Holiday Cottages   map 7/412

On a warm summer evening, away
from traffic, we negotiated high
banked lanes typical of this part of
Devon en route to revisit four properties that are very popular with
readers. **Sleeping 6, 4, 4** and **4**, they
have been sympathetically converted
from farm buildings. *Warren* and
Halcyon are suitable for wheelchairs.
A special feature is the indoor heated
swimming pool: lovely warm water,
wall pictures/hangings, underwater

*We admired exposed beams, good beds,
pretty covers, books and games.*

lighting. A mile away, amid farmland, are *1 and 2 South Hill Cottages*,
refurbished, semi-detached, spacious cottages **sleeping 4**. *We like these
immensely.* They are secluded and enjoy good views and privacy, off-road
parking, shared garden, private patio, and open log fire. TV. Dogs welcome (small charge). Linen provided. Home cooked food (Stowford).
Babysitting. ETC Three Stars. Cost: £190 to £490. Details/brochure: Sally
and David Milsom, Stowford Lodge, Langtree, Torrington, North Devon
EX38 8NU. Telephone Langtree (01805) 601540, fax 601487.

www.stowford.dial.pipex.com   email: stowford@dial.pipex.com

Hartland, near Bideford/Clovelly
Downe Cottages

Checking our maps very carefully, glad to be free of holiday traffic, we left main roads behind and soon picked up the smell of the sea before arriving at this absolutely pristine arrangement of eight converted farm properties around what is probably the neatest and tidiest one-time farmyard we have ever seen. And these top notch exteriors are more than matched by the faultless interiors.

Certainly one of the half-dozen best groups of cottages in this part of the West Country.

Interiors are all 'just so', and so (unusually) are the surroundings...

It is just a mile from the rugged Atlantic Cove – never more dramatic than in the winter, and in itself an excuse for an out-of-season break at Downe Cottages – and just a woodland walk away from Hartland Abbey and its famous gardens. It's also an easy walk to the North Devon Coastal Path. These are really 'away-from-it-all' places without being uncomfortably remote.

With the unusual advantage of covered parking in a smartly renovated stone barn, each cottage is as comfortable as a five star hotel – but with more guaranteed privacy and quiet than you ever get in a hotel – and an impressive attention to detail on the part of the extremely painstaking owners, as well as absolute cleanliness. Among so many good things we noted were log burners or living-flame gas stoves in each (plus oil-fired central heating), five foot wide beds (increasingly requested by readers) in every double except one, masses of space and a total lack of clutter. Showers only throughout. We visited on a bright and breezy early summer day and found the interiors warm and inviting, the whole place humming along beautifully.

The cottages are charmingly named. *Japonica, Hydrangea, Clematis* and *Vine* all **sleep just 2** in a double, *Honeysuckle* **just 2** via a 4' 6" double and a single. *Jasmine* and *Ivy* each **sleep 4** in a double and a twin. *Wistaria* **sleeps up to 6** in a double and two twins. Every bedroom is en-suite.

TVs/video players, with a selection of videos. Logs (where applicable), linen and towels included. Cots, high chairs and basic household items. Non-allergenic pillows available. Not suitable for pets. Cost: about £350 to £990. Details from Jeremy and Lynda Roe, Downe House, Hartland, Devon EX39 6DA. Telephone/fax (01237) 441881.

www.downecottages.com

email: jeremy@downecottages.com

Croyde and beyond
Marsdens Cottage Holidays*

This is a very impressive agency. An intimate knowledge of North Devon, and a policy of personally inspecting properties annually, has paid off. In the 19 years in which they have featured in this guide, *no comments other than glowing reports and praise have come our way.*

The standard of properties managed by Marsdens improves each year, helped by people's increasing awareness of North Devon – a little quieter, more rugged than its southern counterpart.

All the properties have English Tourism Council star gradings, up to Five, and the agency itself is the largest in the West Country that has a policy of having all its properties inspected. Dishwashers, microwaves, pools (even in some properties that are close to beaches) are commonplace. Around half the 200 or so on Mardens's books are in and around Croyde, a small charming village of thatch, with dunes between it and Croyde Bay's wide sandy beach. The rest are scattered across the area from the small sandy resort of Instow around the coastline to Exmoor.

The Round House, Ilfracombe: a fascinating house, with superb gardens.

The most impressive Parkgate Farm properties are new for 2002...

The Mill House (**sleeps 10**), a 16th century listed mill house, stands right on the water's edge of Lee Bay. Furnished with antiques, it retains the benefits of modern living, the kitchen having been refitted with electric double oven, hob, microwave, fridge/freezer, dishwasher, washing machine and pine table.

The original milling room is still there, while an inglenook fireplace, bread ovens and even a boathouse add to the atmosphere, along with the sound of crashing waves. Oh yes, and there are loads of books on smuggling and other salty sea tales there for you to read.

Another newcomer, *Vention* (**sleeps 11/12**), is a spectacular stone-built house in an equally spectacular position – adjacent to Putsborough Sands, with direct access on to the beach. With its spacious rooms – there are six bedrooms for starters – terraced lawned gardens to the rear and several patios overlooking the beach at the front, this must be first choice for a large family party.

The same can be said for *Rhu* (**sleeps 12**), another ocean-side property looking across Saunton Sands and the famous championship golf course. Extensively re-furbished, it has just under an acre of gardens. (Saunton has over six miles of sands and a nature reserve in the dunes.)

258

Beech Cottage, at Combe Martin, has a big garden and cosily sleeps just 2...

The Bungalow is one of many Marsdens properties with exceptional views...

Four outstanding cottages at Parkgate Farm, near Barnstaple (*Walnut, Maple, Mulberry* and *Oak*), new for 2002, have been created from a range of stone barns, and beautifully furnished by the interior-designer owners. With great views, they **sleep 6, 8, 6 and 12**.

Another notable property is *The Bungalow,* located proudly on Baggy Point, one of the headlands forming Croyde Bay, with panoramic views across to Clovelly and Hartland. Equipped to an exceptional standard, the accommodation is comfortable and welcoming. The master bedroom has en-suite jacuzzi/spa bath, separate shower cubicle and there's a further twin bedded room with en-suite shower. If you are looking for a quiet holiday **for 2**, *Beech Cottage*, at Combe Martin, could be the answer. Detached, with a large private garden and patio, the cottage adjoins farmland and is equipped throughout to ETC Four Star standard.

The prestigious *Clifton Court* development (ETC Four Stars) has a heated indoor pool and direct access to the National Trust coastal path to Putsborough Sands. And for sheer novelty value, *The Round House*, Ilfracombe, takes some beating. **Sleeping 10**, it really is built in a complete circle, the result of a bet in 1910 between two local builders, one not believing it could be done. The evidence remains today, with the third storey a rotunda room with a 360 degree view over Ilfracombe and beyond. Six bedrooms, three reception rooms and fine gardens make this another ideal family home. It is Three Stars.

Maps with detailed directions to all properties are provided. Details and a outstanding colour brochure available from Marsdens, 2 The Square, Braunton, Devon EX33 2JB. Telephone (01271) 813777, fax 813664. **www.marsdens.co.uk   email: holidays@marsdens.co.uk**

Rhu is a beauty, usefully sleeping up to 12, and with a most impressive view across Saunton Sands...

Vention Cottage is right on a spectacular beach and, sleeping up to 12, is a great choice for a large family group...

259

Watermouth, near Ilfracombe
Widmouth Farm Cottages

This has so much going for it. First, there's the extraordinary location, looking down on to a private beach (a two minute downhill walk through pastureland from the cottages themselves) and one of the most impressive stretches of the North Devon Coastal Footpath. Then there are the very reasonable prices (in an area that can be expensive) for ten rather cosy, unpretentiously comfortable cottages, **sleeping from 2 to 6**. And there are the animals that in themselves can make a memorable holiday for children – there are sheep (some tame), goats, rabbits, guinea pigs, ducks,

What a location! Here one is looking over some of the cottages towards the sea...   *...and here looking from the sea and the beach up towards the cottages.*

chickens and plenty of wildlife: for example, there's a good chance (especially from the cottages, a very good vantage point) of seeing seals sporting off the coast.

The enthusiastic new owners have brought this harmonious group of cottages up to 21st century standards, and during a 2001 visit we found them warm and comfortable, well carpeted, with a good use of space. Two have coal effect gas fires, as well as central heating. We especially liked these, called *Partridge* and *Pheasant*, which are semi-detached halves of a house of character built circa 1800. Each **sleeps 6**.

Heron and *Kingfisher* both **sleep 4 'plus 1'**, *The Round Barn* (an interesting conversion, overlooking the gardens) and *Kestrel* both **sleep 4**. *Swallow* and *Martin* also **sleep 4**, with a cot available in each. *Robin* and *Wren* both **sleep 2** only, in double bedrooms.

In spite of its impressive location – many readers ask us about this – Widmouth Farm is not at all remote. It is set well back from and below the road that runs westwards to Ilfracombe, so one has 'the best of both worlds', with easy access also to Ilfracombe itself, Exmoor, several superb beaches, Ilfracombe Golf Club and nearby Watermouth Castle. It's a good place for children to make new friends.

TVs. Home cooked meals available. Dogs are 'very welcome'. Linen provided and towels available on request. Short breaks. All are ETC Three Stars except Robin, which has Two on account of its small bedroom.

Details/brochure from Jeremy and Elizabeth Sansom, Widmouth Farm, Watermouth, North Devon EX34 9RX. Telephone (01271) 863743.

www. widmouthfarmcottages.co.uk
email: holiday@widmouthfarmcottages.co.uk

Combe Martin, near Ilfracombe
Wheel Farm Country Cottages

For thirteen years this has been one of the most popular groups of cottages featured in this guide. During a 2001 revisit we met readers (a young couple with a small baby) staying in one of the cottages and asked what they liked most about Wheel Farm. They said: 'It's private, but we don't feel cut off. It's in the country but near the sea, and we love the gardens. Our cottage is light, bright and cosy.'

Nestling in a sheltered valley close to the picturesque village of Combe Martin, near beautiful, wide, sandy beaches such as Woolacombe's (fif-

Stable and Linhay: everything is 'just so', and the North Devon location is a delight.

Every cottage has a beautifully planned and reliably comfortable interior.

teen minutes' drive) and Croyde (twenty minutes), and overlooking Exmoor National Park, Wheel Farm provides an ideal holiday setting for all the family. The eleven acres of grounds have award-winning gardens, patios, millponds (fenced), grassland and wooded copse walks.

Converted from an old water mill (the wheel still remains) and barns, the cottages have exposed stone walls and beams, rustic charm, and yet provide all modern amenities. All have full gas central heating, microwaves, TVs, videos and dishwashers (except those just for 2).

Four of the cottages have four-poster beds; six have wood-burning stoves. They are furnished to a high standard with Victorian farmhouse antique and pine furniture, deep upholstered suites, good quality fitted carpets and drapes. They range from cosy units designed **for 2** to bigger ones that spaciously **accommodate 6**, plus cots. Facilities include an impressive heated indoor swimming pool, sauna, mini fitness room, LTA standard tennis court, children's playground – all free of charge.

Linen and mid week maid service are included, towels are available for hire. Laundry room with token-operated washers and dryers. A selection of groceries can be provided for arrival and hand baked pies, pastries and cakes are available. Arrangements can be made for baby sitting, tennis tuition, restaurant reservations, taxis, riding, golf and cycling. ETC Four Stars. 'Regret no pets.' TVs. Cost: £220 to £1150; short breaks available low season only. Colour brochure available from Mr and Mrs J G Robertson, Wheel Farm Country Cottages, Berry Down 16, Combe Martin, North Devon EX34 0NT. Telephone (01271) 882100. Fax 883120.

www.wheelfarmcottages.co.uk
email: holidays@wheelfarmcotages.co.uk

Goodleigh, near Barnstaple
Willesleigh Farm

Well placed for discovering North Devon and Exmoor, this is an 86-acre working dairy, beef and sheep farm, and visitors are welcome to watch the Jersey cows being milked and their calves fed. It is just three miles from Barnstaple and within ten miles of Exmoor and the beautiful wide sandy beaches of Saunton and Woolacombe. On the ground floor of

A cottage of comfort and character in a pretty, leafy part of the country ...

The Gatehouse is a large double – with ensuite shower room – and two large twin rooms and bathroom. It has its own games room with snooker, wendy house and lots of books. A staircase leads up to a huge, beamed sitting room/diner with sloping ceiling, very comfy chairs, more books, tasteful pictures, TV and video. There is a well equipped, light and spacious, beamed kitchen and a utility room with washer/drier.

The heated indoor swimming pool is available from early May until late October. Dogs are welcome. Electricity, linen and personal towels included. **Sleeps 2 to 6** plus cot. ETC Four Stars. Cost: about £167 to £688. Details from Mrs Anne Esmond-Cole, Willesleigh Farm, Goodleigh, Barnstaple, North Devon EX32 7NA. Telephone/fax Barnstaple (01271) 343763.

High Bickington, near Barnstaple   map 7/419
Country Ways

Readers first alerted us to these three cottages, converted from old farm buildings. We thought them delightful, and they are now very much a part of the 'cottage guide' family. Away even from the little-used lane that passes this working farm, deep in the country, close to the Prices' own property, *The Cuckoo's Nest*, **sleeping 6**, *The Stables*, **sleeping 4**,

Finding this super threesome in deepest North Devon was a joy. ETC Four Stars.

and *The Den*, **sleeping 2**, are a fine balance between 21st century comforts and rusticity (good, expensive sofas and well chosen curtains, for example). Opposite, a matter of yards from, the owners' home, we liked their exceptional spaciousness and the attention to detail. In Cuckoo's Nest we noticed a five foot double bed. There are rural views and absolute peace and quiet. Children will love the farmyard animals, especially the rare-breeds piglets. Linen and towels included. TVs/videos, even a gym. Well behaved dogs by arrangement. Cost: about £170 to £595. Details from Kate Price, Little Knowle Farm, High Bickington, Umberleigh, North Devon EX37 9BJ. Telephone (01769) 560503. **www.devon-holiday.co.uk email: kate.price@virgin.net**

Exford, near Minehead
Barn Cottage

Featured in this guide *for 20 years without a break*, this is a charmer. We revisited the stone cottage in the summer of 2001, taking the quiet, narrow lane that snakes intriguingly away from the interesting village of Exford, only about three quarters of a mile away. It is scrupulously maintained, tastefully and comfortably furnished, and as attractive inside as

Once a barn, this cottage is light, spacious, tasteful and very inviting.

it is out. It really was a barn originally, and is accordingly spacious. We are particularly fond of it, partly because it is *very reasonably priced*. With its dark green fabrics, contrasting with plain white walls and light pine doors, it is one of those cottages we would happily move into ourselves. Of the two bedrooms, one is downstairs, the other upstairs – as is the charming, beamed, dual aspect sitting-room (to get upstairs you ascend an unusual spiral staircase). The kitchen/diner is well equipped. The cottage is surrounded by fields and woodland, and the brown rolling moors of the National Park (the smallest in Britain) are close.

Television. Cost: about £165 to £285. Dogs by arrangement. Further details are available from Mrs Bindon, Higher Mill, Exford, Minehead, Somerset. Telephone Exford (01643) 831347.

King's Nympton, near South Molton
Venn Farm Cottages

This 50-acre, traditional, working farm deep in rolling Devonshire countryside (**map 7/421**) is ideal for children, on account of the goats, the inquisitive farm-cats and the clucking chickens, along with the farm activities that friendly owner Isla Martin organises on a daily basis, and the wooden playground where they can make new friends. The four

Warm, comfortable and scrupulously clean – a most inviting place for families.

conversions, like pretty maids all in a row, are individual yet have similarities such as excellent beds, pleasing colour schemes, well designed kitchens (open plan with the sitting room/diner), thoughtful lighting, tasteful furnishings and superb views – in one case through the main door rather than a front-facing window. In short, interiors are stylish and comfortable. The largest cottage, furthest from the farmhouse, has a downstairs twin room and cloakroom, plus double, twin and bathroom upstairs.

Sleep 4 to 6. TV. Dogs welcome. Linen provided. Cost: £120 to £500. Details from Isla Martin, Venn Farm, King's Nympton, Umberleigh, North Devon EX37 9TR. Telephone South Molton (01769) 572448.

www.bmvenn.demon.co.uk

Brendon, near Lynmouth
Rockford Lodge

It has been featured in this guide for almost 20 years, and we have always had a great fondness for this cottage.

So it was a pleasure in the summer of 2001 to leave our car in the main part of the hamlet of Rockford (just a pub and a few cottages) and walk a few yards over a footbridge across the tumbling river East Lyn to see Rockford Lodge again and to meet the very happy people staying in it.

A regular reader of *The Good Holiday Cottage Guide* has compiled a 'top ten' of his favourite cottages, and includes this in it. Like us, he enjoys places that ramble a bit, and have something of a farmhousey character. Tucked away in a secret, wooded valley on the edge of mysterious Exmoor, Rockford has a big kitchen with a cosy Aga, fitted carpets, lots of books, paintings and a very big, carpeted upstairs bathroom. The river that rushes past the garden fence does not do so loudly enough to keep one awake! The footpaths in the beautiful woods outside the conservatory-like 'river room' beckon one for walks. Described over the years by readers as 'a genuine home from home'...'wonderfully well equipped'...'the setting is marvellous', the cottage is used quite frequently by the owners themselves. **Sleeps 6 plus cot.**

Many years in this guide, Rockford Lodge has a most unusual situation....

...whereby you park your car and then cross a river via a footbridge. Delightful!

Dogs are welcome but not cats. TV. Cost: about £320 to £580. Further details available from Mrs E M Adnitt, 82 The Row, Lane End, High Wycombe, Buckinghamshire HP14 3JU. Telephone (01494) 882609.

Important note: we cannot vouch for every property on an agency's books, but only those we have seen. Most agents have at least a handful of modest properties that appeal only to a very specific market (for example, fishermen, walkers and stalkers), or sometimes properties at the extreme edge of the region they deal with that are not typical of what they offer. But in principle the agencies we feature are notably reliable and conscientious...

osemundy Cottages, Cornwall. Two distinctively different but very handy locations close to the uch-loved Cornish coast; considerate owners, very high standards of comfort. Page 240.

ooke Farm, Cornwall. Extremely effective farm-building conversions, high standards, a rare e for detail and an impeccable sense of taste – all in all, absolutely top notch! Page 245.

ineshop Cottages, Cornwall. Exceptionally ell situated, long featured by us. Page 243.

Gullrock, Cornwall. A short stroll from Port Gaverne's rather secret sandy beach. Page 239.

egeath, Cornwall. Snug, unpretentious, uch liked by many of our readers. Page 242.

Cant Cove, Cornwall. Overlooking the Camel estuary, these really are 'last word'. Page 250.

Colour section B, Page 1

265

Penrose Burden, Cornwall. Charming owners, fine stone cottages. Page 248/249.

Braddon Cottages, Devon. Peaceful country an escape from rush and bustle. Page 273

Marsdens Holidays, North Devon. Widely admired specialists in a very appealing but never overrun part of the West Country: an exceptional agency, with 'no duds'. Pages 258/259.

Widmouth Farm, North Devon. Warm, cosy cottages, virtually a private beach. Page 260.

Mill Field, North Devon. One of our all-time personal favourites (great views!). Page 256.

Wheel Farm, North Devon. A pool that families love, a tennis court, award-winning gardens, and a good range of very well cared for cottages – near the sea but very rural too. Page 261.

Colour section B, Page 2

lebe House Cottages, Devon/Cornwall. The gardens are exquisite, the cottages all ETC Four ar graded and retaining original features. There's even a bar and restaurant. Page 254.

ooder Manor, Devon. You could hardly get oser to the heart of Dartmoor. Page 280.

Horry Mill, Devon. A much-loved cottage, an amazing wooded location. Page 283.

igher Bowden, South Devon. Such a lot to er, deep in the 'South Hams'. Page 282.

Jean Bartlett Holidays, South Devon. By or near the coast, with several gems. Page 295.

he Thatched Cottage Company, East Devon. An amazing, hand picked collection of picture-stcard cottages, jam-packed with character and, in some cases, history too. Page 292.

Helpful Holidays – Devon, Cornwall and beyond. This West Country specialist is virtually a household name. They have some beauties on their books, such as this house by the water...

...as well as 'roses-round-the-door' thatched cottages, deeply rural places with marvellous vistas, and this 400-year-old stunner that was once used by Francis Drake. Pages 288-290.

Drupe Farm, Devon. Very superior conversions round a tidily landscaped courtyard, in this guide for seventeen years, and consistently good reader reports. Page 294.

Compton Pool, Devon. Deep in the country and yet close to the sea, these well converted and attractive cottages are especially popular among families with small children. Page 287.

...ete Estate Cottages, Devon. These are exceptional: impressively situated and well cared for, on ...grand 5000-acre estate – certainly among our readers' all-time favourites. Page 278.

...oles Manor, Dorset. Sandy beaches close, ...autiful countryside around. Page 296.

East Stoke House, Somerset. The kind of place our readers really appreciate. Page 301.

...Town For All Seasons', Devon. Great ...ews from apartments and cottages. Page 298.

Foxhills Properties. A helpful New Forest agency, with high standards. Page 307.

...ekes, East Susssex. 'Incomparable'... 'unique'...and much loved. Page 310.

Swiss Chalet, Herefordshire. A rare, romantic hideaway for two, by a river. Page 345.

Colour section B, Page 5

Docklow, Herefordshire. On a hot summer day the pool is a joy. Page 333.

Owlpen, Gloucestershire. A place where rural England has stood still. Page 326.

Combermere Abbey Cottages, Shropshire. Much admired, utterly stylish cottages on a very accessible country estate, with tennis, croquet, woodland walks, fishing and more. Page 319.

Wye Lea, Herefordshire. An incomparable attention to detail, with many facilities and high standards of comfort; a pleasant, rural location near Ross-on-Wye (with salmon fishing)...

...and cottages that are as comfortable as multi-starred hotels. The seriously good restaurant and the seductive swimming pool have become highlights in themselves. Pages 324-325.

Rock House, Herefordshire. We've stayed in this spacious family house. Page 329.

Stanton Court, Gloucestershire. Superb conversions, a sense of history. Pages 348/349.

Westwood House, Worcestershire. An elegant setting, fine gardens. Page 330

Courtyard Cottages, Gloucestershire. Real country house style, full of history. Page 331.

Knightcote Farm, Worcestershire. Really top notch standards here. Page 364.

The Mill, Oxfordshire. The ancient mill race is a much appreciated feature. Page 356.

Views Farm Barns, Oxfordshire. Rural, but very handy for Oxford. Page 363.

Wenrisc, Oxfordshire. Charming owners, a little known, very quiet village. Page 355.

Colour section B, Page 7

You get so much more with Landranger®

from Ordnance Survey®

Covering the whole country at the detailed scale of 1:50 000 (2 cm to 1 km or 1¼ inches to 1 mile) the Landranger series has all you need to really get to know an area including:

- tourist information
- picnic areas and viewpoints
- selected places of interest
- rights of way information for England and Wales

Maps, Atlases and Guides

For more information about Ordnance Survey products and services call our

Customer Information HelpLine on 08456 05 05 05
Quote reference A4398
E-mail custinfo@ordsvy.gov.uk

Or visit our Web site at www.ordsvy.gov.uk

Ordnance Survey, the OS Symbol and Landranger are registered trade marks of Ordnance Survey, the national mapping agency of Great Britain.

Ordnance Survey®

...linking you to the real world

Braddon, near Holsworthy
Braddon Cottages

When we revisited here in 2001 a party of Germans had taken over all the cottages, but so well spaced out are they that the place could have been deserted. At the end of a long drive, near the Devon/Cornwall border, there are six properties, separate, detached, surrounded by 150 acres of meadow and wood, with access to

Tucked well away from any noisy roads...

500 acres of woodland adjoining. All have woodburners (free wood) and fine views to the south over the well stocked three-acre fishing lake. Fishing free, reserved for residents. *The Linhaye* and *Lake House* are large, purpose-built houses **sleeping 12 plus 2**, each convertible into two self-contained, sound-proofed parts. Microwave, dishwasher, washing machine, drier, gas central heating, double glazing, barbecues. There's an all-weather summer house near the lake, an all-weather tennis court, games room with full size snooker table, even a small licensed shop. TV/videos, payphones. Linen/towels provided. Well behaved dogs welcome. Bargain breaks. ETC Three Stars. Cost: £90 to £1000, from £60 2ppn. Details: George and Anne Ridge, Braddon, Ashwater, Beaworthy, Devon EX21 5EP. Telephone/fax (01409) 211350.

www.braddoncottages.co.uk

Ashwater, near Beaworthy   map 7/426
Blagdon Farm Country Holidays

This is 'a dream location', about 20 minutes by car inland from the seaside resort of Bude and the surfers' paradise of Widemouth Bay, and in easy striking distance of Bodmin Moor and Exmoor. Not yet seen by us – we will visit in 2002 – Blagdon Farm offers eight very comfortable cottages (ETC Four/Five Stars), all south-facing and overlooking the two-and-a-half acre lake and the

This comes very highly recommended...

woods beyond, and set in 30 acres. This is stocked with rainbow trout, and is ideal for beginners to try their hand. Blagdon Farm is extremely suitable for disabled guests, as the owners are attuned to such holiday-makers' particular requirements. There are TVs, a very warm indoor pool, a bar/restaurant, an adventure playground, and more.

Washing machines, tumble driers, microwaves. Pets welcome, linen and towels included. Cost: about £240 to £700. Disabled access Category 1. Details: David and Sue Tucker, Blagdon Farm Country Holidays, Ashwater, Beaworthy, Devon EX21 5DF. Telephone (01409) 211509. Fax 211510.

www.blagdon-farm.co.uk   email: info@blagdon-farm.co.uk

Welcombe, nr Bideford/Beaford, nr Winkleigh
Linton Farm/Mill Cottage

Linton Farm, an 18th century farmhouse within its own lawned garden of an acre, is only half a mile from North Devon's spectacular coastline. In a secluded hamlet, the house is comfortable and roomy, **sleeping 8**, with, for example, inglenook fireplaces, original features and some antique furniture. There is a small playroom, with toys, to keep children happy and a slide and climbing frame outside with lots of space for ball games. *Mill Cottage*, close to the River Torridge in Tarka the Otter country, and also in rural seclusion, with a large garden, is cosy, 17th century, comfortably furnished and well equipped. You enter through a sun room into a beamed living room with wood burner; a second sitting room, also with woodburner, leads to a beamed, modern kitchen/dining room with a door leading into the garden, complete with its own Wendy house! The cottage **sleeps 7** in two double rooms, a bunk room and a single. Great Torrington is five miles away, the coast twelve.

Linton Farm: a fine 18th century building, just half a mile from a superb coastline...

English Country Cottages, Stoney Bank, Earby, Barnoldswick BB94 0AA. Telephone (0870) 5851155. You can also dial-a-brochure: (0870) 5851111. **www.english-country-cottages.co.uk   Ref EMA 94.**

Bratton, near Minehead   map 7/428
Woodcombe Lodges

We like the way these two cosy stone cottages and four spacious timber lodges are poised on the edge of the Exmoor National Park, a few minutes' walk or seconds by car from deep countryside. In the lee of the owners' country house, but hidden, the group of purpose built chalet style properties have delightful views towards Exmoor itself, are well spaced and roomy. We met a family in *Cedar* (**sleeps 4/5**), who said 'It is so nice to think we have such a super place to come home to at the end of the day'.

Very nicely situated close to Exmoor...

A couple we met in *Rose Cottage*, adjoining the main house, said 'We like it so much that we are staying put today'. We saw their neat little nest, **just for 2** (a good double bedroom), good carpets, a well planned galley kitchen, set in attractive gardens. A nice touch: there is a nine hole putting green, with croquet also available.

ETC Four Stars. Dogs welcome. Linen and towels available. Cost: about £105 to £420. Details from Stephen Joyce, PO Box 21, Hertford, Hertfordshire SG14 2DD. Telephone (014388) 69489.

Exmoor (near Dulverton)
Draydon Cottages

We were captivated by the beautiful view south over the Barle Valley when we first came upon the tucked-away set of seven cottages five minutes' drive from the little time-stands-still town of Dulverton. Once barns belonging to Draydon Farm, the cottages are all roomy and painstakingly designed and furnished, most of them on an open-plan basis. They have either one or *Cottages of comfort and character in a hilly, leafy part of the country ...*

two bedrooms. We noted deep sofas, Velux windows and lots of pine. Four cottages have en-suite bathrooms and *Cottages 1* and *2* even have a whirlpool bath. Linen and towels are provided. In fact there are no hidden extras. Full marks to the owners for including 'everything' here – that is, all heating and electricity. All are English Tourism Council Four Stars. The atmosphere, with horses next door, is 'farmy' but it is not a muck-and-smells place. **Sleep 2 to 4 'plus 2'.** TVs. Dogs welcome. Short breaks. Cost: £170 to £435. Details from Karen Bennett, St Anthony's Close, Ottery St Mary, Devon EX11 1EN. Telephone (01404) 812859.

www.escapetoexmoor.co.uk email: karen@draydon.fsnet.co.uk

Dunster, near Minehead
map 7/430
Duddings Holiday Cottages

Four miles inland from Minehead – though more about Exmoor's leafy glades and deer-haunted, bracken-covered hillsides – and about five minutes by car from pretty Dunster and its castle, these mostly look con-genially on to a convivial courtyard. We revisited in 2001, and were especially impressed with *West Wing*, **sleeping 10/12**, and the very cosy *Exford* and *The Annexe*. All twelve *Upgraded year by year by the owners...*

cottages, each with its own patio, have been converted from a variety of old farm buildings, and we liked the cottagey comfort, the mod cons and the rusticity: original oak beams and exposed stone walls, for example. There's a warm indoor pool, tennis, table tennis, a pool table, trout fishing and a nine hole putting green. Eight have ETC Three Stars, four have Four. **Sleep from 2 to 12**. TV. Dogs welcome. Linen but not towels included. Cost: approximately £175 to £1510, plus electricity. Further details are available from Mr and Mrs Tilke, Timberscombe, near Dunster, Somerset TA24 7TB. Telephone (01643) 841123. Fax 841165.

www.duddings.co.uk email: Richard@Duddings.co.uk

275

Sandyway (Exmoor National Park)
Barkham

Exmoor is an 'away from it all' place to start with, but arriving at Barkham is a tonic for anyone tired of the cut and thrust of city life. With the home of the laid-back and friendly owners taking up part of the three sided courtyard, the two sides are made up of three cottages and a gallery. The whole thing is reached via an intriguing little lane off what's not a very busy country road anyway.

Better yet, the cottages look down over a beautifully landscaped garden, a labour of love of many years, sloping valley-wise downhill, with trees on each side. In all there are twelve acres of trees, streams and meadows, and there is even a three-storeyed treehouse.

Readers have enthused about Barkham, with such comments as 'We were treated like one of the family'...'an ideal base, with friendly local pubs'...'so quiet and peaceful' – just three recommendations we have had for this place, whose self-catering cottages and very comfortable, thickly carpeted 'bed and breakfast' in the 200 year old farmhouse are complemented by an art gallery, concerts and residential masterclasses that centre round as appealing a recital room as you'll find this side of Aldeburgh and Snape.

The three cottages, furnished with antiques, are comfortable, 'cottagey' but not twee conversions from two stone barns, all with stunning views down that private valley. They are *Old Copse,* **sleeping 5**, *Turnip Close*, **sleeping 4** and *Dobbins Close*, **sleeping 6**.

The residential musical courses have featured such well known names in

This is a delightful place, and the fact that Exmoor is right on the doorstep is a big bonus for the visitor...

There is more to Barkham than meets the eye! Concerts and an art gallery seldom enjoy such a setting...

the musical world as pianist Philip Fowke, singer Jean Rigby and Radio Three presenter Stephanie Hughes, with accommodation available in the cottages or in the house. (See also Page 14.)

Linen, gas and electricity included, central heating extra; washing machines, microwaves, TV and videos. Pets welcome in Dobbins Close. ETC Four Stars. Cost: £270 to £550. Details of accommodation and musical events from John and Penny Adie, Barkham, Sandyway, Exmoor, Devon EX36 3LU. Telephone/fax (01643) 831370.

www.exmoor-vacations.co.uk
email: adie.exmoor@btinternet.com

Beacon, near Honiton
Red Doors Cottages

We see some extraordinary places during our research for *The Good Holiday Cottage Guide*, but these really gave us something 'to write home about'. Though only three easy miles from the useful small town of Honiton they are deep in the country – among the Blackdown Hills, an Area of Outstanding Natural Beauty.

Fitting very harmoniously into its surroundings is Grade II* listed Red Doors farmhouse and its group of recently restored cottages. The delightful *Farmhouse* itself, rambling in the nicest way and hitherto occupied by the owners (who now live a mile away) has become available from the 2002 season. The thatched house **sleeps up to 8** in two doubles and two twins, and among so many other appealing features is a woodburner in the drawing room and a splendid four-oven Aga.

There are six other cottages, two thatched, **sleeping from 2 to 6**, with an indoor and well heated swimming pool, a games barn, a 'secret garden', a play area, a croquet lawn and much more. All but one has a woodburner – so cosy on a chilly day. We looked into several at random and thought them so full of style, character and comfort – the sort of places where (even though there is lots to see and do around here) people tend to stay put just to enjoy their surroundings. We especially liked *Swallows Loft*, an ultra-modern *tour de force*.

You can enjoy excellent walking from your doorstep or explore the unspoilt East Devon coastline, about 30 minutes' drive away.

This is the splendid Farmhouse, a highly desirable base for a large family holiday.

The super kitchen in Cider Barn is typical of Red Doors's tremendous sense of style.

A typical comment about Red Doors comes from Gwen Done, of Northampton: 'Our cottages (we took more than one for a family get-together) were fabulous, the best we have ever found. And the Rushtons are such nice hosts.'

Short breaks. TV. Central heating. Linen and towels are included. Dogs are welcome by arrangement. Cost: for the cottages, about £395 to £925, for The Farmhouse, about £695 to £1350. Further details/brochures are available from Sarah Rushton, Red Doors, Beacon, East Devon EX14 4TX. Telephone/fax (01404) 890067.

www.reddoors.co.uk
email: info@reddoors.co.uk

Mothecombe, near Plymouth
The Flete Estate

Each of the properties on The Flete Estate enjoys a quite memorable situation and the estate itself has 5,000 acres of impressive scenery, an abundance of wildlife, wading sea birds, open meadows and thick woodland. To cap it all, near its northernmost point stands a particularly imposing and romantic castle, and down a lane from that is a very pretty, very private cottage – plus a little detached lodge – that we really liked. This is *Flete Mill Cottage*, easy on the eye and comfortable, **sleeping 3** (including a five foot bed) **plus 2** in the lodge.

We have known and admired the other properties here for many years. *Coastguard Cottages* enjoy a breathtaking position directly overlooking a huge sandy beach just 20 yards away. They stand alone, with ever-changing sea views and peace and quiet. There are good modern kitchens and bathrooms (they all have showers and baths), three bedrooms upstairs, two with sea views. One **sleeps 6**, two **sleep 8**. *Nepeans Cottage*, **sleeping 10**, is in the heart of beautiful woods down a path which you think is going on for ever. Quite isolated, it is almost chapel-like in appearance, with its arched ground floor and dormer windows. Once a gamekeeper's cottage, it has lots of appeal and plenty of space and comfort: you are guaranteed privacy. There is a large sitting room with open fire and a modern kitchen and bathroom.

The elegantly furnished *Efford House* overlooks the wide Erme estuary. **Sleeping 12**, it stands in its own grounds with gardens down to the river. There are two large and beautifully decorated sitting rooms, each with big Georgian windows looking over the estuary. Twelve people can stay here in great comfort: there are five bedrooms on the first and two on the sec-

Coastguard Cottages: are these the best situated in the whole West Country?

Flete Mill Cottage is a neat, tidy and most attractive recent addition.

ond floors, and two bathrooms, one of which has 'a huge and sumptuous shower'. There is a large kitchen with split-level oven, all modern appliances, and a walk-in larder; also a utility room.

Cost: about £300 to £1500. TV. Washing machines, tumble driers, dishwashers, food processors, microwaves. Dogs by arrangement. Linen hire. ETC Three to Five Stars. Open all year. Short breaks. Details/brochure from The Flete Estate, Mothecombe, Holbeton, Plymouth, Devon. Telephone Holbeton (01752) 830253, fax 830500.

www.flete.co.uk email: cottages@flete.co.uk

Okehampton
Fourwinds

You'll be impressed as you sweep into the spacious driveway of this handsome 1860s property (now three substantial holiday homes), and even more impressed by how sumptuously comfortable, warm and well insulated they are. There really has been 'no expense spared' in the con-

Sumptuous interiors, easy to get to...

version, and it's not surprising they've acquired a huge following in a short time. This has been helped along by the superior pets' corner, where children love to meet tame pigmy goats and chickens, all of which have their own names, ducks and a goose. There are safe and enclosed gardens. (You won't get lost here, as the A30 dual carriageway runs close. But it's out of sight: the view from the cottages' front windows is of rolling hills that beckon walkers.) Two-storeyed *Tor View* **sleeps 4 'plus 2'**, *Brokan,* a first floor apartment, **sleeps 8 'plus 2'**, and *Orkney,* a ground floor apartment, **sleeps 4**. But note: the latter two can be opened up to make one large property for **up to 14**. TVs. Linen/towels included. Baby sitting. Welcome pack, laundry facilities. ETC Four Stars. Cost: about £250 to £525. Details: Sue Collins, Fourwinds, Tavistock Road, Okehampton, Devon EX20 4LX. Telephone (01837) 55785. Mobile 07816 093332. **email: fourwinds@eclipse.co.uk**

Drewsteignton (Dartmoor) map 7/438
Michaelmas Cottage/The Gardener's Cottage

Here are the ingredients of a really memorable Devon holiday. Said one reader: "A truly wonderful cottage – delightful gardens.' Another said: Magical – everything one could wish for'. One can choose from two adjoining Grade II listed thatched cottages, both ETC Four Star, respectively **sleeping 6 and 3**. They are in a splendid setting within the National Park, and are near the vil-

Well placed for enjoying Dartmoor...

lage (a good pub and Post Office/shop). Each has a delightful walled garden, an inglenook fireplace with woodburner, oil fired central heating, beamed rooms, antique furniture and many special touches that make them homes from home. They share a good-sized heated outdoor swimming pool, further gardens, a croquet lawn, and a paddock with a friendly 'pensioner' pony and free range rare-breed hens. Warmth, comfort and the proximity to superb walking make these all-year-round favourites.

TV/videos. Telephones. Dogs welcome. Linen, towels, electricity, heating and logs included. Cost: about £195 to £625. Details from Anthony and Angela Thomas, Netherton Vine, Drewsteignton, Exeter EX6 6RB. Telephone/fax (01647) 281602.

Widecombe-in-the-Moor
Wooder Manor

Here is a beautiful, peaceful place, surrounded by woodland, moor and granite tors, and just half a mile down a quiet and level country lane from famous Widecombe-in-the-Moor. Angela Bell has been renting out cottages on the family's 150-acre farm in the heart of Dartmoor for several years. The seven properties vary in style and size, being conver-

Dartmoor retains a special magic, and these properties are at its heart...

sions of an old coach-house and stables beside the Bells' large farmhouse. *Wooder House* **sleeps 12** in five bedrooms; its decor and furnishings are, as throughout, comfortable and relaxing. Two cottages **sleep 6 to 7**, the others **sleep 4**. The location is ideal for walking, fishing, canoeing, cycling or riding; stabling and grazing are available for guests' horses.

Reductions are offered off-peak for under-occupancy. Central heating, laundry room; bed linen by arrangement; microwaves, TV, metered electricity; cots and highchairs available free; log fires in *Honeybags* and Wooder House. ETC Three Stars. Dogs possible by arrangement. Cost: about £160 to £900. Further details from Angela Bell, Wooder Manor, Widecombe-in-the-Moor, Newton Abbot, Devon TQ13 7TR. Telephone/fax (01364) 621391.

The internet is all very well, but nothing quite beats putting your feet up with a sheaf of glossy cottage brochures...

Modbury, Ivybridge
Oldaport Farm Cottages

Delightfully tucked away into one of the leafy coombes of the South Hams, this could be miles from any-where, although quiet and unspoilt Wonwell Beach is only a mile and a half away. Cathy Evans runs the four cottages and the 70-acre farm, over-looking the beautiful Erme estuary. A great deal of thought and care has

You could be 'miles from anywhere', but Salcombe and Kingsbridge are handy....

gone into these conversions. Three cottages, **sleeping 2/4, 6, 6**, were created from the old stone cowshed and dairy. The fourth, *Orchard* – single storeyed and **just for 2** – overlooks the paddock where miniature Shetland ponies graze beside chickens and ducks. Latch doors, pine furniture and comfortable furnishings convey the right mood, and there are plenty of games and books. The farm is famous for its championship Lleyn sheep. The South Coastal footpath is nearby, and so is Dartmoor. ETC Four Stars. Laundry room, payphone.

TV. Bedlinen included. Cost: £149 to £441. Dogs welcome low/mid season. Short breaks, low season. Details from Miss C M Evans, Oldaport Farm Cottages, Modbury, Ivybridge, Devon PL21 0TG. Telephone (01548) 830842. Fax 830998.

www.oldaport.dial.pipex.com   email: cathy.evans@dial.pipex.com

Membury, near Axminster   map 7/442
Cider Room Cottage

This very special place is absolutely traditional, with much of its original character intact: an increasingly rare find. And if you fancy being deep in the rolling Devon/Somerset border country, next to the family-in-residence but with plenty of privacy, you will like this as much as we do. The location is rural and peaceful, but not isolated, and the cottage is neat and

'The real thing', lots of books and a good use of the available space...

attractive: it will suit people who prefer an individual cottage to being part of a complex. The views of green, hilly farmland are delightful, and there are ducks, dogs, cats and pet Vietnamese pot-bellied pigs to delight small children. Candlelit meals can be enjoyed in the owners' home. The cottage has a spacious, comfortable stone-flagged and carpeted sitting room, two bedrooms, lots of beams, rustic stone walls (there is a shower-room, not bath). We spotted lots of books, fresh flowers and, especially upstairs, a skilful use of the available space.

TV. Dogs by arrangement. Cost: £135 to £255. Details from Pat and David Steele, Hasland Farm, Membury, Axminster, Devon EX13 7JF. Telephone (01404) 881558. Fax 881834.

Higher Bowden, near Dartmouth
Higher Bowden Cottages

This attractive place has a warm, almost Mediterranean, ambiance, enhanced by a landscape garden of parkland proportions, complete with the gentle sound of running water. Add a heated indoor swimming pool, spa bath, sauna and gymnasium, not to mention a full-sized snooker room with a slate bed table, and a floodlit all-weather tennis court, and you could be forgiven for assuming you were staying at a large well run family hotel. But then Tony England and his wife Anita did exactly that in the Lake District before putting their talent for providing top-class hospitality to a different use. The result is that rare combination of easy comfort plus something extra, including Anita's own health and beauty salon. It retains a strong year-round appeal. The Englands have now been joined by their daughter Monica and her husband Paul Khosla, who are responsible for the day-to-day management.

Nor can you fault the location: sheltered in a south facing hillside in the South Hams, the thirteen cottages, converted from 17th century farm buildings, are just a mile from the award-winning Blackpool Sands and will appeal to both young and old. There's a playroom for under fives, two playgrounds, and many cottages have secure terraces or gardens.

We looked specifically at the courtyard cluster, of which *Little Bowden Cottage*, a perfect holiday hideaway **sleeping 2**, brimming with character and with an old stone fireplace, is indicative of the variety on offer.

The tennis court and the gardens help enhance the family hotel feeling.

We were particularly taken with Rose Cottage, a deluxe conversion.

Particularly attractive is the courtyard itself, dating back some 300 years and laid out so that each cottage has a virtually self-contained garden.

At a lower level are five more cottages, **each sleeping 6**, converted from what were known as 'the old workshops' into deluxe properties. Of these, the delightful *Rose Cottage* has three bedrooms, one with a queen-sized double bed and en-suite shower cubicle, one with twin beds and one with full-sized bunk beds as well as a separate family bathroom.

Bedlinen, personal towels and basic cleaning requirements supplied; electricity by meter; direct dial telephone and satellite television (the availability of sport has proved an asset in wet weather). Cost: approximately £257 to £1521. Further details are available from Monica and Paul Khosla, Higher Bowden, near Dartmouth, South Devon TQ6 0LH. Telephone (01803) 770745. Fax (01803) 770262.

www.higherbowden.com   email: cottages@higherbowden.com

Hollocombe, near Chulmleigh
Horry Mill Cottage

First featured in our 2001 guide, this caught on immediately with readers. Like us, they appreciated a remote rural scene that is as true today as it was in a faded photo on the wall of this cob-style cottage. It **sleeps 6** in two bedrooms with double beds, plus one with a twin, and there is also a child's room, with a cot or a 2ft 6in bed. The fully equipped bathroom has a free-standing electric

We loved the absolute peace and quiet, and have heard how warm and genuine a welcome guests receive here...

shower. We admired the huge inglenook fireplace and bread oven in the sitting-room, also the small south facing sun parlour with grapevine. There is a well equipped kitchen and dining-room seating six and high chair. An open fire, with logs provided free, complements oil fired central heating. The Hodgsons will collect local dishes ordered in Crediton, or elsewhere. Pophams restaurant, with a national reputation, is close by.

Linen and towels provided. Television, video and stereo/CD player. Dogs welcome. Non-smokers preferred. Cost: from £220 to £450. Details from Sonia and Simon Hodgson, Horry Mill, Hollocombe, Chulmleigh, Devon EX18 7QH. Telephone (01769) 520266.
www.horrymill.com   email: sonia@horrymill.com

Winkleigh and Talaton   map 7/446/448
Higher Westcott/The School House

Blakes have many thatched cottages on their books, and one that comes strongly recommended by readers is *Higher Westcott*. The 16th century thatched, Grade II listed farmhouse, **sleeping 12 'plus 2'**, has so much in its favour, such as being situated within nine acres of farmland, with a number of original features, oil paintings and watercolours. (Ref 4909) *The School House* (Ref CP93) very conveniently **sleeping up to 8,** is nicely situated down a quiet lane

The School House, sleeping up to 8, is in Talaton, near Exeter. Detached, it incorporates original details.

that leads to a 12th century church. There are large, enclosed gardens with (a first for us) clock golf. Not suitable for pets. Sidmouth, a genteel family seaside resort, is only a short drive away.

For details of these and similar properties: Blakes, Stoney Bank Road, Earby, Barnoldswick BB94 0BL. To book: (08700) 708090. Brochures: (08700) 708099. **Ref BM090.**

Live search and book: www.blakes-cottages.co.uk

Rattery, near Totnes
Knowle Farm

Lynn and Richard Micklewright have created a paradise for pet-loving youngsters by putting into practice everything they themselves learned as experienced self-caterers. Just open your cottage door and a veritable Dr Doolittle collection of chickens, ducks, pigs, rabbits and donkeys will parade before you. Then there is the outdoor play area, with swings and slides, and one of the best indoor playrooms for under fives we have seen, including a ballpool, slide and toys. There is a genuine attempt here to answer children's needs, without neglecting adults. This is reflected in the cottages, converted from stone and slate barns with wood burning stoves.

Moncks Green, **sleeping 6** plus cot, has one double with four-poster, one twin and one bunk-bedded room downstairs including bathroom/wc with shower. Upstairs, a large living-room, with a high ceiling and exposed trusses, commands impressive views; off this is the dining-room with a shower-room/toilet. *Applecross*, **sleeping 4** plus cot, has one double and

Set in 44 acres, the farm offers tennis and swimming, as well as a whole host of pets.

You can expect fine views and plenty of room for your family in all the cottages.

one bunk room downstairs with bathroom/toilet with shower. Again there are good views from the upstairs living/dining room. *Clematis*, **sleeping 2** plus child or cot, is a cosy single-storey cottage with a wood panelled ceiling in the living/dining room area, full of character like the others. *Woodbine* (**sleeps 8** plus cots) is suited to two families. Downstairs has a galleried living/dining area with high ceiling and bags of exposed beams and trusses, one double bedroom, with four-poster and en-suite facilities, and one twin-bedded room. The first floor gallery sports a gorgeous sitting area, a double and a bunk room, plus bathroom/wc with shower. *Post Box*, a 16th century thatched cottage in a nearby village **sleeps 4** plus cot. Very pretty with old beams and a stone fireplace, this has double and twin rooms upstairs, kitchen, living/dining area, bathroom/toilet with shower downstairs, and its own private garden.

The farm, set in 44 acres, also offers a 36 by 16 feet heated outdoor swimming pool, and an all weather tennis court. Dartmoor is only about five minutes away, the coast about half an hour. Not suitable for pets; electricity and heating by meter; duvets (with linen) supplied; TV; highchairs, cots and stair gates. Cost: from about £150 to £1020. Details from Lynn and Richard Micklewright, Knowle Farm, Rattery, near Totnes, Devon TQ10 9JY. Telephone/fax (01364) 73914.

website – www.knowle-farm.co.uk email: holiday@knowle-farm.co.uk

Salcombe, near Kingsbridge
Salcombe Holiday Homes*

This expertly-run specialist agency operates exclusively in and around the most popular resort in Devon's South Hams, at the southernmost tip of the county.

Salcombe has an exceptionally pleasant climate and is surely one of the country's most beautiful sailing and fishing centres. The properties under the umbrella of Salcombe Holiday Homes are run to exacting standards by the welcoming and professional Tim and Ginny Windibank, and we know that members of staff *visit each property prior to every arrival.*

The agency's portfolio includes *Island Cottage,* which **sleeps 8**, has been beautifully refurbished and is very close to both the quays and car/boat parks. The cottage has views of the creek and retains much of the original character. One of the agency's most popular properties, *Topside*, **sleeps 8** and is hidden away behind the main street. A nice surprise is that it has a heated outdoor swimming pool and secluded patio and terrace.

Salcombe is full of character cottages, and two of these that were new to Salcombe Holiday Homes last year are proving very popular. *Aune Cottage* (**sleeps 4**) has a charming garden with estuary views. It is in a narrow lane just a minute's walk from the main pontoons. *Hope Cottage*

Aune Cottage is in a quiet part of town, but is near the water...

No 3 Rockside has inspiring views of the river estuary...

is in a quiet part of town, within easy reach of the shops, car parks and the water. It **sleeps 5** and has a very appealing garden.

Another special place is *3 Rockside*, the top floor apartment in a listed building, with spectacular views up and down the estuary from the garden and the main rooms. **Sleeps 4.**

This excellent agency's portfolio also includes many cosy cottages and flats for 2/4 or more that are ideal for short breaks out of high season. Out of season the agency offers reduced rates for short stays on many properties and changeover dates can often be adjusted to your needs.

Salcombe is indeed a place for all seasons, offering an excellent selection of shops, galleries, restaurants and pubs.

For a detailed brochure, with line drawings, contact Salcombe Holiday Homes, 3 Island Square, Island Street, Salcombe, Devon TQ8 8DP. Telephone Salcombe (01548) 843485. Fax 843489.

www.salcombe.co.uk   email: shh@salcombe.co.uk

Devon: coast and country
Toad Hall Cottages*

With a very high proportion of clients who become regulars, this cottage letting agency has on its books *some of the most beautifully situated coastal and inland cottages anywhere in Britain*. The agency deals, however, exclusively with Devon. Twice we have spent a day looking at a selection of properties, most recently, the handsome, quiet *Brownscombe Farm*, on the edge of rural Huntshaw, in North Devon, **sleeping up to 9**.

A reader from South London told us during 2000 that she had had 'the English holiday of a lifetime' with a group of friends at *Riverside House*, in the village of Tuckenhay. **Sleeps 10**. Most rooms overlook the water.

Previously, when it was hot inland but with a breeeze off the water, we drove to *Maelcombe House*, in an exquisite high location overlooking the sea at East Prawle, with good bathing and easy access to the beach (marvellous rock pools). There are two spacious apartments and a wing of the handsome house, **sleeping 6, 6** and **4/6** respectively.

Particularly memorable was *Cliff Cottage*, so close to the water in the picture postcard village of Dittisham that at low tide you feel you could reach out and choose a crab for your tea. We sat on the balcony and watched the traffic: weekenders' sailing dinghies, floating gin palaces, little ferries, working fishing boats and wheeling gulls. **Sleeping 6**, the cottage has those fabulous views from (smallish) front bedrooms, a big and convivial sitting room, a huge rear garden with fruit trees. Nearby, also on the water, 400-year-old *Smuggler's Cottage,* full of 'old world' character, is thatched and has views from almost every room. **Sleeps up to 8**.

Then, via narrow and winding lanes bordered by high banks, we went to see *Eeyore's House* and *Alice Cottage*. They were once owned by the grandson of A A Milne ('Christopher Robin went down with Alice'...) but that is just part of their nostalgic charm. They are exceptionally quiet, private and comfortable, with many personal touches.

Every Toad Hall staff member knows every cottage. About half the properties accept dogs and many have open fires. Their full colour brochure is exceptionally good. Descriptions are detailed, and we like the way cottages are put into the context of their surrounding area. Details/brochure from Toad Hall Cottages, Elliott House, Church Street, Kingsbridge, South Devon TQ7 1BY. Telephone (01548) 853089. Fax 853086. **www.toadhallcottages.com email: thc@toadhallcottages.com**

Cliff Cottage: you are close enough to the water to choose a crab for your tea...

Alice Cottage, in a tiny hamlet, was the home of the real-life Christopher Robin...

Compton Pool, near Torquay
Compton Pool Farm Cottages

This much-admired place has a lot going for it: most notably perhaps the pleasure of being both deep in the country *and* very close to the seaside.

It is about ten minutes' drive from the centre of Torquay, but is entirely rural, with easy access to Torbay. Inland, Dartmoor is a short drive away.

There is plenty for guests to do, with wildlife parks, a rare breeds farm, a butterfly farm, steam railways, learning to sail. There is a warm indoor swimming pool to enjoy, and a tennis court on site.

One of our colleagues stayed at Compton Pool with a child of 20 months one recent summer, and reported favourably on 'so many things to do' and liked the proximity of a couple of pubs serving good food (they also welcomed children) – trying to keep the 'self' out of 'self-catering'.

We spoke to a young family who were on their second visit and staying in *Stable Cottage,* which overlooks the courtyard. Their children loved fussing over the free-range chickens and the very warm (85°) indoor swimming pool, and their parents appreciated the safe, enclosed environment.

A notably child-friendly place with, not surprisingly, many return visitors. (We have heard of children just wanting to stay put for a fortnight.)

Families have been known to spend hours in the very warm swimming pool. And one reader wrote to us to say that her daughter had learnt to swim here...

Among the many specific things going for Compton Pool that we have noted over the years are the sandpit for toddlers, the large lawn for games of football, a games barn with table football, pool table, dartboard and leaflets detailing local places of interest, a shed full of ride-on toys for younger children, babysitting by local girls, the hotel down the road that does take-away meals, the delivery of milk, newspapers and groceries.

Compton Pool Farm is a comfortable, friendly size with nine cottages and one very comfortable modern caravan in the orchard. There are cottages to suit all families. The *Old Barn, Cider House* and *Garden Cottage,* which are the largest, **sleeping up to 8** with two bathrooms/showers, are ideal for large families or for inviting grandparents or friends.

Televisions. Not suitable for pets. Highchairs, cots and stairgates available. Linen provided, with beds made up, and towels are available. Cost: about £200 to £826. Details and a good information folder from John and Margaret Phipps, Compton Pool Farm, Compton, Devon TQ13 1TA. Telephone (01803) 872241. Fax (01803) 874012.

www.comptonpool.co.uk email: info@comptonpool.co.uk

The West Country
Helpful Holidays*

We're always impressed by the way this long established organisation balances pictures and text in its lively brochure. You get a very good visual impression and lots of detail of the 450 or so cottages on the agency's books.

But that's typical of this considerate, user-friendly and aptly named organisation. Euan, Su and Moray Bowater, who are at its helm, are known throughout the cottage letting industry to be uncompromising about standards. It has been our pleasure to know and feature 'Helpful' (as it is widely known) for over fifteen years now without a break, and we have never heard anything other than praise from readers.

The Bowaters' priority has always been to find out what individual people want to do on holiday – walk, sit on the beach, ride, fish, birdwatch or whatever – and direct them to the place and accommodation to suit their tastes and purses. They believe in saying what places and properties are really like – warts and all – and have an exceptional variety, from smart boat houses and 'beach houses' to historic country houses, as well as picture-book thatched cottages.

Helpful's properties are spread all over the West Country from Land's End to Somerset and Dorset – seaside and inland. And a glance at their unconventional brochure will soon confirm the 'truth will out' philosophy. It reads like the pages of a 'Which' report.

During the summer of 2001, after following a winding country lane, we visited the impressive *Sheafhayne,* in the beautiful farming country of the Devon/Somerset border. It is a piece of English history beautifully encapsulated in a fine manor house which was once the shooting lodge of Sir Francis Drake's country estate. It is not a museum-piece, but a thoroughly welcoming and comfortably informal home-from-home. We met an extended family plus a group of friends really enjoying the place, which, remarkably, **sleeps up to 24**. It is rambling in the nicest way, with several oak panelled rooms, and bedrooms tucked away up unexpected flights of stairs at the end of half secret passageways. Delightful!

We have also been recommended to, and in 2002 will visit, the extraordinary *Sandridge Barton*, which 'Helpful' (not given to exaggeration) describe as 'sensational'. It is a fabulous Georgian mansion overlooking the Dart Estuary, with an indoor swimming pool any middle-ranking Roman emperor would have been proud of. The house **sleeps up to 12.**

This Grade 1 listed property is both full of history and prettily, quietly situated.

This beautiful Miller's House (Grade II listed) is near Ilminster.

288

Another delightful journey of discovery led us to *Lower Elsford*, near Lustleigh. It is a classic rural Devonshire enclave, four skilful barn conversions adjacent to the owners' house in 35 acres of garden and farmland, from which at certain points it is possible to see the sea. Among many other good things, we admired deep sofas, woodburners, high ceilings, good quality rugs and table lamps, and many charming personal details. All is done with great style. A well heated indoor swimming pool in a converted piggery (we loved the piggy murals!) even has an open fire: a first for us! There are lots of animals for children to make friends with. **Sleep 2 to 6**.

Then, just outside nearby Manaton, we visited an exquisite Grade 1 listed, part-13th century 'upper hall', full of fascinating original details. **Sleeps 2**.

Beyond the River Tamar that separates Cornwall from Devon, and in a tucked away corner that many travellers scurrying westwards miss, we found *Clift House*, an absolute delight. It is beautifully situated on one of the creeks that feed into Plymouth Sound. Partly 13th century, with a wing added shortly after the Civil War, it has masses of character, and **sleeps up to 11**.

Helpful is increasingly strong on large houses for large parties. These include a brilliantly converted barn (with ten bedrooms and ten bathrooms) which has superb views of the River Dart, and two former hotels, both superbly situated: one overlooks the yacht anchorage in Newton Ferrers, South Devon, and has a civil wedding licence, the other is in St Agnes, on Cornwall's north coast of sandy surfing beaches. Also in Cornwall, not far from the Camel estuary, is *Tregarden*, a splendid Elizabethan manor house, **sleeping 20**.

New for 2002 are three supremely well sited, very high quality sea-view houses, all of them **sleeping 10 or more people**. These are near Prawle Point and Salcombe, in southernmost Devon, and Mevagissey, in Cornwall.

In the River Tamar valley is the 15th century manor house pictured below left, and on Dartmoor is *Brimpts Barn*, near Dartmeet, **sleeping 32**. On offer are activities that include horse-riding, canoeing, rock climbing, mountain biking, orienteering, abseiling, caving and rough or clay pigeon shooting.

Increasingly, Helpful Holidays has houses with their own indoor swimming pool. One is in fascinating Boscastle, Cornwall (busy in summer, moody and magnificent in autumn and winter). Another is attached to a Grade II listed thatched former farmhouse in Chideock, south-west Dorset.

This fine, elegant, spacious Grade II listed house sleeps 14 people.

This little jewel is near Kingsbridge, on Devon's South Hams.

We have had glowing reports of cottages with spectacular views in South Devon, a converted boathouse overlooking a Cornish creek, excellent new apartments virtually on the enormous sandy beach at Bigbury-on-Sea, opposite Burgh Island, and a brand new bungalow overlooking the beach just outside Falmouth.

In Somerset, they have cottages, farmhouses and a superb country house on Exmoor and on the slopes of the Quantock Hills. These include a gamekeeper's cottage secluded among pines on the side of a combe, a Grade II listed miller's house in the county's lush farming centre, and a converted apple store from which you can walk to the tops of the Mendips. In Dorset they have cottages in the vales of Blackmore and Stour, and close to Abbotsbury with its swannery.

Naturally they have many cottages in and around Chagford, their very popular little home town on Dartmoor's edge, and in its neighbour, Drewsteignton, a village above the dramatic River Teign valley, near amazing Castle Drogo. Here are six classic thatched cottages, one facing a heated swimming pool in a walled garden. All have the great attraction of open fires or woodburners.

Another splendid country house is *Parnacott*, eight miles from Bude with its sandy beaches and a cliff-walking/bird-watching coast. Amid peaceful grounds of 32 acres, the big house, in the family for 400 years, is quite beautiful and full of character. It **sleeps 14**.

The Bowaters are 'owners' themselves – slumbering under a traditional thatched roof in the Teign Valley below Castle Drogo is their *Gibhouse,* in its peaceful gardens beside a stream and with superb views of green, rolling hills.

Recently Helpful Holidays have moved office converting an abandoned chapel in Chagford. The conversion is much admired and visitors are very welcome.

Weekly prices range from about £105 to £4500. Dogs are welcome in many properties. Details are available from Helpful Holidays, Chagford, Devon TQ13 8AW. Telephone (01647) 433593. Fax (01647) 433694. Or have a look at their website:

www.helpfulholidays.com

email: help@helpfulholidays.com

An idyllically situated cottage near Castle Drogo above.

Parnacott slumbers amid 32 acres, and sleeps no fewer than 14 people.

This fabulous house, sleeping up to ten, is near Mevagissey, in Cornwall...

Dawlish
Shell Cove House Apartments and Lobster Cottage

Ever popular, this substantial and most attractive country house, whose well cared for grounds extend to the cliff edge, embraces several much liked, superbly positioned apartments in a very pleasant setting. Via a private path, guests have access to what is effectively a private beach.

We have met holidaymakers whose enthusiasm for and loyalty to the place is such that they have returned year after year for the past *30* years! Some of them are people who considered buying a place of their own locally, but can't really see the point when they have Shell Cove!

There is such a lot going for guests here, with four acres of timbered grounds to stroll and picnic in and a bird hide gazebo from where you might spot visiting dolphins. There's a hard tennis court, a large heated swimming and toddlers' pool, badminton and croquet lawns, garden and barbecue. Not least, for adults and children who want to get away from each other, there is a large basement games room/hideaway.

People who like the situation, appreciate the extremely friendly welcome from the resident family owners, and enjoy all that Shell Cove has to offer can book their own cottage: either *Lobster Cottage,* **sleeping up to 10** or *Crab-pot Cottage.* Both cottages stand in the grounds of the main house with secluded patios but are a short stroll through the grounds to all the facilities of the main house.

The apartments **sleep 2 to 6.** We noticed good carpeting, deep sofas and armchairs, good quality beds, well planned kitchens with microwave ovens and dishwashers in the larger units, and lovely sea views. Most have their own sunny patios with garden furniture for dining *al fresco.*

Open all year, with lovely spring gardens, the apartments are warm with central heating included. They are popular all year round, and one of our readers referred to 'an oasis of peace and beauty' outside the main season.

Sleep 2 to 10. Linen and towels are included. A maid service is available. There are televisions, videos, a swimming pool, a tennis court, badminton, croquet, indoor games room, bird hide, children's playground and, of course, the beach. Dogs are usually allowed by arrangement. Special short breaks. Central heating. Cost: approximately £200 to £1300. For further details and a good brochure please contact Mrs G Jameson, Shell Cove House, Old Teignmouth Road, Dawlish, Devon EX7 0NJ. Telephone/fax (01626) 862523.

A fine, beautifully-run house with many fans, and an excellent repeat business. Definitely a place to make new friends: both children and adults love it ...

A super, and virtually private, beach lies just below Shell Cove.

Otterton and around
The Thatched Cottage Company*

We know Gill and Robin Barlow from the time they ran an enclave of the
finest cottages anywhere in Cornwall, maintained to superlatively high
standards that 'led the way' for would-be top notch cottage owners. They
deal mainly with chic thatched and in several cases very historic properties, all of them within easy striking distance of the coastline recently designated as a World Heritage Site.

From their base in Otterton, in east Devon, they have built up a portfolio
of just half a dozen cottages, all of them ETC Five Stars, all contained in
an especially eye-catching brochure concentrating on interior photos.

This is where holiday dreams could come true, with picture-postcard thatch...

...set off by some superb interiors: comfy, but with the original character retained.

In *Squirrel* for example, **sleeping 5** in a double (five foot bed), a twin and
a single, we loved the genuinely cottagey ambience, the light, lemony
fabrics and decor, the pale deep pile carpets, the superbly fitted kitchen.

In *Pheasant,* a spacious thatched house, full of beams and with many
original features retained, we admired a particularly inviting sitting room
with well chosen lamps, another outstandingly good kitchen, a five foot
bed in the main bedroom (with just a single as well, the cottage **sleeps 3** –
although the impression is of a bigger place).

In *The Old Granary*, part of a conversion of the outbuildings of what was
once a monastery and more recently a farm, **sleeping just 2** in a double,
we liked the different levels, the brick arches of the original granary, the
log burner, the sense of privacy while being part of a small community.

There is also, for example, *Christopher's Farmhouse*, a fine traditional
Devon 'longhouse' in two acres, just a mile from the sea. It **sleeps 6**;
within the farmhouse but separate and private, is a 2-person unit, *The
Tannery*, and there are also two small cottages within the grounds. (For
large scale get-togethers, all four can be taken together.)

Though when we visited in the summer of 2001 not all the cottages were
up and running, we greatly admired what had already been achieved.

TVs/videos. Dogs are welcome in some properties. Linen and towels are
included. Cost: about £300 to £1250. Further details and a copy of that
very good brochure from Gill Barlow, The Thatched Cottage Company,
56 Fore Street, Otterton, Devon EX9 7HB. Telephone (01395) 567676.
Fax (01395) 567440.

www.thethatchedcottagecompany.com

Sidbury, near Sidmouth
Court Cottage

Unassuming but still comfortable, and used from time to time by the owners, this pleasant place has featured in our guide for over ten years. During our most recent revisit we met some regular guests happily installed. Secreted away in a corner of a comparatively little-known village, the quiet cottage has fitted carpets, a good-sized sitting room (lots of books), a kitchen with a walk-in pantry, and a 'power shower'. There

Tucked away in a large village and therefore not remote, this is nevertheless quiet and feels very private...

are three bedrooms, one (with double-bed) spacious and with good views beyond the village proper, and masses of cupboard space. The second bedroom has twin beds, and this, too, is uncramped. Adding greatly to the character of the cottage is the third bedroom with beamed ceiling. The south facing garden is enclosed by high walls, making it sheltered and private.

Sleeps 5. TV. Unsuitable for pets. Cost: between £190 to £360 per week, depending on when you go, with winter lets considered. Further details available from Allen Cummings, 82 Pitts Lane, Earley, Reading RG6 1BU. Telephone (0118) 966 6073.

Sidbury, near Sidmouth   map 7/458
Lower Knapp Farm

Just five miles from the nicely old-fashioned family seaside resort of Sidmouth, under half an hour from Lyme Regis, and with a good sandy beach at easy-to-get-to-Exmouth, it's no surprise that Lower Knapp's twelve cottages have a strong following. With Four ETC Stars, sixteen acres of land, a nearby donkey sanctuary children love, it is much

A very family-orientated place, but you can also be 'as private as you like'...

appreciated by families. A Mr Chapel from Southampton likes the 'all dogs welcome' policy, and the fact that while this can be quite a sociable place you can be as private as you like. A Mrs Lowry from Middlesex loves the unlimited-access swimming pool. In fact, her children learnt to swim there. There is a useful range of accommodation, from properties **sleeping 2** up to one **sleeping 9 'plus 2'**, and it is of course possible to rent more than one. TVs. Linen and towels included. Pets welcome. Children's play area. Cost: about £165 to £1115. Details/brochure from John Baxter, Lower Knapp Farm, Sidbury, Sidmouth, Devon EX10 0QN. Telephone (freecall) 0800 915 7847. Fax (01404) 871597.

www.knappfarm-holidays.co.uk   email: lowknapp@aol.com

Colaton Raleigh, near Sidmouth
Drupe Farm Cottages

With its kind and professional welcome, gardens that are usually a blaze of colour, and spacious and very comfortable properties, it is no surprise that this excellent base from which to explore the delights of Devon has featured in these pages without a single complaint for eighteen years. The clever conversion of old farm buildings round a central, sympathetically landscaped courtyard is – on a quiet day – slightly reminiscent of some monastic close.

Visitors with children will appreciate the safe adventure playground which adjoins open fields, the converted barn with skittles, badminton, basketball, extra barbecue and the indoor sandpit/toys/activities for toddlers. There are also a games room and a laundry room.

There is nothing cramped about the accommodation in any of the fifteen units, whose spaciousness is enhanced by high ceilings (though some bedrooms have sloping attic roofs). Most of the bedrooms look down into the central courtyard. We noticed good quality fitted carpets and especially roomy sitting rooms. These are not particularly cottagey but are well suited to people not averse to a few creature comforts: central heating, well fitted kitchen-diners as part of the living area, televisions and videos. A most welcoming and professional manager is on hand to provide local information and make sure everything inside the 'cottage' is just so. One unit is especially interesting and especially private: sympa-

We have always appreciated the effective marriage of traditional farm buildings and purpose-built accommodation here.

This unit, at one corner of the complex, has a fascinating, almost circular sitting room, looking out on to greenery.

thetic conversion of part of the original building has left an almost-round sitting room which looks on to greenery. Over recent years, the cottages have been completely and beautifully renovated to a very high standard, including 'fixtures and fittings', and are ETC Four Stars. **Sleep 2 to 8**.

Dogs welcome (extra charge). TV/video. Linen, electricity and gas central heating included. Cost: about £180 to £595. Open all year, and short breaks available, September to April.

Further details and a very full brochure, with a welcome floor-plan of the whole complex, from Drupe Farm, Colaton Raleigh, Sidmouth, Devon. Telephone Colaton Raleigh (01395) 568838. Fax (01395) 567882.

www.drupefarm.co.uk   **email: mail@drupefarm.co.uk**

Beer
Jean Bartlett Cottage Holidays*

Based in a famous place and concentrating very cannily on a specific and much loved area, this medium-sized agency has featured in these pages for many years and been described in glowing terms by so many holiday-makers, with never a complaint: 'thoughtful and efficient people, very desirable locations, some outstandingly good cottages'. They handle properties from Honiton to the coast of East Devon and West Dorset: some very grand, some quite modest and inexpensive. We have visited about a dozen, most within sight of the sea and one or two right on it.

On our most recent visit we looked at *Hope* and *Creole* cottages, both former fishermen's houses with beautiful gardens, right in the centre of Beer village; at *Chapel Cottage*, a quietly situated thatched beauty just inland; at *Westgate Cottage*, the wing of a part-16th century 'hall house' with a number of original features such as a huge fireplace; and at *The Belvedere* and *The Look Out*, spacious and most appealing apartments, with sea views, right at the heart of Beer.

Hope and Creole (**sleeping 5/6**) are furnished to permanent home standards and are much admired by passers-by. They have good sized sitting rooms with deep sofas and chairs, upholstered window seats and an original beamed fireplace. Both have modern kitchens, three bedrooms and a bathroom, plus the benefit of a private parking space.

For guests seeking absolute top-of-the-range accommodation, the agency offers several English Tourism Council Five Star-rated properties including medieval *Sutton Barton*, which accommodates up to twenty guests in six bedrooms. It has seven bathrooms! There is *The Warren*, a part-Georgian property with a tennis court close to Woodbury Common, and *Steppes Barn* – a spacious barn conversion near the River Axe, which has plenty of space for guests who wish to bring a boat.

Picture-book villages such as Branscombe are a short drive, as are the resorts of Sidmouth and Lyme Regis. Costs range from about £150 to £2000. Dogs accepted in about half the properties by arrangement. Details and brochures from Jean Bartlett Holidays, Fore Street, Beer, Devon EX12 3JJ. Telephone Seaton (01297) 23221. Fax (01297) 23303.

www.jeanbartlett.com

email: holidays@jeanbartlett.com

Hope and Creole Cottages offer a rare chance to be based in the heart of Beer.

Sutton Barton not only sleeps 20 people but is an ETC Five Star property...

Maiden Newton, near Dorchester
Lancombe Country Cottages

Far from the madding crowd, deep in Dorset's Hardy Country, these traditional flint and brick properties have a fine reputation, enhanced by an eagerness to please, such as the supply of local maps and a welcome pinta on arrival. The coast is about ten miles away, and nearby Maiden Newton has a very good restaurant. Formerly barns, and surrounded by farmland, the cottages are set off by manicured flower beds and a big

Spotless, 'ship-shape', superbly situated, with panoramic views to boot ...

walled garden. At the back is a shared, safely enclosed, grassy area, and a leisure centre with heated indoor swimming pool and sauna. The neat, easy-to-maintain interiors **sleep 2 to 5**. All the cottages are named after local rivers: *Bride*, **for 2**, has a four-poster and is a favourite of honeymooners. *Frome* is the largest, **sleeping 5**. Laundry room with deep freeze. TV/video; central heating; payphone; linen and towels. Cost: £219 to £599. Open all year. Three night autumn to spring breaks: £126 to £219. ETC Four Stars. Details: Janet Schofield, Lancombe Farm, Maiden Newton, Dorchester, Dorset DT2 0HU. Telephone/fax (01300) 320562.

www.lancombe.co.uk email: lancombe@talk21.com

Corfe Castle
Scoles Manor Colour sect B, P5

Another great location: the most romantic view of Corfe Castle, framed between the Purbeck Hills. Close to the castle, these three cottages (**map 7/462**) have been imaginatively created within a long barn/dairy. They have large windows, pine furniture, smart fitted kitchens and such features as

Very much geared to families, for example with children's playgrounds and babysitting...

exposed stone walls and oak beams. Owners Peter and Belinda Bell live in the adjoining manor house. The thirty-acre estate, at the end of a 600-yard farm track, is home to shaggy Highland cattle, ducks, bantams and doves. And the Purbeck Way footpath to Corfe Castle or the sea passes by the property. There are sandy beaches at Studland and Swanage, a short drive, or you can walk to small coves. A cosy pub is just two fields away. All are ETC Four Stars. Single-storeyed *Dairy* has four double rooms and two bathrooms, *Great Barn* three double rooms (two bathrooms), *Little Barn* two bedrooms (one with bunk beds). Central heating, bedlinen, payphones, starter pack of groceries, babysitting. Open all year. Cost: £210 to £925. Short breaks. Details: Peter and Belinda Bell, Scoles Manor, Kingston, Corfe Castle, Dorset BH20 5LG. Telephone (01929) 480312. Fax 481237. **www.scoles.co.uk email: peter@scoles.co.uk**

Coastal Dorset
Dorset Coastal Cottages*

This agency specialises in old, traditional properties: the 50-plus cottages and barn conversions on their books fit the bill. Many are thatched and have open fires and all are in, or near, villages close to the unspoilt coast between Studland and Lyme Regis. Charles and Jennie Smith, who run Dorset Coastal Cottages,

Milton Cottage, Winfrith Newburgh, has two attractively beamy bedrooms.

know what appeals to lovers of the countryside, as well as the spectacular coastal path. We really like *Milton Cottage*, Winfrith Newburgh, **sleeping 4**, a pretty brick and thatched cottage with two beamy bedrooms and a small garden: not suitable for young children. And *No 3 Coastguards Cottages,* Kimmeridge, 300 yards from the beach, **sleeps 6/8** plus cot.

Costs, including all electricity/gas etc, from £200 to £375 for 2, to £605 to £1255 for 12. Short breaks, minimum three nights. Dogs, where permitted, £10 a week each. Linen/towels included in most, cots/highchairs in many. TV/video; well equipped kitchens with washing machine, freezer, microwave unless specified otherwise. Details from Dorset Coastal Cottages, The Manor House, Winfrith Newburgh, Dorchester, Dorset DT2 8JR. Telephone (0800) 9804070. Fax 01305 854988.

www.dorsetcoastalcottages.com

Cerne Abbas, near Dorchester
Hilfield Manor   map 7/465

Readers who went a couple of years ago to the Sherborne/Dorchester area with an American relative tracing his roots stayed in two of the cottages (*Peter Brooke* and *Dampier Lodge*) at Hilfield Manor, at Cerne Abbas (a place famous for its 'rude' giant carved into the hillside). In this most effective conversion of coach house and stables, our correspondents much appreciated the king-size bed and the

The Hilfield Manor properties have been sympathetically converted...

wood-burning stove in Peter Brooke (Ref 1718), which **sleeps 3**, the 'fabulous' gardens, in which peacocks strut across the lawns, and the secret garden, which has high hedges that come in useful when it's time for barbecues and sunbathing. Dampier Lodge (Ref E1717) **sleeps 4** in a double and a twin; *Castle Coach House* has an open plan sitting room/dining room with a fitted kitchen area, and an unusual spiral staircase to a galleried double bedroom. **Sleeps 2.** (Ref E1719).

Hoseasons Holidays, Lowestoft NR32 2LW. For real-time availability and on-line booking: Telephone 0870 534 2342. Fax 0870 902 2090.

www.hoseasons.co.uk   email: mail@hoseasons.co.uk

Dartmouth
A Town For All Seasons*

We know large parts of Britain 'inside out', but until (in 2001) we checked out Tessa Angles's holiday cottage agency had never seen Dartmouth. With the sun sparkling on the sea, packed pleasure boats puttering up the river, and cream and brown trains transporting people on the restored Dart Valley Railway, it's very special.

This is a delightful corner of Devon, which has a good number of holiday homes (some self-contained houses, many apartments), the best of which are looked after by the highly professional and welcoming Tessa Angles and her small staff.

We looked at a cross section of what she has available, all of them with the sort of view that could keep one sitting quietly in a bay window or on a balcony – just gazing at the river and the town – for hours on end.

We looked first at the almost-palatial, very roomy, rather modern apartment (*Property 186* in the brochure), memorable not only for its views from front windows and its balcony, but among many other good things charming local pictures and prints, dark pink, deep-cushioned sofas, lots of mirrors. We noticed thoughtful lighting, lots of books and also, glancing at Tessa Angles's price structure, that in the winter months the apartment is a real bargain. But this applies to most of her properties.

We also saw *Property 156*, above the town. On three storeys, it has amazing views. We noted rugs on a fitted sitting room carpet. There is old and new pine, top-quality curtains. The sitting room is a very good size. Best of all was *Property 53*, a remarkable detached property (with fabulous views of course) with lots of privacy. **Sleeping 8**, it is about 100 years old, although you would probably not guess that, as it has been very effectively modernised. With high ceilings, it is memorable for its paved deck, accessible from the good sized sitting room. Unusually for the generally tightly-packed Dartmouth properties, it has a substantial sheltered garden. There is a king-sized bed in the main bedroom, a modern kitchen.

Several properties accept pets. Details and a copy of the Tessa Angles brochure from Keith and Tessa Angles, 1A Lower Street, Dartmouth, Devon TQ6 9AJ. Telephone (01803) 833082. Fax 835224.

www.tangles-dartmouth-hols-devon.co.uk
email: tessa@dartmouth-holcots.com

A good number of the Tessa Angles properties are high above Dartmouth...

...and those that aren't mostly have easy access to this extraordinary town.

Lyme Regis, Charmouth and around
Lyme Bay Holidays*

Featured in our guide for seven years now, this well established agency has brought loads of encouraging reports (recently from a Hertfordshire couple with a small grand-daughter in tow, who were very content with their small cottage near the beach). We also know the enthusiastic new owners have brought renewed energy to the organisation. Most of their properties come within a ten mile radius of quiet, sandy, slightly old fashioned Charmouth, which is itself one of Dorset's best kept secrets, and of the genteel little seaside resort of Lyme Regis. Some feature in or near historic Beaminster and Bridport.

We ourselves made a recent extended visit. Our first call was to see two properties in Charmouth itself. One was *Sea Horse Apartment*, a sumptuously comfortable, absolutely clean and smart property **sleeping 4**, with views of the beach through big windows. Secondly, in some contrast but extremely appealing in its way, we saw a spacious detached family house called *Penderel*, **sleeping 7 plus 1** plus cot. We liked the big rooms, the open fire, the quietness – even though Charmouth's high street is only a matter of yards away.

We then drove for about ten minutes out of the village to discover, tucked prettily away near Rocombe, in a secret, miniature valley, a picture-postcard thatched cottage in which on a blustery day a couple were very cosily installed (it sleeps **just 2**, but we admired a very large kitchen/diner). Dating back in part to the 16th century, this charming property has a third of an acre garden.

On the agenda for our next visit there are seven properties along the 'Marine Parade' seafront at Lyme Regis and its famous harbour area known as 'The Cobb'. Two of the most appealing are *Benwick Cottage*, pictured below, and *The Lenton Apartment*, which features a south-facing first floor balcony that has a complete and unobstructed view of the exceptional bay.

Dogs are welcome in a good handful of the 110 to 120 properties. For a copy of the brochure, with good colour line drawings and precise descriptions, write to David Matthews, Lyme Bay Holidays, 44 Church Street, Lyme Regis, Dorset DT7 3DA. Telephone (01297) 443363, fax 445576. Freepost SWB20289, Lyme Regis, Dorset DT7 3BF.

www.lymebayholidays.co.uk

Pretty Benwick is likely to have been familiar to Jane Austen, who loved Lyme.

This pretty thatched cottage makes a cosy hideaway for two people...

299

Somerset
The Big House

Absolutely in line with a huge and recent demand for big and *very big* houses, this much-talked-about organisation has on its books just three substantial properties in the grand country house tradition.

The idea of a weekend or a week away from the everyday world, with friends, family or colleagues taking over the kind of baronial mansion that most people only see when they visit a National Trust house or 'A Stately Home of England' has become '*the* thing'.

All three properties are within three miles of each other, very easily accessible from the M5 motorway.

In the summer of 2001 we looked at part-13th century Grade II listed *Gerbestone Manor House*, at the foot of the wooded slopes of the Blackdown Hills, marvelling among much else at the sumptuously comfortable drawing room, with its superb open fire, at the magnificent panelled dining hall, also with a huge open fire, that seats up to 50 people. (Fifty? Yes: it is possible to rent all three houses and to dine here together.) The house actually **sleeps up to 24**. There is a tennis court, an outdoor pool, a lake for fishing, and a sauna.

Journalist colleagues (Sally Shalam of the *Evening Standard*, Richard Pendlebury of the *Daily Mail*) have visited and stayed at the elegant and substantial Palladian *Tone Dale House*. Built in 1797, it has huge bedrooms, four acres of restored gardens, and oozes character.

One house-party guest dining at Tone Dale speaks of 20-plus people 'utterly defeated' by a gargantuan shepherd's pie and apple crumble. But there are much more sophisicated menus than that, perhaps for that special Saturday night gourmet dinner. From July 2002, it will be possible for **up to 28 people** to sleep here.

On a less grand scale, but nevertheless a substantial house of great character, **sleeping up to 18 people**, *Wellisford Farm House* has open fires, a convivial farmhouse style kitchen with Aga, impressive gardens.

In true house party style all kinds of activity can be laid on for Big House guests, such as clay pigeon shooting and riding.

For details and/or copies of well illustrated separate brochures, contact Ben Fox, The Big House, Tone Dale House, Wellington, Somerset TA21 0EZ. Telephone (01823) 662673. Fax 663558.

At Tone Dale House (above left), and Gerbestone Manor (above right)...

...traditional country house living meets 21st century facilities and comforts.

Motcombe, near Shaftesbury
The Dairy House

Just two miles from Shaftesbury (famous for cobbled Gold Hill), Motcombe is a long village of stone and brick houses. On its outskirts, set back from the modest road to the village, is handsome Dairy House, a recent conversion of an original building into one of the finest holiday homes (spacious, light, bright and absolutely pristine) that we have

This was one of the very best finds during our 2001 investigations...

seen in this part of the country. Completed only in late 2001, and therefore bang up to date in terms of facilities, the Dairy House is accessible to disabled people (one – ground-floor – bedroom has an en suite wheel-in shower.) It also has full central heating, a woodburner-style gas fire in the living room, a Rayburn, *three* TVs (one with ITV digital), freezer and phone. With a delightful and very private patio garden, it **sleeps up to 8** in four bedrooms. ETC grading pending, but we expect Five Stars. Complimentary membership of a local sports centre and swimming pool. Linen, towels, heating, lighting and even dishwasher tablets included. One pet by arrangement. Details: Gilbert and Sue Archdale, Church Farm, Motcombe, Shaftesbury, Dorset SP7 9NT. Telephone/fax (01747) 850968. **www.thedairyhouse.com email: enquiries@thedairyhouse.com**

Stoke sub Hamdon, near Yeovil map 7/473
East Stoke House (Coach House) Colour section B, Page 5

In sleepiest Somerset, this is the sort of place to bring a faraway look to the eyes of people who seek an idyllic, rural England that is increasingly hard to find. Most ingredients are there: formal gardens, with a fine outdoor swimming pool, a championship-size tennis court, croquet, a kitchen garden that guests can take advantage of, long leafy walks without needing to leave the 40-acre estate. With an enclosed exterior glass stairway The Coach House is a

A most skilful and sympathetic conversion, deeply rural but actually not far off the beaten track...

conversion at first floor level of the original, an integral part of the glorious estate that embraces a ten-acre soft fruit farm. It can be let as a whole, **sleeping up to 8 'plus 4 in two sofa beds'**, or two separate (and private) units. TV/video/radio, CD player. Linen and towels are included. Not suitable for dogs. Cost: £500 to £1175. Details and brochures from Simon and Melanie Shuldham, East Stoke House, Stoke sub Hamdon, near Yeovil, Somerset TA14 67UF. Telephone (01935) 822300. Fax 824596. **www.PerfectGetaway.co.uk email: info@PerfectGetaway.co.uk**

South and West
Hideaways*

This is certainly one of the three or four best regional cottage letting agencies in the country. Its reputation is very high indeed, and it has a has some of the best cottages around. Many of them are picture-book places suspended in time: a splendid way to catch the flavour of one of England's most unspoilt corners.

Based between Salisbury and Shaftesbury, Hideaways is strongest where Wiltshire blends lazily with Dorset and Hampshire; it also extends into Cornwall and Devon, with a good selection of properties in the Heart of England, and more besides.

During 2001 for example we visited a rare instance of a quite excellent cottage in the Forest of Dean, where (in one of England's best-kept-secret places) really good self catering is thin on the ground. *Arlin Cottage* is

The Lodge, deep in the New Forest, is a fabulous place – absolutely right for our sort of reader. It sleeps up to 7...

We came across Shedrick Cottage right on its own in deep Dorset countryside. The owners use it from time to time...

quite outstanding, with, among other good things, a superbly equipped family kitchen overlooking fields and woods, and a charming sitting room. **Sleeps up to 10** (maximum 8 adults).

Tucked away in the New Forest (when we visited, we needed the help of a passing postman to find it!) *The Lodge,* near Fordingbridge, is a sunny three-bedroom thatched cottage which shares the owners' three-acre landscaped woodland garden. With distant views over the Forest from its balcony and terrace, this is a *real* hideaway which we reckon visitors will be reluctant to leave. **Sleeps 6/7.** Also in the New Forest, near Lymington, *Rose Cottage,* **sleeping 3,** has been restored by an interior designer to provide exceptional accommodation: hand carved oak doors and Portuguese wall tiles are features of the sitting room.

On a previous Wiltshire-Dorset visit we were impressed, among others, by *Shedrick,* a 17th-century thatched cottage situated on its own deep in the Dorset countryside near Chard, which lost none of its character (oak beams, low ceilings) when it was modernised, partly for their own use. So it has a cosy atmosphere and the convenience of a large fitted kitchen. The three bedrooms (**sleeping 6**) are a double with ensuite shower room/wc, a double with a brass bed, and a twin. There is a small garden with a secluded patio area and barbecue.

Kate's Cottage at Winterbourne Kingston (**sleeps 5**) is available Friday-

Friday. Over 200 years old, it lies along a track on the edge of the village and has a pleasant enclosed garden. It is well placed for visiting some of the most spectacular stretches of coastline in England, around Lulworth Cove, Durdle Door, Swanage and Studland Bay.

On a previous visit we admired a fine example of a pretty, traditional thatched cottage called *The Old Stable,* **sleeping 4**, in the meandering village of Rockbourne. Here we met a young German family enjoying their stay. We noticed an open fire, antique furniture, deep carpets, well planned lighting. In a nearby village, *The Coach House* is superb, standing opposite the former village rectory and incorporating several very attractive features, including a particularly impressive, heavily beamed and timbered bedroom with sloping ceilings. **Sleeps 2 'plus 2'.**

Among other excellent Hideaways properties we know personally are *Academy Cottage* at Tisbury, a Chilmark stone built thatched cottage, dating back some 400 years. There are three bedrooms, beamed ceilings and an inglenook in the 35 foot lounge. There's plenty of room **for 6**.

The Old Stable is in the very attractive village of Rockbourne, in Hampshire. It has an open fire and several antiques.

It has 'our sort of interior': retaining a lot of the original character, but not embarrassed by modern comforts...

The several properties in South East England on the books of this thriving and expanding organisation (which made its name in its home territory of Wiltshire but is impressing readers with what it is doing elsewhere) include two on a large country estate near Oxted, in Surrey. Tandridge Priory belies the fact that it is just 35 minutes from London by train from Oxted village, only a mile and a half away: especially when people staying at either *Tandridge Priory Cottage* or in *Tandridge Priory Wing* – respectively tucked behind and part of the main house – stroll through the extensive grounds which embrace three lakes, pasture and woodland, they feel a thousand miles from the metropolis. The cottage is detached, **sleeps 5** in a double, a twin and a single, has its own small garden and welcomes dogs. The Priory Wing has high ceilings and full length curtains. It **sleeps 4/5** in a family room and a twin. Not suitable for dogs.

In Kent, *Firtree Cottage* is rather special. **Sleeping 6**, plus cot, it is a former millworker's cottage, with a spacious sitting room and an open fire, which in itself makes the cottage a good choice for, say, autumn visits to the nearby and autumnally beautiful Weald of Kent.

Details of these and other properties from Hideaways, Chapel House, Luke Street, Berwick St John, Shaftesbury, Dorset SP7 0HQ. Telephone Donhead (01747) 828000, fax 829090.

www.hideaways.co.uk   email: enq@hideaways.co.uk

Chew Magna, near Bristol   map 7/459
Chew Hill Farm Cottages

Enjoying excellent views over Chew Valley Lake or the Mendip Hills, Mrs Lyons's three welcoming cottages are comfortable, clean, bright and very spacious. They have lots of privacy and have featured in *The Good Holiday Cottage Guide* since its very beginning. Nearby Chew Magna is a charming place. Close to the sweeping Mendips, they are well placed for visiting exquisite Bath,

Twenty years in this guide, and never the suggestion of a complaint...

Cheddar Gorge and Wookey Hole, and Bristol, with its theatres and shops. In *Bailiff's House*, which **sleeps 6**, we admired the big kitchen with its smart units, washing machine and microwave, the very large triple aspect sitting room and separate dining room. There are private gardens. The pleasantly high-ceilinged *West Lodge* is Victorian and **sleeps 4** in a double and two singles. *East Lodge* **sleeps 6** and has a 22 ft long sitting room.

TVs. Linen provided, towels for hire. Dogs possible by arrangement. Cost: £195 to £500. ETC Three Stars. Details from Mrs S Lyons, Chew Hill Farm, Chew Magna, Bristol, North Somerset BS40 8QP. Telephone (01275) 332496; mobile (07831) 117186. Fax (01275) 332496.

Poole   map 7/476
Fisherman's Quay

Readers are always bowled over by this. With wide, uninterrupted views of Poole Harbour (said to be the second largest natural harbour in the world), from which car ferries run to the Channel Islands and to France, this three storeyed house is in a spectacular location. Looking down over

Take binoculars to make the most of the extraordinary wide-ranging views...

the impressive Fisherman's Harbour, two balconies offer an extraordinary vantage point from which to watch every type of waterborne activity – not least, the skills of the pilots guiding huge ships to their berths near Poole Quay – itself bustling with smaller craft and pubs, restaurants, galleries, shops and museums. There are two double rooms, one en-suite, and one twin, main bathroom (both bathrooms have showers), a first floor sitting room with those panoramic views, a well fitted kitchen, dining area, a ground-floor cloakroom, patio and barbecue. Not suitable for pets, infirm or very elderly people, or very young children.

Non smokers preferred. Parking space and integral garage. Central heating included. Cost: £300 to £600. Further details from Dr D Halliday, 1 Grange Drive, Horsforth, Leeds, West Yorkshire LS18 5EQ. Telephone Leeds (0113) 258^0^47.

South and South East

If you glance at the map it looks easily accessible and probably well trodden, but much of this corner of England remains hidden away and secret. Really good properties are hard to come by, but those we have located do seem to get our readers speaking in nostalgic terms – or rather of that strong combination of old fashioned charm and 21st century comfort. We remember the smell of wood-smoke on autumn days, undulating hop fields, 'tile hung' cottages, sleepy red-roofed villages beneath wooded escarpments, manicured topiary gardens. Within easy reach of several of the cottages featured in this section are Winston Churchill's Chartwell, near Westerham, Knole House, at Sevenoaks, Sissinghurst Castle, the celebrated Pantiles, in Tunbridge Wells – perhaps the most elegant 'shopping precinct' in England – the historic Cinque Ports. It's scattered with castles of the toy-fort kind – Bodiam, Hastings, Arundel, Leeds, Hever – and great cathedrals such as Winchester, Chichester and Canterbury (we would even include Guildford's: plain Jane from the outside, exquisite inside). It is also the most fruitful corner of Britain for antique-hunters, with a good sprinkling of old-fashioned tea shops, many in gabled old towns that have defied the depredations of developers. And we have noticed in readers an enthusiasm for including Paris in their 'interesting days out' portfolio – for it's an easy matter to pick up a train at Ashford and have lunch in Montmartre instead of, say, Winchelsea.

Milford-on-Sea
Windmill Cottage   map 2/478

For years one of the everlasting hits of *The Good Holiday Cottage Guide*, this neat, tidy, modern, Georgian-style red brick house seems pleasantly in keeping with the rest of Milford-on-Sea, whose village green and 'character shops' maintain a sense of bygone and rather genteel charm. The house is a joy, and had newly laid carpets and repainted walls when we last visited. The through sitting/dining room has a bow window to the front and French windows to the enclosed back garden. Every electric appliance is in the neat kitchen, including a washing machine, fridge-freezer, tumble drier and microwave. There are three bedrooms (one double, one twin, one small single). **Sleeps up to 5.** There is a modern bathroom, and ample parking space plus a garage in a nearby block. The New Forest, Lymington and Bournemouth are all within easy reach. Village shops are a seven minute walk, and cliffs, together with a pebbly beach, are three minutes by car.

This is a modern, clean and tidy house with everything you could need to give you a virtually chore-free holiday...

Cost: about £210 to £515. TV. Dogs are welcome at £8 each. All linen is included, as well as heat and lighting. Incoming telephone. ETC Three Stars. Further details from Mrs S M Perham, Danescourt, Kivernell Road, Milford-on-Sea, Lymington, Hampshire SO41 0PQ. Telephone Lymington (01590) 643516. Fax 641255.

Lymington
New Forest Cottages*

You'd hardly find a more appealing spot to base a holiday letting agency. From their office on a neat, cobbled slope leading down to Lymington's quayside, this well established and very welcoming organisation handles around a hundred carefully vetted properties.

Several are deep in the New Forest, such as *Hillview,* a substantial house (**sleeping 9**), located near Linwood, in rolling, open forest. The house stands in mature gardens of about an acre, and has extensive facilities on the ground floor, which makes it suitable for elderly or disabled guests.

Also in the forest is *Dell Cottage* (**sleeps 5 'plus 2'**), tucked away along a lane, yet within five minutes' walk of a country pub and just a short drive

The Bee Garden, in the village of Norley Wood, is – typically for this agency – full of character and charm.

Park Farm Cottage is another thatched gem, of which there are many on the agency's books.

from Lyndhurst. It includes a ground-floor annexe with double put-u-up, kitchenette and shower room, so this too would suit two families. Deer and ponies graze beside its good-sized, secluded garden.

Facing Lymington's Town Quay and the fishing boats, yachts and cabin-cruisers on the river is a stylish second floor flat in *Admiral's Court.* The large sitting room/diner has a picture window and a glazed enclosed balcony. **Sleeps 6**. A few miles west at Milford on Sea, a Spanish-style house (**sleeps 8**), part of a modern terrace development by Christchurch Bay, has direct access to the beach and views of the Isle of Wight.

Rose Cottage (**sleeps 7**), on the edge of Lymington, is close to a bird sanctuary on the coast with lovely walks, yet is only a short drive from the picturesque town centre and its lively Saturday street market. Between Lymington and Beaulieu, *Bee Garden* is a spacious thatched bungalow, **sleeping 6**, in the tiny village of Norley Wood: it has a pleasant open plan sitting/dining room and a spacious and well-screened garden. Ponies also graze immediately outside *Badgers Walk Cottage,* a bungalow (**sleeping 4**) in the forest outside Burley. *Hawthorne Cottage,* on the outskirts of Brockenhurst, is a delightful Victorian cottage (**sleeping 3**) overlooking a sweep of open forest – perfect for a romantic week.

Details and a colour brochure can be obtained from New Forest Cottages, Ridgeway Rents, 4 Quay Hill, Lymington, Hampshire SO41 3AR. Telephone Lymington (01590) 679655. Fax 670989.

www.newforestcottages.co.uk

The New Forest
Foxhills Properties*

With fewer than 20 very much hand-picked properties in the New Forest, Foxhills is personally supervised by Jan Puttock. The standard of decoration and facilities is high, and the range on offer is quite wide. *Forest Glade* (**sleeping 4**), near Bartley, has some of the forest's ponies as near-neighbours, as the forest is only an arm's length from the back door. Thatched, detached *Clarifont* (**sleeping 4**), near Cadnam, is attractive

In five acres, the outstanding Forest Glade looks on to paddocks and lawns. Delightfully, the back door opens straight on to the forest itself.

and has its own garden. *Lynwood*, in Lyndhurst, **sleeping 8**, lies in one of the best residential areas of the leafy town, and is just a short walk to the heart of the forest. *Glengariff*, **sleeping 2**, in Landford, is a purpose-built holiday flat within a large garden and paddock.

Cost: approximately £195 to £530, including heating. Dogs and even ponies are welcome at several properties. Further details are available from Jan Puttock, Foxhills Properties, The Old Vicarage, Netley Marsh, Southampton, Hampshire SO4 2GX. Telephone/fax 023-80 869444.

www.foxhills-properties.co.uk   email: foxhills@i12.com

Amport, near Andover   map 2/482
The Thatched Barn

In an area short of quality properties, this quickly caught on among readers. In the heart of the rural Test Valley, it's well-placed for exploring Salisbury and Winchester, and just a few miles from the New Forest. Sharing the owners' large, attractive garden, it has been converted from the stables end of their 17th-century house, the home of the Marquis of Winchester's estate manager until

Properties are hard to come by in Hampshire's sought-after Test Valley...

1870, when the Marquis gambled away everything, including the entire village of Amport. Cleverly converted and carpeted throughout, it has a cosy double bedroom and smartly tiled bathroom in the eaves up a steep, narrow open staircase. It rises from the beamed lounge, which also has round dining table and settee bed. Most visitors eat in the kitchen overlooking the big garden. Linen, central heating included; TV, microwave; washing machine available; use of the large garden with Wendy house and swings. Short breaks; credit cards accepted. One dog possible by arrangement. **Sleeps 3**. Cost: about £200 to £350. Details: Carolyn Mallam, Broadwater, Amport, near Andover, Hampshire SP11 8AY. Telephone/fax: (01264) 772240. **email: carolyn@dmac.co.uk**

Hunston, near Chichester
Hunston Mill

In an acre of ground on the Selsey to Chichester road, about half a mile south of the village of Hunston, the tower of the old mill has been partially rebuilt to provide two flats, **each suitable for 2 adults,** and this accommodation is unique in that you can stand in the centre of the living room and see into every room – kitchen, bathroom, bedroom! For the

We have stayed here – it's comfortable, without any loss of character...

building is virtually circular. Also available are *Stable Cottage* and *Coach House Cottage,* a pair of semi-detached dwellings whose earlier usage is evident from their names. **Each sleeps up to 5** in two bedrooms, with separate kitchens and fully-equipped modern bathrooms on the ground floor. And *Engine House* conveniently and inexpensively **sleeps 2**. All living rooms at Hunston Mill have TV, and there are games and books. You will find kitchen basics – soap, sugar, tea, coffee and more. There's a summer house, Wendy House, garden chairs, putting, croquet, barbecue. Cost: about £165 to £375; winter breaks. ETC Four Stars. Details from Tricia and Richard Beeny, Hunston Mill, Chichester, West Sussex PO20 6AU. Telephone Chichester (01243) 783375, fax (01243) 785179.
www.hunstonmill.co.uk   email: hunston.mill@virgin.net

Telscombe Village, near Lewes   map 2/485
The Coach House

We really liked this property, and it caught our readers' imagination too: three *re*-booked within twelve months of their first stay. Two miles from the coast, Telscombe is a sheltered South Downs village, with immediate access to walks with spectacular views. With Newhaven four miles away, it's easy to make day trips to France. The Coach House is a skil-

Great style in an area short of cottages.

fully converted flint and oak beamed cottage with generous accommodation – ETC Four Stars. The large, comfortable, open-plan living area, with rugs, TV/video, stereo and woodburning stove, has a wide, half-spiral oak staircase leading to two bedrooms: one double, the other a twin. Downstairs, french doors lead into a south-facing walled garden. Linen supplied, towels for hire, cots/highchair provided free. Central heating and hot water included. Well behaved dogs welcome. **Sleeps 4** plus one extra on a sofa bed. Cost: £350 to £550; off season mini-breaks £263.

Details: Best of Sussex, Windmill Lodge, Vicarage Lane, Rottingdean, Brighton, Sussex BN2 7HD. Telephone (01273) 308779. Fax 390211.
www.bestofbrighton.co.uk   email: brightoncottages@pavilion.co.uk

Wadhurst, near Tunbridge Wells
The Hoppers Hut/Carters Cottage

Enjoying their superb location, and happy about their ETC Four Stars, the owners of these peaceful cottages emphasise that they are ideal for people who appreciate solitude. They are deep in rural East Sussex but only 50 yards from Bewl Water, a man-made reservoir famous for trout fishing. Ponies and chickens roam and sheep graze in the fields around. *Hoppers* **sleeps 4/5** in a five foot double and a twin, with a further

Peace and quiet on the water. Perhaps our favourite part of Sussex...

sleeping space in the roof area above the twin. The cottage is cosy, and has a fully equipped kitchen. The sitting room has French windows on to the patio, and a garden. *Carter's Cottage* is **for 2** plus cot. Facilities similar to Hoppers: fitted kitchen, Velux windows upstairs, splendid views, private terrace. Readers say 'views and peace superb'...'idyllic'...'home from home comfort'. Shared games room, laundry room. Horse riding nearby. Woodburners. TV and radio; payphone; linen included. Details: Mrs M Bentsen, Newbarn, Wards Lane, Wadhurst, East Sussex TN5 6HP. Telephone (01892) 782042.

www.bewlwatercottages.com email: bentsen@bewlwatercottages.com

---

Winton Street, near Alfriston
Danny Cottage   map 2/487

This is exceptional. It is 'something to write home about'! For up a quiet country lane one would not normally happen across, we discovered one of those lovingly-cared for jewels that make putting this guide together so rewarding. Our notebook states: 'a rhapsody in local red brick'...'a very pretty, regularly tended half acre garden, with a wood at the end that is a

This is pure delight – one of our all-time favourite cottages. Grab it while you can!

sanctuary for wildlife, including badgers'...'low ceilings, lots of beams, understated white painted walls, attractive paintings, thoughtfully arranged lighting'...'fabulous views from two bedrooms'. There's central heating *and* a woodburner; the kitchen is both inviting and very well appointed, with antique pieces, a well chosen carpet. (The garden has a vegetable plot which guests are invited to 'harvest'.)

ETC Five Stars. **Sleeps 5 'plus a child'.** Well behaved dogs are welcome. Linen and towels are included. Two TVs, video, hi-fi, radio. Telephone. Cost: about £450 to £750. Details from Michael and Kitty Ann, France Hill, Alfriston, East Sussex BN26 5XN. Telephone/fax (01323) 870406.

www.dannycottage.co.uk   email: contact@dannycottage.co.uk

Chiddingly, near Hailsham
Pekes

We use the word sparingly, but – yes! – this place is unique. Five distinctively different properties in and around the romantic-looking Tudor manor house (home to the owners) have enchanted hundreds of our readers over the years. They enjoy the use of such amenities as a jacuzzi, a sauna, a solarium and an indoor swimming pool building, memorable for its flowers and hanging plants. There is a tennis and a badminton court.

The most recent addition to the quintet is a 1930s building called *Mounts View*, with stunning rural views from the good sized sitting room, off which there is a dining alcove (very 1930s!). We like this detail: all the lights have dimmer switches. **Sleeps 6 plus 2.**

The humblest property is the tiny, tile-hung *Gate Cottage*, with central heating. Up the steep staircase are a double and a twin bedded room with room for 2 more on a bed-settee. (The cottage recently underwent extensive improvements, including the addition of a pretty little front entrance porch and the enlarging of the kitchen.)

All the cottages have well equipped kitchens: washing machines, tumble dryers, mixers and dishwashers. *Tudor View,* much improved for 2002, is close to the main house, has an open fire and a smart kitchen/diner. The twin bedroom leads into the double bedroom, with a door on to the patio and garden. **Sleeps 5 plus 2.**

The Oast House has a porticoed entrance leading into a biggish hall and a large, circular dining room. The kitchen has a table big enough for the largest get-together; the sitting room has French windows on to the garden. The green-covered stairs and big landing lead to the master bedroom with an enormous four-poster bed. There is a second large circular family room with a double and two singles, a twin bedroom and a very small single. **Sleeps 7 plus 5**. *The Wing* is unusually shaped, with a smart kitchen and several intriguingly inter-connecting rooms. **Sleeps 5**.

Cost: Oast House £1050 to £1350; Cottages and Wing £375 to £725. Mounts View £735 to £945. Short breaks: Oast House £650 to £785. Cottages and Wing £205 to £405. Mounts View £425 to £575. TVs. Children welcome, dogs by arrangement. Central heating. Linen for hire. ETC Three/Four Stars. Details from Eva Morris, 'Pekes', 124 Elm Park Mansions, Park Walk, London SW10 0AR. Telephone 020-7352-8088. Fax 020 7352-8125. Also (01825) 872229, Saturday to Monday. **email: pekes.afa@virgin.net**

A fine Tudor manor house, with a non-Tudor swimming pool and tennis court.

All the cottages have their own special character: Tudor View is most popular.

Golden Green, near Tonbridge
Goldhill Mill Cottages

These have been festooned with awards. They have won the South East England Tourism Self Catering Holiday of the Year Award Four Times (including 2001) and twice received the Silver Award in the English Tourism Council's England For Excellence Self Catering 'Oscars'.

We saw *Figtree Cottage* recently for the first time. It is difficult to imagine the site was once pigsties, for this seemingly small property opens into a spacious high ceilinged, south facing, living-room with a large comfortable sofa that converts to a double bed, an open log burner and dining area. We loved the pigs over the fireplace, the use of reclaimed bricks, tiles and oak beams. **Sleeps 2** plus child.

Figtree clicks in neatly with its big brothers. We have previously praised *Ciderpress Cottage,* converted from a pair of Tudor barns, **sleeping 4 plus an occasional 2** on a sleeping gallery, for its soft furnishings, good paintings and antiques, also its curtained gallery reached by apple ladder from the living-room. There is a top-notch kitchen, and a master bedroom equipped with en suite bathroom, as is the second bedroom.

Walnut Tree: quiet and full of character. The little garden faces on to the river.

Sympathetic interiors: a blend of contemporary comfort with the original.

Walnut Tree Cottage, likewise converted from the old cowshed in a group of buildings dating back to the Tudor period, rightly enjoys a reputation for its close carpeted comfort, linked with its colour coordinated duvets and curtains, and is congenially lit with wall lamps. Attractive water colours hang on pastel walls. There's a seriously comfortable three piece suite and a free-standing log fire in the living room, a wrought-iron spiral staircase to the upper floor (contained within the roof space, with exposed beams), and a 'last word' kitchen. **Sleeps 6** – each of the three (two five-foot doubles, one twin) bedrooms has an en suite bathroom. Immediately outside is the charming garden by the river, the mill stream, the swans.

All three stand within the 20-acre grounds surrounding Goldhill Mill, mentioned in the Domesday Book. And each carries the ETC's top Five Stars grading. Figtree is also rated Category 2 in the ETC's National Accessible Scheme; Walnut Tree and Ciderpress are Category 3.

Non smokers please. TV/video. Telephone. Linen/towels provided. Barbecue available. Floodlit tennis court. Cost: £225 to £750. Details: Shirley and Vernon Cole, Goldhill Mill, Golden Green, Tonbridge, Kent TN11 0BA. Telephone Hadlow (01732) 851626; fax (01732) 851881.

www.goldhillmillcottages.co.uk   email:vernon.cole@virgin.net

Goudhurst
Three Chimneys Farm

This is a set-up of great style, much praised by readers. In glorious countryside, at the end of a mile-long track, this is a real hideaway – but only about an hour from London. One can walk or cycle into the nearby forest, or stay on the farm,

We'd put these among 'Kent's finest'...

feed the ducks, perhaps play tennis or croquet. These beautifully furnished cottages are equipped to a very high standard: all have automatic washer/driers, dishwashers, microwaves, fridge freezers, televisions, coffee makers, hair driers, telephones (incoming and outgoing), bathrooms with bath *and* shower, and more. There is electric heating (included between May and October), plus woodburners. Specifically, *Starvegoose* **sleeps 2**, *Sheepwash* and *Chalybeate* **sleep 4**, *Marshalls* **sleeps 4 'plus 2'**, *Spoonlets* **sleeps 7**. You might wish to stay put, but if not, you'll find much to see: charming Goudhurst is two miles away, and within ten miles are Sissinghurst, Scotney, Great Dixter and Batemans. Dogs are welcome in one cottage. Linen included, towels for hire. Cost: about £200 to £600. ETC Four Stars. Details from Marion Fuller, Three Chimneys Farm, Goudhurst, Kent TN17 2RA. Telephone/fax (01580) 212175.

www.threechimneysfarm.co.uk
email:Marionfuller@threechimneysfarm.co.uk

East Peckham, near Tonbridge   map 2/493
Pippins Barn/Middle Cottage

We arrived to see these at dusk on a September day, and with their soft lights and deep sofas, thought how warm, cosy and altogether inviting they were. We noticed good sized rooms, well equipped kitchens, a fine attention to detail in the conversion of these original farm buildings. *Pippins Barn*, on one level, **sleeps 4**, in two bedrooms, one with a double, the other full size bunk beds (with

Lots of comfort, well placed for touring.

choice of a sofa bed instead in the sitting room). Large front garden, smaller rear. With a large open plan living room, *Middle Cottage* **sleeps 4** in two bedrooms, one double with double wardrobe, the other a twin with built-in wardrobe. There is a third cottage, *Oakweir*, which **sleeps 5**. All are ETC Four Stars. Gardens set off the properties nicely. Linen/towels included. Centrally heated, all fuel included. TV. Audio system. Well behaved dogs welcome. Non-smokers please.

Details from Garden of England Cottages, 189a High Street, Tonbridge, Kent TN9 1BX. Telephone (01732) 369168. Fax 358817.

www.gardenofenglandcottages.co.uk
email: holidays@gardenofenglandcottages.co.uk

Appledore
Ashby Farms Cottages

Touching on the Weald of Kent, close to the hauntingly beautiful Romney Marsh, the Ashby Farms cottages are an all-too-rare chance to stay in this corner of the Kent and Sussex border country.

We revisited during 2000, renewing our earlier acquaintance with *Roughlands*, outside Woodchurch. It is a conventional detached bungalow, quite roomy and blissfully quiet, with pleasant open views and gardens back and front. Fully fitted modern kitchen and bathroom. There is a twin and double-bedded room, with a bed available for a 5th person.

Only a hundred yards away but completely hidden in woodland the specially designed and pine built *Fishermen's Lodges* (**sleep 6**) reminded us of Scandinavia, even down to the setting, close to two isolated fishing lakes. The familiar A-shape encompasses a large double bed sleeping area reached by an open rung wooden ladder. On the main level are two twin bedrooms, bathroom and a modern well-fitted, galley-style kitchen. Sliding patio doors open on to a large wooden verandah. There are pinewood walls and furnishings, full carpeting, and the lounge/dining area benefits from the full height of the lodge.

Numbers 2, 3 and 4 Spring Cottages, in the adjacent small village of Kenardington, are within a terrace of brick-built dwellings (a shepherd lives in the other one). Each **sleeps 5** in three bedrooms reached by steepish stairs. They are simply furnished, but bright and attractive, have modern kitchens and bathrooms, fitted carpets and TVs. Fine rural views from the rear. Pretty front gardens.

On the road leading into Appledore is a semi-detached cottage called *65 The Street*, unpretentious but with a good-sized kitchen and a modern bathroom. Modestly furnished, **sleeping up to 5** in three bedrooms, it is well placed for those who like to be close to the shops, of which Appledore's are intriguingly individual. There is a neat garden at the back, and attractive rural views.

Dogs welcome. Fishing permits are available at £40 per week for a family of 4 (also by the day), and rough shooting at £10 a day. Linen and towels for hire. Further details from Ashby Farms Ltd, Place Farm, Kenardington, Ashford, Kent TN26 2LZ. Telephone Appledore (01233) 733332. Fax 733326.

www.ashbyfarms.com   email: info@ashbyfarms.com

Fishermen's Lodges: Scandinavian flair, close to two isolated fishing lakes. Easy-to-maintain interiors.

Spring Cottages: No frills, but clean, tidy, and bright.

Eastwell Manor, near Ashford
Eastwell Mews

Featured by us for the first time in 2001, Eastwell Manor quickly caught the eye of readers looking for five star comfort enhanced by superb facilities. A Mrs Gray of Beaconsfield, Buckinghamshire, joined friends for dinner (in the hotel itself) who were staying in one of the cottages within the hotel grounds, and was full of praise, 'especially for the tennis court'.

The recently converted Eastwell Mews cottages are only a short walk from the fine hotel itself and thus the award-winning, wood-panelled dining room and convivial bars are easily accessible to all guests. There is even closer access to the impressive new Pavilion: see below.

This is perhaps 'the best of both worlds': absolute privacy in one's own accommodation, up to five star hotel standard, with quick and easy access to another aspect of good living. A place for a special weekend or a longer stay in which to lap up all there is to see in this historic corner of

The hotel itself is the focal point here.

But the fine cottages are a match for it.

England. There are nineteen *Courtyard Apartments* or *Country Cottages*, arranged to offer one, two or three bedrooms. They provide spacious and extensive accommodation with ensuite bathrooms, kitchen, dining and living rooms. All are superbly furnished, with quality fabrics and linen.

The Pavilion is one of the finest fitness and leisure complexes we have seen. Within its 30,000 square feet there is a 20 metre heated pool and a spa that incorporates steam room, sauna, jacuzzi and hydrotherapy pool. Upstairs is the state-of-the-art gymnasium, 'Dreams', the beauty therapy salon and 'Silks', the relaxation lounge. The Brasserie restaurant and cocktail bar is sophisticated but informal, but has the Eastwell stamp. There is also a beautiful 20 metre outdoor pool for use in summer, with jacuzzi and sun beds. All these facilities are available to residents and most are included in the cost of the accommodation. A massive advantage is that the Eurostar terminal at Ashford (Paris under three hours) is only a few minutes' drive, the Eurotunnel terminal just 20 minutes' drive. The channel ports of Dover and Folkestone are only half an hour's drive.

Eastwell Manor is a four star hotel and the cottages can be rented on a self catering basis or a hotel basis. Satellite TV, video, fax and ISDN in all cottages. Well behaved dogs are welcome. Cost on a weekly basis is from £500 to £900 and short breaks start from £350. Details and brochures from Eastwell Manor, Eastwell Park, Boughton Lees, Ashford, Kent TN25 4HR. Telephone (01233) 213000. Fax: (01233) 635530.

www.eastwellmanor.co.uk   email: Eastwell@btinternet.com

Marden, near Tunbridge Wells
Redstock

A warm, well organised Kent base...

There's a shortage of really good cottage accommodation in this part of Kent, and we were delighted to track down Redstock. On the edge of Marden village (it has a railway station: only 55 minutes to London), and overlooking fields, the well carpeted, warm, comfortable, very well arranged house is used part of the year by the owner herself. (Some of our readers deliberately choose properties for that very reason, knowing everything they need will be to hand). It has so many good things going for it, such as a coal effect gas fire in the inviting sitting room (there is also very efficient central heating), a well equipped galley-style kitchen, air conditioning that comes into its own during our increasingly hot summers, a neat dining room with patio doors on to the garden. Which is safely enclosed, regularly tended, and has garden furniture.

All four bedrooms are spacious, and include two doubles – one is en-suite. **Sleeps 9**. TVs/video/audio system. Piano. Linen and towels are included. English Tourism Council Four Stars. Pets by arrangement. Cost: about £450 to £700. Details from Lesley Atkin: telephone (01622) 831607. Fax/voicemail: (0870) 133 6742. Mobile: (07801) 697789.

www.redstock.force9.co.uk
email: LesleyAtkin@redstock.force9.net

Do let us know about properties of ours you've liked, and others you'd recommend. Also about places that did not come up to scratch...

315

Cotswolds, Heart of England, Home Counties

Just two or three hours' drive from London, it's a small miracle that the Cotswolds have survived the ups and downs of the 20th century intact and unspoiled. Old walled gardens, honey-coloured villages snug within rolling green valleys, clear rivers and shallow trout streams, sturdy manor houses and fine churches built by rich wool merchants: the Cotswolds stretch from Gloucester and Herefordshire in the west, to Bath in the south, and to Oxford in the east, passing close to the fertile Vale of Evesham on the way. Probably the most popular village of all is Bourton-on-the-Water, where small stone footbridges cross a clear stream. Lovely too, and less commercialised, are the Slaughters (Upper and Lower), Moreton-in-Marsh, the straggly village of Blockley, imposing Broadway, little-known Winchcombe. There's Cirencester, with its huge Roman amphitheatre, and Stratford-upon-Avon is probably closer than you think. To the west and the north is country known as the 'Heart of England'. You'll see ruined abbeys and dramatic castles, half timbered buildings, acres of cider-apple orchards. To the east are the Chilterns, the upper reaches of the Thames, rural Hertfordshire and a range of undiscovered country that is 'so near but so far'.

Newcastle, near Clun
map 9/497
Gwilts Barn: The Eyrie

This exquisitely situated and (under new owners) ever more comfortable cottage makes a quiet and romantic hideaway **for 2** (though there is a sofa bed that would be fine for a child, perhaps even an adult). We have featured it for many years, and recently met those new owners, who occasionally use the next door property. We enjoy the winding drive up into the hills straddling the English/-Welsh border on which the cottage

The well planned garden is a special feature of this superbly located cottage.

lies: actually just inside England, with lovely views and good walks. Also, Offa's Dyke, a ditch and rampart built by the King of Mercia in 784, is close by. All on one first floor level, with correspondingly inspiring views, The Eyrie (well named) is inexpensive, especially as the view alone must be worth £100 a week. It has a 4' 6" double, shower, not bath, electric central heating, a recently installed woodburning stove that in itself guarantees autumn and winter bookings, a sitting-out and patio area.

Apart from the fabulous immediate surroundings, there is also easy access to attractive Ludlow, Shrewsbury and Llandrindod Wells.

One well behaved dog welcome by arrangement. TV. Linen, towels, electricity included. Cost: about £200 to £300. Details from Dick Sharratt, 17 Goldsmiths Avenue, Warwick CV34 6JA. Telephone (01926) 412291. Fax 412856. Or at weekends (01588) 640065.

Richards Castle, near Ludlow
The Barn

We thought this would make a romantic and idyllic hideaway **for 2,** though it can actually **sleep up to 4.** With panoramic views, at the end of a leafy drive that leads uphill to the owners' house, *The Barn* is indeed a converted barn, timber clad, skilfully done. It is a little gem, with a charming sitting room more spacious than you would think possible from the

Marvellous views, and lovely traffic-free walks and bike rides from the doorstep...

modest but attractive exterior, a 'deck' leading to an orchard and garden, two smallish but cosy bedrooms, which respectively have a double bed and *a four foot double plus a single sleeping platform.* A well equipped kitchen-diner is incorporated within the living room. We were pleased to note a glass fronted woodburning stove – effective and trouble-free (logs included), but with that lovely glow that 'makes' a room – thoughtful lighting, absolute peace and quiet. Organic vegetables and free-range eggs are often available. TV. Electricity, linen and towels included. Not suitable for dogs. Non smokers preferred. ETC Four Stars. Cost: about £195 to £380. Details from Sue and Peter Plant, Ryecroft, Richards Castle, near Ludlow, Shropshire SY8 4EU. Telephone/fax (01584) 831224.

www.ludlow.org.uk/ryecroft email: ryecroftbarn@hotmail.com

Clun, near Ludlow
Dick Turpin Cottage, at Cockford Hall

map 9/500

This is an absolute charmer. From the private drive winding uphill through parkland we spotted a handsome house where bed and breakfast is available. To the side, a stone barn has been converted into a holiday house – pure delight. We admired pictures and prints that would grace an art gallery, well chosen rugs, a

Visiting this wittily and lovingly cared-for cottage made for a memorable trip!

state of the art hi-fi (with speakers in *all* rooms, including the wittily designed bathroom). There is a log fire *and* central heating. Splendid walks start from the doorstep (within the properties' 20 acres you might spy buzzards, badgers, red kites), with dramatic Offa's Dyke about three miles away, and a well placed picnic table on high ground with spectacular views. ETC Five Stars. **Sleeps 2.** Short breaks. Private water. Unsuitable for dogs. Bedlinen and towels included. TV. Cost: £395 to £575. Details from Roger Wren, Cockford Hall, Clun, Craven Arms, Shropshire SY7 8LR. Telephone (01588) 640327. Fax 640881.

www.go2.co.uk/cockfordhall/ email: cockford.hall@virgin.net

Onibury, near Craven Arms
Hazel Cottage

Rural but not remote (some of our readers dislike being in 'the middle of nowhere') this cottage has an abiding charm. On our most recent visit, for example, we met very contented Dutch guests. It is a semi-detached, but private, Victorian beauty on a quiet lane. The owners, who live close, are landscape gardeners, so the surroundings are delightful. As well as being cosy and

An increasingly rare example of a really 'traditional' (but comfortable) cottage.

altogether comfortable and inviting – we found good beds, lots of warmth – the interior is like a museum, with many of the original features retained in the upgrading to 21st century standards. For example, we noticed a rare Victorian copper sink, solid brass taps, an original bread oven, Victorian wall lights, antique fireplaces, some good quality lace-trimmed bedlinen, pretty rugs, and many knick-knacks. It is ETC Three Stars: we'd have thought Four. There is a well equipped kitchen, including washer/drier, food mixer, and more. No dogs. Television. Linen is included. Cost: approximately £150 to £385. Further details are available from Mrs Rachel Sanders, Duxmoor Farm, Onibury, near Craven Arms, Shropshire SY7 9BQ. Telephone Bromfield (01584) 856342.

Pitchford, near Shrewsbury   map 9/502
Pitchford Estate

On a summer's day in deepest rural Shropshire we discovered a neat and attractive 19th century mock-Tudor/neo-Gothic gate-lodge (*South Lodge*) on the edge of a small village, with very little traffic, and then one of the most impressive barn conversions, called *Windy Mundy Farm*, that we have ever seen. The former has plenty of character both inside and

Windy Mundy Farm: we were absolutely bowled over by this stylish conversion...

out. It is very 'cottagey' and has an open fire. **Sleeps 4**. The latter is a sumptuous, fascinating, spacious architectural *tour de force* **sleeping up to 14**. It has an extraordinary central, hooded fireplace, huge floor to ceiling windows from which to enjoy the rural views (we could also imagine sitting by the fire on a winter afternoon, watching the light fading), three downstairs doubles and further bedrooms upstairs. Well behaved dogs are welcome in Windy Mundy Farm, but not South Lodge, where there is a badger set in the garden. TVs/videos/radios/CD players. Linen and towels. Further details from James Nason, 12 Moreton Terrace, London SW1V 2NX. Telephone 020-7838 4855.

www.pitchfordestate.com   email: stay@pitchfordestate.com

Whitchurch
Combermere Abbey Cottages

These are beauties: full of history, full of style. It's no surprise that they were Silver Award Winners in the 2000 English Tourism Council's 'England for Excellence' scheme and outright winners of the 2000 Heart of England Self Catering Award. Readers have been deeply impressed by the ten superb cottages (*available, incidentally, for weddings*) created in the Jacobean-style stable block of Combermere Abbey, a 12th century monastery on an 1100 acre country estate. They surround a large cobbled courtyard, some facing on to it, others looking on to parkland or walled gardens. One of these has a tennis court and croquet lawn. There's extensive woodland to explore, a 160 acre lake for fishing or swimming, a Wendy house, bikes for hire.

It is all the brainchild of Sarah Callander Beckett (she and her husband live in the original abbey). Her interest in design has led to each cottage

Discovering this tranquil and historic place, and its superlative cottages...

...is the sort of thing that makes producing this guide so worthwhile.

being decorated and furnished in its own very distinctive style by leading designers. For example, *Poole Cottage* is in the Thomas Dare 'rustic' style, and the interior of *Empress Cottage* was inspired by Elizabeth of Austria, who once lived at Combermere.

The cottages, **sleeping 4, 5, 6 or 8,** all have wood-burning or gas-flame fires and ultra-modern kitchens and bathrooms. We loved *Garnock* (French Provencal) whose second bedroom has windows looking down on the sitting-room. Its main bedroom has a dressing room and bathroom.

We especially remember *Cotton* (Indian/colonial), originally the coachman's house, with a magnificent teak four-poster bed and a sitting room overlooking a private garden; *Becket* is spacious, with (to us) a unique African theme; *Callander* was inspired by Scotland, with newly designed tartans that give it great style. Home-made dishes are available from a freezer. You can order 'The Combermere Supper', from a special menu, and have dinner waiting on arrival. And there is 'The Shropshire Hamper' – a selection of award-winning local food for, say, a first-day brunch.

Five cottages are 'no smoking'. All are ETC Five Stars. Cost: £380 to £1000 per week; short breaks available. Dogs welcome. Linen and towels included. TVs. Details and an excellent brochure are available from The Administrator, Combermere Abbey Cottages, Whitchurch, Shropshire SY13 4AJ. Telephone (01948) 662876; fax 660920.

www.combermereabbey.co.uk email: cottages@combermereabbey.co.uk

Trefonen, near Oswestry
Ivy House

This is really outstanding. A short drive from the ancient Welsh-border town of Oswestry, not far from a well used country road but tucked away virtually out of sight and earshot, the house was a revelation. It easily deserves its top tourist board grading. Most lovingly renovated and cared for, with an exceptional eye for colour and design and a great sense of style, it is a beauty. It is very private without feeling isolated, and the 18th century farmhouse has been brought up to 21st century standards of comfort without any loss of character. It is spacious and uncluttered, but manages to be cosy too, and a number of original features have been retained. Nothing is out of place, everything is well planned.

The sitting room is precisely the sort of place (this crops up during discussions with readers) that makes people happy to be 'at home' in their cottage rather than out and about all day. We noticed well chosen pictures, many of them local, irresistible books on shelves, reading lamps, candles. On the floor (throughout much of the cottage) is attractive, practical coir matting set off by rugs. Most usefully, there is a ground-floor shower room.

On the first floor, there is a double bedroom with an antique king sized four poster, two twins – one with a zip link, which we always recommend to owners starting out, because they can make a six foot double when required – a bathroom with over-bath shower.

Situated in its own garden, in what is effectively its own valley, with a

Prettily white against the green, the cottage is on the edge of pastureland.

Inside, everything is both easy on the eye and very comfortable indeed.

small river, this makes an excellent touring location. Prettily white against many shades of green, the cottage stands on its own on the edge of pastureland on which sheep and cattle graze.

With the Welsh border just three miles away, you have the best of both worlds. Llangollen is less than half an hour via quiet country lanes, Chirk Castle closer still, history-rich Chester (the best preserved original city walls in Britain, great shops, impressive black and white architecture) just over half an hour.

TV; CD player; dishwasher; payphone. **Sleeps 6**. Not suitable for pets. Linen and towels included. Welsh Tourism Council Five Stars. Cost: about £425 to £850. Further details from Owen Morris, Llwyn y Maen Cottages, Llwyn y Maen, near Oswestry, Shropshire SY10 9DD. Telephone/fax (01691) 653557.

Frampton-on-Severn, near Gloucester
The Orangery

One of the most remarkable properties we feature, this 18th century 'garden house' is Grade I listed. We like to approach it the 'impressive' way, past the early-Georgian mansion that is Frampton Court and alongside a lily-strewn, carp-rich, ornamental canal. Guests in this fascinating property do have access to these gardens and grounds but also

If you have a feeling for history you are sure to appreciate this rarity...

have their own side entrance, giving on to the delightful and unspoilt estate-village, itself in a conservation area. The interior is fascinating and 'comfortable': you should not expect Versailles. We are impressed by the tiled fireplaces in the (south-facing) drawing room and dining room, by the antique furniture in everyday use, by the spiral staircase, by the fabrics based on the 'Frampton Flora' painted by five sisters in the 1800s.

Cost: about £405 to £580 per week. **Sleeps 8**. Long weekends possible. TV/video. Central heating. Well-behaved dogs welcome. Details from the Secretary, Frampton Court Estate Office, Frampton-on-Severn, Gloucestershire. Telephone/fax Gloucester (01452) 740698.

email: clifford.fce@farming.co.uk

Howle Hill, near Ross-on-Wye
Old Kilns   map 9/506

We rate Ross-on-Wye very highly, but it can get 'busy', and it is pleasant to be based quietly out of the town. *Old Kilns*, ten minutes' drive from Ross, is a good bet, a substantial barn conversion which can be used as two properties. If you take the two properties together they will **sleep up to 14**, but separately they **sleep up to 8** and **up to 6** respec-

A great location, flexible accommodation.

tively in four doubles and two twin rooms in total. The whole property (in six acres of land) struck us as clean and tidy, and is warmly carpeted. We liked the crimson-upholstered cosy sitting room in the bigger house, where we also noticed lots of books, a good sized TV and video, a narrow staircase to the first floor bedrooms. Moving through to 'the other house' you come to a larger sitting room. There is another TV and video and a smallish but well appointed kitchen, a bathroom with jacuzzi, and a four poster in the main bedroom. There is an open fire in each. Dogs are welcome. Linen and towels for hire. Barbecue. Ample parking. Cost: (for example, for 4 in spring) £350. Further details are available from Mrs H I Smith, Old Kilns, Howle Hill, Ross-on-Wye, Herefordshire HR9 5SP. Telephone/fax (01989) 562051.

Stanton Lacy, near Ludlow
Sutton Court Farm Cottages

Tired of trunk-road traffic, we were glad to turn off on to quiet side roads en route to revisit these very comfortably converted stone farm buildings, grouped congenially around as pristine a 'farmyard' as you will find outside a child's Ladybird book. Although this is no longer a working farm, it is surrounded by farming activity. The lambs in the paddock in the spring are an endless source of entertainment. The cottages enjoy peace and quiet in an idyllic situation close to the owners' half-timbered farmhouse and provide an exceptionally comfortable base for exploring the quiet Shropshire countryside and the historic market town of Ludlow only five miles away. Many varied attractions are within easy reach: ruined castles, black and white villages, gardens, farms, shops and markets.

The six cottages (*Barleycorn, Woodsage, Sweetbriar, Hazelnut, Holly* and *Honeysuckle*, **sleeping 4, 6, 4, 4, 2 and 2** respectively) are comfortably furnished in country pine style, with wood burners in Barleycorn and Woodsage. The four family-sized cottages each have their own unique colour scheme and atmosphere created through well chosen pictures, dried flowers and ornaments. There are fitted carpets, night storage heating and electric blankets for the winter months. Holly is all on the ground floor, carefully designed with the frail and disabled (wheelchair users accompanied) in mind. Honeysuckle is a first floor apartment, **cosy for 2**, with chairs outside to enjoy the evening sunshine. They contain all you expect, as they have the ETC's desirable Four Stars classification.

There is an information room, payphone, laundry facilities and a simple games room. Horse riding, cycle hire, trout fishing and golf are nearby. A service offering home cooked evening meals delivered to your door, or a

The original farmyard – and the farm itself – were never quite so handsome!

Exceptionally warm, pretty interiors: all are lovely places 'to come home to'.

cream tea for the afternoon, can be provided given 24 hours' notice. Christmas and New Year are special here, with real Christmas trees, decorations and mince pies awaiting visitors who return time and again.

The cottages are open all year round and also offer bed and breakfast and short breaks from two nights. One well behaved pet by arrangement in some cottages. Cot and highchair available. Cost: from £195 to £475 (linen, towels, electricity and logs included). Details from Jane and Alan Cronin, Sutton Court Farm, Little Sutton, Stanton Lacy, Ludlow, Shropshire SY8 2AJ. Telephone (01584) 861305, fax 861441.

www.go2.co.uk/suttoncourtfarm   email: suttoncourtfarm@hotmail.com

Royal Forest of Dean
Oatfield Farmhouse and Cottages

Much encouraged by glowing reader-reports of the hospitality extended by owners Pennie and Julian Berrisford we recently revisited Oatfield on a lovely summer's day and found everything ticking over perfectly. We admired again the excellent conversions, the individuality of each cottage, the harmonious colour schemes, the warmth, comfort and quiet (one is miles away from any through-traffic). We met some very contented guests. One of them had just been down to admire the River Severn, a short walk or a few minutes' drive away, and had not passed another car.

Oatfield goes from strength to strength, having won the prize for Gloucestershire in the prestigious Rural Enterprise Awards, third prize in the British Guild of Travel Writers annual awards, and achieving Four/Five Stars grading from the English Tourism Council.

There are six cottages, **sleeping between 2 and 8**, within the converted 300-year-old farm buildings, with their castle-thick walls and immense roof beams. *Pimpernel* incorporates a superb 17th century barn, which makes this excellent large cottage especially attractive to groups. The cottages are equipped with top-of-the-range fittings: antique and character furniture, TV/video and radio, microwave, all year round central heating, woodburners and four poster beds in four, full linen, hairdryer, soaps and shampoos and a comprehensive range of kitchen supplies. Each bedroom has its own bathroom or shower room (Pimpernel has a double jacuzzi and *Betony* a king-size), and one cottage has been discreetly designed for a wheelchair user. We really like *Meadowsweet* **(sleeps 4)** and the spacious Betony **(sleeping 8)**, the latter slightly more old-fashioned than the others but very comfortable.

There is a six-acre old cider orchard, and Oatfield adjoins undisturbed ancient woodland and clifftop walks along the River Severn. An all-weather tennis court and croquet lawn provide outdoor activities and there is an excellent games room. Dogs are welcome by arrangement. Cost: approximately £235 to £850 per week, all inclusive, depending on

A fine tennis court, fringed by gardens.   *Reliably warm and very comfy interiors...*

which cottage and when. Short breaks available. Further details, in a most attractively produced brochure, can be obtained from Pennie and Julian Berrisford, Oatfield House Farm, Etloe, Blakeney, Gloucestershire GL15 4AY. Telephone/fax Dean (01594) 510372.

www.oatfieldfarm.co.uk

Ross-on-Wye
Wye Lea

A Mr Thompson of Portsmouth wrote to us about Wye Lea's 'warm welcome and excellent facilities'...about 'the idyllic surroundings in a beautiful area'. He also said 'we have told all our friends about this paradise near Ross-on-Wye'. But that was just one of several reader-letters that endorse what we and so many others feel about these properties.

It is indeed a special place, run with loving care and total professionalism, and we, as well as friends, colleagues and readers of this book such as those quoted above, have stayed here.

Only two and a half miles out of Ross-on-Wye, a historic town that is a gateway to the Cotswolds, the Forest of Dean and South Wales, Wye Lea is so peacefully and beautifully positioned that one can stroll across fields and downhill towards the glorious, wide River Wye itself.

Owners Colin and Sally Bateman have created a leisure club and an impressive indoor swimming pool, heated to a minimum of 84 degrees (even if the outside temperature is minus 5), meaning that, with the warm cottage interiors, Wye Lea is a good bet for spring, autumn and winter holidays, as well as short breaks. There is a five-seater jacuzzi, a six-seater steam room and solarium, an indoor games room with table tennis, pool table, football table, toys for small children and video machines, a fitness centre with half a dozen specialist machines, a massage room and a range of beauty treatments, and a full sized snooker table.

There are also two hard tennis courts, both of which are floodlit, a nine hole putting course and a full-size croquet lawn, and a much admired restaurant. During our most recent visit we treated ourselves to dinner here ('treated' being the essential word, as the restaurant has quickly

When we suggested this was a 'Five Star' set-up, one reader said 'I'd give it ten!'.

Families love it here, as there is always so much going on...

become one of the best in Herefordshire). All the dishes in the restaurant can also be served in the cottages. *See Page 14 for further details.*

There is a comprehensive play area with giant chess, draughts and shuffleboard, plus treehouse, swings, slide, seesaw, climbing frames, hopscotch, a rocking seat and swingball. You'll find skittles, shuttleball and a five-a-side football pitch.

The Batemans can arrange balloon and microlite trips, rough shooting, clay pigeon shooting, horse riding and canoeing.

Colin and Sally Bateman's first main task of the day is the feeding of greediest pigmy goat we have ever met! And, of course, visiting children – and mums and dads – are encouraged to join them. Guests are free to roam the 17-acre parkland overlooking the river.

Linhay is a ground floor cottage suitable for accompanied disabled people by dint of doorways wide enough for a wheelchair and the absence of steps. **Sleeps up to 4**. (Linhay, *Horseshoe* – **sleeps up to 4** – and *Dobbin* – **sleeps 4** – have been converted from old stable buildings, and are separate from the main development of half a dozen cottages set back from the road behind lawns.) Away from the main development is the detached *Squirrels*, **sleeping up to 6**, with masses of space. It has its own landscaped garden with paved terrace and a natural pond. There are two other water gardens, one with a fountain cascading into the pool below; the second a rock and water garden on the south side of the swimming pool.

The 'main development' is Bramble Court. It embraces six two-storey cottages that display the same sense of space and the same superlative furnishings as in the other properties mentioned, and an apartment. As elsewhere at Wye Lea there is more space than you would normally find. Cottages within Bramble Court include *Archway Apartment* (**3**), *Blueberry* (**4**), *Brock* (**4**), *Chestnut* (**4**), *Finch* (**4**), *Silvermoons* (**6**), *Summerhaze* (**6**). Two self contained apartment suites occupy the first floor of the east and west wings of Wye Lea House. These are *Peartree* (**2**) and *Wisteria* (**3**). Being on the first floor they both have fine views. They are also slightly cheaper to rent.

All the cottages, as shown in the handsome colour brochure and a super twelve-minute video, have two baths or shower rooms. All but one have en-suite master bedrooms, dishwashers, microwaves, fridge-freezers, central heating, satellite TV and video. Bedlinen and towels are included. Small conferences can be accommodated.

All the comforts of a fine hotel, with the great advantage of independence...

Interiors are particularly well thought out, and verge on the sumptuous!

There are special rates during the winter months for cottages occupied by only 2 people, and all-inclusive short breaks, with English breakfast and *à la carte* dinner. And Christmas (with all the trimmings) and New Year are memorable here. Details and an excellent brochure from Colin and Sally Bateman, Wye Lea, Bridstow, Ross-on-Wye, Herefordshire HR9 6PZ. Telephone (01989) 562880. Fax (01989) 768881.

www.wyelea.co.uk
email: enquire@wyelea.co.uk

325

Owlpen, near Uley
Owlpen Manor Cottages

This is a small corner of England at its most nostalgic and unspoiled. No traffic, nothing that jars. Just honey coloured cottages and the focal point of the whole place that is the grand manor house. In *The Good Holiday Cottage Guide* since its inception in 1983, we often think of Owlpen's softly enfolding hills, its mellow buildings, its woods and pastures. It seems locked in time, a million miles from the rat-race.

The nine cottages, and fine Tudor manor house where owners Nicholas and Karin Mander live, complement the idyll. The cottages are scattered throughout the many-acred valley, along a lane here, up a track there, in sight of the main house, or tucked away in the woods. Our special favourites are the *Grist Mill* (**sleeps 8/9**) – we've stayed in it – and *Woodwells* (**sleeps 6**), but on a late summer day we also visited again *Summerfield* (**sleeps 2**), *Marlings End* (**sleeps 6**), *The Court House* (**sleeps 4**), *Peter's Nest* (**sleeps 2**), *Tithe Barn* (**sleeps 2**), *Manor Farm* (**sleeps 4**) and *Over Court* (**sleeps 5**). The latter two can be let as one large family house **sleeping 9**, with two sitting rooms and two bathrooms.

We have visited the most impressive restaurant, where visitors to the manor house rub shoulders with cottage guests. In a converted old cider house, this has a sophisticated, rather imaginative range of dishes – a cross between a smart restaurant for an occasion and a cosy pub – and is notably comfortable.

The Manor House and three of the properties are officially 'listed' as buildings of architectural and historic interest, but their intrinsic charm is much enhanced by contemporary comfort and cosiness, and an exceptional flair for decor, fabrics and furnishings. There are remote control TVs, radio/alarms, antiques, telephones, hairdryers and food mixers in all cottages (some also have dishwashers, microwaves, freezers, log fires and four-poster beds), and an on-site laundry service. All the cottages have ETC Four Stars except (because it is smaller) Tithe Barn, which has Three. They have central heating and are welcoming (with tea-trays and chocolates). Our most recent visit reminded us of the lovely paintings, the deep sofas, the good quality fabrics and the king-size beds.

For a copy of the exceptionally attractive colour brochure, write to Nicholas and Karin Mander, Owlpen, near Dursley, Gloucestershire GL11 5BZ. Telephone Dursley (01453) 860261. Fax (01453) 860819. **www.owlpen.com email: sales@owlpen.com**

The Grist Mill is an outstanding property in an exceptional set-up.

Owlpen, featured by us for twenty years, is like a forgotten corner of England.

Goodrich, near Ross-on-Wye
Mainoaks Farm

We turned off a country road, followed an even less frequented lane and arrived at a quiet enclave of well converted stone built farm cottages, rather like a small hamlet. Each has its own character, ranging from 'bijou' to 'farmhousey and rambling'. Close to the banks of the River Wye (a river boat trip can be delightful on a hot summer day), and within sight of the world famous Yat Rock, they vary usefully in size –

An amazing, picture-postcard location – best spotted from the air (if you can!).

Cider Mill, for example, **sleeps up to 7**. We noted a number of appealing features: a woodburning stove in *Peregrine*, which we also thought had 'a nice family atmosphere', and a cruck beam in the bedrooms; Cider Mill's big, convivial dining table; the four poster bed in *Huntsham* (**sleeps 4**); the upstairs sitting room in *The Malthouse* (an 'upside-down' house, so designed to make the most of the view).

TV. Short breaks. Dogs by arrangement. English Tourism Council Three/Four Stars. Linen and towels included. Cost: about £200 to £650. Details from Patricia Unwin, Hill House, Chase End, Bromesberrow, Ledbury, Herefordshire HR8 1SE. Telephone (01531) 650448.

Catbrook, near Tintern
Foxes Reach   map 9/513

This is a real gem of a cottage, with the bonus of being just a mile and a half from romantically ruined Tintern Abbey, and well placed for visiting the Forest of Dean (great walking and cycling), the frontier castles of Raglan and Chepstow, the Three Choirs Festival, Nelson's Monmouth. But you might want to stay put, for this is a charmer. We liked the cot-

Cyclists and walkers especially will love this superbly well located property...

tagey interior, the quality carpeting, the nice lighting, the well chosen pictures and prints, the small but well stocked garden, the woodburner in the appealing sitting room, the wrought iron beds in all the light, bright bedrooms (two doubles and two twins: the cottage **sleeps 6**). and the two bathrooms. There is a newly fitted kitchen, with an open-plan dining area.

TV/video/CD stereo. One well behaved dog welcome; fabulous hacking makes it worth using the owners' stable for your horse. WTB Five Stars. Linen and towels are included. Cost: £170 to £480. Details from Fiona Wilton, Ty Gwyn, Catbrook, near Chepstow, Monmouthshire. Telephone/fax (01600) 860341.

www.traveltrainingservices.com   email:wilton@globalnet.co.uk

St Weonards, near Ross-on-Wye
Treago Castle Cottages

Our particular readers really seem to go for rural Herefordshire. Those country lanes leading nowhere in particular, cattle grazing against a background of low hills and softly enveloping woods, sleepy black and white timbered or sandstone villages that seem hardly to have changed for hundreds of years.

We know they also appreciate the four cottages – each with its own special character – in the grounds of the 500 year old Treago Castle, and like meeting Sir Richard Mynors, present head of a family that has occupied the castle for all those centuries without a break, along with his wife Fiona.

The cottages are very worthwhile in themselves, but practical and comfy rather than fussy and frilly, and it is a bonus to have an irresistible 34-feet long indoor swimming pool, heated to 82 degrees F. This is open all year,

All the properties are in the grounds of 500 year old Treago Castle, held by the same family for all those centuries...

Each is as private and self contained as you like, but, usefully, three can be linked to sleep 20 under the same roof...

one of a number of reasons Treago is a great place for 'out of season' holidays and short breaks. We also love the five acres of garden, which include an arboretum, a walled garden, and *even a vineyard* (both red and white wine is produced here, and is available for guests to buy).

We looked first at *Butlers*, a neat and tidy apartment, with a good use of space. **Sleeping just 2** in a double, it is quite a bargain outside the main season. Then at *The Stables*, **sleeping 4**, a first floor apartment with a woodburner and french doors that open directly on to part of that impressive garden, with woods and good walks at the back. This can link up with *The Coach House*, **sleeping 4 'plus 2'**.

This in turn can be linked with the most impressive *Looseboxes*, with more good things about it than we have room to describe. These include a private garden, and a superb, newly carpeted first floor sitting room (there is even a lift to it!) *with a grand piano*. **Sleeps 10** plus 2 cots.

Clearly all these apartments can be booked independently, but a huge advantage at Treago is that several or all of the properties can be rented as one. *This is a great bonus for big groups of up to 22*.

Dogs welcome, TVs. Linen included (towels for hire for overseas visitors). Cost: about £208 to £1123 (slightly higher at Christmas/New Year). Details from Sir Richard and Lady Mynors, Treago Castle Cottages, St Weonards, Herefordshire HR2 8QB. Telephone/fax (01981) 580208.

www.treago.co.uk   email: fiona.mynors@cmail.co.uk

Carey Dene, near Ross-on-Wye
Carey Dene and Rock House

With the River Wye just across the field (it can easily be seen from the front bedrooms), and the well-known Cottage of Content pub close by, *Carey Dene* is a cleverly converted 18th century farm building, transformed into one of the pleasantest and most tastefully appointed cottages we have seen.

A few miles further is the historic, unspoilt town of Ross-on-Wye. Featured here since the guide first hit the bookshelves back in 1983, Carey Dene also suits people who like to make border raids into Wales (the Welsh border country is lovely) but be back in time for tea.

This is 'so nice to come home to': a fine large sitting room (triple aspect) with night storage heaters and a handsome wood-burning stove for which logs are provided free, south-facing French windows leading on to a patio sun-trap, and good books to read. There is a neat, well equipped kitchen, an open style staircase up to two bedrooms, one double-bedded and one, with great character and a clever use of the space available, twin-bedded. There are pretty duvets and excellent bathroom fittings.

Rock House, owner Mrs Price's second, and much bigger, house on offer across the little lane is even more full of character. When we first saw it we described 'masses of space; absolute peace and quiet', and as we later stayed here for a few days ourselves, we can vouch for it. There's a dishwasher and microwave in the large kitchen and a big utility room adjacent with washing machine. There is a very comfortable lounge, which is triple aspect (gorgeous, hilly countryside views), and we noticed table lamps, attractive pictures and prints and a good selection of books in a

Tasteful, neat and cosy Carey Dene is a joy, with lots of character and style...   *...and we are heartened by knowing how many of our readers are pleased by it.*

bookcase. There is some very interesting furniture and lots of personal touches that help to make this a cut above most. All is quietness and comfort, and the bedrooms are deep carpeted and spacious, all with good views – well, actually, better views than downstairs! **Sleeps 6/8** – and there is oil-fired central heating.

TV. Dogs are welcome. Electricity, towels and linen included. Baby-sitting available. Cost: £170 to £295 (Carey Dene), £200 to £400 (Rock House). Cot/highchair available. ETC Three Stars. Further details can be obtained from Mrs Rita Price, Folly Farm, Holme Lacy, Hereford HR2 6LS. Telephone/fax Holme Lacy (01432) 870259.

email: ritamprice@aol.com

West Malvern
The Cottages at Westwood House

Graced by elegant period homes in a heavily wooded setting, with fabulous views of the Severn Vale, Malvern is one of our favourite towns.

In West Malvern, a few minutes from the centre of Great Malvern and standing high, half way up the Worcestershire Beacon, Westwood House is a handsome Regency house in its own grounds. It is the focal point of some of the best self catering we know.

We recently revisited its four properties (there are three cottages and a flat in the main house) and had never seen things looking so good.

We remember the adjoining *Ostlers* and *Coachmans* cottages for their old pine, antiques and plain walls that enhance pretty pictures, old prints and quality fitted carpets. Each is a little gem, and **sleeps 4** (with a shower, not a bath). They are deceptively spacious, with a good-sized kitchen/diner and sitting room.

In its own quiet garden is the largest of the cottages, *Westwood,* which has panoramic 30 mile views of the Welsh mountains. **Sleeping 6** in three double bedrooms (two of them are on the ground floor), this traditional Malvern stone cottage has lots of stripped original pine, a delightful kitchen and a new bathroom. (And we loved the scented honeysuckle round the porch!)

Butlers, a very generous ground floor flat **for 2** in the main house, has stunning views from its elegant bay-windowed drawing room. (We were impressed by the pictures and especially the prints.) It offers the comfort of a bath *and* shower, a new kitchen and its own courtyard and patio.

Coachmans and Ostlers are 'the real thing': traditional but very comfortable.

Each interior has been exquisitely, even fastidiously, decorated and furnished...

Dogs and other pets are not allowed. Cost: about £220 to £530.

Westwood and Butlers details from Jill Wright, Westwood House, West Malvern, Worcestershire WR14 4DS. Telephone (01684) 892308. Fax (01684) 892882.

Ostlers and Coachmans details from Jane Staddon, Mistletoe House, 31 Highfield Rd, Malvern WR14 1HR. Telephone/fax (01684) 578004.

email: davidwrighttrans@cs.com
or **john.staddon@lineone.net**

Tewkesbury
Courtyard Cottages, Upper Court

For a start, the location is enviable: Kemerton is a charming Cotswold village (one of the most appealing in the region) at the foot of Bredon Hill, and it is a pleasure in itself to follow a quiet lane for a couple of hundred yards towards the church and the grand Georgian manor house that is Upper Court.

The house's fifteen acres of garden and grounds (featured in the National Gardens Scheme) are idyllic, and embrace a watermill mentioned in the Domesday Survey, a lovely lake and a dovecote. As the Herfords have an antique business, the cottages are full of antique furniture. Beds are made up for your arrival; there are plenty of towels, and you can order 'Cordon Bleu' home cooked meals to be brought to your door (and washed up!).

Guests can enjoy the outdoor all-weather tennis court and table tennis, an outdoor pool in June, July and August, or croquet. A major attraction is the beautiful lake, a two acre wilderness that is home to wildfowl, swans, heron, ducks and geese. You can take the boat out, row around the two islands, have a picnic, barbecue or just enjoy the pleasant surroundings.

In this splendid location on the edge of the Cotswolds and the fruitful Vale of Evesham, it's just a stroll down the lane to the village shop or the Crown restaurant. And you are well placed for Cheltenham races, Sudeley Castle and Broadway.

Specifically, *The Courtyard Cottage* **sleeps 7/8**; *The Coach House* **sleeps up to 10/11,** and incorporates an amazing 45 foot square sitting room/dining room that can easily seat two or three dozen people for a special occasion, for example when used as a reception room for the two previous properties plus *The Stables,* which **sleeps 5** in a ground floor bedroom that would suit less mobile people (half tester bed) and a double upstairs with an extra single bed. There is a fireplace with wood-burning stove.

Cottages in the lee of the big house...   *...but private and self contained.*

Most recently available is *Watermill*, **sleeping up to 8**. It has its own little garden, which leads directly on to the lake. Also quite new, the *Garden Flat* sleeps **just 2**.

The cottages range from ETC Three to Five Stars. Linen and towels included. TVs. Cost: about £275 to £1465. Short breaks. Further details from Bill and Diana Herford, Upper Court, Kemerton, near Tewkesbury, Gloucestershire GL20 7HY. Telephone (01386) 725351. Fax 725472.

www.uppercourt.co.uk   email: diana@uppercourt.co.uk

How Caple, near Ross-on-Wye
Cider Mill Cottage/Gardener's Cottage

Dusk was descending as we arrived to see Sue Farr's two cottages (both are close to her own home, but private and separate). *Cider Mill* (**sleeping 4**) is especially cosy and nicely lit – we met two couples very comfortably installed – and with a most inviting, high ceilinged, beamy sitting room with a big log-burning fire in an inglenook, carpets and rugs. The very well equipped farmhouse-style kitchen has a stable door leading to a terrace and rose garden.

Gardener's Cottage (**sleeping up to 8 in a twin and two doubles,** one with a king-sized bed) is particularly spacious, very much a family house, with lots of beams, good carpeting, and, again, a most appealing sitting room with three deep sofas as well as armchairs, lots of books and an open fire. There are french windows on to the garden. The separate dining room has a dining table seating eight – thus helping to create one of the most convivial properties we know.

Cider Mill is a converted 17th century building...

...as appealing inside as it is outside, and very cosy too.

TVs. Well behaved dogs welcome. Linen and towels included. Cider Mill Cottage is Wales Tourist Board Five Stars, Gardener's Four. No smoking in Cider Mill. Cost: about £280 to £600. Details from Sue Farr, Garraway House, How Caple, Herefordshire HR1 4SS. Telephone (01989) 740253.

www.holidaybank.co.uk
For availability: **www.holidaybank.co.uk/uk/heuk/h0542.htm**
email: suefarrHowcap@compuserve.com

Do ask whether short breaks are available in cottages that appeal, even when owners don't advertise this. Even in summer, agencies and individual owners are often pleased to arrange two or three days.

Do note that 'dogs welcome' usually (though not always) applies to other pets too. But please

Don't turn up with three Alsatians when you have had enough trouble persuading a cottage-owner to accept a Pekinese.

Docklow, near Leominster
Docklow Manor

Featured in this guide for 20 years, and much praised by readers, Docklow is like a small village. There's plenty of privacy in and around the several cottages, and cars are relegated to a leafy car park. With resident ducks fussing about, and cottagey gardens, time seems to have stood still for a hundred years.

The surrounding countryside is a springboard for surrounding beauty spots: the Brecons and Black Mountains, the Malvern Hills, Stratford and the Cotswolds, the historic half timbered market towns of Ludlow, Leominster and Ledbury, the timeless Welsh border towns and castles.

The sandstone cottages are grouped round a walled pond, visited by clucking hens, a peacock and friendly cats. The rest of the garden is typically Victorian, with a number of unusual shrubs and flowers and ten acres to explore. (An intriguing woodland walk starts from one of the cottages.) Better yet, all Docklow guests have the use of the nicely tucked away outdoor swimming pool.

As an example of the cottages that are available, *Tanglefoot Cottage* (**sleeping 5/6**) has been extended, redesigned and extensively renovated, but retains its old beams. It has a superbly fitted kitchen with split level cooker, fridge freezer, dishwasher, washing machine and tumble drier. It has two bathrooms and a feature that holidaymakers seem to appreciate

Staying at Docklow is like being part of a traditional English village.

Cottage interiors are comfortable, warm, quiet and have plenty of character.

more and more – an open fire. On summer evenings one can enjoy a barbecue in the private garden, which is where we met very contented first-time guests during our last visit, in 2000.

We also admired the renovation of *Limetree Cottage* (**5 people**) to the same standard as Tanglefoot. We met regular visitors relaxing in the conservatory and watched the ducks on Limetree's own pond garden.

Cost: about £312 to £588. Low season three-night weekends: £177, with an extra night free mid-week. Details from Malcolm and Carol Ormerod, Docklow Manor, Docklow, near Leominster, Herefordshire HR6 0RX. Telephone (01568) 760643.

www.docklow-manor.co.uk
email: enquiries@docklow-manor.co.uk

Blockley, near Moreton-in-Marsh
Lower Farm Cottages

Blockley, one of the handsomest large Cotswold villages we know, is much sought-after by holiday cottage fanciers. Their expectations are fulfilled in this mini-hamlet of cottages at pretty-as-a-picture Lower Farm (not a working farm: no muck, tractors or smells) as so much goes into making guests comfortable.

We've had nothing but praise from readers for the *nineteen* years during which we have featured these exceptional, superbly maintained and extremely well cared for properties. We have treated ourselves to a short break here and understood why people rave about them. Impeccably converted from a group of period farm buildings, they are a credit to the Cotswolds and to tourism in general, and, better yet, are within walking distance of a convenient and congenial hotel and restaurant.

There are also three newly available houses in a row (rather too grand to be called cottages!). Called *Littlebrook*, *Stepping Stones* and *Riverbank*, they are superb, with too many good things to detail here. But, for example, we noted good carpets, top notch furniture of the reproduction antique style, lamps, pictures, books. They all **sleep 4**.

We explored Lower Farm's gardens and especially enjoyed the bubbling stream that borders one side of them. We also admired exceptionally comfortable interiors, soft furnishings in various shades of brown, plain white walls, and noted several visitors' book comments: 'A lovely escape from the rat-race'...'Ten out of ten'...'We are in love with Lower Farm and

Superlatively high standards, even in (generally excellent) Cotswold terms.

The gardens are very much a feature: we've never seen a leaf out of place!

Blockley'...'Duck down duvets: great!'...'Totally outstanding, totally serene'. Several times people mentioned the ducks (no immediate connection by the way with the duck-down duvets!) by name, for a feature of Lower Farm's grounds is the duck pond. It was also notable how frequently people who have found Lower Farm return time and time again.

We spent a lot of time inside these delightfully quiet and neat cottages. We noticed pottery, plants and dried flowers, prints, paintings and old photographs. Some rooms have fitted carpets, others have rugs scattered over parquet floors. Bedrooms are charming, with illuminated wardrobes and continental duvets (all linen and towels are provided), and kitchens have food mixers, electric cookers and microwaves as well as all the essentials. The largest cottages have dishwashers and freezers. There is full central heating, TV/video and also twice weekly maid service.

Of the nine cottages, six were converted from the original farm buildings, and retain many old features, such as original Cotswold stone and large mullioned windows. *Toad Hall,* the largest, full of old world grand-eur, and *Badger's Den* both **sleep 6** in two twins and one double bedroom; *Mole's,* **sleeping 5,** has a double, a twin and a single bedroom.

Otter's Abode is a **4 person** cottage with an enormous sense of space derived from the exposed timbered roof and open-plan kitchen, dining and living area broken by a central spiral staircase leading to a gallery and the double bedroom. The downstairs twin bedroom is particularly suitable for elderly people. *Willow End,* once the granary, also **houses 4** people

Interiors are never 'over the top', but well planned and utterly comfortable.	*We love the careful blend of privacy and the sense of being part of a community.*

and has much more the ambiance of a traditional English country cottage.

Ratty's Retreat is a perfect **2 person** hideaway. The tastefully furnished 'design style' living room enjoys a delightful view of the grounds and the parish church beyond. This view is shared by the main bedroom, which comes complete with a Victorian half-tester bed, with bathroom en-suite, on a gallery floor reached by a spiral staircase. A stone mullioned window reaches from the floor to the eaves of the cottage.

The grounds of Lower Farm consist of two and a half acres, mostly lawn, bounded by a willow-shaded brook, and made doubly tempting by the provision of croquet and – with children in mind – a small dinghy in the stream, and a range of outdoor children's games.

This is Britain at its most picturesque, a world of mellow stone villages, historic houses, fine cities such as Cheltenham, Worcester and Oxford and other places of interest: the Cotswold Wildlife Park, Chedworth Roman Villa, the Wildfowl Trust at Slimbridge and the Royal Shakespeare Theatre at Stratford-upon-Avon are all within an easy drive, generally free of heavy traffic.

Cost: about £245 to £629, depending on which cottage and when booked. Short breaks are available out of season from £150. English Tourism Council Four Stars. Not suitable for dogs. Further details and a colour brochure are available from Katie Batchelor, Lower Farm Cottages, Blockley, Moreton-in-Marsh, Gloucestershire GL56 9DP. Telephone/fax Blockley (01386) 700237.

Video available on request.

www.lower-farm.co.uk
email: lowerfarm@hotmail.com

Calmsden, near Cirencester
The Tallet Holiday Cottages

A memorable find! This lovely, light, spacious, beautifully situated property was one of the most outstanding finds of a recent Cotswolds visit. On a warm summer afternoon it was a pleasure in itself to locate it at the end of a series of narrow country lanes that see almost no traffic.

It is a delight, and we would love to stay in it ourselves. Ideal for a group, this clever conversion by Nicholas and Vanessa Arbuthnott (he is an architect, she a fabric designer) **sleeps up to 12**. The twosome that makes up the dozen comes by way of a double room adjacent to the family's own property.

To help you get your bearings, the family home is on one side of the inner courtyard that in itself contributes so much character to the house, the holiday property – actually a converted cow byre and barn – on the other.

'Calmsden' is right: this is a peaceful, beautifully located place to unwind in...

...with stylish, spacious, well planned interiors. We rate this very highly.

Also attached to the Arbuthnotts' own house is Vanessa Arbuthnott's studio: her designs are on the fabrics, ceramic tiles and much else around the house. Among many good things are a huge drawing room, with lots of lamps that in the evening help turn this splendid property into something even more welcoming and charming, and lovely paintings and prints. Most rooms are at least double aspect. All the five main bedrooms have singles that can be pushed together, meaning that as doubles and not singles they are six foot wide beds.

When we visited, the Arbuthnotts' offspring were sporting in a children's pool in the garden, the visitors' part of which is very good sized and includes a raised swimming pool, a football pitch, badminton and more. Visiting children will love the chance to meet the ducks, the goats and the chickens. Definitely one of our 'top twenty'. ETC Five Stars.

A real bonus is that Kemble train station is just fifteen minutes' drive away, with direct links to London Paddington.

Linen and towels included. Pets welcome. Non-smokers preferred. Cost: about £517 to £1150. Details from Mr and Mrs Arbuthnott, The Tallet, Calmsden, near Cirencester, Gloucestershire GL7 5ET. Telephone/fax (01285) 831437.

www. thetallet.demon.co.uk
email: vanessa@thetallet.demon.co.uk

...hall, Warwickshire. A very good use of ...ace, a pleasant rural enclave. Page 352.

The Old Dairy, Gloucestershire. This is one in a hundred, the view rarer still. Page 351.

...eath Farm Cottages, Oxfordshire. Fine ...ildings, superlative interiors. Page 362.

Garden Cottage, Gloucestershire. Quiet, elegant, roomy, rather understated. Page 361.

...all Farm, Worcestershire. The location is perfect for seeing the Cotswolds, the Heart of ...gland, Shakespeare Country, the Welsh Marches. Nice people, fine properties. Page 350.

...vat Trust, Shropshire. If you like that magical combination of historical associations and ...mfortable living, this organisation (devoted to restoring old properties) might suit. Page 20.

Rural Retreats, The Cotswolds and beyond. They are known world-wide for the charm and comfor their cottages, and have a famous attention to detail. We've stayed in several...

...including three of the gems pictured here. Not once in fifteen years have we had a complaint from our readers about any aspect of the organisation's properties.

Interiors have lots to do with deep sofas, soft lighting via heavy and expensive table lamps, th pile carpets, kitchens more up to date than many Rural Retreats clients have in their own hom

Several properties offer quite formal living, and are likely to impress passing friends and fam and almost all the cottages are picture-postcard-pretty. Main feature: pages 346/347.

lakes Cottages – main features on Pages 30/31, 141 and 209 – is one of four or five 'household-name' agencies in the country. It has 'properties with facilities', many rural gems...

...and several properties ideal for extended families, such as this (above left) near the shores of lake Ullswater and 'a little treasure', which we know well, in lovely grounds in deepest Norfolk.

...mong the Scottish properties is this grand mansion, with cottages, on the Ayrshire coast, and in the north east) another fine house. It sleeps 12, and it even has a Bechstein grand piano.

Wales, among so many properties of historic interest and charm, are this watermill near Llangollen and this beauty – full of literary associations –near Portmeirion...

Colour section C, Page 3

Connemara Coastal Cottages, based in Co Galway, is shaping up to be one of the best 'hands on' agencies in the country. This well situated house is at Claddaghduff, Co Galway. Page 37

Killarney Lakeland Cottages, Co Kerry. A peaceful spot near a bustling town. Built in tradition style, and interiors combine a flavour of the old Ireland with 21st century comforts...Page 370

Manor Kilbride, Co Wicklow. Just one of several outstanding cottages here. Page 376.

'Village and Country', Co Clare. Superb interiors, in a village or by the water. Page 3

Culduff Cottages, Co Mayo. Rather old-fashioned, but full of character. Page 374.

Grayling, Co Clare. This was one of the nice finds of a recent Irish journey. Page 374.

Colour section C, Page 4

340

*glish Country Cottages (main features, Pages 22/23, 123 and 171) conveniently covers England
1 Wales in one brochure. It is a household name at home and abroad, with thatched gems galore…*

*nd, as immediately above, cottages and houses that seem to typify what's available on Scotland's
hs and sea shores, and, for example, the softer surroundings of the Cotswolds.*

*eir Welsh programme is much appreciated by the tourist board, and they seem to have secured
ny of the most appealing 'traditional' cottages, as above. Also above, right: 'just another pool'!*

*over the British Isles, their range is huge, but they are known for their properties of character,
toric interest and comfort. Above left, in rural Derbyshire; right, on the shores of Windermere.*

Colour section C, Page 5

National Trust Cottages are one of the great success stories of the past few years. By definiti virtually all their properties are full of character and rich in historical associations...

And also by definition, properties are in interesting locations. Those featured here are (top) Norfolk and, above, Scotland and Northern Ireland. Main feature: Pages 18/19.

Hoseasons Country Cottages is a major player on the national-agency scene, with a particul impressive brochure that combines interior and exterior photographs.

Here is just a handful of their ever-increasing portfolio of excellent cottages in (from top left Suffolk, North Norfolk, West Sussex and South Devon. Main feature: Pages 22/23.

untry Holidays (main feature on Pages 26/27) have a bigger selection of individual cottages
n any other operator in Britain, so even holidaymakers wanting variety tend to be regulars.

ey love this castle (above left) in north east Scotland – there is an apartment within the castle
d a coachyard conversion in the grounds – and this classic beauty in Dorset...

iong people's thatched dreams-come-true are those pictured above. Left, a 300-year-old
mhouse in Derbyshire, and, right, a beauty near Helston, in Cornwall.

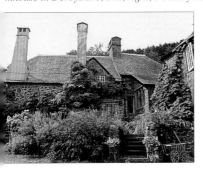

ese two are in Somerset: a conversion of three barns, with the shared pool, and a superbly
ated house of great character near Porlock, with views over the Bristol Channel.

With over 9,000 dream cottages…

ENGLAND • WALES • SCOTLAND • IRELAND • FRANCE

…where will you escape to next?

There has never been a wider choice of superb self-catering cottages for you to discover. Plan your escape now to some of the most beautiful properties situated in the most sought after locations.

All our cottages are regularly inspected and graded so you can always expect quality properties, with excellent facilities – a real home from home. From quaint, romantic hideaways in beautiful rural settings, to spectacular sea, lake and mountain locations, superbly appointed, many with pools, just waiting to welcome you.

Over 9,000 cottages @ one address
Visit www.cottages4you.co.uk where you can search through all of our properties, which will allow you to choose the one that is perfect for you. It's simple to use and many of our properties have a virtual tour, allowing you to discover your dream get-away before you leave home.

So visit www.cottages4you.co.uk now to discover your perfect holiday cottage

cottages4you

Duntisbourne, near Cirencester
The Old Cottage

There's something satisfying about dropping down into a low-lying village, three quarters hidden from the world, to claim one's holiday cottage. And if arriving at The Old Cottage was a pleasure, seeing inside was even more so. This is a charmer, with so many good things about it. Such as two separate staircases, one of our favourite cottage features, a very cosy, warmly carpeted sitting

This is a real winner, in a hidden-away but easily accessible village of character.

room with a woodburner in an inglenook fireplace, and the original bread oven. Better yet, the separate dining room has an open fire. (The cottage is sometimes used by the owners, meaning you'll find 'everything you need'.) The well-cared-for garden is raised above street level, and thus more private. **Sleeps 4** in two en suite doubles, and a small property across the sleepy lane offers accommodation **for 2**, and a double garage.

Details from Gill Simpson, Church Barn, Hawling, near Cheltenham, Gloucestershire GL54 5TA. Telephone/fax (01451) 850118.

www.cottageguide.co.uk/cotswoldcottages
email: simpson@glos68.fsnet.co.uk

Canon Frome, near Ledbury
The Swiss Chalet   map 9/527

Beside a weir in the River Frome, The Swiss Chalet is one of the most delightful and amusing holiday cottages we have ever seen. It has the makings of a most romantic stay **for 2**. From a very comfortable, but naturally not large, double bedroom, on the ground floor, you ascend a 'ship's ladder' to the first floor where, amid considerable comfort, you can hide yourselves from the world. From a

This is one of the most romantic places we know: you can hide yourselves away!

balcony overlooking the water (where some people swim) you will almost certainly see kingfishers (there is even a bench right by the water's edge) and in late autumn see salmon jumping the weir. There are deep and comfortable sofa/chairs, a kitchenette with dining bar, lots of warmth, a high beamed ceiling: all this adds up to a remarkable holiday retreat.

TV. Dogs by arrangement. Cost: about £163 to £333. Linen provided. Full details are available from Julian and Lorna Rutherford, Mill Cottage, Canon Frome, Ledbury, Herefordshire HR8 2TD. Telephone (01531) 670506 or (07778) 591899.

http://freespace.virgin.net/julian.rutherford/

The Cotswolds and beyond
Rural Retreats*

Rural Retreats is a household name in the holiday cottage industry. It is particularly known and admired for dependably comfortable, rather chic, extremely well maintained, top bracket cottages.

It is probably best known for its Cotswold properties, but actually has an impressive (and growing) presence in many beautiful corners of Britain including Cumbria, Cornwall, Devon, Dorset, Herefordshire, Kent, Suffolk, the Yorkshire Dales and Scotland.

In fifteen years we have had nothing but fulsome praise from readers. *Every single property is of a very good standard*, with notably comfortable and harmonious interiors, and many are 'little palaces'.

You'll always find a 'welcome pack' of cheese, wine, fruit, bread, etc, and you'll find little touches in the decor – hard to encompass here, though we think of handsome table lamps, expensive curtains, good quality rugs, pretty bedspreads, all distinctively in the Rural Retreats' style. You'll find some four poster or brass beds, wood burning stoves and open fires, antique furniture, an uncompromising standard of cleanliness.

During several visits to the Cotswolds, Shakespeare Country and the Welsh borders we have visited Northwick Park, near Rural Retreats' head office. Here, in the lee of a great country mansion a number of cottages and cottage suites have been created, and we saw two of those on the agency's books. In *4 John Rushout Court,* **sleeping 4**, we noted: an uncluttered and bright interior, an absolute commitment to neatness and cleanliness, very thoughtful lighting, coal effect gas fire, deep sofas, mirrors, well chosen pictures, a super kitchen, seductively comfortable beds. Suitable for dogs.

In Bourton-on-the-Hill, away from the main road, *Lower Barn* , **sleeping 5**, is exquisite. We would recommend it to the most discriminating cottage-goer. Among so many good things we loved the big, convivial dining table, the sumptuous beamed sitting room with wood stove and piano.

The exterior of John Rushout Court fits happily into its country-mansion setting...

Stocks Barn, in the Cotswolds, is like something out of 'Homes and Gardens'...

In the pleasant village of Cleeve Prior, on the edge of the Cotswolds near Bidford on Avon, we saw a converted barn that is memorable even in the context of Rural Retreats. *Stock's Barn* is like something straight out of the pages of 'Homes and Gardens': wonderful ancient oak beams (and, generally, a very skilful preservation of many other original features), a kitchen of character that combines the best of mod cons with a farmhousey ambiance: don't forget your Rick Steins and your Keith Floyds, for you're bound to want to cook ambitious family meals during your stay. **Sleeps 8**.

We have stayed in a modest-sounding cottage (called *The Hovels*) in the Cotswold village of Longborough, just ten minutes' drive from the exquisite Batsford Arboretum, which on a golden afternoon we had almost to ourselves. Rather 'Scandinavian' in ambiance, it has a small but cosy sitting room and a spacious conservatory that opens on to an enclosed, well tended garden. **Sleeps 4** in two twin bedrooms. We haven't stayed in the winter months, but would love to do so in order to luxuriate in front of the open front wood-burning stove.

We have not previously written much about Rural Retreats' East Anglian properties, but they have some gems, two of which have particularly caught our eye. These are *The Priory*, **sleeping 8**, near King's Lynn, a Tudor mansion that has been exquisitely furnished, and *Red Roofs*, **sleeping 7/8**, a many-timbered Grade II beauty near attractive Eye. It is a gem, in deepest Suffolk – a classic 16th century Suffolk longhouse: just walking into it is like a trip by time-machine.

Rural Retreats offer all year round what they call their 'hotel facility': you choose which days of the week you arrive and leave (minimum stay for most is two days). Each of the properties has a number of services, which can include a dinner delivery service and baby-sitting. In the north Cotswolds cottages carry membership of a local country club with a range of sports and leisure activities.

There are televisions in all cottages, all linen/towels, electricity or gas central heating, payphones, washing machines, tumble dryers, logs for the open fires, babysitting and free weekly cleaning (additional cleaning is usually available by arrangement). Children are welcome in most, and there is usually no restriction on dogs.

A sumptuous brochure (one of the best we know) is available from Rural Retreats, Station Road, Blockley, Moreton-in-Marsh, Gloucestershire GL56 9DZ. Telephone (01386) 701177. Fax 701178.

The Priory, near King's Lynn, is one of several historic East Anglian beauties...

...as is Red Roofs, in half an acre of rural Suffolk, and near a famous restaurant...

www.ruralretreats.co.uk
email: info@ruralretreats.co.uk

347

Stanton, near Broadway
Stanton Court Cottages

Twenty years in this guide, and never anything but praise from several hundred satisfied readers. It must be due to the magical combination of picture-postcard attractiveness and an uncompromising attention to guests' comfort and warmth.

The more we see of this idyllic arrangement of cottages (and two rather grand apartments) the more we are impressed. Most recently we stayed in the most romantic of all the cottages, *Peach*, a delightful hideaway **for 2**, with a galleried bedroom. On a perfect early summer evening, with children sporting in the open air pool, we could hardly tear ourselves away from the exceptional gardens, but we had an appointment in the excellent pub at the top of the hill at the end of this exquisite little village. We would certainly put it among our top two or three Cotswold favourites.

The atmosphere is perfect, friendly but private when you want it to be, the picture-postcard golden stone village of Stanton a perfect backdrop. Stanton lies close to the wooded lip of the Cotswold escarpment, surrounded by some of the richest greenery in England. As you approach, you hardly notice this cluster of cottages: they seem more like a natural crop of rock than something installed by man. The village main street has hardly changed since it was first built in the 16th century.

The cottages are grouped around the courtyard of the village's principal house, which was built by Elizabeth I's chamberlain. Its garden, sheltered by ancient trees, notably some majestic yews, is mostly lawn, backing on the village churchyard. Since the house was built on such a grand scale, the parts of the original complex that have been transformed into self-contained units are mostly quite spacious.

We could write a book about these fine cottages, but, in brief, *Courtyard*

We admire the way modern comfort has been combined with original features.

This superb Elizabethan mansion is quite a focal point for the cottages.

Cottage is closest to the imposing entrance gates, **sleeps 4** in one double and one twin and has good views of the surrounding countryside, especially the imposing Malvern Hills. In little Peach, the bigger two-storeyed *Rosemary* and delightfully spacious, single-storeyed *Shenberrow* we came away with an impression, among other things, of big, comfortable beds, expensive and elegant tables and standard-lamps, deep sofas in subtle, modern colours. We admired so much of the detail and attention to comfort and remember especially Peach's unusual conservatory (the fruit is a bonus for summer visitors!) and its inviting open fireplace. The cottage is, incidentally, on three levels, with a galleried bedroom that has a romantic atmosphere. We were especially delighted by Rosemary, with its high pitched roof, its brass bedsteads in one of the twin rooms, more of those deep sofas and wing chairs. It **sleeps 6** in a double and two twins. Shenberrow, another fairly recent addition to the Stanton family, also has charm: it **sleeps 4**, has two bathrooms and is suitable for wheelchair-bound guests. On the early summer evening of one recent visit, the manicured gardens were especially memorable.

Paddock used to be the potting shed. The original stone walls and occasional outcrop of historic timbers are featured here, and, in fact, recur throughout most of the cottages. It offers one-level accommodation, and so is suitable for the elderly or the handicapped. It **sleeps 2** in a twin or double (ie zip-link beds), and also has a double sofa bed in the (quite spacious) sitting/dining room. As with all the cottages, it comes fully equipped with linen and towels and has full gas central heating, TV, and a telephone. Paddock can, in fact, be combined with Peach to **sleep 4**. *Studio Cottage* continues the chunky wooden beam theme. It too has quarry tiled floors and a large walk-in pantry that puts the cottage's interior into its true perspective. You'll find the dining room and large sitting room (with lovely views) equipped with a convertible settee. Parties of **up to 7** can be accommodated in *Garden*, actually a first floor flat, in three bedrooms (a double and two twins), two with their own hand basins, and there is an enormous lounge, along with a grandfather clock, antique pine furniture, and co-ordinated soft furnishings.

Another of our favourites, though we would happily stay in any one of the Stanton Court properties, is *The Granary*, characterised by a huge lounge, with a stone fireplace, and a bold craftsman-built modern wooden staircase, leading to the beamed roof gallery corridor, off which the three bedrooms lead. It is a house of enormous character.

Stanton Court also has its own tennis court, another popular activity, and

The cottages manage to be impressive and intimate at the same time.

The village is a delight, and Stanton Court, at one end, is its pride and joy.

a heated outdoor pool. There is a centrally heated games room, an imaginatively laid out children's adventure playground, a laundry room and a new reception area. A range of inexpensive food is available in the cottages, and there is even an off-licence. ETC Four Stars.

Cost: about £315 to £888 per week, including heating and electricity. Well behaved dogs welcome – maximum two per cottage. Details from Stanton Court, Stanton, near Broadway, Worcestershire WR12 7NE. Telephone Stanton (01386) 584527. Fax 584682.

www.stantoncourt.co.uk   email: sales@stantoncourt.co.uk

Sedgeberrow, near Evesham
Hall Farm Cottages

Clustered together at the heart of the pleasant village of Sedgeberrow, with extensive gardens and a grass tennis court, these cottages are reliably warm, scrupulously maintained, 'cottagey' but modern enough to suit people's demands.

We have stayed in most of them, and much enjoyed and appreciated each and every one. Collectively, they are definitely among our Top Twenty, and we find the owners among the most welcoming and helpful we know.

The location is exceptional, on the right side of the Cotswolds for touring: Stratford-upon-Avon to the north-east, the secret Welsh border country and the apple orchards of Herefordshire to the north-west. The fertile Vale of Evesham is at hand: pick your own strawberries, raspberries, plums, apples and vegetables. Not to be missed during the month of May is the local asparagus.

The biggest house of all, *Moat Path Cottage*, is one of several properties grouped around a green, a spacious and nicely self-contained place. There is a particularly charming upstairs attic bedroom. **Sleeps 6**.

Adjoining is *Stable Yard Cottage,* of similar design. Both properties have bedrooms and bathrooms on the ground floor, making them suitable for partially disabled guests. Smaller cottages face on to a large lawn, and we have enjoyed afternoon tea there – comfortable garden furniture is supplied – after a day's touring.

A feature common to all the properties – lots of books on shelves and furniture of character, including some antiques. Guests have use of the owners' heated swimming pool (a short distance away on their farm, within the same quiet and attractive village) and there are horses and donkeys.

Award-winning conversions of old farm buidings, up to 21st century standards...

...with interiors that combine a 'cottagey' quality with contemporary needs.

Cost: about £185 to £520, depending on which property you choose, and when. Not suitable for dogs. English Tourism Council (in most cottages) Four Stars. Bedlinen and towels provided. TV.

Further details and brochure available from Daphne Stow, Hall Farm Country Holidays, Sedgeberrow, Evesham, Worcestershire WR11 6UB. Telephone/fax Evesham (01386) 881298.

email: daphnestow@aol.com

Cleeve Hill, near Winchcombe
The Old Dairy

We revisited in 2001, to confirm that not only does this cottage have what must be one of the best views in England, with panoramic vistas over the Severn Vale as far as the Black Mountains, but that it is also a delightful *tour de force* done to a superlative standard. We arrived after negotiating a narrow track from the turning off a high point on the Winchcombe to Cheltenham road,

English Tourism Council Four Stars: a fabulous cottage with breathtaking views.

snaking past the owners' house and climbing even higher. In four acres of unspoiled meadowland, it is a joy. We especially like the huge sitting room, its wood burning stove and oak floor, the vaulted ceiling and the gallery at one end. Downstairs, from that main room you go through to a stylish kitchen. A thoughtfully planned bathroom leads to a pristine double bedroom (ensuite). Upstairs are two twin rooms, and another bathroom. The house is light and bright and, appropriately, it is heated partly by solar panels. **Sleeps up to 8** (including the use of a futon).

TV/video. Linen and towels included. Not suitable for pets. Cost: about £300 to £700. Details from Rickie and Jennie Gauld, Slades Farm, Bushcombe Lane, Cleeve Hill, Cheltenham, Gloucestershire GL52 3PN. Telephone/fax (01242) 676003. Mobile 07860 598323.

www.btinternet.com/~cotswoldcottages
email: rickieg@btinternet.com

Oldcroft, near Lydney   map: 9/531
Cider Press Cottage

The Forest of Dean is one of those 'best kept secrets', and because it's rater hidden away and not very commercially minded, really good self catering is hard to come by. This (a reader put us on to it) is outstanding. In four acres, it is on the edge of the forest, and there is very good walking and cycling. Specifically, there are two doubles, both of them with king sized beds, and a twin. Pets are

A very useful base for the Forest of Dean, with easy access to South Wales...

welcome, and there is Category 2 accessibility for disabled people. English Tourism Council Four Stars: a very reliable classification.

More details from Hoseasons Holidays, Lowestoft, Suffolk NR32 2LW. Telephone (01502) 501515. Fax 584962.

For on-line booking and 'real time' availability: **www. hoseasons.co.uk**
email: mail@hoseasons.co.uk

351

Exhall, near Alcester
Glebe Farm

We admire the use of space in the conversion at Glebe Farm of one-time barns that stand around three sides of a traditional farmyard. Of the ten properties, five are single storeyed cottages, *The Stable* is a sizeable, two storeyed, and chintzily comfortable house with lots of beams and lots of warmth (shower

Neat and warm cottages well placed for Shakespeare Country and the Marches.

only, not bath). One of the cottages, *Mill Meer,* is suitable for people with limited mobility. Most recently available within a handsome converted barn, are *Duck Pond* and *Goose*, deliberately made for flexibility. There are two apartments done to a very high standard in a separate, detached one-time cartshed, called *The Granary* and *The Cart Hovel*. The very welcoming owners (who have stylish bed and breakfast, including a four-poster) offer complete access to the extensive gardens, and encourage visiting children to fuss over the ducks and geese. There is a small shop exclusively for guests (provisions, souvenirs, maps and guides), a laundry and a payphone. One dog per cottage welcome. TV. All linen and towels, electricity and heating included. Cost: about £140 to £500. Further details from John and Margaret Canning, Exhall, near Alcester, Warwickshire B49 6EA. Telephone/fax Stratford-upon-Avon (01789) 772202.

Buckland, near Broadway   map 9/534
Hillside Cottage/The Bothy

We've featured these for years, and enjoyed a revisit in 2001. At the very end of picture-postcard Buckland's village street (it's a no-through-road) you continue uphill to locate two comfortable, private, self contained 'upside down' houses (they have first floor sitting rooms) that are adjacent to but have a separate drive-way from the owner's home. From those sitting rooms you look down

Comfortable and warm, not frilly...

on the outer reaches of this leafy, honey-coloured village. We like the beamed ceilings, the open fires, the comparative roominess, the comfy sofas. One of *Bothy's* bedrooms has a four-poster, and Bothy and *Hillside Cottage* both **sleep 4**. There is a good sized indoor heated pool available all day, and a garden with barbecue area. A bonus for walkers: the Cotswold Way is yards from the cottages. TV with teletext. Linen/towels included. ETC Four Stars. Dogs welcome. Cost: about £216 to £480. Details from Charles A Edmondson, Burhill, Buckland, Worcestershire WR12 7LY. Telephone Broadway (01386) 858842. Fax (01386) 853900.

www.pepegarden.co.uk   email: info@pepegarden.co.uk

Condicote, near Stow-on-the-Wold
Flagstone Farm Cottages

In one of the more high lying parts of the Cotswolds (neatly maintained farms, panoramic views, a different atmosphere from the hidden-away honey-coloured villages), we discovered this cluster of skilfully converted former farm properties looked after with energy and a flair for interior comfort by Ann Whitney.

Just two miles from Stow-on-the-Wold, at the end of a private and well maintained drive off the road, and from a distance looking like a traditional and prosperous farmstead – the ten acres of grassland and four acres of woodland are freely available to guests – there are six cottages, which most usefully vary in size and are very appropriate for, say, extended families wanting to take more than one property. They are nicely juxtaposed but not uncomfortably close to each other, and we enjoyed strolling from one to the other and in two or three cases meeting people happily installed. All have been finished to the highest standards of comfort, warmth and insulation, and we were impressed by the way original features such as beams and details within stonework have been retained. Throughout, there are quality carpets, curtains and other soft furnishings. Kitchens for example are handmade out of old pine.

Broadway **sleeps 14** in two five-foot four-posters, one double and four twins; *Stanton* **sleeps 12** in four twins and two doubles (a five foot four-poster in the master bedroom); *The Farmhouse* **sleeps 8** in three twins and a double; *Snowshill* and *Bibury* **sleep 6** in a double and two twins; *Clematis* **sleeps 2** in a five foot four-poster. A cot is available in each.

The cottages are altogether so warm and inviting that you may want to stay put for a week or longer, but if not, there is so much to see. Such as

A substantial farmstead has been given a marvellous new lease of life...

...and transformed into cottages of varying sizes but consistent quality.

the Cotswold gems (Chipping Campden, Broadway, Burford) and lesser known delights (Upper Slaughter, Stanton); a bit further afield is Shakespeare Country, Herefordshire, Worcestershire, the Welsh borders.

TVs and videos. One dog welcome in each cottage. Linen and towels included. Hard tennis court. Pitch and putt. Snooker and table tennis. Croquet and badminton. Bicycles for hire. Cost: about £150 to £1550. Details and a well illustrated brochure from Ann Whitney, Flagstone Farm Cottages, Condicote, Stow-on-the-Wold, Gloucestershire GL54 1ER. Telephone/fax (01451) 832215.

www.cotswoldfarmhouse.com email: awhitney@btclick.com

353

Winchcombe
Sudeley Castle Country Cottages

We love to revisit Winchcombe. Not only is it one of our favourite small Cotswold towns, but it adjoins Sudeley Castle, much visited for its exquisite interior and its fabulous gardens. There is a further bonus, for the tranquil 1200 acre Sudeley estate embraces – just five minutes' pleasant stroll from the castle itself – a cluster of fourteen holiday properties finished to high standards, each with its own individual character.

We revisited in 2001, *partly to see the newly available Cooper's Hill Barn and Studio (see opposite page)*, but also to look again at a selection of the main group of cottages. We really like the combination of privacy, total peace and quiet, 21st century comfort and powerful historical associations, and the fact that each property has its own character and is not 'done to a formula'.

Note: cottage guests have complimentary unlimited access to the castle and gardens during normal opening hours. Grouped around a central courtyard so neat, clean and tidy it always seems to us as if it is swept twice daily, there are Cottages and Mews Cottages, The King's Apartments and The Mill Court.

We have stayed in *Oliver Cromwell*, **sleeping 4**, which is one of the Mill Court properties, and remember lots of light and space, lots of beams, a two storeyed arrangement with a twin and a spacious double bedroom. We also remember the impressive *Lady Jane Grey*, **sleeping 5**, in a double, a twin and a single, with a sitting room that opens on to a small patio and a shared garden. We also found *Queen's Cottage* and *Emma Dent*, **sleeping 4 and 5** respectively, are interesting and comfortable, the former

A sympathetic conversion of old buildings into very comfortable cottages...

...and a rare chance to stay so close to such an impressive and historic place...

a clever and practical conversion of the estate's original engine house.

The two Mews Cottages are full of history, overlook the gardens and the river, and have open fires. Other property names are intriguing: *Anne Boleyn, Queen Mary, George III, Prince Rupert*. For Sudeley's famous associations run like a thread through the history of England. Not suitable for pets. Cost: about £191 to £648. Details from The Cottage Administrator, Sudeley Castle, Winchcombe, Gloucestershire GL54 5JD. Telephone (01242) 602308. Fax 602959.

www.sudeleycastle.co.uk email: marketing@sudeley.org.uk

Winchcombe
Sudeley Castle: Cooper's Hill Barn and Studio

The high point of our 2001 visit to the castle was seeing both the quietly situated *Barn* and *Studio* that are very much part of the estate (though nicely tucked away) and still used by the family themselves: a limited number of weeks are available however to outside guests.

We thought they were irresistible – one of those memorable places that make putting this guide together so worthwhile even after 20 years. The Barn has an especially appealing 'sunken' sitting room, giving on to a deck with garden furniture and looking on to a small wooded valley and a stream; the whole property is surrounded by fields, with inspiring views from most windows. There are two ensuite bedrooms at either end of the property, accessed by separate staircases, so they are just right for two couples. Both are ensuite. There is a five-foot double in one, a pair of zip-link singles in the other that can make up that great sybaritic luxury, a six-foot-wide bed. We loved the deep, squishy sofas, the pictures, the weighty table lamps, the woodburning stove – in brief, the style.

The Studio, across the yard, can accommodate two further guests and is not let separately, so privacy is assured. This has long been used as an artist's studio by Lady Ashcombe, and is high ceilinged, bright and airy, with a galleried twin bedroom (not zip-linked).

Sleeps up to 6. Cost: about £750 to £950. Further information as detailed on the opposite page.

Swinbrook, near Burford   Colour section B, Page 7
Summer Haze/Wenrisc Cottage   map 9/539

These cottages make for a memorable holiday, right from the warm welcome. Tucked away quietly on the edge of one of those Cotswold villages that most people probably never come across, they are smallish but excellent. Their appeal is great: for example, one has a fine open fire, the other a good quality woodburning stove. Both have much going for them, not least the meadow view, the good books, parlour games, cleverly lit alcoves, excellent fabrics and soft furnishings.

Kind, considerate owners, a quiet location on the edge of a little known village...

Specifically, *Summer Haze* **sleeps 4** in a pretty double and a twin and is on three levels, with the kitchen opening on to a steep, charming garden. *Wenrisc Cottage Apartment* is a delightful and warm hideaway **just for 2,** built into the hillside with its own secluded part of the rambling garden.

TVs. Dogs by arrangement. Cost: approximately £140 to £250, depending, as always, on 'which' and 'when'. For further details, contact the Picken family, 'Upper Wenrisc', Swinbrook, Burford, Oxfordshire OX18 4EE. Telephone Burford (01993) 823272.

Burford
The Mill

Our most recent visit to these cottages, among the best in the Cotswolds, was to meet the new owners, who have already made their mark with a rare attention to detail, colour and style. Just a five minute walk from Burford's high street, and thus very convenient for walking to the shops, restaurants and pubs, they have featured here for sixteen years.

An 18th century watermill, lovingly restored and straddling an arm of the Windrush, stands on the edge of the delightful and popular small town. *Tail Race Cottage,* one of five self-catering units nestling around The Mill, is especially cosy. It **sleeps 5**. There's a bright kitchen opening on to a small patio beside the water, a most welcoming living room with a log stove, comfortably furnished and filled with country antiques, books and interesting original pictures. The main bedroom has a modern four-poster bed; there's central heating and a new and pristine white shower-room.

There are two well equipped apartments, one above the other, in what was once a cabinet maker's workshop. The ground floor unit, with two bedrooms and a living room full of 'bygones' and books, has a balcony overlooking the millstream. This is *Windrush,* and it **sleeps 4**. Above it, *Millstream* is smaller, with just one bedroom, a shower instead of a bathroom, but lots of light, a small balcony and the busily rippling waters of The Mill's tail race. This flat is a great favourite with honeymooners – though it has a double *and* a single bed.

Looking out over the secluded garden and the wooded wilderness beyond are *Cider Press* and *Lime Tree,* two substantial studio flats of great charm. Cider Press **sleeps 2,** while Lime Tree has a double bed for parents and a sleeping platform tucked up under the steeply-sloping roof, which is

Really good cottages, such as these, are a great rarity in much loved Burford.

Interiors have been much upgraded by the new owners, with attention to detail.

much enjoyed by children in the 5 to 15 age range.

The Mill provides free bikes for guests, fishing on the River Windrush nearby, a boat in which to explore the river, a laundry room with drying facilities and central heating.

Cost: property for 2, £190 to £334; property for 5, £265 to £492. Open all year. Winter-breaks from £129 for three nights for 2 people. TVs/videos. Central heating. Dogs are welcome by arrangement. Further details from Tony and Pat Waddell, The Mill, Witney Street, Burford, Oxfordshire OX18 4RX. Telephone Burford (01993) 822379. Fax (01993) 822759.

www.themillatburford.co.uk email:cottages@themillatburford.co.uk

Bruern, near Chipping Norton
Bruern Stable Cottages

The handsome village of Bruern seemed perfect, with its manicured grass and its tidy verges, when we first saw it one quiet, silent, misty autumn morning with nothing at all to spoil the mood. Outwardly unchanged for a couple of centuries, it comes as no surprise that so many people return to stay in one of the ten cottages prettily arranged on three sides of a courtyard at the heart of this very special, very 'English' place.

It is also no surprise that Bruern Stable Cottages won the English Tourist Board's much respected Self Catering Award in the England for Excellence scheme in 1998 because, having seen literally thousands of cottage interiors on our travels during the last twenty years, we definitely rate these exceptionally highly.

Each is like a mini-stately home, with open fires, particularly attractive, soft and subtle lighting, deep sofas, fine paintings and prints, many antiques, good quality rugs and carpets, five-foot four-poster beds in sev-

This is the sort of place that gives self-catering in Britain a good name...

Standards are very high indeed, but there is nothing stuffy or formal here...

eral cases, show-house kitchens, the sort of bathrooms you would find in discreet, expensive Mayfair hotels. The whole place seems to reflect the care with which it is run, and there are lots of those little touches that mean so much, such as well chosen books and games, frozen (but home-cooked) dishes, maid service and baby sitting, and a welcome hamper.

We looked at most of the cottages (all but one named after famous racecourses) while they were being prepared for new guests. Each has its own character, as well as its own particular fans, and they **sleep from 2 to 8**.

The main communal gardens are lovely, and each cottage also has at least its own private terrace, while several have their own enclosed garden. All have TVs, video players and hi-fis. Linen and towels are included, and there is a choice of blankets or duvets. Direct dial phones. Games room. Children's play area. Shared use (at specific times) of a heated outdoor swiming pool and hard tennis court. ETC Five Stars. Not suitable for pets. Changeover day is Friday.

Cost: about £309 (for the small cottage out of season) to £1215 (for the biggest in high season). Details and an outstandingly good brochure from the Hon Judy Astor, Bruern Stable Cottages, Red Brick House, Bruern, Chipping Norton, Oxfordshire OX7 6PY. Telephone (01993) 830415. Fax 831750. Mobile 07802 182092.

www.Bruern.co.uk   email: judy.astor@btconnect.com

The Cotswolds
Manor Cottages and Cotswold Retreats*

Though long established, this cottage letting agency was new to the guide in 2000. But it quickly picked up a following among readers looking for properties in the 'tourist honeypot' parts of the amazingly well preserved Cotswolds – though the agency has a good number of cottages that are off the beaten Cotswold track.

So there are cottages in such famous places as Burford, Stow-on-the-Wold and Bourton-on-the-Water, and some real delights in other villages (a couple of which we only recently discovered for ourselves while checking out Manor Cottages properties).

These include *Green View Cottage,* **sleeping up to 8**, in one of our own favourite Cotswold villages – Little Barrington. Overlooking the charmingly hillocky village green, known for its wild flowers and grasses, it has beams and an open fire in an inglenook. We especially liked a newly available barn conversion, *Cottage Barn*, in the attractive village of

Cottage Barn is a skilful modern conversion, but nicely 'in keeping'.

Green View Cottage, Little Barrington – a village nicely off the beaten track...

Longborough, near Stow-on-the-Wold. Pristinely clean and tidy, the property is furnished in a unique oriental style and has a conservatory and private garden. **Sleeps 6** in a double and two twin bedrooms.

We very much liked *Arley Cottage* in Hook Norton (a most appealing village we had never visited before), where we met the charming and most welcoming owner. This is no 16th century golden stone Cotswold gem, but a small bungalow in the grounds of the owners' beautiful garden (though very private), with fabulous views. Sleeps **just 2** in a double bed.

With only about 50 cottages, and no great desire to become a large organisation, Angela Richards is a very 'hands-on' agent, who welcomes the demanding and very particular type of holidaymaker.

Most sleep **from 2 to 4/5**, with a sprinkling of cottages that will take **6/7**. Because of the location of the Cotswolds and the demand from London weekenders, among others, short breaks are often available at a sensible price. Dogs and other pets are welcome in about half the properties. Brochure/details from Angela Richards, Manor Cottages and Cotswold Retreats, Priory Mews, 33A Priory Lane, Burford OX18 4SG. Telephone (01993) 824252. Fax 824443.

www.manorcottages.co.uk
email: mancott@netcomuk.co.uk

Duck End, near Stanton Harcourt
Akers

In every edition of this guide we research there are three or four properties that stand out. In 2000 this was one of them, and one year on, Akers remains memorable – one in a thousand.

On the outskirts of the attractive scattered South Oxfordshire village of Stanton Harcourt, in a hamlet of twelve thatched houses called Duck End, and itself thatched (and Grade 11 listed), the house is quite hard to locate (which we like). It is very quiet and, while full of modern comforts, reminiscent of a slower, less frantic age. It is stylish and sensitively handled, with that magical blend of original features and 21st century comforts.

Rambling and labyrinthine in the nicest way, it has the special charm of a traditional farmhouse. There are two staircases, one at each end of the building: children love this, as it makes for thrilling games of hide and seek. They will also love the (third floor) bedroom in the attic, where there is also a spacious third bathroom.

Here are some specifics. The kitchen/diner, roughly in the centre of the house, which is appealing in itself, is outstanding, just right for convivial family get-togethers.('Where shall we go tomorrow? Oxford? Bourton-on-the-Water? Upper Slaughter? Blenheim Palace?' All are close.)

It has the huge advantage of a big stone inglenook fireplace that because it is such a focal point effectively makes the kitchen into a third reception room, the others being a sitting room at the village end of the house, overlooking the gravelled driveway and a delightful, spacious drawing room at the garden end, with south-facing french windows on to a duck pond and an island frequented by wildfowl. There are five bedrooms.

A cross between 'a country house' and a holiday cottage: a lovely find indeed...

The three acres of garden are the icing on a very special cake...

The garden is exceptional. We can imagine families making full use of it on a summer day: a meadow with trees and shrubs, lawns, fruit trees and more: three lovely acres in all. (We love this message in the brochure: 'There are fresh herbs for the kitchen and apple trees to plunder'!)

TVs/video/CD player. **Sleeps up to 9/10**. ETC Five Stars, of course. Linen and towels included. Pets and smokers welcome. Cost: about £750 to £1400. Details from Barbara Harding, Lower Farm, Duck End Lane, Stanton Harcourt, Oxfordshire OX8 1RX. Telephone (01865) 881553.

www.oxfordshirecottages.com
email: barbaraharding@yahoo.co.uk

Cottage in the Country*
(Incorporating Cottage Holidays)

This effective regional agency has as its main patch the Cotswolds, Berkshire and the Thames Valley, with a nod to Buckinghamshire and Hertfordshire, Worcestershire, Herefordshire, much of Shropshire and the Welsh borders.

'Cottage in the Country' has always appealed strongly to overseas visitors looking for 'the real England', as well as holidaymakers from within the UK. Oxford, Stratford-upon-Avon, Warwick and Windsor are among the places that attract. We have also directed many a reader who appreciates the special charms of the Welsh borders to the organisation.

Among 'Cottage in the Country' places we have stayed in or fancy for ourselves is a detached property in the grounds of the owners' home in one of the best liked small towns in the Cotswolds, Moreton-in-Marsh. It **sleeps 4** in a twin and a double. We also admire *March Font Cottage*, in the village of Weston-on-Avon, just four miles from Stratford-upon-Avon,

March Font Cottage is a fine converted barn in the village of Weston-on-Avon, just four miles from Stratford...

Home Farm Stable was one of our most memorable discoveries during a recent exploration of Cotswold properties...

or nearby *Hurnberry*. Both are converted barns, furnished and equipped to a high standard, and **sleep 5/6 and 4/5** respectively. The village itself borders the river, and one can walk all the way into Stratford.

It is not easy to find the right kind of cottage in Malvern, because it is so sought-after for permanent homes, but *The Coach House*, just five minutes' walk from the centre of this marvellously characterful and well preserved former spa town, is very worthwhile. It **sleeps 4/6**, and there is a private and secluded garden.

There are houses in 'Royal' Windsor, as well as Datchet and Henley: all three are on the Thames. Also in the Thames Valley, there is the two storeyed wing of a handsome Georgian house at Walton-on-Thames. All these are easily accessible by train from central London.

The majority of properties on the books of Cottage in the Country are English Tourism Council graded, including some with Five Stars.

For a copy of the agency's brochure contact 'Cottage in the Country/- Cottage Holidays', Forest Gate, Frog Lane, Milton-under-Wychwood, Oxfordshire OX7 6JZ. Telephone (01993) 831495, fax 831095.

www.cottageinthecountry.co.uk

email: ghc@cottageinthecountry.co.uk

Little Faringdon, near Lechlade
Langford House Cottages   Colour section C, Page 1

A matter of yards from a fine but understated manor house are some of the most lovingly tended properties we have seen in Britain. Each has character, is comfortable, warm and spacious with an open fire. For a real treat, and most likely to appeal to our readers, *Garden Cottage* (**sleeping 4**) is superb, certainly one of the 'top 20' in this guide, and not expensive considering how much style it exudes. Owner Lady de Mauley

The elegant drawing room is light, bright and full of style, but comfortable with it...

admits that she would be very happy to retire here, and we don't blame her: a spacious garden – hence the name – an elegant 31 foot long drawing room on to that garden, large and altogether excellent bedrooms and other reception rooms. There's an open fire *and* a wood-burning stove, antiques, great comfort and lots of atmosphere. Bright and sunny in summer, cosy in winter, it's private, quiet, and suitable for wheelchair-bound visitors. Cost: approximately £150 to £550. Not suitable for dogs. TVs. Details and a useful leaflet from The Lady de Mauley, Langford House, Little Faringdon, Lechlade, Gloucestershire GL7 3QN. Telephone Faringdon (01367) 252210. Fax (01367) 252577.

Churchill, near Chipping Norton   map 9/545
The Little Cottage

Picturesque, quiet and little-known Churchill, on the eastern edge of the Cotswolds, comprises a fine church, a village green and a quantity of traditional, honey-coloured stone cottages, of which this (in the middle of a terrace of three and on a B-road that doesn't seem to carry much traffic) is one. Highly graded by the tourist board, it has a wood burning

This little cottage is neat, comfy and in good order, with its own pretty garden.

stove, oak beams, a cosy sitting room enhanced by good quality, co-ordinated Liberty furnishings, adjacent to a well planned kitchen that in turn leads to a very pretty garden. There's lots of pine, a sofa bed in the separate dining room should it be needed, a metal, not plastic, bath in a good-sized bathroom and a charming twin bedroom.

Small TV. Dogs not welcome. Central heating over which guests have complete control. Linen/towels included. Cost: about £195 to £295 for **2 plus 2**. Short breaks off-season: three nights for £145. Details from David and Jacky Sheppard, Gables Cottage, Junction Road, Churchill, Oxfordshire OX7 6NW. Telephone Kingham (01608) 658674.

www.littlecottage.co.uk

Swerford, near Chipping Norton
Heath Farm Cottages

Even compared with the many admirable holiday cottages we feature, these properties are extremely impressive. They are a superlatively comfortable and thoughtfully equipped quintet, any one of which would make an excellent base from which to explore the whole of the unspoilt Cotswolds, the glories of Oxfordshire (the ancient university, Blenheim Palace, the Thames) and, further afield, Shakespeare Country.

There's a pretty, flower-filled courtyard with a mature water garden, 70 acres of farm and woodland readily accessible, extraordinary views of large tracts of rural Oxfordshire from the courtyard and some windows of the four golden ironstone cottages, and exceptional interiors.

David Barbour, who with his wife Nena has created such a haven of comfort at Heath Farm, is a master craftsman with his own joinery business. For example, all the interior doors and the windows, the kitchen units and much of the furniture is hand-made *on site*: a joy to see. (In one of the larger properties, attached to the Barbours' own house, we admired handsome hand-made high backed dining chairs in elm from the farm itself.)

Beechnut and *Hazelnut* **sleep 2/3 and 2** respectively. They are compact, comfortable and private, with rugs, expensive small sofas, cosy lamps, a skilful use of space. Across the courtyard are *Chestnut* and *Walnut*, each **sleeping '2 plus 2'** via a sofa bed. They are exceptional by any standards, with lots of space, a six foot double bed in the latter, big windows, rugs on slate floors. Walnut is a little palace, with a big sitting room, fabulous views (it's on two floors), a magnificent dining table, exposed stone walls, handsome beams, a superb bathroom.

Most recently available is *Cobnut*, **sleeping 4** in two ensuite twins/doubles (that is, zip-link beds). Among so many good things, they have extraordinary views from the master bedroom.

All have open fires for which logs are provided. ETC Four Stars. Electricity, central heating, linen and towels included. Non smokers only. 'Sorry, no pets.' Cost: £238 to £505 (Christmas/New Year cost extra). Credit cards accepted. Details/brochure from David and Nena Barbour, Heath Farm, Swerford, near Chipping Norton, Oxfordshire OX7 4BN. Telephone Great Tew (01608) 683270/683204. Fax 683222.

www.heathfarm.com
email: barbours@heathfarm.com

Award-winning properties, effectively all ETC Four Stars...

...are outstanding, among much else, for the craftsmanship of the interiors.

Great Milton, near Oxford
Views Farm Barns

Within easy striking distance of Oxford – yet in a part of Oxfordshire that many people miss, and popular with overseas visitors wanting to be equidistant from London and Cheltenham, these extremely sympathetic barn conversions are also close to one of Britain's most exalted restaurants, *'Le Manoir aux Quat' Saisons'*. They are well planned, full of charming touches and versatile in terms of the accommodation offered.

Ranged on two sides of a gravelled and paved courtyard, but well insulated and private, they are well organised and do not feel at all cramped. We found them sensitively lit, and admired well chosen pictures, 'country style' interiors, with lots of pine, upholstered cane easy chairs and sofas.

We have seen all six cottages, and find them all brimming with comfort and character. But do check the brochure and make your requirements known to the owners to make sure you choose the right property. *Sanfoin View,* for example, has an excellent arrangement to suit disabled people

Reliably comfortable (and not at all expensive) properties grouped around a gravelled and paved courtyard.

Interior of Rye View, one of two cottages that have recently acquired patios from which there are fine country views...

whereby the sitting room has an optional bed available. **Sleeps 3.** There's an unusually large bathroom with wheelchair access. We especially liked *Wheat View*, **sleeping 2,** typically well designed, an extremely cosy smallish sitting room, exposed stone walls, good books on shelves. Like *Rye View* (**sleeps 3**), this property is actually on two storeys, and is therefore closer to the more traditional cottage. Sanfoin View, Rye View and *Clover View* have patios where you can sit and take in the good views.

All the cottages are quiet (a road runs by, but there is much less traffic on it than you might at first think), and make good bases for seeing, as well as Oxford, the Cotswolds, Windsor, Henley, Blenheim Palace and Stratford-upon-Avon. Walkers are well placed for joining the Ridgeway Path at – for example – Streatley, railway buffs are just a short drive from the Didcot Railway museum, and the great country houses of Stonor Park and Nuneham are close.

ETC Four Stars. Televisions. Dogs are welcome. Full central heating and constant hot water is provided by a straw burner! Cost: approximately £200 to £360. Local fishing – permits available free of charge. Further details and a good colour leaflet can be obtained from Mr and Mrs C Peers, Views Farm Barns, Great Milton, Oxfordshire OX9 7NW. Telephone Great Milton (01844) 279352. Fax 279362.

363

East Hagbourne
The Oast House, Manor Farm

On the edge of the village of East Hagbourne, half way between the 12th century church and the farmhouse where owner Robin Harries lives, *The Oast House* stands quietly below the Berkshire Downs. It is more spacious than its outside Virginia creeper-covered appearance suggests, and has five bedrooms. (The one on the ground floor, though often used as a study or second living room, makes an ideal unit for someone of limited mobility.) The

We have always liked this a lot – even members of a large group can 'get away from each other'...

master bedroom has a five foot bed. The living room has a Victorian style gas fired stove as a very appealing back-up to the full central heating. On the ground floor there is also a separate dining room, a modern kitchen which includes a dishwasher, and a utility room with washing machine and drier, a shower and a third loo.

Sleeps 8. TV/video plus satellite TV. Not suitable for dogs. This excellent house is English Tourism Council Four Stars. Further details are available from Robin Harries, Manor Farm, East Hagbourne, Oxfordshire. Telephone/fax Didcot (01235) 815005.

Knightcote, near Leamington Spa   map 9/549
Knightcote Farm Cottages   Colour section B, Page 7

We revisited these cottages, whose interiors are so well planned, spacious, well-insulated, in 2001. Surrounded by the owners' 500 acre farm, with easy back-road access to main roads (out of earshot), we've long admired the superlative quality of single storeyed *Home Cottage* (**sleeping 6**), two storeyed *Ploughman's Rest* (**sleeping 6/7**) and *Sleep Late Cottage* – a nice name! – **sleep-**

Absolutely superb interiors in every case.

ing 4. It's not surprising they've won the Self Catering Cottage of the Year Award (Heart of England Tourist Board) and the Godiva Award for Tourism. These have now been joined by the recently completed *Chestnut Cottage*, **sleeping 4**, to the same standard, feeling private and rural. (Along with Home, it has wheelchair access.) We also saw the smart new function room available to cottage guests. Dogs possible. Linen/towels included. TVs/videos. Home cooked meals. Cost: £310 to £595. Short breaks from £217. Details: Fiona Walker, Knightcote, near Leamington Spa, Warwickshire CV47 2EF. Telephone (01295) 770637. Fax 770135.

www.farmcottages.com   email: fionawalker@farmcottages.com

Ireland

A few years ago Ireland was seen as a bit of a backwater, albeit with devotees in America, the UK and parts of mainland Europe. Now it is very 'mainstream' indeed, with a flourishing tourist industry. Its varied landscapes, its history, its music, its hospitable people are just some of the elements that make up one of the most appealing destinations anywhere.

Among much else during recent journeys we remember the sun setting on a warm evening over the Atlantic on the bleakly beautiful coast of Connemara, finding 'b and b' en route between cottage visits in a slightly faded but still grand Georgian country mansion, stopping for a drink on a hot afternoon in a whitewashed 17th century pub (miraculously 'unreconstructed') in the-middle-of-nowhere.

We think of the deep, deep green of the countryside bordering the coast of North Antrim, of the mystical quality of the early-morning light over Lake Killarney, and of the wild blue mountains of Connemara. Of putting the world to rights in one of the fabulous sea-food restaurants in this land of Murphy's and honey. Almost everywhere you look you have that powerful combination of history (great castles, stately homes), marvellous golf, fishing, beaches and scenic walks, and comfortable places to stay.

We are not fishermen, but remember seeing anglers' eyes lighting up over a candlelit dinner in romantic Delphi Lodge, among the dramatic hills of the Galway-Connemara border, when describing their day's battles with salmon. We are reminded of clambering over the Giant's Causeway in County Antrim, westering 'home' to a cottage by the sea, of sunbathing in a County Clare garden, of watching the sun setting over the water.

Nowhere is very far from anywhere else, although we do hear from readers who enjoy 'two-centre' Irish holidays. One family, regular users of the book but first time visitors to Ireland, stayed at Woodstown, Waterford, partly for a wedding, then had a week in a thatched cottage at Kinvara, perfectly poised for explorations of Galway, the Connemara National Park, and, over the border in Co Clare, 'the Burren'. This is an amazing lunar landscape, mile upon silent mile of limestone pavements that 5000 years ago were inhabited by Ireland's first people. But the Burren is not bleak: 1000 species of plants grow here wild, some only found elsewhere on the shores of the Mediterranean and in the Arctic.

We would stick our necks out and say that if you have only a weekend to spend in Ireland the strongest contender among places to go and things to see is the 'Ring of Kerry', which is within a day's drive (there are coach tours too, from Killarney, for example). Starting from the limpid Lakes of Killarney, most people drive towards the lush ravines of Glengariff, look out for the fantastic view from Skellig Rocks from roller-coaster roads, listen to the silence of the forest at Gougane Barra, marvel as the sun sets behind the mountains that fringe Bantry Bay.

Note: when telephoning Ireland you should dial your own international prefix (eg 00) then 353 followed by the area code (eg 51, not 051), then the number. Within Ireland, however, you should prefix the area code with '0', eg 051. Note also: a small number of contact phone numbers in this section are UK ones.

The South of Ireland
Country Cottages in Ireland*

Year by year, the 'Country Cottages in Ireland' brochure is one of the two or three most spectacular we know. Rich in colour and full of atmosphere, it cleverly conveys the essence of what makes this beautiful and historic country so popular – increasingly so – among travellers.

Over 440 properties are featured across the country. Many are among those westerly counties memorable for spectacular cliffs, springy turf carpeted by wild flowers, technicolour sunsets and vast golden sands. Less well known regions are featured too, from the rocky headlands of Donegal and the hills of Wicklow to the fabulous beaches of the south.

We have had enthusiastic reader reports of *Moriaty's Farmhouse*, at Caherdaniel, Co Kerry, not least for the marvellous views, its privacy and tranquillity, and its proximity (a mile and half) to excellent sandy

Moriarty's Farmhouse has fabulous, panoramic sea and mountain views...

Thatched Cottage is a rare example of the original style: no plastic in sight!

beaches. It **sleeps 5** in considerable comfort. Ref ZFX (*map 10/550*). One of our inspectors has roots in Co Kerry, where the agency has other well located cottages. These include fabuously situated *Gleesk House*, near Sneem (*map 10/551*), in a hundred acres and with *its own coral strand and shoreline*. It **sleeps 6 'plus 2'**. Ref YCN.

There are cottages and apartments in Kinsale (*map 10/552*), which is known as 'the gourmet capital of Ireland', with some of the best seafood restaurants in Europe. These include apartments in *The Grove*, plus a small cottage **just for 2**, all with memorable views of Kinsale harbour (ref ZAN). A short drive from Kinsale, there are several properties in beautifully situated Courtmacsherry (*map 10/553*), on one of the prettiest parts of the coast, including *Bayview Cottage*, an 'upside down' house with fine views of the water (ref ZAV).

And during our travels we have met readers of this guide while they stayed in the handsome, spacious and, unusually, modern country mansion called *Redhills House* (Ref ZM8), in 250 acres of parkland in Co Cavan. **Sleeps 8 (*map 10/554*).**

For a copy of the exceptional brochure, phone 0870 585 1166. To book any of the cottages featured here, phone 0870 585 1177. Country Cottages in Ireland, Stoney Bank, Earby, Barnoldswick BB94 0AA.

www.cottages-in-ireland.co.uk

Quote ref. IMA94

Ballineen, near Bantry/Cork
Manch House

Seeing the two self contained apartments in this beautiful late Georgian mansion, deep in lovely countryside and under an hour from Bantry Bay, was a pleasure. They offer a rare chance to experience country house living, but with total independence. Guests are welcome to walk where they please, in the woods or by the river, on the 300-acre estate. Private salmon and trout fishing available by

Kind and considerate hosts in a grand setting: a touch of old Ireland indeed...

arrangement. *The South Apartment* **sleeps 2**, with bedsitting room, choice of twin beds or king size double, the windows look south across the river valley. *The East Wing Apartment* **sleeps 4** in two twin bedrooms with handbasins; its kitchen/dining room is large and fully equipped. The sitting room also faces south across the Bandon valley. Both apartments have a shower room with handbasin and toilet. TVs. Heating, light, linen and towels included. Not suitable for dogs. Cost: about £280 to £605, dependent on when you go. Details from Con (Cornelius) Conner, Manch House, Ballineen, Co Cork. Telephone (353) 23 47256. Fax 47276.

www.manchhouse.com email: con@manchhouse.com

Bantry map 10/563
Whiddy Holiday Homes

We rate these very highly. On board a small passenger ferry you cross beautiful Bantry Bay, fringed by green hills, to Whiddy Island. Ten minutes on the water, a world away. Depending on which of the three most appealing cottages is yours (usefully, their owners live on the

This private, self contained, very nicely furnished cottage overlooks Bantry Bay.

island in summer), you might be driven a couple of miles along a bumpy track, past a freshwater lake with a rowing boat freely available to cottage guests, past hedges of scarlet fuchsia that are a summer trademark of the west of Ireland. All three are utterly quiet, all with sea views 'to die for'. Rowing on the lake, exploring every nook and cranny of the island by bike or on foot, climbing to the eerily beautiful, deserted Napoleonic fort, eating and drinking in the congenial 'open all hours' pub-restaurant would fill a happy week or, in good weather, a fortnight of serious unwinding. Fishing and sailing can be arranged without difficulty.

Linen and towels included. TV. Dogs welcome. Cost: about IR£185 to IR£545. Brochures and booking details available from Greta Steenssens, Roddam 67, B-2880, Bornem, Belgium. Telephone (32) (3) 8896111. Fax 8894171. In Ireland: (353) (27) 51739. Fax 51069.

Hoseasons Country Cottages*
(Ireland)

Hoseasons (main feature: Pages 24 to 25) have made a huge impact on the holiday cottage scene in the last few years, and have picked up on the current popularity of Ireland by developing a quality programme there.

On our list to see in 2002 is *Joy's Farmhouse* (*map 10/565*), a rare chance to stay on the 21-square mile, dramatically scenic Valentia Island, linked to the mainland by a road bridge. There is an acre of garden, inspiring views and, better yet, an open fire plus (in the kitchen) a woodburner. **Sleeps 6**. Brochure ref R1068.

We have had rave reports of *Dunmanus House*, overlooking Dunmanus Bay, in County Cork (*map 10/566*). With fabulous sea views, it **sleeps 8** but can be organised to sleep more than as many again. Within the spacious interior there are so many good things, including an open fire, a snooker table and, in one bedroom, a five foot double bed. Ref R1006.

Ross Castle: a grand estate, comfortable stable and courtyard properties.

Sheeaun Cottage is 'the real thing': a sympathetically renovated period piece...

A colleague has stayed at *Johnstown Cottage* (Ref R1081), in Co Tipperary, appreciating its traditional thatch and its views of Lough Derg (*map 10/567*), and a reader reported on *Hillside Farm Lodge* (Ref R1004), near Kenmare, Co Kerry. It is a comfortable family house in 60 acres (*map 10/568*).

But even by Hoseasons standards the properties at magnificent Ross Castle (*map 10/569*), between Galway City and the coast of Connemara, are special. In a commanding position in 30 acres of grounds, the castle has six self catering properties: two are within the castle courtyard, four have been converted from former stables. The biggest, *David's Cottage*, **sleeps 8**, other accommodation **2, 4 or 6**. Refs R1043-R1047 and R1122.

Among exquisitely located individual cottages is *Sheeaun Cottage,* in Connemara (Ref 1082). It is a rare example of a renovated traditional cottage, just half a mile from the sea (*map 10/570*). Also just half a mile from the beach at Inch, *Ard na Pairce* (**sleeping 6**), has fabulous views of Dingle Bay (*map 10/571*). Ref R1019.

Details from Hoseasons Holidays Ltd, Lowestoft NR32 2LW. Telephone 0870 534 2342. Fax 0870 902 2090.

On-line booking and 'real time' availability on the web:
www.hoseasons.co.uk   email: mail@hoseasons.co.uk

Kinvara, near Galway
Dunguaire Thatched Cottages

Quite simply, these four imposing thatched and white-washed cottages (overlooking an inlet of Galway Bay and ancient Dunguaire Castle) are among the most impressive we've seen in Ireland. We revisited recently, and found everything fine. The village (pubs and restaurants) is just a five minute walk and one is well situated for trips to The Burren and romantic Connemara. Set back from the road on rising ground, the cottages are in a congenial arrangement

With Shannon Airport just an hour away, consider a short winter break, costing only about £100 for six people.

but feel private. Each is spacious and comfortable, with high ceilings, dark beams, wide landings, is quiet and has a woodburning stove and storage radiators with 'boosters', most attractive fabrics and pretty duvet covers. There are three bedrooms (one double, two twins). Each has two bathrooms and good beds. A peak-season week costs about £350 to £475. TV. All linen and towels. Details from Jim and Mary Barr, Dunguaire Thatched Cottages, Kinvara, Co Galway. Telephone/fax (outside Ireland) your own international prefix plus (353) 91 637247.

www.kinvaraonline.com

Ballyvaughan
Village and Country Holiday Homes

Colour section C, Page 4

map 10/573

These are rather special. Surrounded by the limestone hills of the Burren, on the shores of Galway Bay, is Ballyvaughan, and, in 'Village and Country Holiday Homes', *some of the best self catering properties we know in Ireland*. The enclave of well appointed cottages (each with its own garden, quiet and private) is located in a courtyard. The welcoming owners also have traditional-

You choose: in a village or by the sea...

style cottages a mile from the village, close to a sandy beach, and there are two apartments, bright, deceptively spacious, within a few yards of the courtyard cottages. All properties have quality fabrics and furnishings, easy-on-the-eye colours, well equipped kitchens. The country houses **sleep 6**, the village properties **4 or 6** (there are two styles, plus the new apartments). TV. Linen. Optional breakfast packs and daily cleaning. Cost: about £IR150 to £IR550. Details from Mr George Quinn, Frances Street, Kilrush, Co Clare. Telephone (353) 65 90 51977. Fax 65 90 52370.

www.ballyvaughan-cottages.com
email:Sales@ballyvaughan-cottages.com

Killarney, Muckross
Killarney Lakeland Cottages

Tourist board research says Killarney is the most popular tourist destination in all of Ireland, and it is usually buzzing with life. Brian O'Shea's thoughtfully landscaped, well-spaced but nevertheless 'villagey' arrangement of nineteen white-painted traditional-style cottages is however in a quiet parkland setting seemingly miles from the town centre (though it is actually quite close).

We revisited most recently while we were roughly at the halfway point of a long but inspiring journey from Bantry Bay to County Clare, and it was a pleasure to get off the road (though the journey is scenic) to spend time in this peaceful, green enclave.

Though they are notable for their mod cons, the cottages (in two separate groups, each prettily surrounded by trees and each resembling a classic Irish village, each private but a well planned distance from its neighbours) do suggest the original inspiration: for example, every one has not only an open fire, but even a much loved peat fire – peat is available from reception. The number each property sleeps varies slightly, **from 4 to 7**.

A very successful marriage of traditional styles and modern comfort...

...in one of the most tranquil (though the town itself is busy!) locations in Ireland.

There is access to two hard tennis courts, a good games room, bikes, and in each cottage TV with multi-channel reception and direct dial telephone. There is also an arrangement with the nearby Gleneagle Hotel, conveniently on the way into Killarney, regarding the use of their swimming pool and leisure centre at a reduced rate. Golf, squash and pony trekking are also available nearby. Not suitable for dogs. Cost: about E195 to E925.

Details/colour leaflet from Brian O'Shea, Killarney Lakeland Cottages, Muckross, Killarney, Co Kerry. Telephone (outside Ireland) – your country's international code plus (353) 64-31538, fax (353) 64 34113.

www.killarney.cottages.com
email:info@killarneycottages.com

Interhome*
(Ireland)

Interhome (see also page 32) have about 100 properties across Ireland.

About 20 miles from the prosperous market town of Mallow, which itself is roughly 20 miles north of Cork, is a detached stone house in grounds of 75 acres (*map 10/575*). Here, surrounded by peace and quiet and with inspiring mountain views, **7 people** can holiday in the picturesque Cork countryside. Shops, a pub, a restaurant and golf are all to be found within five miles. Ref J4380/100.

Portmagee, a quiet fishing village on the most south western tip of the Iveragh peninsula, just off the beautiful Ring of Kerry, nestles by the Atlantic Sea. It is a perfect spot to relax or, for the more energetic, there's golf, fishing, or a chance to see the sights. Directly by the sea, and thus with stunning views of sea and hills, is a detached house **sleeping 8**. The

Just off the Ring of Kerry, right by the sea and with good views, this is one of four...

This beauty on Achill Island is less than a mile from a sandy Blue Flag beach...

living/dining room has a slate open fireplace (turf/peat provided free) and sea views. This four star house (*map 10/576*) has top quality furnishings, a patio and a shared communal garden leading to the water's edge where you can fish and paddle. Ref J4532/100.

In County Mayo, on the outskirts of 'The Neale' (close to Connemara, Westport and Galway) a traditional, thatched cottage **sleeps 3**. Recently renovated, it is tastefully furnished and quietly situated in rolling country-side (*map 10/577*). There are two open fires, a garden, bicycles and a wide range of literature. Ref J6511/100.

Still in Co Mayo, Achill is Ireland's largest island, off its west coast. The narrow strip of sea separating it from the mainland is now bridged and open to traffic. Achill has wild and varied scenery, with mountains, open moorland and dramatic cliffs. There are excellent beaches hereabouts and some awe-inspiring coastline.

In a quiet position surrounded by fields, yet within half a mile of the sea and blue flag sandy beach, pub and restaurant **6 people** can stay in a four star detached house in Dugort, in the north of the island (*map 10/579*). Ref J6540/100.

Details from Interhome Ltd, 383 Richmond Road, Twickenham TW1 2EF. Telephone 020 8891 1294; fax 020 8891 5331.

www.interhome.co.uk

email: info@interhome.co.uk

Delphi, North Connemara
Boathouse Cottages/Wren's Cottage

We have visited some extraordinary places in our researches for this guide, and Delphi certainly numbers among the most romantic and memorable. It is located in a beautiful mountain location, reminiscent of a idealised classical 18th century landscape: great looming hills, misty valleys, rushing rivers, dark woods. If you are tired or under stress, a few days in this magical place will restore you. Serious fishermen probably know Delphi, and walkers should consider it. It is a wildlife paradise, known for wild flowers, otters, peregrine falcons, pine martens and badgers.

We have stayed, and will return as soon as we can. The location? You will find it where western Mayo nudges into Connemara, a few miles north of Leenane.

Almost adjacent to elegant Delphi Lodge, the original four cottages are very cosy, quite unpretentious, with deep chairs and sofas, lots of antique

Boathouse Cottages were our first discovery: full of character and charm. We met a Dutch family in residence, and they loved the cottage and its location.

Wren's Cottage, newly renovated, is the pride and joy of the Delphi ownership. Idyllically, it overlooks the lough, and is bound to attract a following of its own.

pine, big open fires (making them a most appealing choice for an autumn or winter break), traditional stone floors with rugs downstairs and carpets upstairs. The four are most attractively bordered by shrubs and old stone walls, and all **sleep 4** in two twins.

In 2001 we also saw a newly restored cottage, *Wren's*. On the approach road to Delphi Lodge, overlooking the lough in the Delphi Valley, it has a greater degree of privacy, and has been furnished and equipped to a very high standard. It **sleeps 6** in three bedrooms.

Linen and towels are included. All have telephone. No TVs. Not suitable for very young children or dogs. Cost: Boathouse Cottages, about IR£295 to IR£450, plus electricity by meter, Wren's Cottage, about IR£495 to IR£695. Further details from Delphi Lodge, Leenane, Co Galway (postal district). Telephone (353) 95 42222. Fax 42296.

Note: Excellent bed and breakfast accommodation is available in Delphi Lodge, and cottage guests may sometimes have candlelit dinners here, usually on a communal basis: such a bonus for lone travellers or people from overseas wanting to make new friends.

www.delphilodge.ie   email: delfish@iol.ie

The South of Ireland
Emerald Cottage Holidays*

Welcome Holidays (see also Pages 10-11) have made huge strides in the last couple of years, and their busy Irish programme – Emerald Cottage Holidays – coincides nicely with a big surge of interest not just in Ireland as a whole but in self catering holidays there. The company's Ireland Cottage Directory will inspire many new visitors.

For example, with its hedgerows of wild fuchsias, wooded hillsides and sudden panoramic views along winding country and coastal roads, County Kerry is the stuff of so many Irish holiday memories. And it happens that in this so-romantic corner of the country Emerald Cottage Holidays have a crop of cottages falling into their 'beautiful' or "lovely' categories (see Pages 10-11).

During a planned 2002 Irish visit we will certainly want to see a 'dream of a cottage' near Waterville, Co Kerry (*map 10/581*). **Sleeping 4**, it is just two miles from the sea, and has impressive views. You can join the Kerry Way from right behind the cottage, and a drive around the Kerry

You can walk to a sandy beach from this 150 year old Co Clare house (sleeps 6).

This beauty near Dingle sleeps up to ten people: an exceptional house and location.

Ring is a 'must do' in this part of Ireland. Ref 5286.

And we will see a thatched cottage, also **sleeping 4**, in an idyllic location just a field away from Loch Corrib, though only ten miles from Galway City (*map 10/582*). Horse riding is available, and there is a pier and boat within a mile. Ref 5225.

We want to mention Wexford, Waterford and Wicklow ('Ballykissangel' country), as they are ideal for the first-time visitor to Ireland from England, especially for the easy ferry access. The scenery is delightful, the beaches are super and many of the towns delightful.

Among so many fine cottages, we recommend a detached charmer at Gorey (Ref 5356), in Co Wexford (**map 10/583**), and a spacious semi-detached property in Ballinaclash, a quiet village in Co Wicklow (Ref 5674). It is just three miles from a train connection to Dublin (**map 10/584**).

Brochures, bookings and other information from Emerald Cottage Holidays, Embsay Mills, Embsay, Skipton, North Yorkshire BD23 6QR. Telephone 01756 697736.

You can book directly on a particularly up to date and sophisticated webite: **www.emerald.cottages.co.uk**

Connemara
Connemara Coastal Cottages*

Knowing how fond we are of Ireland, an American reader wrote to us to say how useful this guide had been in finding properties there of character, and described the locations she had loved most. We quickly realised that in most cases she meant Connemara: 'romantic sunsets over the water, endless beaches, marvellous seafood'. During our most recent Irish visit we spent time with a small, personally run agency we'd heard excellent reports of, and saw a good handful of

This appealing agency has on its books some very impressive properties indeed. And almost without exception, they are beautifully situated. Pictured: Ref 117.

the properties on their books. For example, two extremely comfortable cottages, pride and joy of the owners, overlooking the water at Cleggan village, and a thickly carpeted cottage (called *Doon House*) attached to the charming owners' house: rural views but, of course, not far from the sea, and a light, bright cottage conversion almost surrounded by water, with fabulous sea and mountain views, called *Ross Point*.

Among the properties we hope to see during a 2002 vsit to this part of Ireland is a substantial two-storeyed stone-built property, *Grace's Cottage,* at Ross Moyard. With the beach only a fifteen-minute walk away, it has great views. **Sleeps 8**. (Brochure Ref 115).

Pets welcome in most. Details of these and other beauties in an excellent loose-leaf brochure from Julia Awcock, Connemara Coastal Cottages, Cloon, Cleggan, Co Galway. Telephone (353) 95 44307.

www.cc-cottages.com email: cccottages@eircom.net

Stop Press

'In brief'

Originally not sure if they were letting for the 2002 season, and now able to confirm that they are, we do not have the space to describe in detail two properties that quickly caught readers' attention when they first appeared in this guide.

They are the private, half hidden away but not remote *Grayling* at New Quay, on the coast of Co Clare. **Sleeping 7**, it is a charmer – one of our best finds on a recent visit to the west of Ireland (Colour section C, Page 4). And at Culduff, near Foxford, Co Mayo, there are three 'traditional' cottages – not showhouses, but warm and comfy, with open fires in two, and 'the real thing'. They **sleep from 4 to 7/8**. (Colour section C, Page 4.)

Ballisodare, near Sligo
Ravens Rock Farm

It looks a bit ordinary as you arrive, but appearances are deceptive. Off a main road into Sligo (but well out of earshot) and therefore easy to find down a private farm track, this is a traditional farmhouse (on a working farm). We met English people putting on their boots prior to climbing among the Ox Mountains. With a separate sitting room, which has an open 'turf' – peat – fire, this a

A genuine farmhouse atmosphere, handy for Sligo and the coast, and for good walking. It is also very modestly priced.

charming place for a family holiday: a touch of old Ireland. **Sleeps up to 6** in two doubles and two single rooms. Dogs welcome. Linen included. TV. Cost: about £180 to £225. Details: Violet Lockhart, Ravens Rock Farm, Stonehall, Ballisodare, Co Sligo. Telephone/fax (353) 71 67495.

Breeogue, near Sligo
Breeogue House   map 10/588

This is not so much a cottage, more a substantial, rather elegant family house about 150 years old. With its deep sofas, most attractive pictures, some antique pieces, lots of space and room for **up to 8 people** in four high ceilinged bedrooms, it is a good base for exploring Sligo and, say,

A handsome family house, a haven to return to after a day's lovely touring...

Mayo and Donegal. Sligo town is only five miles away. There is an open fire in the light and spacious drawing room which overlooks an orchard, and central heating. **Sleeps 8**. Linen and towels included. Not suitable for dogs. Cost: about £320 to £400. Details: Mrs E MacLoughlin, Breeogue House, Breeogue, Knockahur, Co Sligo. Telephone (01438) 869489.

Redhills, near Cavan
Redhills House   map 10/587

This is an impressive modern house in 250 acres of beautiful parkland, with a private lake. There's an elegant drawing room/conservatory with a log fire, a spacious dining room with an open fire, four twin bedrooms. (Two of the bedrooms open

Unusually, a modern country mansion...

out on to a balcony with delightful views over the park: superb!) TV. Pets welcome. Linen, not towels, included. Details from Mrs J Patton, Millvale House, Tullyvin, Co Cavan. Telephone (national code plus (353) 49 555 3213. Fax 49 555 3307.

Doonbeg, near Kilkee
Aran View

Aran View, on the coast north of Kilkee, is a modest-seeming modern bungalow that is in fact a delightful place. Set back from a quiet lane, it is well named, for there are inspiring views of the Aran islands and, in the middle distance, views of the Atlantic shore and irresistible seaside walks. (You can take boat trips from Doolin, in Co Clare.) The cottage's very cosy sitting room/dining

A modestly priced, superbly well situated, quiet property with super views.

room is graced by a picture window through which to enjoy the view and the fabulous sunsets. One of the two double rooms has the same wonderful view. Usefully, the bungalow **sleeps 8** altogether, in two doubles and two twins, and is deceptively spacious. We felt it would make a fine base from which to explore a region that is exceptional even in Irish terms.

Further details from Miss A Haugh, Monaskeha, Clonlara, Co Clare. Telephone (353) 61 354793.

Manor Kilbride, near Blessington
The Manor Cottages   map 10/590   Colour section C, Page 4

On a handsome estate that embraces pastures where cattle graze and forty acres of woodland border a river, here are four quite outstanding cottages close to an impressive early 19th century manor house. At opposite ends of a large courtyard stand *Wood* and *Herds* cottages. The latter, for example, **sleeps 4/6**, with two doubles and a double sofa bed in the sitting room, stone walls, attractive timber floors and (as in the other cottages) some antique pieces. Thirdly, *Anvil Lodge* stands in an outer courtyard. It has the same sleeping

Here, as so often, it is those 'extras' that make all the difference: antiques, access to forty acres of woodland, use of the owners' indoor swimming pool...

accommodation as the previous two, but a very large living room which overlooks the river. And, finally, there is a gate lodge (*River Lodge*) with just one double bedroom.

Each has a dishwasher, phone, central heating and open fire, plus a small garden with barbecue. There is wheelchair access in Herds. Use by arrangement of the owners' indoor heated swimming pool.

Well behaved pets by arrangement. Cost: about £350 to £500 per week. Linen and towels are included. Details/brochure from Mrs Cully, The Manor, Manor Kilbride, Co Wicklow. Telephone (national code: 353) 1 4582105. Fax 4582607.

Waterford
Woodstown House Country Estate

This is self catering at a very stylish level, either attached to or within a short stroll across lawns from a fine country house slumbering in 35 acres of wooded parkland. (The latter properties are part of a sympathetically converted arrangement on three sides of a paved stable courtyard, with a charming fountain.)

What the two separate types of accommodation have in common is expensively appointed interiors, peace and quiet and, in brief, the ingredients of a holiday to be remembered.

It is just a short walk through the trees until you come to the edge of the lovely, sheltered, sandy Woodstown Beach where, if you arrive early in the morning, you may see racehorses in training galloping on the sands.

We have actually stayed in *Number One, Dower House*, attached to the main house, and much appreciated the spacious sitting room off which there is a well appointed kitchen, a smart bathroom and a twin bedroom. A second, double, bedroom, with antique furniture, is down a corridor. There are elegant paintings, a big open fire (all the properties here have open fires *and* central heating, a patio, deep armchairs and sofas, and most have ensuite bedrooms). One house is 'wheelchair friendly'.

A particularly attractive feature is the double hard-core tennis court contained within the confines of the original walled vegetable garden. This stands close to the *Courtyard Cottages*, which are neat and appointed in four-star hotel style with colour co-ordinated fabrics. All are two storeyed with not large but comfortable bedrooms. On a bright and sunny summer morning they were all light and bright, and spotlessly clean. We noticed lots of pine, good quality sofas, armchairs, carpets and curtains.

(The properties all have a Bord Failte four-star grading). All have direct-dial phones, TV, open log fires, microwave, dishwasher, washing-machine/dryer. Good shore fishing, coarse and game fishing are available; an equestrian centre and an outdoor adventure centre are close.

There are also *ten* excellent golf courses to be found within a ten to forty minute drive. Not suitable for dogs. Cost: about £200 to £510.

Further details and an excellent brochure are available from Ann Cusack, Woodstown House Country Estate, Woodstown, Co Waterford. Telephone (353) 51 382611, fax 382644.

Email: woodstown@granville-hotel.ie

These are very smart stable conversions set off beautifully by parkland...

This is very stylish living indeed, but at a most reasonable cost...

Killyleagh, (Strangford Lough)
Killyleagh Castle Towers

Northern Ireland is one of the historically most interesting and scenically beautiful parts of Europe. These apartments could be an ideal jumping off point from which to explore it...

This is an amazing place in an amazing location. Killyleagh Castle is the oldest inhabited castle in Ireland and has been the home of the Hamilton family since 1604. The Towers were built in 1620 and the larger centre tower was built in 1860 by Lord Dufferin who presented it to his father-in-law when he married the eldest daughter of the Castle. Within, there are three self-catering apartments and one small studio room. The two towers which form the corners of the defences of the courtyard in front of the castle each **sleep 4**, the centre *Gatehouse* **sleeps 5**. *The Studio Room* has one double bed and a bathroom and can very usefully act an an annexe for any of the other apartments. There is parking inside the castle courtyard. Killyleagh is ideally situated for golfing, fishing, riding and sailing. Or you may prefer visiting stately homes and gardens, bird watching, swimming (there is a swimming pool in the garden that can be made available by arrangement) or leisurely driving around the beautiful countryside. Full details of these and other activities are available in the Towers. Excellent meals and entertainment are to be found only a hundred yards away at The Dufferin Arms Hotel.

All are equipped with TVs, bedlinen, towels, 'fridge, washing machine and dryer. Dogs are accepted, though there is a small extra charge. Cost: from about £205 to £355.

Details from Lieut Col Denys Rowan-Hamilton, Killyleagh Castle, Co Down BT30 9QA. Telephone/fax (02844) 828261.

Getting to Ireland

The larger agencies featured in this section carry advice about travelling to your holiday cottage in Ireland, and can usually make bookings for you and offer advantageous ferry rates. There are nine ferry routes from Scotland and Wales, with the route from Swansea to Cork being the best known for cutting out a lot of the driving for people based in the southern half of England.

Our favourite way to travel to Ireland is to fly and then hire a car. Flights can be cheap, especially if you are flexible enough to fit in with special offers, and Ryanair, famously hard to contact directly, now work with travel agents. Car hire rates are competitive.

Cottages4You

The internet seems to have settled down into down into something that's more functional than fun. Useful among much else for checking local services, some kinds of shopping, booking with low cost airlines and – yes! – holiday accommodation, especially at the last minute. But dinner party conversations have moved on...

Among accommodation providers however The Holiday Cottage Group's *Cottages4You* bucks the trend, and this highly sophisticated website is a pleasure to use, well designed and full of interest. With all 9000 of the properties within the group on the site (that is, English Country Cottages, Blakes, Country Holidays, Country Cottages in Ireland and Country Cottages in France) this is a real feast of information and even entertainment.

If cottage hunters don't see what they want on this site it probably isn't available anywhere!

A good proportion of properties offer a fascinating virtual tour; there's a checklist of specific requirements (such as an open fire, a nearby pub, a swimming pool and suitability for pets), and an instant price and availability panel that cuts out the niggly question: Have we missed the boat? Up to the minute special offers, perhaps during those quieter booking periods, add flavouring.

See the advertisement on Page 8 of Colour section C.

advertisement feature

Special Categories
A quick reference

Over the years we have received many requests from readers for specific information. These usually boil down to such things as 'This cottage looks nice, but can you confirm it has a swimming pool?'... 'How far away is it from the sea?'... 'There seems to be a railway station quite near, but are there taxis or will the cottage owners pick us up and take us back?'

None of this is a value judgement, as many of our very best cottages scarcely score at all in these lists. Please note that agencies are not included as it is assumed that most of them can offer properties that include some or even most of the facilities featured.

1. *In a village or town location.*
2. *Beside a lake, a loch, a lough, a river, the sea.*
3. *Within about five miles of the sea.*
4. *Deeply rural and/or fairly remote.*
5. *Home cooked food available (including freezer food).*
6. *Access by rail or owner will collect from train.*
7. *Owner/manager living on site or immediately adjacent.*
8. *On working farm.*
9. *Suitable for people with limited mobility.*
10. *Suitable for disabled (using ETC or RADAR criteria).*
11. *Big houses, suitable for two or more families (say, 9/10)*
12. *Swimming pool on site or immediately adjacent.*
13. *Open fires/coal or woodburning stoves.*
14. *Tennis court on site.*
15. *Special play/entertainment facilities for children.*

* An asterisk indicates that the facility applies to some properties only.

NB. Some readers have asked us to indicate cottages that are available for short breaks either in winter or summer, but our records show that four out of five owners or agents can oblige. It is worth phoning about short breaks even at the height of the season, as even the most sought-after cottages may offer last minute cancellations...

	1	2	3	4	5	6	7	8	9	10	11	12	13	14	15
East Anglia/E Midlands/Shires															
Blue Barn Cottage			✓	✓			✓	✓			✓		✓		
Bolding Way	✓		✓				✓		✓♦		✓		✓♦		
Bones Cottage	✓		✓				✓								
Brancaster Farms Cottages			✓				✓	✓		✓♦	✓♦		✓	✓	
Carpenters Cottages, No.6	✓		✓												
Chantry	✓	✓													
Claire's Cottage	✓			✓											
Clippesby Holiday Cottages			✓		✓		✓		✓♦	✓♦		✓	✓♦	✓	✓
Edith Weston Cottage Holidays	✓												✓		
Gladwins Farm Cottages					✓								✓	✓	
Grange Farm Cottages	✓		✓	✓		✓	✓	✓							
Grove Cottages, The			✓				✓								
Grove Cottages, The				✓			✓		✓				✓		
Ivy House Farm				✓		✓	✓	✓	✓	✓♦	✓	✓	✓		✓
Jenny's Cottage	✓		✓										✓		
Long Gores			✓	✓			✓						✓		✓
Mockbeggars Flat					✓	✓	✓								
Old Farmhouse, The				✓			✓		✓				✓		
Park Hall Cottages			✓	✓		✓	✓	✓					✓		✓
Peartree Cottage	✓	✓											✓		
Peddars Cottage	✓						✓						✓		
Poppyland Holiday Cottages	✓	✓								✓♦			✓♦		
Premiere Marina Cottages	✓	✓							✓♦		✓	✓			
Sandpiper	✓	✓♦	✓♦										✓		
Stubbs Cottages			✓♦	✓			✓	✓	✓♦				✓♦		
Sunnyside Cottage	✓		✓												
Thaxted Holiday Cottages	✓						✓								
Vere Lodge				✓	✓		✓		✓		✓	✓	✓♦	✓	✓
Vista/Carpenters Cottages	✓	✓											✓		
White Horse Farm Barns	✓		✓	✓			✓		✓				✓		
Wood Farm Cottages				✓			✓	✓	✓				✓♦		✓
Wood Lodge				✓								✓	✓		
Yorkshire and The Peaks															
Beech Farm Cottages	✓						✓		✓♦		✓	✓			✓
Cam Beck	✓	✓											✓		
Clematis and Well Cottages	✓♦												✓♦		
Cliff House	✓				✓		✓					✓	✓♦	✓	✓
Close Cottage				✓	✓	✓	✓						✓		
Cote Bank Farm Cottages				✓		✓	✓	✓	✓				✓		
Cotterill Farm Cottages						✓	✓						✓♦		
Cressbrook Hall Cottages		✓		✓	✓		✓		✓	✓	✓		✓		✓
Dalegarth & The Ghyll Cottages	✓					✓	✓		✓	✓		✓			
Dalehead Court	✓			✓		✓	✓								
Darwin Lake Properties		✓		✓			✓								
Dinmore Cottages							✓		✓	✓			✓		
Farsyde Mews Cottages		✓	✓		✓♦		✓	✓				✓♦	✓♦		
Field House				✓			✓						✓		
Fold Farm Cottages	✓			✓			✓	✓					✓		
Hawthorn Cottage			✓	✓								✓	✓		
Hayloft, The				✓			✓						✓		
Headon Farm Cottages				✓			✓						✓		
Holestone Moor Barns				✓		✓	✓		✓		✓		✓		
Honeysuckle & Brook Cottages							✓	✓					✓		
Hopton Hall	✓	✓					✓				✓	✓	✓		
Knockerdown Farm Cottages	✓			✓			✓		✓		✓	✓	✓♦		✓
Layhead Farm Cottages				✓		✓		✓	✓♦		✓♦		✓		
Old Cote Cottage				✓			✓	✓							

	1	2	3	4	5	6	7	8	9	10	11	12	13	14	15
Rudstone Walk Farm Cottages					✓	✓	✓	✓	✓						
Sarah's Cottage	✓			✓		✓	✓								
Shatton Hall Farm Cottages				✓			✓						✓	✓	
Shepherd's Cottage				✓									✓		
Slade House Farm				✓			✓				✓		✓		
Sparrow Hall Holiday Cottages								✓	✓♦			✓	✓		
Swaledale Cottages	✓♦			✓♦			✓♦				✓♦		✓♦		
Thiernswood Cottage	✓			✓♦			✓♦		✓		✓♦		✓♦		
Townend Cottage	✓						✓						✓		
Wasps Nest Cottages	✓					✓	✓						✓		
White Rose Holiday Cottages	✓		✓♦			✓	✓♦		✓♦				✓♦		
Wolfscote Grange Cottages		✓		✓	✓		✓	✓			✓				
Wraycroft Cottages	✓	✓					✓		✓♦				✓♦	✓	
Wrea Head House Cottages			✓			✓	✓		✓	✓	✓	✓			✓
York Lakeside Lodges		✓					✓			✓♦					✓

Northumberland and Durham

	1	2	3	4	5	6	7	8	9	10	11	12	13	14	15
Akeld Manor & Cottages				✓	✓		✓				✓♦				
Bastle House	✓			✓	✓	✓	✓	✓					✓		
Beacon Hill Farm Cottages							✓	✓	✓♦	✓♦		✓	✓	✓	✓
Blue Bell Farm Cottages	✓	✓	✓			✓	✓	✓♦							✓
Boot & Shoe Cottage		✓		✓	✓		✓						✓		
Breamish Valley Cottages				✓			✓		✓				✓♦		
Common House Farm				✓			✓		✓						
Cresswell Wing				✓			✓				✓			✓	
Farmhouse, The				✓			✓						✓		
Grove House		✓		✓	✓		✓						✓		
Old Byre, The				✓	✓		✓	✓	✓	✓	✓		✓		✓
Old Smithy, The				✓			✓	✓	✓				✓		
Outchester & Ross Farm Cottages			✓	✓	✓		✓	✓		✓♦			✓		
Pele Tower, The							✓						✓		
Shepherd's Cottage				✓	✓		✓	✓	✓				✓		
Shilbottle Town Foot Farm	✓		✓			✓	✓	✓	✓		✓	✓	✓	✓	✓
Stables, The & The Byre				✓	✓	✓	✓	✓	✓				✓		
West Lodge/Stables/Coachhouse/Bee Cott			✓	✓	✓		✓				✓		✓		

Scotland

	1	2	3	4	5	6	7	8	9	10	11	12	13	14	15
Achnacroish			✓♦	✓♦			✓♦						✓♦		
Appin Holiday Homes		✓♦	✓♦				✓♦	✓♦							
Ardblair Castle Cottages						✓♦	✓♦	✓♦			✓♦				
Ardtulloch	✓♦												✓		
Armadale Castle Cottages			✓	✓	✓			✓	✓						
Attadale				✓		✓	✓	✓			✓		✓		
Balnakilly Log Cabins/Cottages		✓		✓			✓	✓	✓♦	✓♦	✓	✓	✓	✓	
Blairquhan		✓		✓			✓	✓	✓♦		✓♦		✓		
Captain's House, The	✓	✓		✓									✓		
Crosswoodhill/Midcrosswood Farm				✓			✓	✓	✓				✓		
Culligran Cottages		✓		✓			✓	✓							
Druimarbin Farmhouse			✓	✓		✓			✓		✓		✓		
Duncrub Holidays				✓	✓	✓	✓	✓♦	✓♦				✓♦		
Duns Castle Cottages		✓		✓	✓		✓				✓		✓♦	✓	
Easter Dalziel Cottages			✓			✓	✓	✓	✓						
Ellary Estate Cottages		✓	✓	✓			✓	✓					✓		
Foulis Castle			✓	✓			✓	✓					✓		
Glengorm Castle			✓	✓		✓	✓	✓	✓				✓♦		
Kilchrist Castle Cottages			✓				✓								
Kintail	✓														
Leckmelm Holiday Cottages		✓♦	✓	✓		✓	✓	✓♦	✓♦		✓♦	✓	✓♦		

	1	2	3	4	5	6	7	8	9	10	11	12	13	14	15
Linsidecroy Steading and Farmhouse		✓		✓					✓•				✓		
Logie Newton Holiday Cottages				✓			✓	✓	✓				✓		
Lorgba Holiday Cottages	✓	✓	✓		✓	✓	✓	✓					✓		
Machrie Hotel Lodges		✓		✓	✓		✓		✓						✓
Mid Fearn Cottages		✓		✓		✓	✓		✓				✓		
Rhuveag		✓		✓							✓		✓		
Seaview Grazings		✓													
Speyside Holiday Houses	✓	✓							✓		✓		✓		
Tomich Holidays				✓			✓	✓				✓			
Torren Cottages		✓	✓	✓					✓						
Torrisdale Castle Cottages		✓	✓	✓			✓	✓	✓•		✓•		✓•		
Wedderburn Castle	✓			✓			✓						✓		

Cumbria/Lancashire

	1	2	3	4	5	6	7	8	9	10	11	12	13	14	15
Bailey Mill Cottage		✓		✓	✓	✓	✓	✓	✓	✓	✓	✓			✓
Bank End Farm Cottages		✓		✓	✓		✓	✓					✓•		
Bassenthwaite Lakeside Lodges		✓										✓			
Bowderbeck		✓		✓											
Coach House, The		✓					✓	✓					✓		
Croftside/Croft Corner							✓		✓•						✓
Daleside Farm Cottages				✓			✓	✓	✓•				✓		✓
Field End Barns		✓•		✓			✓		✓		✓		✓		
Heaning, The						✓	✓				✓				
Hollens Farm Cottages	✓	✓		✓	✓		✓						✓		
Howscales				✓		✓	✓		✓	✓					
Kirkland Hall Cottages				✓			✓				✓		✓		
Land Ends		✓		✓			✓		✓						
Long Byres				✓	✓	✓	✓	✓							
Longlands at Cartmel			✓	✓	✓	✓	✓		✓•	✓•		✓	✓•		
Loweswater Holiday Cottages	✓•	✓•		✓			✓		✓•				✓•		
Manse, The	✓		✓												
Matson Ground Estate Cottages				✓•			✓•				✓•		✓•		
Monkhouse Hill Cottages						✓			✓•	✓•	✓•		✓•		✓
Mossgill Loft	✓						✓						✓	✓	
No 1 Greta Cottage	✓	✓													
No 4 Green Cross Cottages	✓					✓									
Oakdene	✓										✓	✓	✓		
Old Coach House, The	✓								✓						
Riverside, The/Garden Cottage	✓	✓											✓•		
Rockery Cottage				✓	✓		✓								
Well Cottage/Green View Lodges	✓					✓	✓		✓				✓•		
Wheelwrights	✓						✓		✓•			✓	✓•	✓	✓

Wales

	1	2	3	4	5	6	7	8	9	10	11	12	13	14	15
Aberdovey Hillside Village	✓	✓				✓	✓								
Blackmoor Farm Holiday Cottages			✓				✓	✓							
Bryn Bras Castle			✓				✓								
Bryn-y-Mor		✓		✓					✓		✓		✓		
Carno			✓				✓		✓•			✓	✓•		
Carreg Coetan	✓		✓												
Cnewr Estate		✓•		✓			✓				✓•		✓		
Derwen & Beth Ruach		✓				✓			✓		✓		✓		✓
Felin Parc, Tan-y-Clogwen		✓	✓	✓							✓•		✓		
Fron Fawr		✓					✓								
Nantcol		✓	✓								✓		✓		
Neuadd Cottages	✓	✓	✓	✓	✓		✓	✓	✓		✓	✓	✓•		✓
Pant Farm & Sanctuary Cottage		✓	✓•	✓			✓	✓					✓•		
Penbryn Bach Cottage			✓	✓			✓						✓		
Penybont Bungalow		✓											✓		
Portmeirion Cottages	✓	✓	✓									✓		✓	

383

	1	2	3	4	5	6	7	8	9	10	11	12	13	14	15
Quality Cottages, Cerbid			✓	✓•			✓•	✓•	✓•				✓•		
Rhos-Ddu			✓	✓			✓	✓					✓•		✓
Rhyd-yr-Eirin	✓		✓	✓									✓		✓
Rosemoor			✓		✓	✓	✓		✓	✓	✓				
Showman's Trailer	✓		✓				✓	✓					✓		
Sir Johns Hill Farm Holiday Cottages	✓		✓	✓	✓		✓						✓		✓
Talcen Foel			✓	✓									✓		
Trallwm Forest Cottages				✓	✓	✓	✓	✓			✓•		✓		
Trenewydd Farm Cottages			✓	✓			✓		✓	✓	✓	✓			✓
West Country															
Badham Farm Holiday Cottages		✓	✓	✓		✓	✓		✓•		✓•			✓	✓
Bamham Farm Cottages							✓		✓		✓•	✓	✓•		✓
Barkham			✓	✓			✓								
Barn Cottage			✓				✓								
Big House Company, The	✓	✓		✓	✓	✓	✓		✓		✓	✓	✓	✓	
Blagdon Farm Country Holidays		✓		✓	✓		✓		✓	✓		✓			✓
Boak Cottage	✓	✓													
Bosinver Cottages			✓			✓		✓	✓•		✓•	✓	✓•	✓	✓
Braddon Cottages		✓		✓			✓					✓	✓	✓	✓
Butler's Cottage			✓	✓			✓	✓					✓		
Cant Cove Cottages		✓	✓	✓			✓		✓		✓		✓	✓	
Chapel & Hockadays Cottages	✓•		✓•	✓•		✓	✓•						✓•		
Chew Hill Farm Holidays			✓				✓	✓							
Cider Room Cottage			✓	✓			✓	✓							
Coach House Cottages			✓	✓	✓		✓				✓	✓	✓	✓	✓
Compton Pool Farm Cottages		✓	✓		✓		✓		✓		✓	✓		✓	✓
Country Ways			✓				✓	✓	✓	✓					✓
Court Cottage	✓		✓						✓						
Dairy Cottages			✓	✓			✓	✓	✓•	✓•		✓			✓
Dairy House, The	✓						✓		✓	✓		✓		✓	
Downe Cottages		✓		✓			✓		✓•				✓		
Draydon Cottages			✓												
Drupe Farm Cottages	✓		✓				✓		✓•		✓				✓
Duddings Holiday Cottages		✓	✓				✓					✓		✓	✓
East Penrest Barn			✓	✓			✓	✓	✓		✓		✓		✓
East Stoke House (Coach House)	✓				✓	✓	✓				✓	✓		✓	
Flete Estate, The		✓	✓	✓	✓	✓	✓		✓		✓		✓		✓
Fourwinds			✓		✓		✓		✓•			✓•	✓		✓
Glebe House Cottages	✓		✓		✓		✓								✓
Gullrock		✓	✓	✓			✓		✓						
Harbour View		✓	✓				✓								
Harbourside	✓	✓	✓	✓									✓		
Higher Bowden			✓				✓					✓	✓	✓	✓
Higher Scarsick			✓				✓	✓					✓		
Horry Mill Cottage			✓				✓	✓					✓		
Jacaranda		✓					✓						✓		
Jews Bank Cottage	✓	✓					✓						✓		
Kennacott Court	✓						✓		✓•		✓•	✓	✓•	✓	✓
Kirk House	✓	✓	✓									✓	✓		✓
Knowle Farm		✓•					✓•	✓•			✓•	✓•	✓•	✓•	✓
Lancombe Country Cottages				✓		✓	✓								
Lower Knapp Farm			✓				✓		✓•		✓•	✓	✓•		✓
Lower Trengale Farm				✓			✓	✓					✓		✓
Manor Cottage			✓	✓	✓		✓						✓		
Marigold/Penny	✓	✓	✓				✓								
Meadow Barn			✓	✓		✓	✓	✓					✓		
Meadow View/Lantern			✓				✓						✓		
Michaelmas Cottage							✓					✓	✓		

	1	2	3	4	5	6	7	8	9	10	11	12	13	14	15
Mill Field Cottage	✓	✓	✓										✓		
Mineshop Holiday Cottages		✓♦	✓	✓			✓				✓♦		✓		
Mudgeon Vean			✓	✓			✓	✓	✓				✓		
North Hill Cottages				✓			✓					✓	✓	✓	✓
Oldaport Farm Cottages			✓	✓	✓		✓	✓	✓♦				✓		
Penrose Burden Cottages		✓		✓	✓		✓	✓		✓			✓		
Pettigrew Cottage	✓	✓					✓						✓		
Red Doors Farm Cottages				✓	✓	✓	✓					✓	✓		✓
Rockford Lodge	✓	✓	✓												
Rooke Farm Cottages		✓					✓	✓					✓		
Rosemundy Cottages	✓		✓		✓♦	✓							✓		✓
Scoles Manor			✓	✓			✓		✓	✓	✓		✓		✓
Sea Meads Holiday Homes		✓	✓				✓				✓				
Shell Cove House		✓	✓			✓	✓		✓♦		✓	✓		✓	✓
St Aubyn Estates Cottages	✓♦	✓♦	✓♦	✓♦			✓♦	✓♦			✓♦		✓♦		✓♦
Stowford Lodge Holiday Cottages				✓	✓		✓		✓			✓	✓		
Thatched Cottage Co., The	✓		✓						✓♦		✓♦		✓♦		✓♦
Tredethick Farm Cottages							✓	✓	✓	✓	✓♦		✓		✓
Trefanny Hill			✓	✓	✓		✓		✓			✓	✓		✓
Tregeath			✓					✓					✓		
Trenant Park Cottages			✓					✓					✓		
Trevathan Farm			✓	✓			✓	✓	✓		✓		✓	✓	✓
Trevorrick Farm Cottages			✓				✓		✓	✓		✓	✓		✓
Treworgey Cottages			✓	✓	✓	✓	✓		✓♦		✓♦	✓	✓		✓
Venn Farm Cottages			✓				✓	✓	✓						
Watersmeet			✓	✓									✓		
Westermill Farm		✓		✓			✓	✓		✓			✓♦		
Wheel Farm Country Cottages			✓		✓		✓		✓♦		✓	✓	✓♦		✓
Widmouth Farm Cottages		✓		✓	✓	✓	✓								✓
Willesleigh Farm							✓	✓	✓			✓	✓		
Willy Wilcox/Quay/Lanlawren	✓♦	✓♦	✓♦	✓♦		✓			✓♦		✓	✓	✓		✓
Wooder Manor			✓				✓	✓	✓♦		✓♦		✓♦		
South and South East															
Ashby Farms Cottages	✓♦	✓♦		✓♦									✓♦		
Ciderpress and Walnut Tree Cottages		✓					✓		✓				✓	✓	
Coach House, The				✓		✓	✓						✓		
Danny Cottage			✓				✓						✓		
Eastwell Mews		✓			✓	✓	✓		✓♦	✓♦		✓		✓	
Hoppers Hut & Carters Cottage	✓	✓		✓	✓	✓	✓		✓				✓		
Hunston Mill			✓				✓	✓					✓♦		✓
Pekes				✓	✓		✓		✓♦		✓♦	✓	✓♦	✓	
Pippin's Barn/Middle Cottage				✓			✓		✓♦				✓♦		
Redstock	✓					✓					✓		✓		
Thatched Barn, The	✓			✓	✓		✓								
Three Chimneys Farm		✓		✓			✓	✓	✓♦		✓♦		✓	✓	
Cotswolds/Heart of England															
Akers	✓										✓		✓		
Barn, The				✓		✓	✓						✓		
Bruern Stable Cottages				✓	✓		✓		✓♦	✓♦	✓♦	✓	✓	✓	✓
Carey Dene & Rock House		✓		✓			✓	✓				✓	✓♦		
Combermere Abbey Cottages		✓		✓	✓	✓	✓	✓					✓	✓	✓
Cyder Barn/Stables Cottage	✓			✓		✓	✓	✓							✓
Dick Turpin Cottage				✓			✓						✓		
Docklow Manor							✓		✓			✓	✓♦	✓	
Flagstone Farm						✓	✓		✓		✓			✓	
Foxes Reach	✓			✓			✓						✓		
Garraway House Holiday Cottages				✓		✓			✓♦				✓		

385

	1	2	3	4	5	6	7	8	9	10	11	12	13	14	15
Glebe Farm							✓		✓						
Gwilts Barn				✓									✓		
Hall Farm Cottages	✓					✓	✓	✓	✓•			✓		✓	
Hazel Cottage							✓								
Heath Farm Cottages				✓			✓						✓		
Hillside Cottage/The Bothy	✓			✓			✓	✓				✓	✓		
Ivy House		✓		✓			✓	✓					✓		
Knightcote Farm Cottages	✓				✓		✓	✓	✓	✓	✓				
Langford House Cottages	✓			✓			✓		✓•				✓•		
Little Cottage, The	✓					✓	✓						✓		
Lower Farm Cottages	✓						✓		✓						✓
Mainoaks Farm				✓									✓		
Mill at Burford, The	✓	✓•					✓				✓•		✓•		
Oast House, The/Manor Farm	✓					✓	✓		✓						
Oatfield Farmhouse & Cottages		✓		✓			✓		✓•				✓•	✓	
Old Cottage, The	✓												✓		
Old Dairy, The						✓	✓				✓		✓		
Old Kilns	✓			✓									✓		✓
Orangery, The	✓					✓					✓				
Owlpen Manor Cottages				✓	✓		✓	✓	✓		✓		✓•		
Pitchford Estate				✓				✓	✓		✓		✓		
Stanton Court Cottages							✓		✓			✓		✓	✓
Sudeley Castle Country Cottages	✓						✓						✓•		
Summer Haze/Wenrisc Cottage	✓						✓						✓		
Sutton Court Farm Cottages				✓	✓		✓		✓•				✓•		
Swiss Chalet, The		✓		✓		✓	✓		✓						
The Mill at Burford	✓	✓					✓		✓•		✓		✓•		
Treago Castle Cottages				✓			✓		✓•		✓•	✓	✓•		
Views Farm Barns				✓			✓	✓	✓•						
Westwood House	✓				✓	✓	✓		✓•						
Wye Lea				✓•		✓	✓		✓•	✓•		✓		✓	✓
Ireland															
Breeogue House	✓		✓	✓			✓						✓		
Carnalee				✓			✓	✓	✓				✓		
Delphi Cottages		✓		✓	✓		✓						✓		
Dunguaire Thatched Cottages	✓	✓	✓	✓			✓		✓•		✓		✓		
Grayling		✓		✓				✓					✓		
Killarney Lakeland Cottages	✓					✓	✓	✓	✓		✓	✓	✓	✓	✓
Killyleagh Castle Towers	✓	✓	✓				✓					✓		✓	
Manch House		✓		✓			✓								
Manor Cottages, The		✓		✓			✓		✓			✓	✓		
Ravens Rock Farm			✓	✓			✓	✓					✓		✓
Village and Country Holiday Homes	✓•	✓•	✓				✓		✓•				✓•		
Whiddy Holiday Homes		✓		✓	✓						✓				

386

Some well-intentioned advice for owners and agents:

Do decide whether pets are welcome or otherwise. Leaving this 'open to negotiation' can mean trying to run with the hare and hunt with the hounds. Owners and holidaymakers end up on edge, wondering if that lively Jack Russell ('yes, we'll only be bringing one small dog') will have more of an impact on a property than a somnolent Rottweiler.

Do take a returnable deposit against damage and dirt. We wish everyone featured in this guide would do this. Inconsiderate tenants will thus be reminded of their responsibilities. (We've never heard of potential customers saying 'we won't go there because they want a deposit: what a cheek'...)

Don't say 'Short walk to sandy beach' if *that* beach is really quicksand, and the nearest one to play ball games on is a fifteen minute drive.

Do give detailed how-to-get-there instructions. Internet cartographic printouts are useful, and local colour is a bonus ('turn left before the Dog and Duck, not after'...'there's a hand made sign opposite the oak tree'...)

Do by all means clean cottages to within an inch of their lives, but do leave salt cellars and pepper pots with their contents intact. It's something few tenants think to bring, and their absence has ruined many a fish supper! Leaving dried herbs and spices is better still.

Do let it be known in your brochure/fact sheet if any single beds are only 2 foot 6 wide or any 'double' beds are only four feet wide.

Do give guests control over the heating (and charge them accordingly). When a gale force wind is blowing the sleet around, it is no consolation to be told when you enquire why the central heating does not appear to be working: 'Good Heavens, it *is* June!'

Do, if practical, place fresh flowers in the cottage, leave out home made cakes and hand-written notes of welcome. It might sound trite, but time and again these items crop up in letters and calls from readers. The ultimate winter-break gesture seems to be, where an open fire or wood-burner is available, lighting that half an hour prior to guests' arrival. With table lamps on, a tea tray waiting, and the wind howling outside, those people will not only come back, but tell their friends...

The following cottages and cottage agencies have appeared in every single edition of The Good Holiday Cottage Guide since it first appeared in 1983.

Joining us in celebrating the **20th edition** of the guide, their longevity (coupled with several visits from us) says a lot about their dedication to high standards and absolute reliability...

Barn Cottage (Exmoor)

Blakes Cottages (A)

Brecon Beacons Holiday Cottages

Chew Hill Farm Cottages

Clark Scott-Harden Holiday Cottages (A) **

Cornish Collection (A)

Classic Cottages (A)

Cote Bank Farm Cottages

Cottage in the Country (A) **

Cottage Life (A) **

(see Heart of the Lakes)

Dalegarth

Docklow Manor

Ecosse Unique (A) **

Ellary Estate Cottages

English Country Cottages (A)

Fron Fawr **

Glebe House Cottages **

Kilchrist Castle Cottages

Leckmelm Holiday Cottages

Long Byres

Longlands at Cartmel **

Lower Farm Cottages

Loweswater Holiday Cottages

Menai Holiday Cottages (A) **

Monkhouse Hill **

Neuadd Cottages

Norfolk Holiday Homes (A)

Owlpen Manor Cottages

Penrose Burden

Quality Cottages Cerbid (A)

Rosemoor **

Shilbottle Town Foot Farm

Stanton Court

Stubbs Cottages

Trallwm Forest Cottages

Trefanny Hill

Wraycroft Cottages

['A' denotes agency and ** indicates that while the cottages in question have appeared continuously in the book, they have undergone a change of owner].

Bed and breakfast/hotel accommodation

The Good Holiday Cottage Guide frequently receives requests from readers wanting information about places to stay en route to distant cottages and for friends and family to stay for a night or two while visiting people staying in a cottage (or apartment, chalet etc). They are sometimes able to stay as extra people in the cottage, but not usually. So we are now including information (in the owners' words) about hotels and 'b & b'...

Mockbeggars Hall, Suffolk. See Page 38.
'ETC 4 diamond, silver award. AA 4 diamond.
A grand, listed Jacobean Manor House set in its own grounds in rolling countryside, with easy access to Ipswich and the delights of Suffolk. Spacious, elegant rooms with modern facilities, affording guests a warm welcome in a friendly and relaxing atmosphere. All bedrooms are en-suite and non-smoking. Brochure available'.
Contact: Priscilla Clayton-Mead, Mockbeggars Hall, Claydon, Ipswich, Suffolk IP6 0AH.
Telephone (01473) 830239. Mobile 0770 262 7770. Fax (01473) 832989.
Email: Pru@mockbeggars.co.uk www.Mockbeggars.co.uk

Gladwins Farm, Suffolk. See Page 39.
'Home-from-home farmhouse B&B in typical Suffolk farmhouse; en-suite rooms, direct dial telephone, lounge area. £60 per night B&B for 2. In the heart of Suffolk's beautiful, rolling Constable Country, with marvellous views. Heated indoor pool, sauna, tennis court. ETC Four Diamonds'.
Contact: Robert and Pauline Dossor, Gladwins Farm, Harpers Hill, Nayland, Suffolk CO6 4NU. Telephone (01206) 262261. Fax 263001.
Email: GladwinsFarm@compuserve.com www.gladwinsfarm.co.uk

High House Farm, Suffolk. See Page 42.
'Beautifully restored 15th century Farmhouse on family run arable farm. Featuring exposed beams and Inglenook fireplaces, spacious and comfortable accommodation. Explore the heart of rural Suffolk, local vineyards, Easton Park Farm, Framlingham and Orford Castles, Parham Air Museum, Saxtead Windmill, Minesmere, Snape Maltings, Woodland Trust and the Heritage Coast. B&B from £22. Reductions for children'.
Contact: Mrs Sarah Kindred, High House Farm, Cransford, Woodbridge, Suffolk IP13 9PD.
Telephone (01728) 663461. Fax 663409.
Email: b&b@highhousefarm.co.uk www.highhousefarm.co.uk

The Grove, Norfolk. See Page 56.
'When in Cromer you can stay at the beautifully situated 18th century
Grove Guest House. You can have bed and breakfast and also a home
cooked evening meal. Price for bed and breakfast is
£25 per person per night'.
Contact: Mr and Mrs Graveling, The Grove,
Overstrand Road, Cromer, Norfolk.
Telephone (01263) 512412. Fax 513416.

Bones Cottage, Norfolk. See Page 61.
'Bed and breakfast accommodation in an idyllic setting between
Blakeney and Cley, on the North Norfolk coast. Only minutes' walk to
Cley marshes and within walking distance of Blakeney harbour. The
accommodation is a private suite, tastefully decorated, with TV, tea/coffee
making facilities, own bathroom and dining hall.
Peaceful location, parking'.
Contact: Mrs R Stocks, Bones Cottage, Hall Lane,
Wiveton, Holt, Norfolk NR25 7TG.
Telephone (01263) 740840. www.bonescottage.co.uk

Rudstone Walk, East Yorkshire. See Page 72.
'The East Yorkshire cottages at Rudstone Walk also offer superb bed and
breakfast accommodation, using the en-suite bedrooms in the courtyard
apartments surrounding the old Yorkshire Farmhouse. Delicious
breakfasts and traditional residents' evening meal-of-the-day are taken 'en
famille' around the large farmhouse dining room table, which easily seats
20 guests. Special 3 night breaks for the price of 2 until end May apply,
as well as special rates for any weekend guests'.
Contact: Rudstone Walk, South Cave, Nr. Beverley,
Brough, East Yorkshire HU15 2AH.
Telephone (01430) 422230. Fax 424552.
Email: office@rudstone-walk.co.uk   www.rudstone-walk.co.uk

Layhead Farm Cottages, North Yorkshire. See Page 91.
'Enjoy peace and tranquillity in The Stables. A newly converted barn
which is self-contained but close to our home. Two comfortable,
tastefully decorated en-suite bedrooms for B&B – one twin, one double.
Delicious Yorkshire breakfasts either cooked for you in the Stables
kitchen or left for you to prepare yourselves. Local organic produce used,
where possible. ETC Four Diamonds'.
Contact: Rosemary Hyslop, Field House, Rathmell,
Settle, North Yorkshire.
Telephone (01729) 840234. Fax (01729) 840775.
Email: rosehyslop@layhead.co.uk www.layhead.co.uk

Cressbrook Hall, Derbyshire. See Page 97.
'Perched high on the south facing Wye Valley, overlooking Cressbrook
Mill and adjacent to beautiful Monsal Dale, historic Cressbrook Hall
(circa 1835) is an impressive family residence standing in rural grounds.
Elegant en-suite B&B is offered in rooms with spectacular views around
the compass. Bakewell five miles, M1 20 miles'.
Cressbrook Hall, Cressbrook, near Buxton, Derbyshire SK17 8SY.
Telephone (01298) 871289. Fax 871845
Email: stay@cressbrookhall.co.uk www.cressbrookhall.co.uk

Park View Farm, Derbyshire. See Page 97.
'Enjoy country house hospitality in our elegant farmhouse set in large
gardens with lovely views overlooking the park that contains the
National Trust's magnificent Kedleston Hall.
Delightful dining room and lovely drawing room overlooking
the south-facing terrace. Delicious breakfasts. Beautifully furnished,
ensuite, four-poster bedrooms. AA Five Diamonds'.
Contact: Linda Adams, Park View Farm, Weston Underwood, Ashbourne,
Derbyshire DE6 4PA.
Telephone/fax (01335) 360352.

Cote Bank Farm, Derbyshire. See Page 103.
'Wake to birdsong, stunning views and the smell of freshly baked bread.
The same care and attention given to guests in Cote Bank Cottages is
lavished on them in our farmhouse. One double, one twin, all en-suite,
TV, tea/coffee trays. B&B from £26. Open March to December'.
Pamela Broadhurst, Cote Bank Farm, Buxworth,
High Peak, Derbyshire SK23 7NP.
Telephone/fax (01663) 750566.
Email: cotebank@btinternet.com

The Stables/The Byre, Durham. See Page 104.
'If you are travelling north or south to or from Scotland, you'll find us
conveniently located 12 miles west of Durham City, just a mile and a half
from the A68 and very private up a farm lane. Our very comfortable
stone barn conversion offers a welcome break, all bedrooms are en-suite
with tea/coffee making facilities; antique and pine furnished.
From £22.50 '.
Contact: Linda Vickers, Greenwell Farm, near Wolsingham,
Tow Law, Co Durham DL13 4PH.
Telephone (01388) 527248. Fax (01388) 526735.
Email: greenwell@farming.co.uk

Machrie Hotel and golf links, Isle of Islay. See Page 144.
'The 'Machrie' lies close to its 15 self-catering cottages. Along with 11
twin rooms and five double rooms, it has two bars, a dining room, a
function room and a private dining room. The food is predominantly
local, with Islay beef, lamb and shellfish a speciality. Bar meals are
served both at lunchtime and in the evening'.
Contact: Machrie Hotel, Port Ellen, Isle of Islay, Argyll PA42 7AN.
Telephone (01496) 302310. Fax 302404.
Email: machrie@machrie.com   www.machrie.com

Daleside Farm, Cumbria. See Page 163.
'Daleside Farm is a 500 acre working sheep farm in a magnificent,
peaceful rural location with wonderful views. It is ideally placed for
exploring the Lake District, the Solway coast, Hadrian's Wall and the
Scottish borders. One family/twin room and one double room, both en-
suite, with tea/coffee making facilities, a beautiful dining room and
visitors' lounge with log fires. Award winner 2000 Keswick in Bloom.
Keswick Tourism Association Country Establishment winner.
ETC Four Diamonds. Cost £23-£25 adults, £12.50 children'.
Contact: Alan and Isabel Teasdale, Daleside Farm, Ireby, Carlisle,
Cumbria CA7 1EW. Telephone (016973) 71268.

Bron Heulog Guest House, Powys. See Page 210.
'Bron Heulog (sunny bank in Welsh). Beautiful Victorian house built in
1861, grandly situated in large garden. Fully restored, with original
features, magnificent curved oak staircase and fireplaces in every room.
Orchid, Sunflower and Bluebell rooms are all recently refurbished with
Victorian style ensuite facilities and offer every comfort to our guests.
Price from £22 - £28 per person/per night'.
Contact: Karon & Ken Raines, Bron Heulog, Waterfall Street,
Llanrhaeadr YM Mochnant, Powys SY10 0JX.
Telephone (01691) 780521.
Email: kraines@enta.net www.kraines.enta.net

Greenbank Countryside Hotel, Cumbria. See Page 155.
'Greenbank Countryside Hotel is adjacent to Rockery Cottage, in an acre
of quiet grounds. Ten double en-suite rooms. Excellent cuisine. Log fires
and superb walking area. The hotel is renowned for its comfort and
hospitality, four miles out of Keswick in an elevated position with
spectacular views. B&B from £30 pppn and DBB from £45 pppn'.
Contact: Jean Wood, Greenbank Countryside Hotel,
Borrowdale, Keswick, Cumbria CA12 5UY.
Telephone (017687) 77215.

Broadwater, Hampshire. See page 307.
'Broadwater is a thatched cottage in a conservation village off the A303. Two twin/double bedrooms, both with en-suite; a guests' sitting/dining room and a cottage garden. Ideal for airports and ferries, Winchester, Salisbury and Stonehenge. Credit cards accepted.
Brochure available. £25 per person'.
Contact: Carolyn Mallam, Broadwater, Amport, near Andover, Hampshire SP11 8AY. Telephone/fax (01264) 772240.
Email: carolyn@dmac.co.uk   www.dmac.co.uk/carolyn

Three Chimneys Farm, Kent. See Page 312.
'Also available at Three Chimneys Farm, Bed & Breakfast. There are two charming rooms, in the unusual spaces found in the oast house. A double room, and a children's room, with bunk beds, sharing their own private bathroom. The double room costs £45 per night, and if there are children, the cost is £70, including a full English breakfast'.
Contact: Marion Fuller, Three Chimneys Farm, Goudhurst,
Kent TN17 2RA. Telephone/fax (01580) 212175.
Email: Marionfuller@threechimneysfarm.co.uk
www.threechimneysfarm.co.uk/

Sutton Court Farm Cottages, Shropshire. See page 322.
'Sutton Court Farm Cottages are also pleased to offer Bed & Breakfast. You will be accommodated in one of our cottages and have full use of all its facilities. Breakfast is offered in our 16th century farmhouse.
Prices £32 pppn (single supplement)'.
Contact: Jane Cronin, Sutton Court Farm, Little Sutton, Stanton Lacy,
Ludlow, Shropshire SY8 2AJ.
Telephone (01584) 861305. Fax (01584) 861441.
Email: suttoncourtfarm@hotmail.com
www.go2.co.uk/suttoncourtfarm

Old Kilns, Ross-on-Wye. See Page 321.
'Set in an elevated rural location, this character house offers excellent accommodation. Bedrooms are spacious, well equipped and include modern en-suite or private facilities. There is a comfortable lounge with open fire. Four-poster beds and jacuzzi. AA Four Diamonds, RAC Four Diamonds and Sparkling Gem Award. Pets and children welcome.
B&B £20-£30 per person inclusive. Dinner optional'.
Contact: Mrs H Smith, Old Kilns, Howle Hill, Ross-on-Wye.
Telephone/fax (01989) 562051.

Upper Court, Gloucestershire. See Page 331.
'As well as offering exceptional cottages, Upper Court is a country house in which bed and breakfast guests can feel 'at home'. Delicious English breakfasts can be served in bed at no extra charge. The guest bedrooms all have either romantic four poster or twin beds – all en-suite. There are magazines to read by the open fire in the drawing room or, in the summer, by the lake with tea or drinks. Breakfast, tea or dinner can be served on the lawn overlooking the lake.'
Contact: Bill and Diana Herford, Upper Court, Kemerton, near Tewkesbury, Gloucestershire GL20 7HY.
Telephone (01386) 725351. Fax 725472.

Glebe Farm, Warwickshire. See Page 352.
'In our quaint old farmhouse, tucked away in one of "Shakespeare's villages" (just ten minutes from Stratford-upon-Avon itself) there are four rooms, including a double with a four poster. They all overlook the Warwickshire countryside towards the Cotswold Hills. There is a large lounge with an open fire, a garden with a wendy house and a swing in the old apple tree.'
Contact: John and Margaret Canning, Exhall, near Alcester, Warwickshire B49 6EA.
Telephone/fax Stratford-upon-Avon (01789) 772202.

Short breaks

A number of readers have asked why our 'special categories' listings make no mention of short breaks, as these are an increasingly important part of the self catering scene. It can however be assumed that nine cottages out of ten that we feature are available for short breaks. Mostly these are for a minimum of two nights. The short breaks season is generally taken to be autumn through to spring, with some tremendous bargains to be had by the increasing numbers of people who appreciate rural Britain in the quieter months...

Maps

The maps on the following pages do not pretend to be a definitive or precise guide to the location of properties featured in the text, and place names are for orientation only. Their inclusion or otherwise is not a comment on whether a town is of tourist interest. So, no letters, please, from Swaffham and Droitwich...

Numbers given on maps do not refer to page numbers in the text but to the map reference at the top of the page. To some extent they are in numerical sequence, and where this cannot be the case readers should only need to look forward or back two or three pages.

Note: numbers underlined on maps denote agencies (which in the main text are marked with an asterisk). With only a few exceptions the locations marked on the map is the letting agency's headquarters, and it is normal for the agency to be strongly or even exclusively represented in that particular region. In the case of the larger regional and the main national agencies, no location reference is given.

Our favourite maps are the ones roughed out by owners themselves, with lots of local detail, such as 'turn left by the old oak tree'...

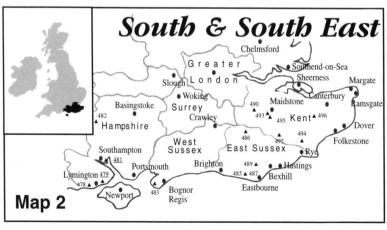

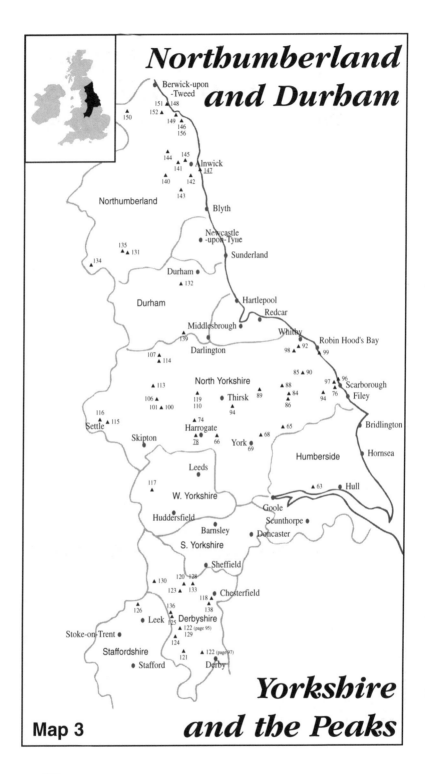

Northumberland and Durham

Berwick-upon-Tweed
151 ▲ 148
152 ▲
150 ▲
149 ▲
146
156

Northumberland

144 ▲ 145 ▲
141 ▲ Alnwick
140 ▲ 142 ▲ 147
143 ▲

Blyth

135 ▲ 131
134 ▲

Newcastle-upon-Tyne
Sunderland

Durham ●
132 ▲

Durham

Hartlepool
Redcar

Middlesbrough ●
139 ▲

Whitby
98 ▲ 92 Robin Hood's Bay
Darlington 99
107 ▲
114 ▲

85 ▲ 90

113 ▲ North Yorkshire 88 ▲ 97 ▲ 96 Scarborough
106 ▲ 119 ▲ Thirsk 89 84 ▲ 94 76 Filey
101 ▲ 100 110 ▲ 86 ▲
94

116 ▲ 74 ▲
115 ▲ Harrogate
Settle 78 66 65 ▲ Bridlington
Skipton York ● 68 ●
69 Hornsea
Humberside

Leeds ●

117 ▲
W. Yorkshire 63 ▲ Hull ●

Huddersfield ● Goole ●
Scunthorpe ●
Barnsley ● Doncaster ●
S. Yorkshire

Sheffield ●

120 128
130 ▲ ▲
123 ▲ 133 118 ▲ Chesterfield ●
136 ▲ 138 ▲
126 ▲ 125
Leek ● Derbyshire
Stoke-on-Trent ● 122 (page 95)
129 ▲
124 ▲
121 ▲ 122 (page 97)
Staffordshire Derby ●
Stafford ●

Yorkshire and the Peaks

Map 3

398

Scotland

Durness
John o'Groats
Tongue
Thurso
Wick
Unapool
Kinbrace
Lybster
Lochinver
Highland
Lairg
Brora
Ullapool 192
181 Inveran
191▲
Dornoch
Gairloch
Invergordon
172
206▲
Lossiemouth
Macduff
Cromarty
202▲ ▲204
Achnasheen
Nairn
Elgin
Buckie
Banff Fraserburgh
Isle of Skye
189
Rothes
Peterhead
Kyle
195▲
185▲
Inverness
Huntly
190
174▲ 179▲
183 Grantown-on-Spey
186▲
199▲
Invermoriston
Aviemore
Grampian
Aberdeen
193▲
Invergarry
Kingussie
Banchory
Mallaig
187
Stonehaven
Fort William
205▲
198▲
200▲
Pitlochry
Brechin
Tobermory
Glencoe
169▲ 166
Montrose
216▲
197▲
Tayside
Mull
Aberfeldy
164▲
Oban
208▲
165▲
Dundee
Arbroath
167
Callander
Perth
St Andrews
Stirling
Fife
Central
Dunoon Dumbarton
North Berwick
Dunbar
210
Greenock
Glasgow
156▲
217
Paisley
Lothian Edinburgh
Eyemouth
Islay
215▲
158 153
154
Arran Irvine
Kilmarnock
Galashiels
Melrose
218▲
157
Kelso
219▲ Campbeltown
Prestwick
Ayr
Strathclyde
Borders
159▲
Girvan
Dumfries
and
Stranraer
Dumfries ● Galloway
162▲
Whithorn
Kirkcudbright

Map 4

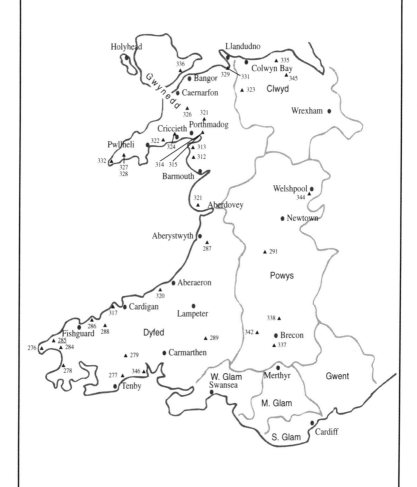

Wales

Holyhead

Llandudno

▲ 335

Colwyn Bay

Gwynedd

436

329

331

345

Bangor

Clwyd

Caernarfon

▲ 323

326

321

Wrexham ●

Criccieth Porthmadog

Pwllheli

322

324

▲ 313

332

▲ 312

327

328

314 315

Barmouth

Welshpool ●
344

321

Aberdovey

● Newtown

Aberystwyth ●
287

▲ 291

Powys

Aberaeron
320

Cardigan
317

Lampeter

Dyfed

286 ▲

288

338 ▲

342 ▲ ● Brecon

Fishguard
285

▲ 289

▲ 337

276 ▲

284

279

● Carmarthen

278

277 346 ▲

Tenby

W. Glam   Merthyr   Gwent

Swansea

M. Glam

S. Glam   Cardiff

Map 5

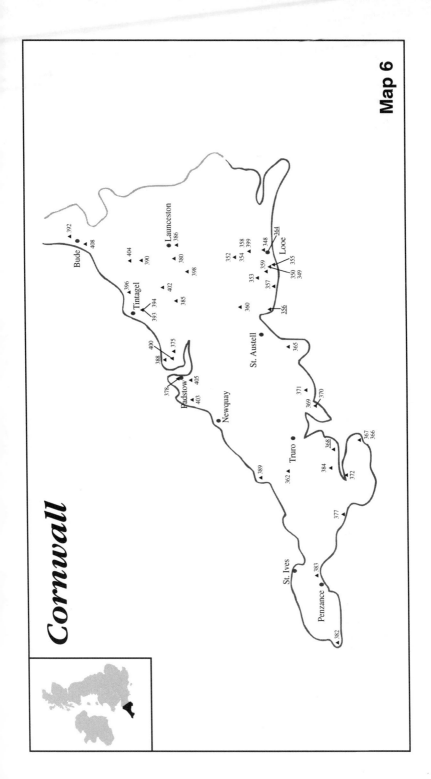

Cornwall

Map 6

Bude

408
392
404
390

Launceston
386
380
398

396
Tintagel
402
393 394
385

352
354 358
353 359 399
357 350 348
349 355
Looe

400
388 375
360
356
364

378 Padstow
405
403

Newquay

St. Austell
365

371
370
369

Truro
362
384
368
367
366
372
377

St. Ives

Penzance
383
382

389

West Country (Devon, Dorset, Somerset, Wiltshire, Avon)

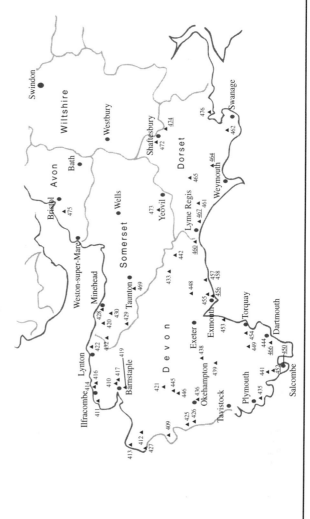

Map 7

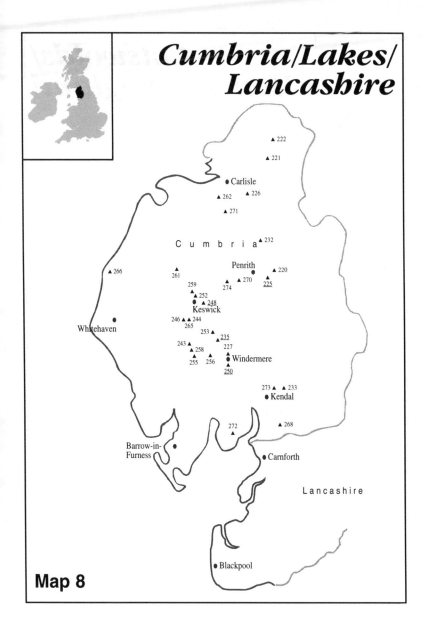

Cumbria/Lakes/ Lancashire

▲ 222

▲ 221

● Carlisle

▲ 262   ▲ 226

▲ 271

C u m b r i a ▲ 232

▲ 266

▲ 261

Penrith
●   ▲ 220
▲ 270 ▲
274   225

259 ▲

▲ 252
● ▲ 248
Keswick

246 ▲▲ 244
265

253 ▲
▲ 235

243 ▲
▲ 258   227

255 ▲   256 ▲   ● Windermere
▲
250

● Whitehaven

273 ▲   ▲ 233
● Kendal

272
▲   ▲ 268

Barrow-in-
Furness   ●
● Carnforth

L a n c a s h i r e

● Blackpool

Map 8

Please note that we cannot vouch for all the properties within the generally very reliable agencies we feature, but only those we describe. When booking through an agency, discuss your requirements in detail, read the brochures carefully, check locations and make sure how many people a property will sleep in comfort – that is, in 'real beds' …

Cotswolds/
Heart of England

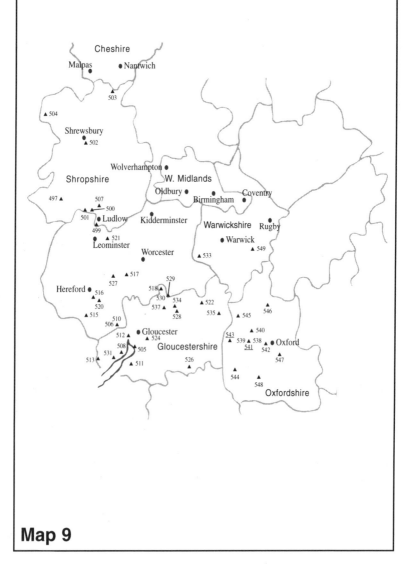

Cheshire

Malpas ● Nantwich

▲ 503

▲ 504

Shrewsbury
● ▲ 502

Wolverhampton ●

Shropshire   W. Midlands

Oldbury ●   Coventry
497 ▲   507   Birmingham ●
        ▲ ▲ 500
501 ●▲ Ludlow   Kidderminster   Warwickshire   Rugby
    499   ● Warwick ▲ 549
● ▲ 521   ▲ 533
Leominster   Worcester

             ▲ 517
        527
Hereford ● 516   518 ▲   529
    ▲   530   ▲ 534
    520   537 ▲ ▲   ▲ 522
 ▲ 515   528   535 ▲   ▲ 545   ▲ 546
  506 ▲ 510
   512 ▲   ● Gloucester   ▲ 540
  508 ▲ 524   543 539 ▲ 538 ● Oxford
513 ● 531 ▲ 505   Gloucestershire   541   542
       ▲ 511   526   547
                              544   ▲
                                   548   Oxfordshire

Map 9

Ireland

Londonderry

Letterkenny

Belfast

Donegal

Killyleagh

Enniskillen

Armagh

Sligo
592

▲ 588
586

Ballina

Dundalk

▲ 554 Navan

579

Castlebar
Westport

580

585

▲ 577

Athlone

Dublin

Clifden

569 582

Dun Laoghaire

570 ▲ ●Galway

590
▲

573 572

Port Laoise

Wicklow

▲ 567

Carlow

Arklow

Ennis
Limerick

589

Wexford

Tipperary

Waterford

Clonmel

591

Tralee

575
▲

571 ▲
Dingle

Killarney

Cork

574

565

581 551 568

552

576

Bantry

562 ▲ 553

550

563

566

Map 10

405

C

Y

Tell it like it is...

Please tell us about your reactions to *The Good Holiday Cottage Guide*, and of any ways in which you feel it could be improved. Tell us too about properties you have stayed in that did not come up to scratch.

Comments

My name/address/phone number is:

Please send to:

Swallow Press, PO Box 21, Hertford, Hertfordshire SG14 2DD.
Telephone (01438) 869489. Fax (01438) 869589.
Email frank@cottageguide.demon.co.uk

I bought/borrowed the guide from:

Don't keep it up your sleeve

Please tell us about holiday properties you know personally or have
stayed in that you think ought to be included in
The Good Holiday Cottage Guide.

Name of property/properties:

Comments:

My name/address/phone number is:

Please send to:

Swallow Press, PO Box 21, Hertford, Herts SG14 2DD.
Telephone (01438) 869489. Fax (01438) 869589.
Email frank@cottageguide.demon.co.uk

I bought/borrowed the guide from:

Sutton, near Buxton
Lower Pethills Farm

Readers caught on very quickly to these most appealing properties (*map 3/126*), agreeing with us that there is 'a warm and welcoming atmosphere, panoramic views, excellent beds, furnishings and equipment, and scrupulous cleanliness'. We saw them for ourselves in the summer of 2000, and agree with her! Converted from

Extremely high standards in a beautiful location, and very reasonably priced...

the stone shippon on a peaceful 32 acre smallholding (sheep and a few hens) in a picturesque valley on the edge of the Peak District, they are a delight. Reached via private farm lanes, and very quiet, with beautiful countryside and excellent walking from the doorstep, they are within easy reach of such attractions as Bakewell, Chatsworth Hall, Tatton Park, Jodrell Bank and the Silk Museum at Macclesfield. Each **sleeps 4 plus 2** in a double and a bunk room, with a sofa-bed in the sitting/dining room. There is full central heating, a shared utility room and a shared rear garden from which there are excellent views. Shower rooms (no baths). Two pets welcome. Televisions. Heating, electricity, bedlinen and towels included. Mountain bikes available for hire. Cost: very reasonable, from £185 to £275; short breaks from £100.

Further details from Greg and Sue Rowson, Lower Pethills Farm, Higher Sutton, Macclesfield, Cheshire SK11 0NJ. Telephone (01260) 252410.

Do note that we cannot vouch for all the properties on the books even of the generally excellent letting agencies we feature, but only those we describe. Holiday cottages are all about 'horses for courses', and most agencies have a number of comparatively basic properties that suit, say, fishermen or youth groups better than they do the typical reader of The Good Holiday Cottage Guide. When booking through an agency, discuss your requirements in detail, read brochures, check locations, check how many people a property will sleep in comfort..

Between half and two thirds of the cottage owners featured in this guide accept dogs, and acceptance of dogs usually but not always means other pets too (a small number exclude cats). Most owners charge extra – usually between £12 and £17 per week per dog – for the inevitable extra wear and tear on properties, though this is without exception much less than what kennels would charge. Please do not arrive with more dogs than you have permission to take, and please do not sneak a dog into a cottage where it is not welcome. Do note that, even when cottage owners say 'No dogs', dog lovers may still find themselves 'among friends': it could be that visiting town dogs may not take well to cottages surrounded by sheep, or that the owners' dogs don't like strange animals.

UK ONE CALL

**Having problems finding the right place?
Call us and we will search for you – you then deal direct with
the owners – NO COMMISSION AND NO FEES**

•••

**Contact us by telephone, fax or email or see our web site
Telephone and fax (+44) 01227 454563
email: team@ukonecall.com
Website: www.ukonecall.com**

•••

**The free availability information service for self catering
holiday properties throughout the UK**

•••

**We have hundreds of houses and apartments on our
database**

•••

UK ONE CALL Ltd, 30 The Crescent, Canterbury, Kent, CT2 7AW

•••

*While we will try to place you with a property featured in this guide, we do
feature others. We will always advise you of the standard of the property as
graded by the Tourist Board or other grading authority.*

•••

**UK One Call Ltd is part of World One Call Ltd with offices
covering also France, Spain and Italy**